Master of Deception

Master of Deception

The Wartime Adventures of Peter Fleming

Alan Ogden

BLOOMSBURY ACADEMIC
LONDON • NEW YORK • OXFORD • NEW DELHI • SYDNEY

BLOOMSBURY ACADEMIC
Bloomsbury Publishing Plc
50 Bedford Square, London, WC1B 3DP, UK
1385 Broadway, New York, NY 10018, USA

BLOOMSBURY, BLOOMSBURY ACADEMIC and the Diana logo are
trademarks of Bloomsbury Publishing Plc

First published in Great Britain 2019
Reprinted by Bloomsbury Academic 2019

A catalogue record for this book is available from the British Library.

ISBN: HB: 978-1-7883-1509-8
           ePDF: 978-1-3501-2409-7
           eBook: 978-1-3501-2408-0

Typeset by Integra Software Services Pvt. Ltd.
Printed and bound in Great Britain

To find out more about our authors and books visit www.bloomsbury.com
and sign up for our newsletters.

I have always believed in doing everything possible in war to mystify
and mislead one's opponent

FM THE EARL WAVELL

INTRODUCTION TO DUDLEY CLARKE'S *SEVEN ASSIGNMENTS*

Hence, when able to attack, we must seem unable;
When using our forces, we must seem inactive;
When we are near, we must make the enemy believe we are far away;
When far away, we must make him believe we are near.

SUN ZI AND *THE ART OF WAR*, FIFTH CENTURY BC

Contents

Charts, maps and plates

Charts

Maps

Plates

Unless otherwise stated, images are in the public domain.

Acknowledgements

I would like to thank Kate and Lucy Fleming for allowing me to research and use extracts from their father's letters and for their kind permissions to use some family photographs; Tina, Nick and Tony Bicat for their collective and often very funny memories of their father; John Ralli for assisting me to construct a wartime portrait of his father Lucas; Christian Stewart-Smith for sending me copies of his great-aunt's (Lady Caccia) letter; Major Philip Wright and Charles Richards for their impeccable proofreading and constructive suggestions; Lady Anne Thorne for presenting me with a copy of her late husband's privately published *Reminiscences*; the Lindsay and Wheatley families for their input on Martin Lindsay; and Duff Hart-Davis for his many kind words of encouragement.

Preface

I first came across Peter Fleming's war when I was writing *Sons of Odysseus*, the story of SOE in Greece. It was but a passing reference to the YAK Mission and it was several years later, when I was working at the Grenadier Guards Archives, that I came across a copy of his full report about that mission that he had used as the basis for 'An Ammunition Train in Greece' in *With the Guards to Mexico!* in 1957.

Once again, when I was writing *Tigers Burning Bright*, the story of SOE in the Far East, the name of Peter Fleming cropped up, this time in the context of the mysterious D. Division. Coupled with the YAK Mission report and his own book *Invasion 1940*, a remarkable picture began to emerge of his extraordinary wartime exploits, first against Germany and then Japan. It was only when I read Sir Michael Howard's official history of British deception in the Second World War and Thaddeus Holt's definitive study of Allied deception – *The Deceivers* – that the magnitude and importance of Fleming's achievements in D. Division came into focus.

Personally requested by General Wavell to set up a deception organization in the Far East, Fleming soon became the mastermind of the British war of deception against Japan. It turned out to be a huge undertaking that required every ounce of his energy and sinew of his intellectual brilliance.

One of Fleming's many admirable qualities was his ability to speak his own mind in the hierarchical and competitive world of the military and intelligence communities. He had no truck with empire building, turf wars or pipe dreams. If he disagreed, he either said so or put his waspish pen to work. This 'informed dissent' made him enemies, yet the clarity of his thinking and his expertise in the arts of deception invariably prevailed and smoothed the ruffled feathers of senior officers.

୶

The world of military and intelligence services is strewn with acronyms that reduce commands, titles and organizations to an alphabet soup seasoned with a sprinkling of full stops. My readers rightly urged me to reduce them to the minimum, so where practical I have spelt them out in full, leaving only a handful which I hope will become familiar through their constant repetition.

Several intelligence agencies cultivated a number of titles as cover to confuse their true identity. The Secret Intelligence Service, often referred to as MI6, conducted its business in the Far East as the Inter-Services Liaison Department: I have called it SIS.

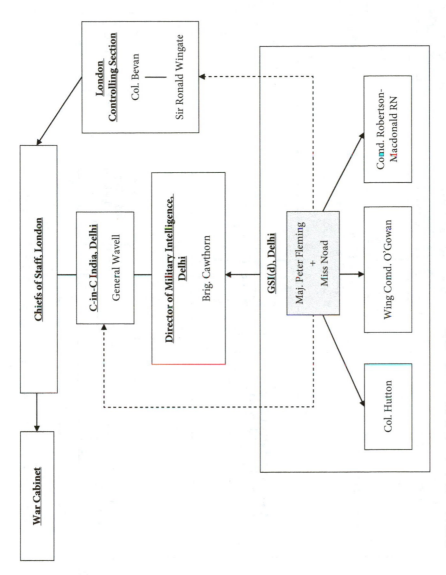

1 D Division: Early days in Delhi, summer 1942.

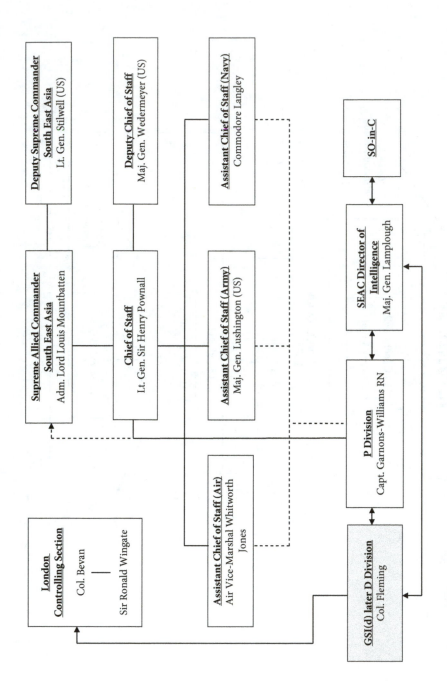

Supreme Allied Commander South East Asia
Adm. Lord Louis Mountbatten

Deputy Supreme Commander South East Asia
Lt. Gen. Stilwell (US)

Chief of Staff
Lt. Gen. Sir Henry Pownall

Deputy Chief of Staff
Maj. Gen. Wedermeyer (US)

Assistant Chief of Staff (Army)
Maj. Gen. Lushington (US)

Assistant Chief of Staff (Navy)
Commodore Langley

Assistant Chief of Staff (Air)
Air Vice-Marshal Whitworth Jones

London
Controlling Section
Col. Bevan

Sir Ronald Wingate

P Division
Capt. Garnons-Williams RN

SEAC Director of Intelligence
Maj. Gen. Lamplough

SO-in-C

GSI(d) later D Division
Col. Fleming

2 D Division: Reorganization into boxes after the arrival of SACSEA, autumn 1943.

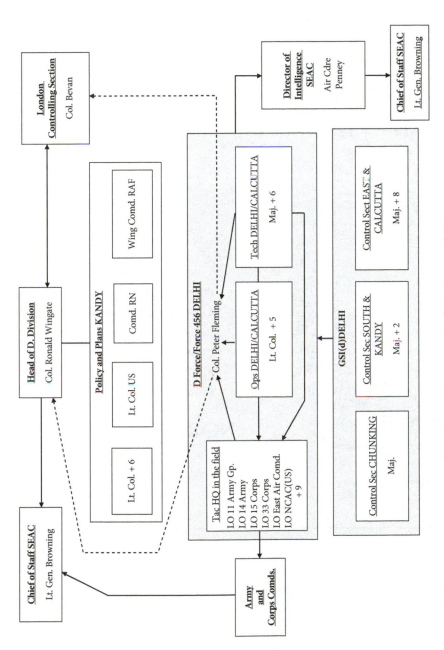

London Controlling Section
Col. Bevan

Director of Intelligence SEAC
Air Cdre Penney

Chief of Staff SEAC
Lt. Gen. Browning

Head of D. Division
Col. Ronald Wingate

Policy and Plans KANDY

| Wing Comd. RAF |
| Comd. RN |
| Lt. Col. US |
| Lt. Col. + 6 |

D Force/Force 456 DELHI
Col. Peter Fleming

Tech DELHI/CALCUTTA
Maj. + 6

Ops DELHI/CALCUTTA
Lt. Col. + 5

Tac HQ in the field
LO 11 Army Gp.
LO 14 Army
LO 15 Corps
LO 33 Corps
LO East Air Comd.
LO NCAC(US)
+ 9

GSI(d)DELHI

Control Sect EAST &
CALCUTTA
Maj. + 8

Control Sec SOUTH &
KANDY
Maj. + 2

Control Sec CHUNKING
Maj.

Chief of Staff SEAC
Lt. Gen. Browning

Army and Corps Comds.

3 D Division: How Fleming retained command and control in the field, January 1945.

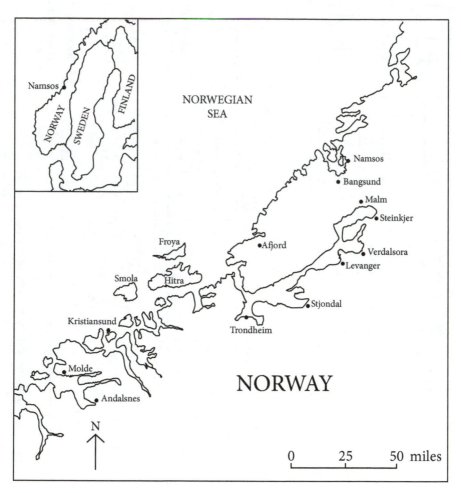

Map 1 Norway 1940

Map 2 Greece 1941

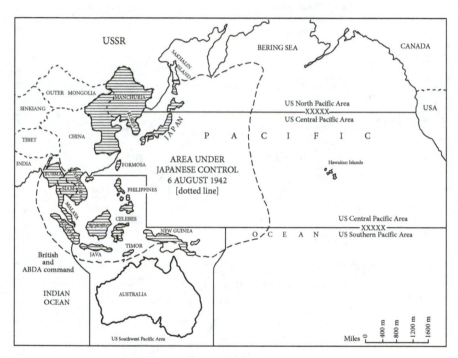

USSR

BERING SEA

CANADA

SAKHALIN ISLAND

OUTER MONGOLIA

MANCHURIA

US North Pacific Area
XXXXX
US Central Pacific Area

USA

SINKIANG

KOREA

JAPAN

TIBET

CHINA

P   A   C   I   F   I   C

INDIA

FORMOSA

AREA UNDER
JAPANESE CONTROL
6 AUGUST 1942
[dotted line]

Hawaiian Islands

BURMA

PHILIPPINES

SIAM

MALAYA

CELEBES

US Central Pacific Area
XXXXX
US Southern Pacific Area

BORNEO

NEW GUINEA

O   C   E   A   N

TIMOR

JAVA

British
and
ABDA command

INDIAN
OCEAN

AUSTRALIA

US Southwest Pacific Area

Miles

400 m

800 m

1200 m

1600 m

Map 3 The war in the Pacific, August 1942

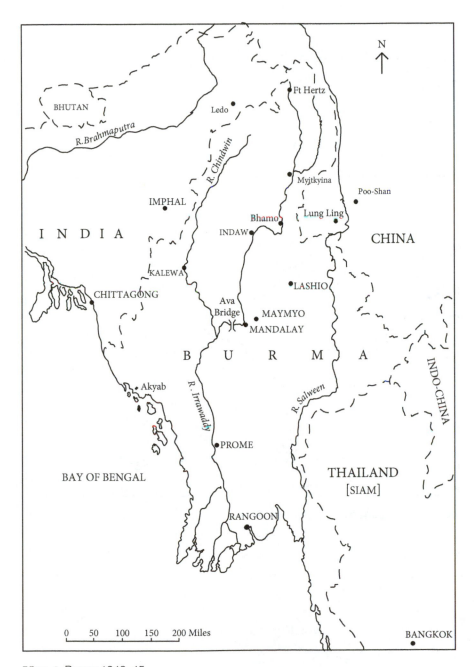

Map 4 Burma 1942–45

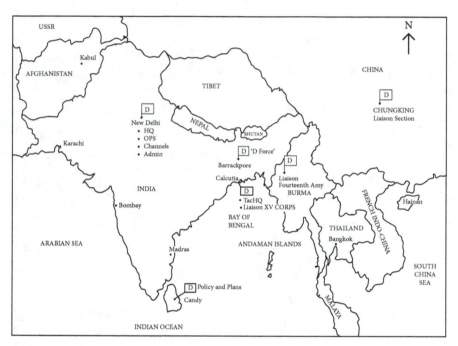

Map 5 D. Division area of operations, 1942–45

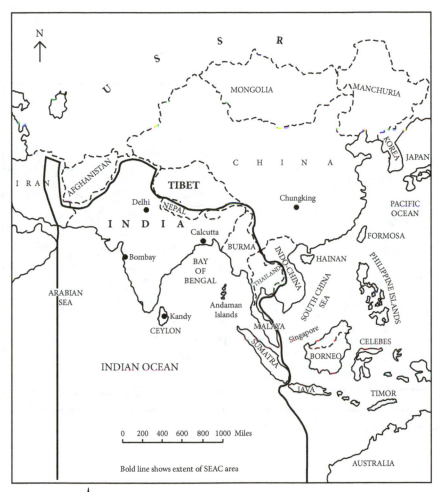

Map 6 SEAC theatre boundaries, 1944–45

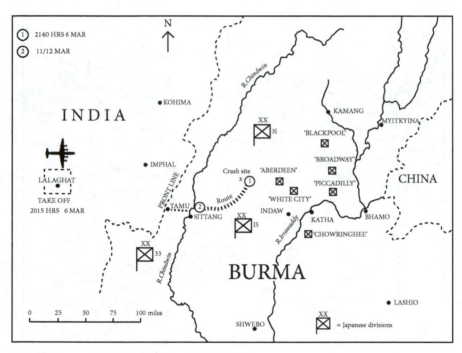

Map 7 Second Chindit expedition, March 1944

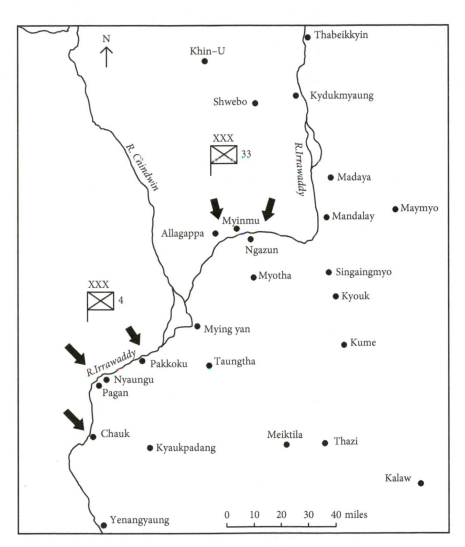

Map 8 Operation Cloak, the crossing of the Irrawaddy

Chapter 1
A new Elizabethan

Peter Fleming was born into a world of Edwardian luxury, an era when Britain was at the apogee of its imperial wealth and status. Yet his grandfather, Robert Fleming, the son of a humble bookkeeper in Dundee, had started work at the age of fourteen as an accountant with a local textile firm[1] and gone on to become one of the shrewdest and most respected investors of his generation, founding both The Scottish American Investment Trust and the merchant bank, Robert Fleming & Co. His son, Valentine, naturally had a very different start in life. Educated at Eton and Oxford where he read law,[2] he became Member of Parliament for Henley at the age of twenty-eight. Married to a beautiful socialite, Evelyn St. Croix Rose, and by now the father of four sons, Valentine joined the Queen's Own Oxfordshire Hussars in 1914 and was in action on the Western Front until his death in the trenches of Guillemont Farm in France in May 1917. He was awarded a posthumous DSO. Abruptly, ten-year-old Peter now found himself head of the family. He had much to live up to. His brother, Ian, who was later to become world famous as the creator of James Bond, was away at boarding school; Richard aged six and Michael aged four were still at home.

Winston Churchill's eulogy for Valentine Fleming was published by *The Times* on 25 May 1917:

> Valentine Fleming was one of those younger Conservatives who easily and naturally combine loyalty to party ties with a broad liberal outlook upon affairs and a total absence of class prejudice.

> He was most earnest and sincere in his desire to make things better for the great body of the people, and had cleared his mind of all particularist tendencies. He was a man of thoughtful and tolerant opinions, which were not the less strongly or clearly held because they were not loudly or frequently asserted.

> He shared the hopes to which so many of his generation respond of a better, fairer, more efficient public life and Parliamentary system arising out of these trials. But events have pursued a different course.

He had everything in the world to make him happy; a delightful home life, active interesting expanding business occupations, contented disposition, a lovable and charming personality. He had more. He had that foundation of spontaneous and almost unconscious self-suppression in the discharge of what he conceived to be his duty without which happiness, however full, is precarious and imperfect. That these qualities are not singular in this generation does not lessen the loss of those in whom they shine.

As the war lengthens and intensifies and the extending lists appear, it seems as if one watched at night a well-loved city whose lights, which burn so bright, which burn so true, are extinguished in the distance in the darkness one by one.

After excelling as a scholar at Eton and winning a scholarship to Christ Church Oxford to read English Literature, when he came down in June 1929 with a 'first', Fleming was sent to America by his family to serve an apprenticeship with a firm of stockbrokers in preparation for joining the family bank in London. Almost as soon as he arrived, Wall Street collapsed, ushering in 'the worst economic blizzard of the century [which] wiped out the fortunes of the rich and the savings of the poor',[3] and after managing to delay his return home by conjuring up hunting trips to the southern states and Central America, he dutifully reported to Robert Fleming & Co in the City of London. Two months in an office in a merchant bank was enough for the free-spirited young man and after a series of job interviews, he landed a position at *The Spectator* as assistant literary editor. At the same time, he joined the Grenadier Guards and on 29 November 1930 was commissioned second lieutenant in the Supplementary Reserve of Officers, a reservist body designed to produce in the event of war a flow of replacement platoon commanders whose life expectancy was traditionally measured in weeks rather than months.

Training with the 2nd Battalion in 1931 (June and July) and 1933 (April and May) was fitted in between journeys to Brazil[4] and China.[5] The genesis of the Brazilian expedition lay in an advert in *The Times* seeking two applicants to 'explore rivers Central Brazil, if possible ascertain fate Colonel Fawcett'. After signing on and recruiting the artist Roger Pettiward,[6] 'very tall, with red hair and a slow quizzical drawl',[7] Fleming managed to be appointed as *The Times'* special correspondent to the British Mato Grosso Expedition as it was officially and rather grandly termed. Its quest was to enquire into the mysterious disappearance of Colonel Percy Fawcett, an irrepressible explorer who deservedly lived up to the idiom 'a legend in his own lifetime'. A friend of Rider Haggard and Arthur Conan Doyle,[8] Fawcett had made seven expeditions to the interior of Brazil between 1906 and 1924, returning to duty in the First World War to command an artillery brigade on the Western Front. In 1925 he set off with his eldest son Jack and Jack's friend Raleigh Rimell in search of the lost city of El Dorado in the Mato Grosso region. In a letter to his younger son Brian, Fawcett described the quest for the city:

I expect the ruins to be monolithic in character, more ancient than the oldest Egyptian discoveries. Judging by inscriptions found in many parts of Brazil, the inhabitants used an alphabetical writing allied to many ancient European and Asian scripts. There are rumours, too, of a strange source of light in the buildings, a phenomenon that filled with terror the Indians who claimed to have seen it.

The central place I call 'Z' – our main objective – is in a valley surmounted by lofty mountains. The valley is about ten miles wide, and the city is on an eminence in the middle of it, approached by a barrelled roadway of stone. The houses are low and windowless, and there is a pyramidal temple. The inhabitants of the place are fairly numerous, they keep domestic animals, and they have well-developed mines in the surrounding hills.

They all vanished, never to be seen or heard of again, and it was assumed that they had been killed by local Indians who were known to be hostile to intruders. The disappearance of the expedition created a whirlwind of speculation, including a theory the colonel had been plucked from his canoe by a giant and exceedingly ravenous anaconda snake lying in wait in a tree above the river. Another version centred on a mysterious old man with long white hair living with an Indian tribe who answered to the name of Fawcett. As lost expeditions go, it was to prove a fertile furrow to plough and promised to yield a bumper harvest of *Boy's Own* adventures.

After the publication of *Brazilian Adventure* in 1933 as well as *Variety*, a collection of his humorous 'essays, sketches and stories' from *The Spectator*, Fleming suddenly found himself in the literary limelight. Two articles in *The Times*[9] – 'The Heart of Brazil' – filed by Fleming as a special correspondent (29 and 30 November 1932), had done much to publicize *Brazilian Adventure*. He explained that their programme had been transformed from 'a full-dress expedition into a more or less happy-go-lucky reconnaissance' on account of a revolution in San Paolo which had put the country into 'a state of pleasurable excitement'. Fleming described the first stage of their journey into the interior as 'a placid, comfortable life' until they reached unexplored territory where, from there on, their 'entry was slapdash and unprofessional'. Weeks of paddling in canoes, manhandling boats down rapids which 'had a much worse reputation than they deserve' and trekking through dense jungle concluded with Fleming's assessment that 'I think this journey was impossible with the resources at our disposal'. If nothing else, although they 'brought back no conclusive proof that Fawcett [was] dead … no one who has seen anything of the region in which he disappeared can entertain the possibility of his survival', the reader was treated to a grand caper reported with a liberal dollop of understatement and laid-back insouciance.

The *Daily Express* enthused 'this is the adventure book which one always dreams of reading and no one ever writes. It must enthral everybody.' 'An extraordinary good book' announced *The Sunday Times*; J.B. Priestley agreed, writing that it 'is the best travel book I have read for a long time'. One of the main reasons for the book's success, Duff Hart-Davis suggested,[10] was Fleming's 'splendidly original attitude. Until he came on the scene, travel and travel books had been treated with excessive reverence and solemnity; but then, with a single, sustained burst of self-mockery, *Brazilian Adventure* blew the whole genre sky-high. Readers – and reviewers – could scarcely believe that a travel book could be so funny.' His choice of Roger Pettiward had proved inspired for 'nothing could have exceeded the composure and resource with which he faced a series of odd and occasionally alarming predicaments'.[11] There is a marked resemblance between Pettiward and 'Boy Endover' in Fleming's 1951 novel *The Sixth Column* – 'a tall, rather stooping young man ... His frivolity was so deep-rooted in him that it partook rather of the nature of a philosophy than of a failing. He appeared to believe that all human institutions, and most human situations, had in them something inherently ridiculous, and that it was his duty to exploit this latent seam of risibility.' At the time of Fleming's death in 1971, over 123,000 hardback copies had been sold.

The one dissenting voice was that of Robert Byron whose book, *First Russia Then Tibet*, had been published two months later and achieved only modest sales. Writing to his mother from Kabul in June 1934, he confided that 'I have just read *Brazilian Adventure* – or part of it. Very disappointing – in fact I have ceased to be jealous.' On the surface, both men had much in common; both had gone to Eton and both were *Times* correspondents covering Russia and Central Asia. Where they parted was in their respective appreciation of architecture. Fleming confessed in *One's Company* that he was 'wholly lacking in either an historical sense or the ability to appreciate architecture' whereas for Byron, buildings old and modern were his all-consuming passion, attracting either lofty praise or biting opprobrium.

In his essay on Evelyn Waugh in *The Art of Travel*, Martin Stannard includes Fleming along with Waugh, Byron and Graham Greene as part of a generation

which liked to see itself more overtly aggressive, irreverent, cosmopolitan and impatiently dismissive of "the old men" who had made the war ... While in the grey light of the thirties, Europe floundered through the Depression towards yet another global disaster, these smart young men provided intelligent light reading which satisfied both political scepticism and a frustrated thirst for the exotic. Hollywood was the "cheap" answer; the new brand of travel writing represented another, more sophisticated, form of escapism which had the greater merit of ostensibly being an attack on escapism.[12]

The Army Reserve was now destined to take a back seat to travel writing or 'swanning' as Fleming described it in a self-mocking tone. Between June

1933 and September 1935, Fleming made two landmark journeys to the Far East which were published as *One's Company* (1934) and *News from Tartary* (1936). Both confirmed his reputation as one of the most engaging writers of his generation. Vita Sackville-West in *The Spectator* called *One's Company* 'a travel book in a thousand' and termed him 'an Elizabethan spirit allied to a modern mind'; the sobriquet 'a modern Elizabethan' stuck. By the time it was out of print in 1946, 90,000 copies had been sold.

Of the two books, *News from Tartary* is the more substantial, describing a journey from Peking to Kashmir 'not only in Marco Polo's footsteps but at Marco Polo's pace'[13] that lasted seven months and covered about 3,500 miles. The route chosen by Fleming and his companion, the Swiss adventurer and writer Ella Maillart, took them westwards across a China torn by civil war to Xinjiang and then south to British India. It had been eight years since any foreigner had crossed Xinjiang. During that time few of those who entered it came out alive. After entering the lands of the Tartars by a little-known route and following the course of the ancient Silk Road, they reached Kashgar before crossing the Pamirs into India. The explorer Lucy Kelaart cherishes it as:

> a story of pure travel – the endless waiting for permissions, evading officials, living from hand to mouth, long days in the saddle or on foot pushing on into the interior of this great unknown region, of fatigue and animal illnesses, courting the small disasters of expedition life … as well as one of bringing back news of the state of affairs in this isolated, unknown, far corner of China and the Chinese, Russian and British interests within it.[14]

Propelled by rave reviews such as Harold Nicolson's verdict in the *Daily Telegraph* that 'no modern writer can equal Peter Fleming as a story-teller, as an astringent narrator of romantic and dangerous voyages through unknown lands', *News from Tartary* went through seven impressions in the first year.

∽

The continuing support of *The Times* played a major role in promoting Fleming's books. On his first journey to China, under his own byline, five articles[15] were published in 1933 including two long articles: 'Communism in China – a First-Hand Enquiry. How Red Areas are Controlled' examined the history of communism in China and its present-day development; 'Life under a Red Regime' analysed the extent of the Chinese Communist movement and ways in which it might evolve in the future. Fleming's conclusion was sanguine:

> As long as the Nanking Government remains in office China as a whole is safe from the Reds; and as long as the Reds stay in their mountains they can defy the whole of China. It is only in some unpredictable crisis – only, say, if the

Nanking Government falls and no effective successor can quickly be found – that the Reds will have their chance. Then, indeed, chaos is come again.

In an entirely different vein, 'A Journey in China: From Shanghai to Canton, an Overland Route' followed Fleming's peregrinations by car, bus, sampan and train and ended with travel tips to adventurous *Times* readers such as 'with enough visiting cards with the traveller's name and status printed on them in Chinese and enough patience (you must never lose face by seeming in a hurry) you can go almost anywhere within reason, and enjoy going there.' *One's Company* was favourably reviewed in *The Times* on 3 August the following year – 'Mr Fleming is always good company. He has a gift for making a landscape visible and an inexhaustible vitality in drawing and caricaturing people encountered.'

After a temporary job in the Talks Department of the BBC, on 24 August 1934 Fleming set off again as a *Times* special correspondent to China, this time accompanied by 'George' and Mogs Gage[16] on the first leg of a trip to Georgia. Four articles under the headline 'Across Russia' appeared in January 1935.[17] The first, 'From Moscow to the Ukraine', datelined Mukden November 1934, contrasted his first visit to Russia in 1931 with the Moscow of 1934 showing 'a marked improvement … streets were cleaner and better paved, queues were shorter and beggars fewer'. A visit to a Park of Culture and Rest, 'a kind of austere and purposeful Coney Island', and attendance at International Youth Day in Red Square where 'half an acre of red bunting appealed to the youth of the world to unite in struggle against this and that', followed by official visits to a collective farm or *kolhoz* outside Kharkov and an agricultural machinery factory in Rostov-on-Don all provided material to showcase the great advances made by Russian society; and all were irreverently qualified by deft observations such as the workers' clubs were 'almost entirely unfrequented' and the children in the *kolhoz* crèche looked 'happy and well, if perhaps a little tired of tourists (for this was a show place)'.

Fleming is more at home in the second instalment 'Shooting in Georgia' when his travel writing persona is given freedom to roam in a two-day journey with the Gages into the mountain fastness to meet the Hevsur tribe, 'a handsome, proud people, a queer oasis of dignity and dour reserve in the desert of Soviet garrulity' and supposedly descendants of Godfrey de Bouillon's Crusaders. On arrival in Tiflis, having discovered that the expedition was nothing but a figment of the imagination of the Moscow state travel agency, Fleming took himself off 'for an amusing fortnight in the mountains of Eastern Georgia' where apart from wounding a *tour* or mountain sheep and killing a large wild boar, the bag 'was confined to a few small deer, a wild cat, several jackals, some pheasants, quail, and pigeon, and a few antelopes'. He comes into his stride at the end of a day's excursion when the hunters cut whatever had been shot into small pieces spitted on green wands and made into shaslik over the ashes of a fire. Then they would sing songs with melodies oriental rather than Slav, and, throwing their long knives on the ground, do fierce firelit dances like a Scottish sword dance before lying down in their *burkas* to sleep ... When we returned to our base in a village one of the men would ask the whole expedition to his house, and there huge quantities of wine and home-made delicacies would be produced, and a *tamada* or toast master appointed to make little speeches before giving the Georgian toast which means "Be the victor!" ... The peasants were kindly and spontaneous people, and the snow-capped mountains among which they lived were of exceptional beauty. Here the drums of propaganda rolled only faintly, and each of the remoter villages had still its own customs, its own dishes, and its own taste in wine.

Aware that the Soviet behemoth had escaped censure in this article, Fleming ended his report at a new restaurant on the way back to Tiflis:

It was the kind of shoddy, characterless institution that you find all over Russia, and as I looked at the redundant posters on the walls, and the mass-produced cutlery, and the bust of Lenin, and the menu on which no variation could be played, I realized that Soviet civilization was marching up to the mountains, and that soon, in the villages we had left, it would all be like this.

Georgia, with its friendly Highland villagers and plentiful food, proved the odd man out for soon, in his next article 'Romance and the Rhumba', Fleming was on the Trans-Caspian Railway to Samarkand and Tashkent.[18] The lights in his carriage failed, resulting in three nights spent in darkness despite the train being full of railway officials heading to a conference on Central Asia Railway Improvements. By day, he carried away 'Fleckerian memories of quizzical Kirghiz women in long-waisted coats of gorgeous colours, of Turcomen whose stature is increased by fantastic fur hats, of kneeling camels and tiny donkeys, of piles of melons and gigantic grapes'. The first to admit that his journey through Russian Central Asia was 'too superficial to enable me to judge whether the autonomy of its republics exists in anything more than their titles', Fleming changed trains and continued his journey on to Novosibirsk and Vladivostok in Siberia, this time on the Turksib Railway.

In the final article, 'Government by Fear', he gave a blunt and no-holds-barred summary of his experiences in Russia, where 'public opinion is rationed and distributed like bread' and whose '170,000,000 citizens ... are governed, in the last analysis, by fear', a fear supervised by the NKVD, multiplied by informants and defined by 'frontiers that are to all intents a prison wall ... Soviet citizenship is a life sentence against which appeals are very rarely successful.' Yet his deductions also revealed a desire for optimism for 'it is on the rising and the coming generations that her hopes of success depend – generations untainted by old ideas, unscarred by civil war, steeped from the cradle in the culture of the new regime, which today has much more than found its feet'.

Based in Peking from 1 January 1935,[19] Fleming filed two stories under the banner of 'An Eye Witness in Mongolia'[20] and a further five grouped as 'A Far Eastern Inquiry: The Japanese in Manchukuo', 'The Threat of Conflict', 'Trade with Manchukuo', 'The Soviet Frontier' and 'The Opium Monopoly' before setting out in February with the Swiss explorer Kini Maillart on an epic journey from Peking to Srinagar in India. Back in England in September, he diligently produced fourteen enticing articles for *The Times*, each at least 2,000 words long. In November and December 1935, *The Times* published them in three batches, starting with 'Hidden Asia (One)': 'To India from Peking'; 'Train and Lorry in China'; 'Ten Anxious Days in Sining'; 'With the Prince of Dzun' and 'Three Months from Peking'. A fortnight later, 'Hidden Asia (Two)' followed: 'Into the Altyn Tagh'; 'The Green Oasis of Cherchen'; 'Under the Union Jack'; 'The Mystery of a Warrior'; 'Interlude at Kashgar' and 'The End of the Journey'. Collectively they amounted to an abridged version of *News from Tartary* which was published the following August.[21]

In January 1937, *The Times* sent Fleming, accompanied by the beautiful actress Celia Johnson[22] whom he had married soon after his return from India, as a foreign correspondent at large on a tour of European capitals (Paris, Rome, Prague, Vienna, Berlin and Moscow). His byline does not appear but the opening paragraph of 'Czech and German – False Alarm of Communism', (29 January 1937) – 'Brightly clad peasants and drably clad townsfolk hurry along country roads and city streets, apparently bent on urgent tasks ...' – and 'New Russians – the Drive for Culture', published on 6 February, suggest his authorship. Then, in February 1938, having persuaded the editor of the significance of the Japanese declaration of war against China, he headed east as an accredited *Times* war correspondent, again taking Celia with him, this time to Burma, China and Japan.

His first story, 'Top Hats in Chungking' (30 April) was an amusing account of the visit of HBM Ambassador, Sir Archibald Clark Kerr, to Chungking to present his letters of credence to the President of the Chinese Republic. On arrival at the airstrip, when 'the twin engines of the Douglas had done their job, the twentieth century receded as the coolies hoisted us with the formal grunted adjurations which chair-bearers have used for hundreds of years in Szechwan [and our] processions wound its way at the pace of the Middle Ages up a zigzag flight of stairs in the steep cliff face'. *The Times* then ran two stories on 'The Burma Road to China' ('In Marco Polo's Steps' and 'Peasant Builders') in May and two more in June, 'Bombed Canton' and 'Prospects in China'. In the latter, Fleming wrote 'at the front Japan will go on winning, and China losing, almost indefinitely. But it is still open to doubt whether Japan's digestive powers are equal to assimilating the fruits of victory without endangering the national wellbeing.' The couple returned in July and it was not to be until 1954 that *The Times* ran another story by Fleming.[23]

As a journalist, Fleming wore two hats. The first, predominantly of clownish design, he donned when writing about his travels, reeling off light-hearted, witty and derring-do pieces to entertain and enthral his readers; the second, a hybrid between a bowler hat and a military cap, was worn when engaged on serious political and military enquiries and gave his work the authority of an expert commentator and perspicacious political analyst. Both would often appear in *The Times* a few days or weeks apart, which served to blur the distinction. The fact was that Fleming, with his keen intellect and love of adventure, was both an avant-garde travel writer and diplomat manqué, preferring to excel at the former with its individual freedoms rather than make his way up through the structured ranks of the Foreign Office or international big business.

⋰⋰

With all three books in circulation in the libraries and drawing rooms of England, it came as no surprise to the Grenadiers when Lieutenant Fleming, now one of England's young and, through his marriage to Celia, most glamourous literary lions, resigned his commission on 7 March 1936. The parting was entirely amicable and his fellow officers waited eagerly for the next adventure of their peripatetic colleague for he was by no means the first Grenadier to roam in far-off places. Indeed, Brigadier George Pereira, a former Grenadier and the first European to walk from Peking to Lhasa, had made many adventurous journeys in Central Asia, China and Tibet before he died aged fifty-eight on the road to Kantze in Sichuan in 1923.[24]

These were heady days for Fleming. In his preface to *When the Going was Good* (1945), Evelyn Waugh recalled that

> these were the years when Mr Peter Fleming went to the Gobi Desert, Mr Graham Greene to the Liberian Hinterland and Robert Byron – vital today, as of old, in our memories; all his exuberant zest in the opportunities of our time now, alas! tragically and untimely quenched – to the ruins of Persia. We turned our backs on civilization. Had we known, we might have lingered with 'Palinurus';[25] had we known that all the seemingly solid, patiently built, gorgeously ornamented structure of Western life was to melt overnight like an ice-castle, leaving only a puddle of mud.

On the centenary of Fleming's birth, the American author Ben Downing, writing in *The New Criterion*,[26] asks what makes him so very readable.

Besides his exciting subject matter, the obvious answer is his prose … I think of the moment in *News from Tartary* when Fleming, fed up with his refractory porters, 'abused them in the dregs of three languages' (namely Chinese, Russian and Turkic), or his evocation in *Bayonets to Lhasa* of the filth of the Tibetan capital: 'Pigs and ravens competed for nameless delicacies in open sewers.' And who else would think to describe a slow train as Fleming does in *One's Company*? 'It was the most irresolute of trains. After maintaining for perhaps twenty minutes its maximum speed of eighteen miles an hour, it would suddenly lose heart and draw up in a siding for a period of introspection.'

To this assessment, one should add his superlative powers of observation that delight the reader with glimpses such as 'four geishas mopped and mowed upon a windswept stage'; 'a tortoise suspended on a string, spinning as aimlessly as a planet above the counter of a fishmonger's stall' (*One's Company*); and 'men … naked to the waist, their shaggy robes gathered in great unwieldy bunches round their middles, the wrinkled tubular sleeves dangling flaccidly like the trunks of dead elephants' (*News from Tartary*).

In 1938, Fleming's uncle, Philip, gifted him the beautiful Nettlebed Estate which lies a few miles to the north-west of Henley-on-Thames. He used this windfall wisely and commissioned the architect Paul Phipps to design a family house at Merrimoles, for by now Celia was expecting a child. Nicholas[27] duly arrived in early January 1939 just as the war clouds gathered over Europe. In May, Fleming rejoined the Grenadier Guards and was reinstated[28] as a lieutenant, with seniority from 18 February 1937. His age made him an awkward fit for he was too old to be a platoon commander and yet he did not have the experience to command a company. 'The chance to fight [with his regiment], it turned out, was denied him – ironically enough by his own individuality. His brilliant intellect, his record of long solitary journeys and his knowledge of the East all marked him out as an ideal agent for intelligence work and special duties.'[29] Indeed, it is probable that Fleming had been on the books of the Secret Intelligence Service (SIS) ever since his first journey to Russia. Earlier that year, he had been interviewed by Major General Frederick Beaumont-Nesbitt, the Deputy Director of Military Operations and Intelligence (and a former Grenadier), as a candidate for Military Intelligence Department One (Research), usually referred to as MIR, the War Office's irregular warfare wing, and so he was immediately sent for specialist intelligence training from 5 to 17 June pending a transfer. Somehow he managed to squeeze in a canoeing holiday with Celia on the Rhône in late June before reporting to the Grenadiers' 2nd Battalion for three weeks' training in July. Subsequently, he was temporarily employed by the Military Intelligence Directorate in August before being appointed to MIR as a General Staff Officer Grade Three with the rank of acting Captain on 6 September. Inadvertently, he thus became a founder member of what was to become the 'top secret' Special Operations Executive or SOE.

His three younger brothers all flocked to the colours. Ian joined the Naval Intelligence Directorate in June 1939 as the personal assistant to its chief, Admiral John Godfrey, and installed himself in the mysterious-sounding Room 39 of the Admiralty. Michael and Richard both became soldiers, the former commissioned into the Oxfordshire and Buckinghamshire Light Infantry and the latter into the Lovat Scouts.

Chapter 2
Plans and more plans

MIR had started life in March 1936 as General Staff (Research), a small section consisting of one major and a secretary which reported directly to the Director of Military Operations and Intelligence. Its first incumbent came up with the idea of the Army Education Corps, the second examined military medicine,[1] but by 1938 their successor, Major Jo Holland of the Royal Engineers, had a more warlike agenda. With a charter to 'research into problems of tactics and organization … in order to collect new ideas on these subjects' and a modus operandi 'to go where they like, talk to whom they like but be kept from files, correspondence and telephone calls',[2] Holland tasked his section to research the subject of guerrilla warfare. Badly wounded in the Irish Troubles of 1919–20, he had first-hand experience of the difficulties of dealing with an insurgency as a member of the occupying power.

After extensive study of the Boer War, the Russian Revolution, the Irish Troubles, the Spanish Civil War and the Sino-Japanese War, in the early part of 1939 the section, now known as MIR, advanced the proposition that guerrilla warfare and other allied activities would prove to be an important feature of the impending war. From the outset it was recognized that the key to all such activities would be the ability to produce the right men when the time came. Accordingly, a personnel section was created to build a list of men with knowledge of languages and countries who were likely to prove effective as guerrilla leaders; it was planned to give them military training as opportunity offered.

Meanwhile, the Directorate of Military Operations and Intelligence had been split in two with Major General Beaumont-Nesbitt now in charge of the new Directorate of Military Intelligence. Consequently, a new charter evolved for MIR:

1   General research as required by the Director of Military Intelligence,
    including examination of preparation of projects involving the
    employment of special or irregular forces to assist or increase the effect
    of normally conducted operations, directly or indirectly.

2   Technical research and production of appliances as required for such projects.

3   The operation of projects as decided between Intelligence and Operations.

4   The collection of intelligence by special means outside the province of other sections of the Military Intelligence Directorate.

Within SIS there was a similar organization called D Section (originally called Section IX), headed up by Major Lawrence Grand, another Royal Engineer, which studied the possibilities for British clandestine action against Germany. Working closely together, Grand and Holland prepared a position paper for Lord Gort,[3] the Chief of the Imperial General Staff, who in turn presented it to Lord Halifax, the Foreign Secretary, on 23 March 1939. This resulted[4] in D Section being given the go-ahead to engage in sabotage and propaganda in the Nazi-occupied Czech borderlands and Austria. The significance of this political green light was not lost on Beaumont-Nesbitt who sent Holland's section to work along D Section in its new offices in Caxton Street. For a short time, the two organizations were merged into D/M Section. It was not a success for the contrast in character and temperament between the two section chiefs led to frequent clashes. At the first opportunity on 3 September 1939, Holland led his men back to the main War Office building in Whitehall, where Fleming pithily observed, 'I seem to be under the War Office but not of the War Office.'[5]

⁊

By now, with war imminent, MIR had become a hothouse of unconventional and exciting ideas. Following a directive from Lord Gort, Holland instructed Lieutenant Colonel Colin Gubbins of the Royal Artillery to write two short pamphlets: 'The Art of Guerrilla Warfare' (22 pages) and 'Partisan Leaders' Handbook' (40 pages) and Major Millis Jefferis, an 'inventive genius'[6] and head of explosives and devices, was tasked to produce a guide on 'How to use Explosives' (16 pages and diagrams). In these simple no-nonsense pamphlets the main common sense principles of guerrilla warfare were laid down and were later adopted by resistance groups throughout Europe and then the Far East.

Fortuitously, Fleming found himself in the Africa and Asia Group, where after an initial 'teething' reshuffle, the other members were Ralph Greg, a barrister and former Black Watch officer who had lost a leg in a big-game hunting expedition in Africa in 1928, and Captain Bill Allen of the Life Guards. An Etonian like Fleming, Allen had been a precocious student and had his first book *The Turks in Europe, a Sketch-Study*, published by John Murray when he was only eighteen.

In the interwar years, Allen had been a peripatetic journalist, first as a special correspondent of the *Morning Post* in the Greco-Turkish War of 1919–22 and then the Rif War of 1925 in Morocco. He had then gone on to travel extensively among the peoples of the Caucasus and Anatolia in the 1920s[7] and 1930s and, together with Sir Oliver Wardrop, Britain's first and only British Chief Commissioner of Transcaucasus, founded the Georgian Historical Society before writing an authoritative *History of the Georgian People* in 1932. In this period of great change and upheaval following the Russian Revolution, his grasp of the complexities of the Caucasus, Turkey, Russia and the Ukraine elevated him to the level of international scholarship; yet, as head of David Allens, one of Britain's oldest outdoor advertising agencies, he also oversaw a very successful business with his two younger brothers.

Allen was soon on his way to Palestine with the 1st Household Cavalry Regiment. On arrival he volunteered to join Orde Wingate's Gideon Force in Abyssinia which Wingate famously later described as 'sick camels and the scum of 1st Cavalry Division'.[8] Like Fleming, Bill Allen could capture 'his sitter' perfectly in words:

> In the evenings he unbent a little. He held the most pronounced Zionist views and was a Hebrew scholar well read in the Scriptures. His big nose and shaggy beard could recall, as he proclaimed the glories of Israel, the ghost of some harassed hill prophet; but the bony structure of the face, the thin, high-bridged line of the nose and the gleam of deep blue eyes declared some old Norse blood soured through Convenanting centuries. His equals were inclined to bait him, and the more easy-going went in fear. But the same fervour that made him goad men to almost superhuman effort insisted later that their courage be recognized.[9]

Fleming was to meet Orde Wingate three years later in India.

In mid-August 1939, MIR hatched a plan to send Fleming, Captain Martin Lindsay and John Keswick to China to explore how assistance could most usefully be rendered to the Chinese in the event of Britain being at war with Japan. Lindsay, who had started off as a regular officer in the Royal Scots Fusiliers, had made a name for himself as a polar explorer; *The Times* of 13 October 1934 decided that 'for daring and success [the 1934 British Trans-Greenland Expedition] will rank high in the long annals of polar exploration'. A book entitled *Sledge* followed and with his new public profile, Lindsay left the Army to pursue a career in politics. The third member of the group, John Keswick, was neither a travel writer nor explorer. As the youngest son of Henry Keswick, the taipan of Jardine Matheson, after completing his education in England he had joined the family business in Hong Kong and knew a great deal about Chinese business and politics.

MIR's plan was thwarted by the Foreign Office which 'produced insuperable political objections' and on 20 September, the China Mission was 'postponed indefinitely'.[10] Notwithstanding this disappointing outcome, Fleming's perspicacious and realistic plan[11] for British military assistance to the Chinese went on to form the foundation of SOE's Chinese strategy and indeed was to influence that of the American OSS. In this report, Fleming demonstrated that he could effortlessly switch from journalese to the terse report writing style required by the military for his fine analytical powers and clarity of expression served the identical needs of both masters.

NOTES ON THE POSSIBILITIES OF BRITISH MILITARY ACTION IN CHINA

1 If a state of war existed – with or without a declaration of war – between Great Britain and Japan, British politico-military objectives would be to a great extent identical to those of China. [Fleming footnote: 'The Japanese are, collectively, a cautious and conservative people. This does not apply to the personnel of either subordinate or high commands in China, whose record during the past two years has been one of spasmodic, often dangerous, but usually successful impetuosity in dealing with the local interests of Western powers. In the event of a major crisis in Europe, whether or not it leads at last to hostilities, it is more than possible that a period of weeks or even months will supervene during which the Japanese armed forces in China will commit isolated acts of war against Great Britain without any formal declaration of war by the Japanese Government.']

2 Chinese objectives are implicit in the policy on which she embarked, after some hesitation, in late July 1937. She has since followed that policy with complete consistency and with more success than was at first apprehended.

3 China's intention is to break, rather than to defeat, Japan. Her method is attrition. If we were involved in war against Japan (and assuming that our principal land forces were engaged, or at any rate contained elsewhere) our logical course would be to accelerate and intensify the process of attrition.

4 These processes, in so far as they are military, have been found to depend largely on what is loosely termed guerrilla warfare. The value and function of the guerrillas was not recognised by the Chinese until after the fall of Nanking in December 1937. Since then considerable attention has been paid, not without success, to increasing their sticking power and effectiveness. [Fleming footnote: 'True guerrillas should, ex-officio, claim and retain the initiative. In some, though not by any means all, sectors in China, the initiative is claimed and exploited by the Japanese garrisons, whose sorties from the walled cities in which they are loosely beleaguered represent the only positive military action normally taken

in those particular areas. The reverse (it is only fair to say) is sometimes true; but not often enough.']

5 Lawrence could not have won his war without Allenby: Allenby could not have won his war without Lawrence. Chinese high strategy recognises that guerrillas can only represent a subsidiary military effort; but that strategy is coloured by the tacit admission that China, however numerous her Lawrences, has nothing equivalent to Allenby – has, in fact, no offensive power capable of producing decisive results in the field.

6 In the Chinese conception, Allenby's role is filled by Time. This is logical and up to a point realistic; but the theory coincides with and justifies much that is ineffective in Chinese military practice. The almost pathological reluctance of the Chinese to take the offensive; their tendency to procrastinate; and their dislike of finality in any form – all these failings are condoned by a conception of high strategy which is, by implication, passive and which largely leaves it to the enemy to destroy himself.

7 The result is an avoidable declaration of the process of attrition. It seems probable that any British military effort in China would most profitably be directed towards eliminating this factor.

8 It also seems probable that this could best be achieved by concentrating at least as much on the fringes as on the centre of the Chinese military organisation. The German military mission, before it was recalled in 1938, enjoyed the confidence of Chiang Kai-shek and had undoubtedly done good work in training his regular troops before war broke out. The Germans appeared, nevertheless, to sacrifice effectiveness by being concentrated overmuch at Headquarters, where they remained – and were sometimes deliberately kept – out of touch with realities in the war areas. A British mission would, of course, need to have a well-manned and influential stronghold at Chiang Kai-shek's Headquarters; but to supply even the best strategic advice and the best technical aid would be of far less practical value than to supply local tactical initiative in as many sectors as possible.

9 Pending the results of a preliminary reconnaissance in China, it is possible to visualise a scheme of intervention developing, very broadly, along the following general lines:

   a Establishment of mission headquarters at Chungking, probably with a liaison and line of communication branch at Kunming, disposing of three or four aircraft (as well as some lorries, etc.) for transportation of stores and personnel.

b   Propaganda. This should not be neglected and should be laid on
at an early stage. The Chinese will be very responsive to the idea of
British co-operation and propaganda, even of the simplest kind, will
greatly improve the mission's chances of getting results out of junior
officers and men.

c   The despatch, probably via Chungking, of small parties of officers,
with a limited number of technical personnel to the Headquarters of
the various 'War Areas', which at present number five [?]. [Fleming
footnote: 'It might be worth considering providing each officer
with a minimum of personal bodyguards, for reasons of 'face' and
convenience. These details (not more than four men, including one
driver per officer) might consist of British-trained Chinese troops, or
of Indian troops, or of (non-Burmese) troops from Upper Burma.']
These sub-missions might operate along (roughly) the following lines:

   i   The senior officer, together with a minimum personnel for liaison,
signals and intelligence, would remain at the Headquarters of his
War Area, where he would endeavour to advise and stimulate the
local Chinese command both directly and (through contact with
British headquarters at Chungking) indirectly.

   ii   His junior officers would make their way, singly or in pairs, to
different sectors either of the 'front' or of the 'occupied' areas.
Their function would be to organise and, where possible, <u>to lead
personally</u> local offensive action against the enemy, particularly in
the more stagnant sectors.

d   The value of even a very small number of British officers going into
action (e.g. on night patrols or raiding parties) with, if not at the head
of, Chinese troops might be expected to be twofold. It would have
a considerable effect (which our propaganda could exploit) on the
Chinese rank and file, who would be pleasurably surprised to find
foreign officers coming with them under fire; and it would be the
surest way to overcome the obstacles of pride, jealousy and 'face'
which will be encountered in local commands. The average Chinese
general will not take kindly to foreign direction or control, however
tactfully imposed on him; but he will view with gratitude, respect and
astonishment a foreign officer who undertakes in person, and with
success, the distasteful task of fighting.

e   On the more technical forms which co-operation with the Chinese
might usefully take, the present writer is not competent to give an
opinion. But we could probably help them and ourselves by teaching
them up-to-date methods of demolition, by building bridges for
them, and by training a certain number of their young officers in

Burma. It is assumed that co-operation in the air will not be available on a scale large enough to make it economic.

10 The following points are implicit or explicit in the foregoing appreciation:

a In the present circumstances, should the Far East become a British theatre of war, our best way of striking at the Japanese on land is by accelerating and intensifying the processes of attrition to which she is being subjected by the Chinese regular and irregular forces.

b This can best be achieved by providing the Chinese with leadership, initiative and the will to attack. Lack of these attributes represents their most serious military weakness. Given these attributes, there is nothing wrong with the fighting qualities of the rank and file.

c The method here proposed is the infiltration of a small number of picked British officers into the Chinese forces, not merely advisers at Headquarters, but as fighting guerrilla leaders.[12] In this connection, liaison with the central Chinese authorities and propaganda directed at the Chinese people as a whole, are matters of considerable importance.

11 In conclusion it may be noted that the obstacles in the path of effective Anglo-Chinese co-operation in the field, however great the goodwill on both sides, will be formidable, various and complex. Given the right men, however, there is no reason why they should not be overcome.

12 The attitude of the Russians towards British military intervention in China would probably require watching.

As to who would be best suited to lead such a mission, Fleming suggested that 'the best material from British sources in China would probably come from such firms as Jardine Matheson, Butterfield and Swire, BAT, APC and ICI.[13] The banks would be unlikely to produce men with the best kind of qualifications, since their employees have, in the nature of things, very little experience of the interior.' He identified the following individuals as 'completely trustworthy men whose services would be of value, if necessary at an early stage'.

a W.J. KESWICK. (Jardines; wife and child in Shanghai; circa 36). Member of Shanghai Municipal Council. Very good man. His contacts and ability as a negotiator would be most valuable at Chiang Kai-shek's HQ.

b A.J. KESWICK. (Jardines; unattached; circa 32). Like his brother, is liked and trusted by most of the important Chinese, and, in addition, would make an excellent local leader or adviser.

c Michael LINDSAY. (Yenching University, Peking; son of the Master of Balliol; unattached [?]; circa 32). During the last 18 months has made three or four fairly extensive trips with guerrillas in the north and has written about them (for *The Times*) with shrewdness and discrimination. I know nothing of his military qualities, but his first-hand experience and his local contacts would clearly be of value. The fact that he has avoided getting into trouble with the Japanese speaks well for his discretion.

d   C.M. McDONALD. (*The Times*' correspondent in Shanghai; wife and child in Shanghai (I think); circa 40). A thorough and reliable man who understands the Chinese and gets on well with them. When bombed on the *Panay* showed great gallantry and resource, but this and other war experiences may have affected him in such a way as to make him more valuable at the centre rather than the fringes.

e   Roger HOLLIS. (MI5; married; circa 34). Did several years in China with BAT. Though he has not been there recently, his judgement of Far Eastern affairs has always impressed me as unusually realistic. His co-operation, or even his comments, might be valuable at an early stage, particularly as he is available in London.

f   Richard FLEMING. (Lieutenant Lovat Scouts; married; circa 29). I have put down my brother's name, because, although he has no experience of China, he is the best potential leader of irregular troops I know.

୬

Fleming's inclusion of Michael Lindsay's name was prescient. Lindsay had arrived in Japanese-occupied Peking in January 1938 to help introduce the Oxford University tutorial system to Yenching University, an American missionary university. On his first spring vacation, together with three Yenching colleagues, he decided to venture into Chinese-controlled territory outside Peking, and stumbled upon the Chinese Communists' Eighth Route Army, which had just started to move into the area. Lindsay returned to the Communist-controlled areas in the summer of 1939[14] when he was asked by the Communists to act as a purchasing agent for their troops, taking advantage of his status as a British citizen who could move relatively freely in Japanese-controlled Peking. Not a fluent Chinese speaker himself, he recruited one of his students, twenty-three-year-old Li Hsiao Li, to help him re-label in Chinese the medical supplies, radio parts, chemicals and other supplies he procured for the Eighth Route Army.

In April 1940, when funding for his position at Yenching temporarily dried up, Lindsay's brother-in-law, Robert Scott, arranged for him to be seconded to the British Embassy as 'press attaché', a position that brought him into close contact with SIS. After six months he returned to Yenching where he resumed smuggling supplies to the Communist army. He married his student accomplice, Li Hsiao Li, in June 1941 and the two just managed to escape the clutches of the Japanese secret police on 8 December as they fled the city. For the next two years Lindsay worked as a radio technology instructor and technical adviser to the Communist Jinchaji Military Region. In March 1944 he decided to move to the Communist Army HQ and after a 500-mile trek with his wife and newborn daughter, he reached Yenan at the end of May. Now the 'Wireless Communications Advisor' to the Third Department of Eighteenth Group Army, he built a high-powered transmitter and established a link with India and North America, one which could bypass the KMT in Chungking.[15]

∽

Written in the expectation that he and Martin Lindsay were as good as on their way to India, Fleming had added an appendix to his note that typified his imaginative approach to solving apparently intractable problems. While clearly playing to his own strengths and those of his peer group of former explorers and hardy travellers, his concept of a self-sustained British force operating along the Russian borderlands was masterful. He even identified the threat from the air as the potential fly in the ointment and looked to the Chinese to offset it:

> While it would clearly be uneconomic, if not impractical, for Great Britain to despatch anything in the nature of an expeditionary force to China, it might be worth strengthening our mission by attaching to it a small formation of regular troops.
>
> The advantages of sending out even (say) one battalion or its equivalent would be:
>
> **a)** Valuable effect on Chinese morale and on the mission's prestige
>
> **b)** Valuable effect on Japanese morale
>
> **c)** Valuable effect (locally) on the actual progress of hostilities
>
> The factor last mentioned may perhaps be scouted as negligible; but I think it probable that a small independent British force of the right type, using the right methods in the right area, would have a nuisance value out of all proportion to its size.
>
> The right area is the Mongolian Corridor – more specifically, the high grasslands to the north and west of the Peking-Kalgan-Paotow Railway. This corridor is of great strategic importance to the Japanese; but since it was over-run at the beginning of the war it has never been strongly held. It is sparsely inhabited country in which the distances are very great. The features (e.g. walled 'key' cities, roads, railways etc.) which in other parts of China offer the Japanese their best footholds and constitute the essential sinews of control, are largely absent or, where they exist, have not the same importance as elsewhere.

It is country which, since the days of Ghenghiz Khan, has been the happy hunting ground of irregular cavalry; and the presence in it of a regiment of British or Indian cavalry would be extremely unwelcome to the Japanese.

Logically, of course, the Mongolian Corridor ought to be a Russian sphere of operations. But in the past two years, whatever may have happened further north, the Russians have never made a diversion there; and in making our dispositions it would be unwise to rely on any positive Russian action in the Far East. At the same time, even with Russia passive, the presence of British troops in the neighbourhood of what is in effect a Russian frontier would be a disturbing omen to the Japanese General Staff.

Another consideration is the possibility of stimulating and acting as spearhead to the large forces of Chinese Moslem cavalry which are normally to be found in the North-Western Provinces and with some of whom (e.g. at Ning Hsia[16]) a British force would automatically come in contact. The Moslems are good fighters, with more dash and fanaticism than ordinary Chinese. Something (but probably not very much) might also be done with the Mongols, whose most valuable function would be as scouts.

The British force should, as indicated above, consist of cavalry or mounted infantry. It should be drawn either from the Indian Army or from one of the tougher British Yeomanry formations (e.g. the Lovat Scouts). It would proceed via Burma dismounted and travel up through China by motor transport. It would procure horses, with the co-operation of the Chinese authorities, on arrival in the north (only the Mongol pony could stand up to the distances and the diet; it would be admirable for our purposes).

Officers and men would have to live hard; to withstand great cold in winter; and, at times, to subsist largely on mutton and flour in various forms.

Such a force, well handled, should have little to fear except from the air. Accurate enemy air reconnaissance would increase its otherwise negligible chances of being caught in a 'comb-out' by mechanised columns; and (more important) effective bombing of the various bases from which it would carry out raids might cripple it, given luck. The possibility of giving it some protection from the air (probably mainly from Chinese sources) accordingly wants consideration.

It should be emphasized that even the minimum force envisaged in these notes could hardly come into action in much under six months from the date on which it was decided to employ it in China.

But it should be remembered that the appearance of a small British force on a Japanese flank would be more likely to have its maximum effect six months after, rather than on, the outbreak of war.

Fleming's idea never saw the light of day but an equivalent initiative, Detachment 204, was set up by Major General Dennys in February 1941 to train an elite Chinese guerrilla force. Once more, as soon as the Foreign Office got wind of it, they immediately decreed that under no circumstances could British personnel fight alongside the Chinese unless war had been declared although a way round this diktat was quickly devised by the formation of the Chinese Commando Group, manned by non-British European officers. Detachment 204 finally deployed in 1942 and after what General Wavell described as 'the most trying circumstances and difficult conditions' it returned to India at the end of the year. They had never once been allowed by the Chinese to attack the Japanese.

∽

With the mission to China well and truly kiboshed by the Foreign Office, life for Fleming at MIR entered a hiatus which, given the comings and goings of his fellow officers to Romania and France, must have been frustrating. Inventive as ever, Fleming busied himself with other projects. The MIR monthly report mentions 'under consideration is a project from Captain Fleming concerning sabotage on a minor scale in mails or freight carried to Germany or Russia by the Trans-Siberian Railway'. It also refers to 'a paper by Captain Fleming has recently been put up to colonel military intelligence embodying a plan for activities at Sinkiang in the event of hostilities in Trans-Caucasus'.

On 14 November, Fleming was sent for three weeks' training with the Warwickshire Yeomanry and returned to duty at MIR on 13 December. Just before Christmas, there was a flurry of activity as various officers,[17] including the prolific polar explorer Andrew Croft, were despatched either direct to Finland or via Stockholm. The next entry for Fleming in the MIR War Diary reads: '10 April Captains Davis and Fleming, Martin Lindsay and Lieutenant F. Carr RN began planning for the landing of guerrilla bands in Norway.' The day before, someone had made a stark entry: 'Invasion of Norway – the lack of intelligence before and after the event proved the need for a very much better intelligence service.' On 12 April, the log reads:

At midday, MIR were asked to send a small reconnaissance party to Namsos to prepare for landing of military contingent under General Mackesy. A hectic afternoon followed and by 02.00 hours the next morning, Fleming and party were ready to go. Their departure was postponed until the next day when they left at midday in a lorry and two taxis for Heston. We wished them well of their thankless task, as, until they reached Namsos, they would not know whether or not the Germans were already there.

Before he left, Fleming lodged the manuscript of *The Flying Visit* with Jonathan Cape. Written that March, it was a comic story of a propaganda flight made by

Hitler over England which went dreadfully wrong when a bomb exploded on the aircraft, resulting in the Führer bailing out over Oxfordshire and ending up locked in the lavatory at Huffham House guarded by Jennings the butler. Laced with real-life politicians such as Churchill and Chamberlain, Fleming justified his frivolous genre by proposing in his introduction that 'a sense of humour and a sense of proportion (or perspective) are essential and happily almost indestructible elements of any civilization'. It was a peculiarly English view of the world and for many provided an uplifting tonic in the dark days of the summer of 1940 when it was published.

When Hitler's deputy, Rudolf Hess, parachuted down to earth from his Messerschmitt on 10 May 1941 and landed on a farm to the south of Glasgow, rarely can there have been a more striking instance of life imitating art. Fleming's whimsical story with David Low's satirical illustrations now became headline news. The fictional and factual quandary for the British Government was remarkably similar. If the British portrayed Hess as mad, they would validate German propaganda. If his peace offer was genuine, they would have appeared as warmongers if they did not respond. So, both in art and life, they chose to say nothing.

Chapter 3

To war in the frozen north

In the early hours of 8 April 1940, Operation WESERÜBUNG, the German invasion of Denmark and Norway, began as the Kriegsmarine put to sea from its Baltic ports and headed north. By the following evening, though far from entrenched, the German command in Norway reported to Berlin that the occupation of Norway had been accomplished 'according to orders'.

In haste, Britain and France cobbled together a counter-move. On 12 April, Task Force AVONMOUTH, consisting of 24 Guards Brigade and 146 Infantry Brigade, sailed from Scapa for Narvik. During the planning process, it became obvious that the city of Trondheim was the key strategic point since once it fell into enemy hands, shipments of precious ore from the northern port of Narvik would have to run the full gauntlet of German firepower. A seaborne landing in the Trondheim area and a direct attack on the city – Operation HAMMER – was the only viable option but from the start, the Secretary of the Chiefs of Staff Committee, General Hastings Ismay, was not confident:

> Amphibious operations require highly trained personnel, a great variety of technical equipment, a detailed knowledge of the points at which the landings are to take place, accurate information about enemy strengths and dispositions, and, perhaps above all, meticulous planning and preparation. In the case of the projected Norwegian expeditions, none of these requirements could be fulfilled.[1]

The final plan adopted by the War Cabinet involved two landings some 300 kilometres apart to the north and west of Trondheim. 146 Infantry Brigade was diverted from Narvik to Namsos and 148 Infantry Brigade was ordered to land at Andalsnes. By quickly expanding these bridgeheads, a pincer movement would result in establishing a defensive front along the roads and railways and thus halt the German advance from Oslo. After landing at Romsdalsfjorden, SICKLEFORCE under Major General Paget was tasked with the capture of

Andalsnes and then to advance to Trondheim; to the north, MAURICEFORCE commanded by Major General Carton De Wiart was to disembark at Namsos (Operation HENRY) and then make his way south to Trondheim where he would meet up with Paget.

For MIR, events in Norway offered a chance to deploy their hand-picked team: Captain Torrance to Narvik, Major Palmer to Trondheim, Captain Munthe to Stavanger and Captain Croft to Bergen. No.13 Military Mission led by Major A.W. Brown and consisting of Captain R.B. Redhead and Sergeant Dahl was despatched from Stockholm on 16 April to Norwegian GHQ to 'encourage every aspect of guerrilla warfare' and to liaise between all British and Norwegian forces.[2] With a large inventory of explosives, MIR's technical wizard Major Jefferis landed with British troops at Andalsnes to blow up strategic targets.[3]

Fleming's No.10 Military Mission, consisting of Captain Martin Lindsay, 2nd Lieutenant Jack Scott-Harston, 2nd Lieutenant Gordon O'Brien Hitching[4] and Sergeants Berriff and Bryant of the Royal Signals, took off in a Sunderland flying boat from Shetland on 13 April and, after the rear gunner had scared off two tailing German aircraft, arrived over Namsos to reconnoitre the area ahead of the arrival of MAURICEFORCE. Fleming wrote in his diary of their dramatic arrival:

Suddenly swinging around a bend, we saw Namsos ahead of us: a little huddle of coloured wooden houses crouched between the mountains and the water. In a few seconds we were circling over it … There was our objective: so near and yet so far, like a toy in a shop window. Smoke rose from its chimneys, trampled snow lay in its streets. A ginger cat walked meditatively down one of them. But apart from the cat there was no sign of life at all … No.10 Military Mission had been ordered, less than 48 hours ago in Whitehall, to find out who was in occupation of Namsos. Here it was, hovering over the place like a kestrel over a rickyard, and for all it knew, Namsos might have been occupied by the Tibetans.

Once they had landed, the mission was able to confirm naval reports from the previous day that the area was clear of German forces but, after setting up their HQ in the Grand Hotel with the help of Captain Edds RM and his party, were unable to contact the destroyers due to a fault on their W/T set.[5] It was only early on 15 April that Fleming managed to get a signal through to the Admiralty:

Norwegian 5 Division HQ at Kvam reports at 23.00 hours 14 April. No enemy north of Hell. They estimate total enemy strength 1,600. Norwegian strength uncertain. Train south from Namsos running to Veral today. Naval landing party will be in a position South of Bangsund and East of Namsos by dawn 15 April. Locals co-operative. Namsos reconnoitred daily by enemy aircraft.

Both Namsos and Bangsund being snow covered, partially evacuated and very small, offer no concealment for considerable force. Local deployment impossible owing to four feet snow before proceeding on sparsely wooded country. Some MT available, no detail yet, rolling stock on single track railway. Southbound movement of any force much larger than one battalion must be slow and conspicuous from air. Namsos at present short of fresh water. Meeting De Wiart dawn 15 April.[6]

General Carton De Wiart VC was a legendary figure in the British Army, especially within MIR as he had led its mission to Poland in 1939 which had narrowly escaped the clutches of the Germans after experiencing the novel realities of a blitzkrieg. Fleming described his appearance as 'distinguished and, thanks partly to a black eye-patch and one empty sleeve, faintly piratical … As a *grand blessé* he was in a class by himself; he was severely wounded eight times and lost his left hand (and eye).'[7]

Now appointed commander of the North-Western Expeditionary Force, De Wiart arrived by flying boat on the afternoon of 15 April only to be greeted by a flight of German Ju88s. The Sunderland pilot manoeuvred his aircraft at high speed over the water of the fjord to present as hard a target as he could to the marauding German aircraft and it was only after an hour and a half that the destroyer HMS *Somali* was able to send a boat to collect the general. His ADC, Lieutenant G.E. Elliott, had been wounded in the attack and returned to Scotland in the flying boat, leaving the general without a staff officer.

On board I found Colonel Peter Fleming and Captain Martin Lindsay, and whoever may have been responsible for sending them I thank him now, for there and then I appropriated them and a better pair never existed. Colonel Peter Fleming from being adventurer and writer turned himself in general factotum number one and was the epitome of [Gilbert and Sullivan's]:

Oh, I am a cook and a Captain bold,
And the Mate of the Nancy brig
And a Bo'sun tight, and a Midshipmite,
And the crew of the Captain's gig!

Captain Martin Lindsay, explorer and traveller, picked up the bits where Peter Fleming left off, and between them they were my idea of perfect staff officers, dispensing entirely with paper.[8]

At 10.00 pm HMS *Somali* put into Namsos under cover of darkness and De Wiart called a conference on board. It was clear to everyone that German air activity posed a serious threat to the imminent landings and in a signal to London dated 01.25 hours 16 April, De Wiart told the Chief of the Imperial General Staff:

Arrived Namsos 16.40 hours but could not board destroyer until 18.15 hours owing to number of enemy aircraft. There is no possibility of landing troops from troopships here on account of enemy air activity. A landing will have to be carried out at night by destroyer. I hope to land two or three battalions on night 16/17 April. Marines will be relieved by then. On night 17/18 April I will land remaining battalion of brigades. 740 enemy are at present at STO DALEN and I hope to have fuller information tomorrow. I hope to attack enemy on 21 April. Chief difficulty at present is enemy air policy. We have no planes here at all. Enemy have been very active and have shadowed destroyer all day and made three raids here. My impression is that they suspect an attempt to land troops as enemy aircraft have been much more active today than yesterday. Concealment of troops by day is very difficult. There is little cover and still a great deal of snow. However if it is essential to advance the sooner it is done the better. I cannot at present judge situation at Trondheim but it will be essential that strong action should be taken as regards enemy air activity when I attack. If there is to be a naval attack at Trondheim and it is successful General Audet should attack as soon as possible after it. If you could inform me of date of this attack it would help decide definite date of my attack.

By 18 April, 146 Brigade had disembarked at Namsos and was beginning to make its way slowly south, moving only at night in line with De Wiart's orders. Much of the credit should go to Fleming for Lieutenant Atwater RN had told Colonel Holland in London that the Navy reckoned that 'Fleming's presence in Namsos had made it possible for him to cut communications with the rest of the country and had thus given the Navy three days' security for landing British and French troops with their stores before the Germans started bombing them'.[9] Fleming had gone ahead on 16 April with Sergeant Bryant to see the Norwegian General Laurantzon at his HQ at Kvam. Before leaving, he signalled the Admiralty:

Reliably reported railway bridge south of Verdal demolished, road bridge still intact 14 April. Confirmed some light troops for FVS landed at Trondheim. Proceeding Norwegian HQ Kvam, full sitrep tomorrow. Thawing but cross country movements off. Inadvisable without skis for probably three weeks. Note: Heavy W/T screening and long distance caused delay in reception.

After being briefed on the disposition and capabilities of the Norwegian forces in the area, Fleming came to the conclusion that with low ammunition states and no artillery, the Norwegians would not be able to make any significant contribution to taking on the advancing Germans. Instead he asked Laurantzon to deploy his ski-troops as a harassing force and sent his signallers with their W/T sets back to Norwegian HQ the next day to assist with communications. They managed to establish a voice link over thirty kilometres and a Morse link over forty kilometres but the overall signals environment was very patchy; at one point by Lake Snaasa, they were down to a one-mile range. Both returned to Namsos on 18 April.

A second wave of Allied troops, 5 Demi Brigade of the French Chasseurs Alpine, disembarked at Namsos on 19 April. Unaware of the cat and mouse game being played by De Wiart and Fleming with the Germans, the French foolishly engaged some enemy aircraft the next morning thereby triggering a devastating bombing raid which turned the town centre into an inferno, destroying a large part of their stores and ammunition. Well equipped for winter warfare, the French dispersed outside the town to the chagrin of De Wiart, who Fleming later recalled, fished around in his pocket for a cigarette, lit one up – no mean feat for a man with one arm – and muttered 'Damn Frogs, they're all the same. One bang and they're off!' For No. 10 Military Mission it had been a disaster:

'Our sets destroyed in Grand Hotel. Civilian telephone exchange destroyed. Bang went remaining skeleton communications inland. Moved out to Grong during night.'[10] With no airstrip in the area and no aircraft carrier immediately available, De Wiart saw 'little chance of carrying out decisive, or indeed, any operations'.

In a signal to London timed at 20.29 hours on 22 April, De Wiart gave his frank assessment of the situation confronting MAURICEFORCE:

Have seen Phillips [commander of 146 Brigade] who has situation in hand. The battalion from Verdal area is retiring. The three companies at Vist are in touch with a strong force of Germans and will attempt retiring tonight to Steinkjer area. Steinkjer has been bombed and completely destroyed. Our men cannot fight off road owing to deep snow, this does not handicap the enemy who is using snow shoes. I have ordered Phillips to retire by the Steinkjer-Namsos road but when enemy discover this move everything on this road will be destroyed and in this weather it will put a very heavy physical strain on the men. I had hoped that by pushing Phillips' brigade south as far as I did, and if a heavy raid on Trondheim had taken place, I might have made a dash for Trondheim but now I clearly cannot do this and I must try and extricate Phillips. When his brigade gets back to Namsos they will find no accommodation, no water, no facilities and the bridge may not be standing. Troops in Veral sector shelled by destroyer today 22 April. I should be grateful if you would let me know what your policy will now be. I much regret to give you such a gloomy view of situation but it is a true one.

Fortunately, poor weather and a lull in German air activity enabled a second group of French troops to land intact with all their stores and equipment and by 25 April the whole of MAURICEFORCE had disembarked.

The underlying situation remained grave. Strong German land attacks against forward British positions in the Steinkjer and Vist areas forced MAURICEFORCE on the defensive. With no sign of an Allied landing at Trondheim, De Wiart became increasingly despondent about 'sitting out like rabbits in the snow'[11] and signalled the War Office on 22 April that he had ordered the 146 Brigade to retire. Being a seasoned campaigner, he sensed that London had no inkling as to what was actually happening on the ground and despatched Fleming on 27 April in a flying boat back to England to report on the seriousness of the situation. On arrival, he was greeted with some surprise for the *Daily Sketch*, acting on information from Stockholm[12] that he had been killed in a bombing raid on the Grand Hotel in Namsos, had run the headline 'Author Killed in Norway', with a picture of Peter and Celia underneath and a short obituary. Such was the lax security at MIR. After delivering his despatches to the War Office, Fleming had a breakfast meeting with Churchill, then still First Lord of the Admiralty, who impressed him as a politician who 'knew how, and how not, to wage a war'.

On his return two days later, Fleming told De Wiart that 'you can really do what you like, for they don't know what they want done'. A chance meeting with Major Johnny Bevan, an intelligence officer with the Expeditionary Force, resulted in a defiant act of deception; the two men concocted some typewritten messages and then left them in a half-burnt state. The reader would be under the impression that the Namsen bridge had been wired to an explosive device on a time-fuse with a dug-in machine gun post covering the line of advance on the road.[13]

The situation was by now unsustainable. Ship-to-shore communications now relied on signal lamps manned by Fleming's two Royal Signallers. The Allied campaign to recapture Trondheim and stem the German advance had ignominiously ground to a halt and was in reverse. The two expeditions were too far apart to mutually support each other and without air cover both were exposed to enemy aircraft at every point along their lines of communications. Late on 27 April, De Wiart received a signal to begin the evacuation of his 6,000-strong force, prioritizing the rescue of men over that of equipment. The 2nd Demi Brigade and 147 Infantry Brigade withdrew together and by 2 May were dug in along the perimeter of the Namsos bridgehead. On the night of 2/3 May, the Navy came to collect them and after a harrowing voyage under constant attack from Stukas, the convoy finally dropped anchor at Scapa Flow on 5 May.[14] The next day, Namsos fell without a shot to the Germans. Four days later, Chamberlain resigned as prime minister, the government fell and Churchill emerged as leader of a wartime coalition.

In their short time together in Norway, Fleming and De Wiart became firm friends as well as comrades in arms. That friendship continued in the latter stages of the war when the two men were together in Chungking in China and was celebrated by Fleming in a witty article called 'Beau Sabreur'. In an affectionate and colourful obituary he wrote[15] on the general's death in 1963, beginning:

> it was to the age of chivalry that Adrian De Wiart properly belonged. He saw life as a list in which honour (when nothing much was happening) and duty (when his country was in peril) engaged him automatically as a contestant. It was once said of him that in the world of action he occupied the same sort of niche that Sir Max Beerbohm occupied in the world of letters; and this was true, for he was in all things a stylist.

De Wiart held a candle to the memory of Fleming in Norway and late in 1944 was heard to tell Mountbatten, 'I can't think what you want with this bloody great staff. I only had Peter Fleming in Norway and was never bothered with bumf at all.'[16]

Chapter 4

A very British guerrilla

Shortly after the evacuation of the British Expeditionary Force from Dunkirk in June 1940, the Secretary of State for War, Anthony Eden, visited XII Corps in Tunbridge Wells, commanded by Lieutenant General Andrew Thorne, a highly decorated Grenadier Guards officer of the First World War.[1] Eden was so appalled by its lack of anti-tank weapons that he immediately reported the situation to Churchill. The prime minister summoned Thorne to lunch at Chequers where he was briefed on the paucity of defences from Greenwich to Hayling Island. Sir John Colville, who as Churchill's private secretary was present at the meeting, noted that 'Thorne thinks 80,000 men will be landed [by the enemy] on the beaches between Thanet and Pevensey'.

Thorne came away from lunch determined to revive an old idea of his about the need to form a stay-behind guerrilla movement in Britain. His mind went back to his years in Berlin and a visit to East Prussia where he had witnessed the value of 'stay-behind' guerrilla bands, who by hiding allowed the enemy to advance over them and then attacked their lines of communication from the rear. He had likewise been impressed by the Wehrmacht's use of camouflage when attending military manoeuvres. Once he had taken command of 1 Guards Brigade on his return to England and after having consulted his friend, the military theorist Sir Basil Liddell Hart, he tested in conjunction with RAF Farnborough two types of camouflage on exercise in the Aldershot area. Using brigade funds, he purchased pea-netting and garden parasols to hide his HQ and to simulate a dummy one.

In his book *Invasion 1940*, Fleming credits Thorne as being 'the first officer to see that it might temporarily be very valuable, and would certainly be better than nothing, if at this stage the enemy in his bridgeheads were harassed by light forces left behind for the purpose.' While an advancing army is not normally bothered by guerrillas,

Thorne expected, if he was pushed back from the coast, to stand and fight, with whatever resources were available, on "the GHQ Line", a large ditch or fosse then being hastily excavated round the southern outskirts of the capital. It seemed to him that if the enemy's attack on this position could be delayed or interfered with by irregulars operating against the German supply-routes and concentration areas, Home Force's chance of repelling it would be, however negligibly, improved.

Shortly after his meeting with Churchill, Thorne got in touch with General Hastings Ismay, Churchill's Chief of Staff. He responded by sending him an officer he considered well qualified to assist him in developing the concept. It was Peter Fleming who, as the author of *Flying Visit*, was much spoken of at the time. The two men knew each other socially – they had met in Berlin in 1934 when Thorne was military attaché to Germany[2] – and an excellent working rapport followed. Charged with this 'sort of unorthodox task which, with its promise of almost schoolboy adventure, appealed to his Buchanesque nature',[3] Fleming was seconded to XII Corps on 25 May to develop a UK stay-behind force in the event of a German invasion.[4] As he later put it, 'I found myself charged with the duty of organizing some sort of guerrilla force which would allow itself to be overrun by the invaders and thereafter harass them to the best of its ability.'[5]

Invasion fever was running high at the time. In his biography of Ian Fleming, Andrew Lycett recounts how Peter Fleming and his brother Ian had been despatched to Southend over the Whitsun weekend of 11/12 May to act as 'official observers' of an imminent German attack on the seaside town that MI5 had been tipped off about. However, instead of a deserted promenade they found the streets full of holidaymakers enjoying the spring bank holiday, and after gazing out at an empty sea from the roof of a hotel, they decamped back to London.

The plan which the new C-in-C Home Forces, General Ironside, presented to the Chiefs of Staff on 25 June for the defence of Britain provided for a 'crust' of troops along the coast to meet the first invaders. Behind them in great depth were mobile columns and static strong points intended to delay the enemy until the mobile columns were brought into action; and, finally, covering London and the industrial areas there was to be a 'GHQ' line in the form of a continuous ditch running from Yorkshire to the Blackwall Tunnel and on to Maidstone and south of London. In a letter to Thorne, Ironside extolled that 'Local Defence Volunteers (LDVs) should be of great use to you for the static defence – shot guns and bombs and those Molotov Cocktails'.[6]

Fleming took Thorne's thinking one stage further. After an area had been overrun, the original concept was for hand-picked members of the Home Guard led by one or two Army officers to emerge from their hiding places and attack the Germans before being killed or captured or possibly making their way back to British lines; in other words, they were almost immediately expendable. By invoking the dictum of an imaginary Chinese general of the fifth century BC –

'a guerrilla without a base is no better than a desperate straggler' – he contended that by constructing elaborate underground hideouts, well stocked with rations, water, W/T sets and explosives, small units of a dozen or so men led by a lieutenant would be able to operate behind enemy lines 'with a sporting chance … of remaining a thorn in the enemy's flesh for weeks or perhaps even in some cases for months'.[7] Approval quickly followed.

Installed in a secluded farmhouse called The Garth at Bilting, a village between Ashford and Canterbury, Fleming established the first regional training centre for stay-behind units, known by the cover name XII Corps Observation Unit. Soon, with the assistance of the ever-resourceful Royal Engineer 'Mad' Mike Calvert, about twenty 'Auxiliary Units' were deployed in underground hideouts across south-east England.

Calvert had been at the Lochailort Special Training School as an instructor in demolitions when he was summoned to the War Office and introduced to Fleming. Although both had been in Norway at the same time, they had started from opposite ends of the pincer movement to surround Trondheim and thus had never met. In his introduction to Calvert's book *Prisoners of Hope*, Fleming described their first meeting:

> He was sitting at a table in a corridor of the War Office; this table acted as a sort of ante-room to the overcrowded office occupied by one of the less orthodox sections of the Military Intelligence Directorate … The stocky, crouched figure … rose up to its feet with simian grace and we shook hands warily; I was one rank senior to him, but he was a regular soldier. As we started to discuss, in the usual pleasantly chimerical way, the special duties for which we had been selected, neither of us was aware that he had found a close and [as far as we can tell] a lifelong friend.

'Briefly, our job was to make Kent and Sussex as unsafe and unpleasant as possible for the Germans if they ever got that far,'[8] recalled Calvert. They started by putting themselves in the position of the invading Germans, 'seeing the towns and villages of Kent and Sussex for the first time and not admiring the scenery but deciding which bridges to cross, which houses to occupy and so on. We then set about mining and booby-trapping all the places we thought the Germans would use.' The next task was to pick the people who could be relied upon 'to find their way to a switch and press it when the Germans came'. These formed the nucleus of a British resistance movement and soon occupied in their spare time a series of well-concealed underground bunkers, stocked with food, water, medical supplies and explosives.

There were moments of hilarious improvisation. Fleming acquired two large bows and a stock of arrows and set about training his small detachment of Lovat Scouts in close-range archery. The idea was to engage the enemy silently in the woods and along the tracks and rides of Kent without giving away their own position and at the same time creating an irrational fear of an army of furtive bowmen in the mind of the German High Command. In the end the only target they engaged was a fallow deer which, despite a lengthy follow-up, they never found. Fleming concluded that 'this was [as far as I know] the nearest the British soldier has come for several centuries to discharging an arrow in anger; and on the whole I think it is probably just as well that in 1940 he never had to come any nearer.'[9]

Part of their remit was to test the defences of the Army and on a famous occasion, Fleming and Calvert planted sticks of gelignite attached to timers in the flowerpots on the terrace of Lieutenant General Bernard Montgomery's V Corps headquarters. The prickly general took it well. When they were recalled to London, Calvert was confident that 'if it had been called to action, the Resistance Army of Kent and Sussex would have had at its core some of the toughest and most determined men' he had ever met. Their farms and their shops and their homes would have been highly dangerous places for any enemy soldier to enter.

On one occasion Calvert recalled that they were visited by several VIPs and, as hosts, offered them lunch.

It was quite nourishing, though not West End standard, and we all sat down round the box of gelignite that we were using as a table. Soon after we had started it began to get dark so I lit a few candles and put them on the box. This was normal practice for Peter and me and we went on eating without giving a second thought to the spluttering candle flames. Looking back, I realize that our guests, not used to living on quite such intimate terms with high explosives, behaved very well in the circumstances. 'I see you like to live dangerously,' was the dry comment made between mouthfuls by General Sir Andrew Thorne.

Colonel Norman Field, who took over from Fleming at The Garth, found him 'a very agreeable man. He had a brilliant brain, was a quick thinker and a wit with a keen sense of humour.' He was full of admiration at what XII Corps Observation Unit had achieved in so short a time.

[Fleming] had to move very fast. He had to get his friends around him to give him a hand. His brother [Richard] brought a platoon of the Lovat Scouts down. He had to requisition vehicles from here there and everywhere, obtain explosives and, more importantly, go and see people in authority whose word he could trust to discuss recruiting leaders. He did all this, but there was very little record of anything. It was done in a hell of a rush. If, for example, after acquiring a suitable recruit, something like an obscure cellar existed in the area, material was just dumped there. The construction of a suitable base would follow.

Fleming recalled in *Invasion 1940* that

> the underground hideouts ... were mostly sited in areas of dense woodland or scrub. They varied in design. Some were merely large dugouts, excavated, roofed and provided with bunks and ventilation by the Royal Engineers. Others made use of existing underground accommodation. One was in the cellars of a house destroyed many years earlier and abandoned; another was made by enlarging the tunnels of a badger's sett in a derelict chalk pit where generations of these animals had made their home; a third consisted, basically, of a huge oval pit, dug in the corner of a deer park to house a small and presumably secret airship during the First World War. The domestic economy of these lairs bore a general resemblance to that of the Lost Boys' subterranean home in the second act of *Peter Pan*.

When General Thorne paid a visit to the Auxiliary Units, his ADC, Ralph Arnold, remembered being met by Fleming who

> led us into the middle of a thick belt of woodland on the hill above Charing. Stumbling along in the dark we presently reached a clearing, and the Corps Commander was challenged to find the entrance to the unit's hideout. We poked about unsuccessfully for a few minutes, and then our guide casually kicked a tree stump. It fell back on a hinge to reveal a hole with a rope ladder dangling into a cavern that had been enlarged from a badger's sett. In this cave, sitting on kegs of explosives and surrounded by weapons, booby-traps, a wireless set and tins of emergency rations, were some Lovat Scouts and half a dozen hand-picked Home Guards ... chosen for their toughness and their knowledge of the countryside.[10]

In mid-June 1940, the concept and implementation of UK stay-behind forces was handed by General Ironside to Brigadier Colin Gubbins, who had commanded the Independent Companies in Norway with distinction. His Chief of Staff, Major Peter Wilkinson, recalled 'first of all we had Peter Fleming, who was already in the woods between here [Charing] and Canterbury. It was decided that his organization was as good a model as any other.' Wilkinson, who had shared an office with Fleming in MIR, remembered that 'he was eight or nine years older than me and one of my schoolboy heroes. I absolutely worshipped him. A very clever man. He turned me from being a very raw schoolboy into a civilized creature in about six months!' Much to Fleming's delight, Andrew Croft was among the twelve regional commanders[11] summoned by Gubbins to a conference shortly after Hitler's 16 July Directive No. 16 for the invasion of England. Although himself a deft hand at harpooning seals in the Arctic, Croft was intrigued by Fleming's inclusion of bows and arrows in his armoury, some tipped with 'a particularly useful poison he had discovered in Brazil'.[12]

After the war, Fleming was realistic about what the Auxiliary Units would have been able to achieve, citing lack of communications as a serious handicap and also the lack of natural camouflage at the onset of winter. With the benefit of hindsight, he also identified the spectre of brutal reprisals from which 'the Germans had no thought of shrinking'. Terrible retribution would have fallen on the families and neighbours of the members of the 'striking force' following their forays against the Germans. That said, 'even assuming the British resistance movement would have melted away in the white heat of German ruthlessness, it might have struck some useful blows before doing so'. Churchill's verdict that the Auxiliary Units were 'a useful addition to the regular forces' remained, in Fleming's opinion, fair and valid.

Never one to draw attention to himself or claim credit for other men's achievements, Fleming was meticulous in thanking Thorne – 'it made all the difference to owe allegiance to a sympathetic and accessible Commander on the spot'.[13] Ironically, Fleming himself never received any official recognition for the strategy and design which he personally drew up for the Auxiliary Units.

On 2 October, a lunch was held to mark the end of MIR as it dissolved into the new intelligence structures of SOE. The occasion represented the gathering[14] of that clan of military thinkers who would continue to break new ground in taking the war to the enemy where he least expected or wanted it. Six would graduate to SOE – Gubbins, Wilkinson, Davies, Greg, Fleming and Perkins. The day before, news came that Fleming's youngest brother, Michael, had died from wounds whilst a POW, having been captured at Dunkirk when he was Adjutant of the 4th Battalion Oxford and Buckingham Light Infantry. Three times mentioned in despatches for gallantry, the loss of Michael weighed heavily on the family; his widow and four young children moved in with Celia at Merrimoles, Fleming's country house on the Nettlebed Estate in Oxfordshire.

William Mackenzie, the SOE historian, concludes that during its brief lifespan,

MIR was certainly extremely successful as a research department in the widest sense. There is always argument about the exact origin of any scheme which proves successful, but it is safe to say that MIR was one of the really live spots in British military organization, and that it launched or helped to launch a number of projects which had an important future. There were, for instance, aid to escaping prisoners (MI9), strategic deception (ISSB and MI10), the Independent Companies, from which came the Commandos, the guerrilla training centre at Lochailort (STS) and the Politico-Military courses at Cambridge. These were all projects that have left a deep mark on our ideas of training and organization for war, which are not likely to be forgotten.[15]

As a member of the MIR hand-picked team, Fleming certainly left his mark as Mike Calvert later acknowledged:

It was good to be in the company of men who were pioneering the type of fighting that had begun to intrigue me: the small force which acted on its own, harried the enemy and upset their balance. Such forces could not win wars alone, of course, and none of us ever pretended they could. But they had tremendous value as the spearhead of a big attack, or the annoying jolt that distracted the enemy from the central front, or the means of destroying a vital strategic point which for some reason or other the main force could not reach. They could dart in quickly and silently from the air, from the sea or on land and do their deadly work before the other side really knew what was going on.[16]

Chapter 5
A Greek tragedy

When MIR was absorbed by the newly formed Special Operations Executive (SOE) in July 1940, Hugh Dalton, Minister of Economic Warfare, sent for Fleming and appointed him head of the YAK Mission tasked to scour Italian POW camps in Egypt for 'anti-fascist' candidates for SOE operations in Axis Italy; indeed, there was even talk of raising a 'Garibaldi division' and 'a charter to collect and train a band of anything up to a thousand Italian desperados'.[1] Installed in Room 808 in the War Office in November, he quickly assembled a team from scratch, casually inviting friends and acquaintances to 'come to Egypt'.[2] One recruit was brother Grenadier Captain Norman Johnstone, who had read modern languages (including Russian) at Oxford. He had joined the Grenadier Guards in 1932 and, after serving for seven years including three years in Egypt with the 3rd Battalion, had been on the point of leaving when war broke out. After active service with the 2nd Battalion in France, he jumped at the opportunity to soldier abroad and close with the enemy albeit at this stage somewhat indirectly. Guardsman Loveday, who had joined the regiment in October 1939 aged 22, came along as Johnstone's orderly: he was in for a surprise.

The other members of the mission were Captain Bill Stirling (Scots Guards), Lieutenant M.R. Norman (Royal Artillery), Second Lieutenant L.O.M. Barstow[3] (Royal Horse Artillery), Second Lieutenant G.R. Randall (Devon and Cornwall Light Infantry), Staff Sergeant Major R. Richardson (Royal Army Service Corps), Corporal W.J. Isted (Royal Engineers), Lance Corporal D.S.A. Turkhand (Royal Signals) and Lance Bombardier P. Clarke (Royal Artillery). After a crash course in irregular warfare at Lochailort and carrying £40,000 in notes and gold sovereigns, the mission sailed from the Clyde in January 1941 and after a complicated journey by sea to Freetown and then Takoradi, they finally reached Cairo by air. No sooner had they arrived than it quickly became clear that judging by the response in the POW camps around Cairo, very few POWs of the 130,000 'in the bag' by February 1941 were remotely interested in the unconventional line of work offered by Fleming.[4]

No 'free' Italian force was ever formed and a frustrating wait for a new assignment followed. Fleming wrote to Celia on 4 March and reported that

Fleming's Foot are at present in a state of stagnation and it is very difficult to see what our destinies are going to be, except they are certain to be very safe. We all live expensively at Shepheard's and I spent my time flapping around and trying to fix things up, which is inordinately difficult whatever the things are … Norman [Johnstone] is a tremendous figure, surrounded by pimps and middlemen of all kinds, their horrible faces kindled with the happy and prosperous memories of peacetime Cairo.[5]

After three weeks of hustling for work during which time Bill Stirling transferred out to work for the CGS,[6] Fleming and his mission found themselves deployed by General Wavell to northern Greece to prepare stay-behind parties in the event of a German invasion 'on [the] lines [of the work] done by him in Kent'.[7]

SOE and its forerunners, Section D and MIR, had been busy in Greece since February 1940 but to little avail. With scant human and financial resources, strategy fell into the 'on a wing and a prayer' category. In May 1940, the 'office' was beefed up with the appointment of a full-time manager, Ian Pirie of Section D, and its numbers increased with the arrival of Major Bill Barbrook of MIR[8] and the archaeologist John Pendlebury, also MIR, whose job was to organize a Cretan resistance movement under his cover of vice consul in Heraklion. In May, another MIR-trained Cambridge archaeologist, Nick Hammond, arrived in Athens only to be refused admission by the Greek authorities who sensed that this heightened level of British clandestine paramilitary activity could compromise their relations with Germany. In November 1940, two young Intelligence Corps officers, Patrick Leigh Fermor and Monty Woodhouse, arrived in Athens as the British Military Mission to Greece, both tasked with reporting on the Greek Army in its defence against the Italian invasion across the Albanian border. Hammond managed to return in March 1941 around the time of Fleming's arrival. With orders to train Greeks as W/T operators and saboteurs, he successfully destroyed the Lake Copais Company's cotton stocks at Haliartus just before the Germans arrived in Athens.

Here is the mission's story as reported by Fleming, who sent a copy of his report to the Regimental Adjutant of the Grenadier Guards, Major Arthur Penn, one of whose duties was to keep track of 'extra-regimentally employed' Grenadier officers dotted around the world. In his own inimitable way, Fleming surpasses the standard military reportage of what, when, where, by whom, to whom, and weaves in a narrative of adventure and excitement laced with spur-of-the-moment decisions, all the time paying homage to the fickle hand of fate that rules over life and death on the battlefield.

REPORT ON VARIOUS MINOR OPERATIONS IN GREECE

The foregoing paragraphs will serve to explain how and why a small training unit supposedly engaged on SOE activities came to undertake a series of miscellaneous duties in the field which had nothing to do with SOE. Our operational role tended to vary, for we were in turn commercial travellers, engine drivers and anti-aircraft artillery personnel. In this report a brief account is given of the various small tasks which came our way.

A. INTRODUCTION

On the orders of the C.-in-C.,[9] Middle East, I proceeded to Greece on 25 March and reported to GOC 'Z' Force.[10] I had under my command four officers and five other ranks on the strength of SOE[11] with three vehicles, a quantity of demolition stores and booby trap devices, and twenty Thompson submachine guns. My orders were to do what I could to organize, train and equip local personnel for post-occupational resistance and sabotage in areas likely to be overrun by the enemy …

The Greek General Staff intimated that they wished me to carry out this task in the Monastir Gap. I accordingly moved up and established a camp on the ridge immediately north of Xinon Heron.[12] For purposes of convenience and security my party were attached to British Advanced HQ where it was known as the Topographical Unit.

Hardly had this camp been pitched when the enemy in considerable strength crossed the Yugoslav frontier and entered the Gap. We now found ourselves immediately behind the British Forward Defence Lines[13] and it was clear that the time factor rendered our task in that area impossible. I accordingly reported to the Brigadier General Staff on 10 April and asked whether there was any capacity in which my personnel and stores could be made useful to the Force. He ordered me to report to … the Chief Royal Engineer, 6 Australian Division, with HQ at Perdika.

B. DISTRIBUTION OF BOOBY TRAP DEVICES

[At Perdika] we demonstrated and handed over to forward Engineer units several thousand 'time pencils', which are a delated action fuse[14] with five delays varying from half an hour to 24 hours. I do not know on what scale or to what effect these simple and efficient devices were employed, but the Sappers seemed glad to get them. Thirty charges were set with them in a petrol dump immediately north of Perdika.

C. DESTRUCTION OF ROLLING STOCK AT AMYNTAIO

Chance reconnaissance by two officers of the Topographical Unit on 11 April revealed that twenty locomotives and approximately 100 coaches had been abandoned in Amyntaio railway station. As the Germans were in possession of both ends of the line, permission was sought and obtained from the Chief Engineer to destroy the rolling stock. A party consisting of Captain Johnstone, the Intelligence Officer of 6 Division HQ and two Australian other ranks arrived at Amyntaio about 10.00 hours on 12 April and began sabotage against locomotives and permanent way.[15] By 20.00 hours all locomotives had been disabled and thirty-one delayed action charges consisting of about 50 lbs. each of Greek dynamite were installed among the rolling stock. One Greek field gun of German origin and a wagon of shells were also destroyed. At 16.00 hours Sergeant Thomas of 4th Hussars, arrived at the station, following an urgent request for engine drivers. By 12.30 hours he had succeeded in getting steam up in one locomotive which was then driven about a quarter of a mile away and run at full speed back into the railway yard. This operation was repeated three times and resulted in the complete destruction of fifteen wagons and a tank engine. In addition, about 30 yards of the permanent way were torn up. Sergeant Thomas acted throughout this operation with coolness and resource and was working under accurate shell fire from 19.30 to 20.00 hours. At 20.30 hours the party withdrew on orders from the Chief Engineer to Perdika, clearing obstructions from the road as it went. The success of this operation was due to the drive and ingenuity of Captain Johnstone.

D. INSTALLATION OF FLAME FOUGASSE AT SERVIA

After the withdrawal to the Aliakmon Line I was ordered by the Chief Engineer to take charge of Flame Fougasses, devices which by means of a small charge throw a sheet of burning oil for a distance of 50 yards. Lieutenant Tyson, Royal Engineers, who had been demonstrating these engines to the Greeks, was attached to my unit for this purpose. Commanders of forward troops however were undisposed to attach technical value to these devices or to make available working parties for their installation; and the only one we did in fact set was sited some distance in front of the British Forward Defence Lines on the Aliakmon bridgehead north of Servia. This Fougasse was installed on the afternoon of 13 April after the Aliakmon bridge and pontoon had been destroyed by the Sappers. Three large barrels of the appropriate mixture of petroleum products were buried and camouflaged in the bank covering the junction at the bridgehead of the road and the track leading up from the pontoon. Refugees were coming across the destroyed bridge on foot and the problem of setting a booby trap which could not be initiated by them but would be initiated by the enemy was solved by the use of a derelict Greek bus. This was placed athwart the road with pressure switched under the wheels connected with the charge. The bus could not be moved by pedestrians but would have to be moved by anyone wishing to get a vehicle past … It is unfortunately impossible to say whether or not this booby trap was initiated by the enemy.

E. REMOVAL OF AMMUNITION TRAIN FROM LARISSA STATION

On 14 April the Chief Engineer ordered me to withdraw to the Larissa area, where on the evening of the 15th we discovered there were two large ammunition trains in No. 353 siding outside the station. The Railway Transport Officer was absent from the station and a certain lack of initiative and control was evident throughout those parts of 81 Base Sub Area[16] adjacent to Larissa, which was being intermittently but heavily bombed. On the morning of 16 April I accordingly sought and obtained from Brigadier Parrington[17] commanding 81 Base Sub Area, permission to attempt to salvage one of the ammunition trains, whose contents (particularly.303 small arms ammunition) I knew to be badly needed further south. Captain Johnstone had acquired a rudimentary knowledge of engine driving during the demolitions at Aliakmon, and a party consisting of myself, Captain Johnstone, 2/Lieutenant Barstow, Guardsman Loveday and Corporal Yannoulatos (who had been attached to me by Captain Prince Peter[18]) began work at 08.30 hours. We obtained a working party of ten other ranks from 81 Base Sub Area to act as brakemen, stokers, etc. There was still no Railway Transport Officer at the station and most of the Greek railway officials were also absent. We were assisted by Lieutenant Reay of the Expeditionary Force Institutes (part of the NAAFI) who had come to Larissa to look for some of his men.

Of approximately twelve locomotives in the station the majority had been damaged by enemy action. There was very little coal available and the water mains had been cut by bombing. The permanent way and sidings had been extensively damaged and continued to sustain damage throughout the day.

Between 08.00 hours and 18.00 hours enemy aircraft made ten bombing attacks on Larissa, in most of which the station received attention. There was a good deal of somewhat aimless machine gunning. The largest force of aircraft engaged was eighteen bombers. Our work received a setback when one of the few heavy bombs used destroyed the line a few yards in front of the engine in which we were attempting to get up steam, rendering it immobile. By the end of the day there was only one intact set of rails running through the station to No. 353 siding.[19]

By the middle of the afternoon we had steam up in a locomotive which appeared to be reasonably sound. Captain Johnstone drove it to No. 353 siding where we attached it to a train of twenty trucks containing 120 tons of ammunition, and 150 tons of petrol. (Owing to the way the train was made up, it was impossible to leave the petrol and take more ammunition.) There were no guards or personnel in charge of the two ammunition trains in the siding.

We took the train back through Larissa station, picked up the brakemen and kit, repelled several Greek boarding parties and at 17.00 hours steamed south from Larissa with Captain Johnstone driving and 2/Lieutenant Barstow stoking. On the eve of our departure, we had the unusual experience of seeing an officer from 81 Base Sub Area (Lieutenant Dibbs) in the station.

Five miles out of Larissa the locomotive, in which our faith appeared to have been misplaced, slowed down owing to loss of pressure and finally stopped. The train began to run backwards downhill towards Larissa, as we had not had an opportunity to instruct the brakemen in their duties.[20] This retrogression was stopped, the brakemen were shown what to do and we started work again on the engine. I sent the other ranks to take cover 400 yards away from the train, as enemy aircraft were taking an interest in us. While we were working on the engine, two low-flying attacks were made on us by single bombers, which seemed to have run out of bombs, but fired their machine guns and cannon copiously. One cannon shell hit the cab of the engine, causing no damage.[21] We engaged the aircraft ineffectively with a Tommy gun.

I sent Loveday and Corporal Yannoulatos back to Larissa on a motor bicycle which we had with us in search of railway experts; but by nightfall it was apparent that our locomotive, which was now short of water, would get us no further. I accordingly sent Captain Johnstone back to Larissa, where he fired another engine. I also sent 2/Lieutenant Barstow forward to the next station to see if he could raise an engine there.

Our problem was finally solved at midnight by the appearance from the south of an entire train transporting personnel of the 2/1 Australian Field Battery, who were looking for their guns and vehicles. The Officer Commanding made contact with Australian Corps HQ, who were now moving into the Larissa area, and decided to take his train back to Doxara until the situation was clarified. His engine took us in tow. We reached Doxara at 07.00 hours on 17 April, got an engine, and proceeded to Pharsala whence I sent another engine north to reinforce the Australian rolling stock.

Throughout the 17th we travelled slowly south. The weather was bad with low cloud and no enemy air activity was noted.

At dawn on the 18th we reached Gravia where I handed over three trucks of ammunition to the Officer Commanding. The remainder of the train was handed over to the Railway Transport Officer at Amfikleia (or Amphykleion) on the instructions of Colonel Goodwin.

While the train was being machine-gunned south of Larissa one other rank lost his nerve and refused to come back to it from the place where he was taking cover; a full report on this casualty has been made to Advanced HQ. On the night of the 17th, one other rank walked in his sleep, fell out of the truck and injured his arm; this man was put on a hospital train at Amfikleia.

Captain Johnstone and 2/Lieutenant Barstow were entirely responsible for getting the train away from Larissa, almost unaided. In difficult circumstances and under fairly frequent attacks from the air, both these officers showed resource, coolness and determination in a very high degree.

F. MISCELLANEOUS DUTIES ON LINES OF COMMUNICATION

The remainder of my unit and stores, under Lieutenant Norman, had meanwhile proceeded to the Lamia area. Here the Lines of Communications organization appeared to be in a somewhat fluid state, and during the 17th-18th, Lieutenant Norman did what he could to fill what appeared to be a gap by:

1   Taking command of three light anti-aircraft guns from Elasson, which were lost, and causing them to shoot at dive-bombers.
2   Forming a petrol dump with 40 tons of petrol which also seemed to be lost.
3   Taking charge of a dump of 25 pounder [artillery] ammunition.[22]
4   Organizing traffic control.

G. DEMOLITIONS ON NAUPAKTOS-AMFISSA ROAD

At 16.00 hours on 22 April, General Wilson[23] ordered me to carry out demolitions north of the Gulf of Corinth, in order to impose as much delay as possible on the German advance following the Greek collapse in the Lannina sector.

I obtained from Major West, Royal Engineers, a party consisting of Lieutenant Bale, Royal Engineers, and four Sappers with two trucks and one ton of high explosives, and sent them under the command of Captain Johnstone to Patras, with orders to get across on the ferry from Psathopyrgos to Nafpaktos early on the 23rd. This party left Athens at 21.00 hours, 2/Lieutenant Barstow and Guardsman Loveday accompanied Captain Johnstone.

I followed at 05.00 hours on the 23rd and the remainder of my unit under Lieutenant Norman at 09.00 hours.

The Greek General Staff, through Brigadier Salisbury-Jones,[24] promised various forms of assistance, including a covering detachment at Missolonghi and two trucks of high explosives. None of these were forthcoming.

West of Nafpaktos there are two alternative roads leading down from Agrinion; but east of Nafpaktos there is only one. Being short of personnel, stores and especially of time, I decided to cut the road thoroughly east of Nafpaktos rather than attempt to deal with the two roads west of it, which did not appear to lend themselves to any decisive form of cutting.

There was no reliable news of the enemy's advance, though periodic waves of apprehension affected the almost continuous stream of retreating Greek troops. One Greek officer, when questioned about the military situation, said: 'There are nothing but white flags between you and the Germans.' Having selected a site for the main demolition eleven miles east of Nafpaktos, I decided, as a precaution against being interrupted by the sudden arrival of enemy vehicles, to do minor damage to both roads west of Nafpaktos. We had supplemented our high explosive stores by obtaining four 250 lb. bombs from Patras aerodrome, and these Captain Johnstone exploded under a small concrete road bridge with only moderate effect, the bridge remaining passable for wheeled traffic. On the alternative road, he and 2/Lieutenant Barstow jammed two lorries together on a narrow bridge and blew the axles off them, creating a satisfactory temporary block.

Meanwhile Lieutenant Bale and his four Sappers, who worked continuously all day, had prepared the main demolition. This consisted of three charges of 200 lbs. of gelignite each, placed saps 2 ft. square, six feet below the road and six feet from the outside of the retaining wall which supported the road on a steep face. The retaining wall was 75 ft. long and the road 21 ft. wide.

The retreat of the Greek Army was greatly retarded by the universal custom of jumping out of your lorry and running 300 yards if you or one of your friends thought he heard an aeroplane. On that day it was no uncommon sight to see several miles of transport immobilized – most of the vehicles being left in the middle of the road – by a solitary reconnaissance plane in the far distance. Nevertheless, the flow of vehicles had dwindled to a trickle by 19.00 hours, and at 19.40 hours I ordered the charges to be blown.

The results of the demolition appeared to be satisfactory. The three craters were approximately 12 ft. deep and varied in width from 12 ft. to 19 ft. (the width of the road being 21 ft). The foundations of the road had been blown away or loosened for a distance of approximately 80 ft. and the site was of a nature to impose very great difficulty on any working party repairing it. Lieutenant Bale reported that this cut would impose a delay of from 48 hours to one week on all vehicles. I do not consider that 48 hours is an over-optimistic estimate.

At 21.00 hours the party withdrew in the ferry, all caiques[25] (approximately six) in Nafpaktos harbour having been sunk with small charges of high explosives.

The only enemy air activity worth recording during the day was three separate attacks, each by eleven dive-bombers, on a Greek steamer lying off Nafpaktos harbour. No direct hits were obtained. The ship was probably damaged by near misses but as she was out of commission already, the course of the war was not affected by these spectacular operations …

I consider that Lieutenant Bale and his men carried out their task with great efficiency. The success of the operation was largely due to their skill and assiduity, and to Captain Johnstone's work on reconnaissance.

H. EVACUATION FROM GREECE

At the request of Mr H.A.Caccia,[26] First Secretary, HBM Legation, Athens, and in the absence of any precise instructions regarding the evacuation of my party which was by now attached to nobody in particular, I embarked my unit, with all our stores, arms and kit, on the SY *Calanthe* at 20.00 hours on 23 April from the Piraeus with a view to providing some measure of anti-aircraft for this vessel. *Calanthe* (Commander Brass, RN[27]) carried some eighty miscellaneous diplomats and civilians,[28] including twenty women and five children, and a Greek crew.

The SY *Calanthe* was no stranger to clandestine operations. She had been chartered by the Royal Engineers to sail to Thessaloniki with a cargo of explosives in early March. The crew of three officers and twenty-five other ranks found the 600 pounds of HE woefully undershot what was needed and the *Calanthe* was despatched back to Athens. When she returned to Thessaloniki in mid-March, she carried 'a further ton of chocolate for Sussex (Captain R. Menzies, RE)' for the destruction of the coastal defences.[29]

Fleming continued his report with a factual description of the harrowing journey by sea that finally saw the mission arrive in Egypt. Many years later, he typed up a copy of his diary entry[30] of the evacuation from Athens; it is altogether a more human and emotional account than the matter-of-fact version of events in his official report. He had seen death close up on his pre-war travels and journalist assignments and in the ill-fated campaign in Norway but this was the first time he had witnessed the deaths of men under his personal command, one of whom was the brother of the wife of his close friend Harold Caccia.

This fragment of a diary, long lost but found and typed out in 1957, begins with the return of a small party under my command which had been ordered by Jumbo Wilson to go and blow the road near Missolonghi to delay the German advance on Athens along the North of the Gulf of Corinth after the capitulation of the Greek Armies on the Albanian front. This advance might have cut off the retreat of our forces on Athens and points South.

Evacuation

… Got into Athens (where no one seems depressed or excited) just before 19.00 hours. Find Oliver [Barstow] and the 3-tonner at the flat. Pack the latter off to Piraeus, followed by the van. Send Oliver on motorbike on recce for 15 cwt [truck] … Give Costopoulos 1,000 Drs, two portable typewriters and a live chicken … Harold Caccia turns up with Barbrook[31] and we all move down to the Piraeus; there had been another alert about 19.00 hours but nothing happened.

Find the *Calanthe*, tubby, one tall funnel, 400 tons, and all our stuff being loaded on board. Nobody seems to know how many passengers there are or who is who. Sail about 20.30 hours through the devastated harbour in a yellow afterglow. Cat jumped off as we left.

We distribute rations and hold a soirée in the stern, where we all sleep very happily on deck. Ship's British personnel Royal Marines under a NCO: bloody, boastful and mostly drunk. Try and restore a little discipline. Norman [Johnstone] and I arrange to wake at dawn as they look unreliable.

There are four Lewis guns, two aft and one on each side of the bridge. The NCO gives us a garrulous demonstration in the morning but I bet he won't be there if there is an attack. We have anchored discreetly in a little bay of Polyaigos, a small island next to Mylos which means windmill and has in fact got little white windmills above the village opposite to us. Nothing is well organized or taken seriously.

I undertake to find three gun crews of one officer and one other rank[32] each; Marines to man the fourth gun. Lovely peaceful day. Clean Tommy guns and check stores, then send Mark [Norman] and Oliver, Sergeant Major [Richardson] and Clarke ashore. I am on rear gun with Isted: Gilbert with Turkhand on middle gun: Norman and Loveday on starboard gun.

Three planes, after much far buzzing, appear in the distance about 11.00 hours. Lord Forbes[33] and a mongrel in RAF uniform leave instantly, two stray women and a few *bouches inutiles* also sent ashore. These include Charles Mott-Radclyffe's servant to whom I give a message for Mark telling him and Oliver to stay where they are and I will signal if I want reliefs. I have a hunch we shall get it this afternoon; 14.00 hours is the time they usually recce Mylos.

Later we hear from some colourful guys in a boat, who sell us 800 eggs and a few nautically minded sheep, that this morning's planes sank two small boats at Mylos. Gin and lime on the bridge and a delicious omelette. Then the shore party turn up for lunch, not having got my message. I tell them both to go back after lunch and stand by with the motorboat. But Oliver pretends to misunderstand and stays around, which I don't find out till later. Mark goes with Gilbert [Randall] and Isted.

Hot afternoon, bathing and reading, the blue water shining back on the underside of the gulls' wings. All quiet save for one or two distant drones (two planes fly straight over island about 14.00 hours) until Norman goes ashore about

17.00 hours. Mark and Gilbert come back, relieving Loveday and Turkhand. We are just going to have a drink at 18.00 hours when trouble begins.

Three bombers come over high but do nothing about us. Then one comes along very low between the islands, half a mile away. We show up fine in the lateral evening sunlight and soon we hear him coming back for us on the other side of the steep white island. Another comes over the bay from the south and we know they are taking trouble and we are for it.

First attack comes over the hill from the east. He slants straight down for us, lets his bombs go far too soon, and they burst on the shore behind and above the women and children. He comes on machine-gunning hard, masthead high, and we engage him, eight men standing nakedly to the tall Lewis gun mountings. You really need a grouse-butt of some kind for this sort of thing. He is shooting short and when he has gone over his tail gunner sprays the water miles beyond us.

I think my gun has jammed but it is only the cocking handle forward. Nobody seems to have been hit. A Marine is coming aft to look at my gun. I send Clarke forward to take his place, then the second bugger comes into the attack, not giving us more than two minutes between doses. This time he has us. We see the white ribbons of smoke or rather I suppose vapour from his machine gun exhausts; they trail below him. He comes at the height of a driven partridge, and I dare say his bullets whistle round us but I don't remember noticing them.

Four bombs come out of him. Our fire has no effect. I think two bombs were short, one a short near miss, and the fourth a direct hit just forward of amidships. For less than a split second I think we have got away with it, and looking round think I see large bits dropping off the plane and have a small spasm of exaltation and shout, 'Look at the bugger, he's hit!' or words to that effect. But the large bits must have been segments of the ship, which reacted violently to the near miss and blew up a second time (the boiler going) immediately afterwards at the direct hit.

The ship flies skywards in the middle. The air is black with smoke, steam, oil and coal. I find myself staggering, holding on to the tilted deck. I suppose my tin hat fell off, as a hunk of the ship fell on my head and made a cut which I noticed later because of the blood. Isted and the Sergeant Major, the black man, are staggering in the murk. Wreckage goes on falling for a long time. We collect lifebelts and chuck the raft over. The buggers are still flying round but they don't machine-gun.

Stupidly assuming that one should leave a sinking ship promptly I put Isted (glad I told him to change his boots for gym shoes) over the side on the raft.

Presently I see him struggling in the water with a mongrel RAF man but the Sergeant Major pulls him out. (Note. Isted was a non-swimmer.)

I have been shouting, 'Anybody hurt? Anybody left forward?' and now I hear somebody yelling. There is a biggish fire amidships, spreading. Then I locate Gilbert swimming about (I imagine I locate Oliver too) and Gilbert after shouting locates Mark somewhere forward and says he is not too good.

I call the Sergeant Major who has climbed back on board and is cutting a boat loose and we go forward for Mark. (There was an interlude before this when I picked up a Tommy gun with the idea that I mustn't leave my arms behind. I also poked about for my battledress and leather jerkin, but without collecting either of them.)

When we go for Mark, I notice that blood has been pouring down my right leg, also from my head, blinding one eye. I think I am hit in the left shoulder but nothing hurts and I have no idea how the wounds came.

The Sergeant Major, who is splendid, comes along and we crawl past the fire, balancing awkwardly on torn upended plates but getting there in the end. We find a black man with black hair, who is unrecognisable as Mark, huddled and bleeding from the head. He says he thinks he can move and the Sergeant Major gets busy on a cradle. I hail Gilbert who is now in a boat, then find myself liable to pass out owing I suppose to loss of blood. Rather than leave two inert bodies to be got over the high bulwark, I tell the Sergeant Major I will send a party up, scramble somehow overboard and slide down a rope.

I am very thirsty and have salvaged a water bottle. Almost but not quite pass out on the floorboards, where I lie for a minute looking up at little soft white clouds, thinking of larches at Merrimoles and feeling in an unreal way that this is what it means to get into trouble at last. A Greek is in the boat shivering with shock. He saddens me and I send him aft. I also bawl out one of the dozy sailors who turns up smoking a cigarette.

Norman turns up and goes up the side of the ship with Turkhand and Loveday and at last Mark comes down in a sling. Nobody has seen Oliver or Clarke.

I tell Gilbert to take us ashore, which is a shorter distance than it was, the ship having drifted. I can get out and made ashore on my own but feel weak and lie down beside a screaming scalded Greek on a rock like a sea urchin's back. Once more the sky and the little clouds and a dream-like feeling.

Nancy [Caccia] looks fierce in a bust-bodice with blood on her cheek. I tell her about Oliver [her brother] but I think she knows already. There are about eight of us stretched on the white rock with the boat burning seventy yards away and small arms ammunition going off continuously like a Chinese feast.

Norman and his party are salvaging stuff from the bows, the flames are all over the stern now. Mrs Blunt, also in a bust-bodice, is being very energetic. Huge faces loom from all angles offering whisky which I refuse and water of which I drink a good deal.

Then someone says the ship is going to blow up, which I say is nonsense, but sure enough it does while we are all being lugged over the tufts of prickly low scrub by kind people trying hard not to be clumsy. I think there must have been some of our high explosive in the stores.

They have sent a boat across to Kimolos and before dusk we all move over. I shiver a good deal, probably from shock, and my leg hurts a bit. Nancy is fine. Try not to think about Oliver. Reach Kimolos, get shifted on to camp beds which are carried uphill under the first stars by gangs of kindly Greeks. We are put in a disused stone hospital, the gift of some benefactor. The scalded man is screaming and we debate giving him a knockout drop, these having been salvaged by Nancy. Many kind Greek ladies drift about, stretcher parties stay to gape, and odd elements drift in for the same purpose. Mark said to be all right but I worry about him.

Lance Corporal Turkhand gives me his pipe and the Sergeant Major his tobacco and I eat a bit of bread and get half washed and my wounds dressed (head, shoulder, leg). Sleep.

24 April?

Mark is tired by getting on. Forbes and the RAF man have spread alarm and on the assumption that the island is going to be razed most people scatter.

A splendid doctor (Captain Forrest-Hay[34]) turns up in a caique from Crete – we can telephone to Crete – at 10.30 hours. With three Passport Control Officers[35] men (Bond, Dillon, Carlisle) who are all good. Sergeant Major makes me a huge crutch and on the evening of this or the next day I get up and hobble around, finding the crutch much more difficult to manage than my leg.

Pretty white village, pretty little harbour. I have one shirt, Oliver's shorts and my shoes. Sergeant Major finds my five-shilling piece in a shirt he scrounges. Beith and RAF men form a Turkey party. They all flap and gas and give a sorry exhibition. Wounded move down into basement …

We got away in the end, after on-and-off loading the wounded on two successive nights (you had to sail by night on account of German air supremacy) but were driven by a crosswind to Santorini, a strange island formed by the tip of a still mildly active volcano. There we transferred to a small Greek steamer which took us to Crete. The wounded and the women and children went on to Alexandria in HM destroyers *Havock* and *Hotspur*.[36]

Back in Egypt, YAK force was wound up. Johnstone left with the main party to England and Fleming followed after a few weeks. In hindsight, it had been a fruitless endeavour, epitomizing the heroic conduct of the desperate days that characterized the over-stretch of the British Army as it strived to stem the seemingly inexorable advance of the Germans as they consolidated their grip on mainland Europe. At the political level, Churchill felt that he had no option other than to order Wavell to commit 65,000 Commonwealth troops to assist Greece under the treaty obligations, irrespective of the doubts expressed by his senior generals who wanted to pursue the campaign against the Italians and Rommel's Afrika Corps in North Africa.

In his obituary of Wavell,[37] Fleming recalled:

I once asked him, towards the end of the war, if he believed that the diversion of German forces to deal with our intervention in Greece had imposed on Hitler's first headlong drive into Russia the small margin of delay which in the event meant that winter caught the Germans just outside Moscow and enabled the Russians to halt their advance. It was a perfectly arguable theory and has since, I believe, been confirmed from German sources; and it was a theory which, since it showed in so favourable a light the long-term results of a quixotic but disastrous adventure, might have been expected to commend itself to the man who had been responsible for the military, though not the political, side of the affair. Wavell's reply was characteristic: 'I've often wondered about that,' he said. 'I imagine Greece did upset the German programme to a certain extent; these diversions always do. But I don't see how anyone can tell at this stage how much effect it really had. We shall know one day, I expect.' He was extraordinarily fair-minded. I doubt if anyone ever knew him to claim even indirectly any credit for himself, except in some trivial context and by way of a joke.

Chapter 6
A summons to India

Joan Bright, who was running the Commander-in-Chief's Special Information Centre in the War Office, remembered Fleming's return to London:

> He walked in as imperturbably as he had walked out of MIR for Namsos that evening many months ago. It was always good to see his square face with its wide smile and to straighten out one's own fevers and uncertainties against his calm acceptance of events and tolerance of human frailty. He was a four-square, basic, solitary sort of person, immune to luxury, to heat or to cold, with a rock-like quality that made him the most staunch of friends and a kindness which made him the least vindictive of enemies.[1]

Fired up by his experiences in Norway and Greece, Fleming put pen to paper to pass on the wisdom he had acquired in dealing with ground attacks by enemy aircraft. He ended it with an appeal to common sense:

> All the foregoing suggestions could be easily and relatively quickly implemented. They do not perhaps amount to very much; but they are commonsense encasures, not councils of perfection, and their aim is the sensible one of (so to speak) inoculating troops while in training against the morale effect of bombing in the field as far as is possible. Being bombed, like having a baby, is not an experience for which completely realistic rehearsal is possible; but much more can be done than is being done at present to give troops and commanders some practical guidance in dealing, not so much with air attack, as with that unnecessarily paralysing factor – the threat of attack from plainly visible aircraft.

His regiment, the Grenadier Guards, was in limbo in England. The three battalions (1st, 2nd and 3rd), who had all fought with the British Expeditionary Force in France,[2] were on home duties and the three recently formed ones[3]

(4th, 5th and 6th) were working up to operational efficiency.[4] On 22 September, Fleming was posted to the London District School of Tactics where he ran the Street Fighting Wing in Battersea.[5] It was an undemanding role and he was able to put together a book of his short stories which Jonathan Cape published as *A Story to Tell* the following year. Dedicated to his late brother Michael whose 'complete disregard for danger and coolness under fire were a wonderful example to all at critical times', he warned his readers in the preface that 'in sum and in essence they [the stories] amount, I'm afraid, only to cheap melodrama; but perhaps even cheap melodrama will provide an acceptable distraction in these days of expensive tragedy. At any rate, I hope it will.' His hope proved well founded.

Apart from being caught speeding at 40 mph along the Queenstown Road on 7 January 1942, he found life as chief instructor dull and uneventful. According to the police report, he breezily said that 'I always exceed the speed limit here every day'. Apprising the Regimental Adjutant of 'the hideous facts', Fleming conceded that 'no other course is open to me than to throw myself at the mercy of the court or into the shark-infested Timor Sea, whichever is handiest at the time'. He was referring to a summons[6] he had received from General Wavell to join him in Java as a Grade Two Staff Officer in the Intelligence Directorate GHQ of the newly formed American-British-Dutch-Australian Command. The diplomat and Japanese scholar Sir George Sansom was already in situ in Batavia as an advisor to the Directorate.

If the picture in England was dire at the beginning of 1942, then the Allied military situation throughout the Far East was little short of catastrophic. China had already been at war with Japan for five long years. After attacking the US fleet at Pearl Harbor on 7 December 1941 and having previously come to an arrangement with Vichy France jointly to garrison Indo-China, on 8 December the Japanese invaded Thailand which capitulated within twenty-four hours and signed an armistice. Using ports and airfields in these countries, the Japanese armed forces quickly launched their offensive against British and Dutch Colonial territories in South East Asia. Hong Kong fell on 25 December, Kuala Lumpur on 11 January 1942, Borneo at the end of January, Singapore on 15 February, Rangoon was evacuated on 7 March and, by the time Fleming arrived, Sumatra was on the point of surrender. The Philippines, jointly defended by the United States and the Philippines Commonwealth, had been invaded on 8 December 1941 and American troops were still engaged in a desperate rearguard action at Corregidor.[7]

The pace of events was such that it was almost impossible to understand what had happened. Within three months the whole of the British and Dutch Far Eastern Empires were gone, including the pivotal and prestigious naval and military base of Singapore; Burma, an appendage of India, lost; Japanese mastery of the eastern seas absolute after the sinking of the battleships *Prince of*

Wales and *Repulse* and the obliteration of the remnants of the British and Dutch Far Eastern fleet in the Battle of the Java Sea.

The manner of the Japanese advance was vividly described by the naval historian, Samuel Morison, as resembling 'the insidious yet irresistible clutching of multiple tentacles. Like some vast octopus it relied on strangling many small points rather than concentration on a vital organ … Each fastened on a small portion of the enemy and, by crippling him locally, finished by killing the entire animal.'[8] Unquestionably the Japanese had used their military assets with great skill, with an impressive display of the correct use of air power in support of maritime and land operations. Yet it was equally clear that the Allied military response to the obvious threat of Japanese aggression had been characterized by complacency and under-investment. Paradoxically, although the Far East colonial possessions of Britain and Holland were among their most valuable financial assets, they were the least defended. The reason was self-evident, namely that in the pre-war climate of appeasement, the structure of imperial governance was predicated on efficient administration and internal political control to maintain commercial and economic stability. Talk of existential threats was inconvenient and rarely heard on the verandahs of colonial club land.

India herself, although her sheer size presented an enormous challenge for any invasion by the Japanese armies now camped on her eastern borders, remained vulnerable to increasing internal dissent and, with a German advance to the oilfields of the Persian Gulf and the Caucasus still a possibility, the Indian Army, like Janus, faced in two directions.

Two days after Wavell's signal arrived, Churchill's Chief of Staff General Sir Hastings Ismay replied 'W/S. Captain R.P. Fleming available … cable grade of suggested appointment and whether he should proceed by air if passage possible'. Leaving England on 17 February on HMS *Indomitable*, it took Fleming a month to reach India. En route, he spent a week in Cairo to confer with Lieutenant Colonel Dudley Wrangel Clarke of 'A' Force, the arch exponent of the art of deception, and one of four men who would have a profound influence on his wartime career.

With a Russian mother, Dudley Clarke was far from a traditional regular officer. A small man with fair hair and blue eyes, he was an excellent raconteur and great company at a party, but as the novelist-turned-intelligence officer Dennis Wheatley observed, 'with a strange quietness about his movements and an uncanny habit of suddenly appearing in a room without anyone having noticed him enter it'.[9] With an extraordinary knowledge of military affairs, he had the ability to see the essentials of a problem and then to put his thoughts clearly and briefly on paper. In that respect, he and Fleming were peas from the same pod.

A protégé of the Chief of the Imperial General Staff General Sir John Dill, Clarke had had a varied career that had taken him to Turkey, Transjordan, Aden, Palestine and East Africa. He had been instrumental in developing the concept of the Commandos which had been very much his own idea in his capacity as Military Assistant to Dill. Indeed, it was his paper on deception of 5 June 1940 that Dill had presented to the prime minister who approved it for submission to the Cabinet which immediately agreed and thus MO9[10] was created. Deeply involved in the early Commando raids – he was nearly killed on the first one – in November 1940 Clarke received a summons from Wavell, who knew him from his reconnaissance of the overland route from Mombasa to Cairo the previous year, to report to Cairo as 'Personal Intelligence Officer (Special Duties) to the Commander-in-Chief'. Behind the title, the job description entailed not only the planning and conduct of deception activities but also the responsibility for training soldiers to evade capture and, if caught, assisting them to escape.[11]

En route to the Middle East, Clarke travelled under the cover of a *Times* correspondent via Madrid where he was detained by the Spanish police on account of his strange choice of clothes, namely wearing a flowery dress, lipstick and a pearl necklace. An alarmed and embarrassed embassy reported the incident to Whitehall[12]:

FROM MADRID TO FOREIGN OFFICE.
18 October 1941.
Following for Sir A. Cadogan.

Dudley Clarke, *The Times* correspondent, arrived in Madrid on 16 October on his way to Egypt via Gibraltar. He informed the Military Attaché that he was also employed by the joint Intelligence Bureau, Near East, and was under the War Office. The Military Attaché and Hamilton-Stokes[13] were particularly struck by his intimate knowledge of military secrets and plans of Naval Intelligence, Middle East. Last night he was arrested in a main street dressed, down to a brassière, as a woman.

The police interpreter, who helped the interrogation of him, informed a member of my staff that he stated that he was a novelist and wanted to study the reactions of men to women in the streets. His luggage contained another complete set of women's clothes, a war correspondent's uniform and a note book with a number of names of people in London in it. Also papers and a roll of super-fine toilet paper which particularly excited the police who are submitting each sheet to chemical tests.

The Consul who saw him this morning found him calm and unconcerned, but he told a different story. He was taking the feminine garments to a lady in Gibraltar and thought that he would try them on for a prank. This hardly squares with the fact that the garments and shoes fitted him.

The interpreter states that the police consider it a homosexual affair, and will probably fine and release him. But the Germans apparently think that they have got on to a first class espionage incident and will certainly make the most of it, either way, I need hardly point out the damage this incident will do to us and *The Times* here. Jokes have already begun about the editor of *The Times* masquerading as a woman. Shall I send Clarke back to London or let him proceed, if and when released?[14]

Clarke was duly released from custody in Spain and made it to Gibraltar and then Cairo. But the fallout continued until the following summer, when the embassy in Madrid was sent an anonymous letter saying the police photo of Clarke dressed as a woman was to be published in a Berlin newspaper 'in order to discredit His Majesty's Embassy'. The response from 'C' – chief of SIS – was: 'We can only await developments in a spirit of calm and resignation.'[15] Clarke's quirky behaviour remains an enigma. His apostasy to the creed of secrecy had been revealed through an act of self-indulgence and, by inference, self-pleasurable folly. There was no justification for the operational mantle of disguise.

As soon as he arrived in Cairo that December, Clarke installed himself in an office in a converted bathroom in Grey Pillars, the GHQ Middle East building, and with the help of one of Wavell's secretaries, immediately set about implementing Plan CAMILLA to wrong-foot the Italian general the Duke of Aosta as to the true direction of Wavell's plan to recapture British Somaliland. By April 1941, the deception business in Middle East Command had burgeoned to such an extent that Clarke needed a cover name of his own ('Advanced HQ "A" Force'), a separate office in a requisitioned brothel in Sharia Kasr-el-Nil, and an establishment of three staff officers,[16] a junior officer as his personal assistant,[17] ten other ranks, a car and four trucks.

In a 1944 paper he prepared for the Americans, Dudley Clarke described the origins of 'A' Force:[18]

'A' Force started under two handicaps … the first handicap was a lack of precedent. Deception on a big scale had never been practised before and it had to prove its worth at the same time as it was trying to find its feet. As a result, the early 'A' Force could only operate freely in the zones of operation of the more imaginative commanders, who, amid the successive adversities of 1941, were prepared to give a trial to anything which offered them a prospect of help. This led the organization extending in an unbalanced way, dependent upon 'selling' itself and inevitably shaped to suit the personalities concerned.

Clarke then explained to the Americans how 'A' Force had 'discovered a few basic facts' during its incubation period:

The first concerns the scope of the organization's activities and, in particular, the directions in which they should be focused. Until this is properly understood there will be a tendency to muddle Deception with Psychological Warfare and even to suggest that the same instrument can serve both purposes. A moment's examination of the aims of the two will show this to be fundamentally unsound, and any attempt to mix both in practice will be highly dangerous. Nevertheless, that danger is often present and is sometimes curiously difficult to dispel. The essential difference lies of course in the audience for whom the two organizations cater. Psychological Warfare starts at the apex of a triangle and endeavours to spread its arms as wide as it can to embrace the broadest possible base. It matters little if many of its audience can detect the origin of their messages, nor if a privileged few can recognize distortion of the truth; its appeal is to the masses and it is unlikely to influence the thoughts or actions of the enlightened inner circles of the General Staff. Deception, on the other hand, works in exactly the opposite way. It starts at the base of the triangle and concentrates its influence towards a single point on the apex; its essential aim is to conceal the origins of its messages by directing them upon this single point from as many different directions as possible. It cares little for the thoughts and actions of the masses, but it must penetrate directly into the innermost circle of all. Its audience is narrowed down to a small handful of individuals, as represented by the senior members of the enemy's Intelligence Staff, and sometimes even to a single individual in the person of the Head of the Intelligence Staff. If they [the deception staff] can influence him to accept as true the evidence they have manufactured for his benefit, then they have accomplished their entire aim, since it is only through the Head of Intelligence that any enemy Commander receives the impression of his opponent upon which he has to base his plan of operation. It is necessary, therefore, that the single-purposeness of any deception machine should be recognized from the start and its shape dictated by the overriding need to concentrate every ounce of its diverse efforts upon that one ultimate target. As a corollary it follows that those who direct the deception machine must have an adequate knowledge of the small group of men on whom all their activities are focused, of their national characteristics, their language, thoughts and professional methods with all their strengths and weaknesses.

It is this note on personalities which leads me to the next principle, which I firmly believe to be the foundation stone in the successful application of deception. Deception is essentially an art and not a science, and those who practise it must be recognized as falling into the category of artists and not artisans. This is, I know, difficult to accept in professional military circles where it is widely believed that the Art of War can be taught to the average educated man even though he may have little aptitude for it. But, nevertheless, I am convinced it is true; and twice in 'A' Force I have seen highly qualified and highly intelligent staff officers of the British Regular Army fail completely to cope with the work, although both did brilliantly afterwards on the Operations Staff. What they lacked was just the sheer ability to create, to make something out of nothing, to conceive their own original notion and then to clothe it with realities until eventually it would appear as a living fact. And, since that is precisely what the deception staff must do all the time, it follows that the art of creation is an essential attribute in all who are charged with such work. To expect those who have not this art to produce the required results will lead to risks beyond that of mere failure.

If this thesis is accepted, it is easy to see why one brain – and one alone – must be left unhampered to direct any one deception plan. It is after all little more than a drama played upon a vast stage, and the author and producer should be given as free a hand in the theatre of war as in the other theatre. (Also, of course, in both they must have the necessary qualifications to justify that confidence.) It is not a bad parallel to compare a Commander in the field with the impresario who wants to mount a successful play in his theatre. He decides on the type of play he wants – drama, comedy, musical, etc. – and instructs an author to produce the script. Having accepted the script, he appoints a producer to mount the play. From that point onwards he may well leave everything else to these two, and look only to the results obtained. Provided these are satisfactory, the impresario who is not himself an author or producer, wisely leaves them to rule the cast, scenery, costumes and all else that goes to make a play. The wise Commander-in-Chief will follow the same example. In his case the matter is simplified in that the head of his deception staff doubles the roles of author and producer. The Commander therefore tells him what sort of deception he needs, examines the plans produced for him with the required aim in view and, once the final version is approved, watches only the results and leaves all else to his specialist. In both peace and war, however, the chief is the best judge of results: in both cases he assesses them by the reactions of the audience (or the enemy), and should succeed to achieve the object he himself has set.

And it is this mention of the 'object' which brings me to the last of the principles I have tried to enunciate. For the theatrical impresario this presents no difficulty – all he wants is to see the audience moved to tears, laughter or rhythm in concert with the play – but to the general it is a problem that merits most careful thought. His audience is the enemy and he alone must decide what he wants them to do. To advance? To withdraw? To thin out or reinforce? Whatever he chooses, the main point is that his 'object' must be to make the enemy DO something. It matters nothing what the enemy THINKS, it is only what he does that can affect the battle. It is therefore wrong, and always wrong, for any Commander to tell his deception staff to work out a play 'to make the enemy think we are going to do so-and-so'. It may be that the plan will succeed but that the enemy will react to it in a totally unexpected way, upon which the Commander will probably blame the deception staff who have in fact produced exactly the results they set out for. It is this boomerang effect which has made many people apprehensive of using the deception weapon, and it cannot be stressed too strongly that, if used in the wrong way, it can prove a real danger. But there is one sure way to avoid any possible risk, and that is to get the OBJECT right. Given a correct 'object', the deception plan may fail but it cannot in any way do harm. Give it a wrong 'object' and it will invariably give wrong results. Our theatrical impresario after all will not attempt to dictate to the author the plot of the play, but that is precisely what the general does who tells his deception staff that he wants the enemy to be made to 'think' something. It assumes a knowledge of the enemy's likely reactions which the deception staff should know from experience very much better than the general. It is for the latter to say what he wants them to do, and for the specialists to decide what the enemy must be made to think in order to induce them to act in the manner required. Perhaps an illustration will explain this best. In the early days of 1941 General Wavell wanted the Italian reserves drawn to the South in order to ease his entry into Northern Abyssinia. He considered this might be done by inducing them to reinforce the captured province of British Somaliland, and he gave instructions for a deception plan to be worked out to persuade the Italians that we were about to invade Somaliland. The plan, innocently ignoring the real object of influencing the location of the enemy's reserves, was entirely successful;[19] but the results were totally unexpected. In the face of the threatened invasion, the Italians evacuated British Somaliland. Not only had General Wavell to draw on his meagre resources to re-occupy the country, but the Italian garrison was freed to swell the forces in the North which were to block our advance at Keren. Had a different object been chosen, quite a different deception plan would have emerged and perhaps a quite different effect produced upon the actions taken by the enemy.

Oversight of strategic deception plans and operations was initially provided by a committee of representatives from the three fighting services, MI5 and SIS under the name the Joint Inter-Services Security Board (ISSB). Set up in February 1940 under the auspices of the Joint Intelligence Sub-Committee of the Chiefs of Staff Committee, it reviewed 'A' Force deception plans once the GOC Middle East had approved them. In the early days of the war, the thrust of ISSB was 'more at concealing our intentions than at persuading the enemy to make a calculated false move of which we could take operational advantage'.[20] This was to change after a series of meetings in October 1941 between Clarke and various War

Cabinet sub-committees and the Chiefs of Staff themselves. The result was the establishment of the London Controlling Section (LCS), a top secret new section under Colonel Oliver Stanley, MC.

Although formally called the Head of the Future Operational Planning Section of the Joint Planning Staff, Stanley was to all effects the Section Commander or 'Controlling Officer' with a brief to plan both cover and deception operations and supervise their execution, calling on the relevant intelligence and military authorities as needed. The 1945 US Joint Security Control's definitions are helpful in differentiating 'cover' and 'deception'.

> Cover consists of planned measures for disguising or concealing an operation against an objective, such measures being directed against an enemy ... deception consists of planned measures for revealing or conveying to the enemy true information (or false information which could be evaluated as true) regarding our strategic plans, strengths, dispositions and tactics, with the purpose of causing him to reach false estimates and to act thereon. Cover conceals truth; deception conveys falsehood. Cover induces non-action; deception induces action. An important distinction must be made between deception activities and psychological warfare which seeks to affect the enemy's frame of mind – to feel that the war is hopeless, that his leaders are incompetent, that his cause is unjust, that the men and the weapons opposing him are irresistible.

His appointment was an inspired choice for not only had he served with the Lancashire Hussars throughout the First World War, winning an MC and Croix de Guerre, but he also had a distinguished political career, serving as Minister of Transport, President of the Board of Trade and Secretary of State for War. The new team – Lieutenant Colonel A.F.R. 'Fritz' Lumby, Captain Hallorhan RN and Wing Commander Dennis Wheatley, the popular novelist – still had to go through the ISSB which was chaired by Colonel Graham; the Naval member was Commander 'Ginger' Lewis, the Air member Wing Commander Byron with MI5 and SIS represented by Lieutenant Colonel Gilbert Lennox and the Home Office by Mr Buckley.[21]

With a number of successful deception operations under his belt, Clarke felt able to fine-tune the deception glossary and this is what he most likely inducted Fleming into.

1   The objective of a deception is not to induce the enemy commander to think something but to induce him to do something (which, of course, includes doing nothing).

2   Your customers are the enemy intelligence services. You need to know how they operate and what information given to them will induce them

to give their commander the estimate of the situation that will cause him to act as you want him to act.

3 Never conduct a deception with no clear objective simply because you can do so.

4 A proper deception plan must have time to take effect – a major operational deception plan may take weeks to percolate through the enemy system; a large-scale strategic one may take months.

5 The most effective deception is one that confirms what the enemy already wants to believe.

6 Building up over time the belief that your forces are stronger than they really are, thus making all sorts of fictitious plans and operations seem plausible to the enemy.

7 It is not necessary to make the enemy actually believe in the false state of affairs that you want to project. It is enough if you can make him so concerned over its likelihood that he feels that he must provide for it.

8 Your goal to induce the enemy to do something does not mean that he has to do it right away. Building up a pattern in his mind that will be the basis for future specific actions is a perfectly legitimate goal e.g. orders of battle.

In May 1942, Wavell, now in India, sent the prime minister a message outlining his concept for centralized strategic deception. While he appreciated the work of ISSB, he found their approach defensive rather than aggressive and wondered whether a policy of 'bold imaginative deception worked between London, Washington and commanders in the field … might show a good dividend, especially in the case of the Japanese'.

Sir Ronald Wingate, Bt., a cousin of the later famous Chindit commander Orde Wingate, was asked by General Ismay to 'sell' the concept to the Chiefs of Staff. He later wrote:

All his life Wavell had been not only a student of the art of modern war, but a student of the art of war throughout the ages. He had used various ruses both on the strategic and tactical planes to deceive the Italians in the Abyssinian War, and he was convinced that the study and application of this art were essential elements in the duties of a commander's planning staff. But he went further: he knew and foresaw that the Second World War would be a world war in all its implications, controlled centrally by the two great antagonists, the Axis and the Allies. Every operation in every part of the world, however distant, and however disparate the conditions, would have its effect on every other operation. Therefore, he argued that if it was possible to deceive the enemy in one theatre, that deception, especially on the strategic plane, could not be effective and might even be dangerous if its effects on operations in other theatres were not controlled.

So the brief ... was to persuade the Chiefs of Staff that the deception or cover plans of theatre commanders must always be co-ordinated by the Chiefs of Staff themselves so that they should not only have the maximum effect in their own theatre, but should fit in with the general plan of campaign of the other theatres.

He [Wavell] was successful, and not only did every theatre commander systematically prepare a cover plan as part of his operational plan, but all these plans were co-ordinated at the centre, and advice was given about any modification that might be necessary to fit in with the general picture.

Around that time, the Chiefs of Staff approved the appointment of Lieutenant Colonel 'Johnny' Bevan, MC, as Controlling Officer of LCS to succeed Oliver Stanley, who had asked to return to political life.[22] His time as Controlling Officer had certainly not been wasted and Operation HARDBOILED, a notional attack on the Norwegian coast, proved to be an invaluable lesson in the art of deception planning and inter-agency co-operation.

Ten years older than Fleming, Johnny Bevan, a stockbroker whose father had been the Chairman of the London Stock Exchange, came from a similar background including an Eton and Oxford education. Both men shared a love of the countryside, especially shooting and fishing. Dennis Wheatley recalled Bevan as

a rather frail-looking man of medium build with sleepy, pale-blue eyes and thin fair hair which turned grey from the strain of the remarkable work he accomplished in the three years following his appointment ... He was a much tougher person than he looked and, despite lack of exercise, managed to keep very fit; except that he suffered badly from bouts of insomnia ... his most notable feature was a very fine forehead, both broad and deep; and one of his greatest assets an extraordinarily attractive smile. During periods of great strain, when he was sleeping particularly badly, he was often irritable and curt ... But, even on those bad days, if one of us made a joke or suggested that he should knock off for a few hours and come out to dinner, that smile which lit up his whole face would immediately flash out.[23]

Bevan had been commissioned in the Huntingdonshire Regiment in 1911 as a Territorial officer and had served for the greater part of the First World War on the Western Front. After the collapse of the Russian Front and Peace of Brest-Litovsk and the resulting transfer of German troops to the West, in early 1918, Field Marshal Sir Henry Wilson appointed him to assess the probable German

Order for Battle for the coming spring offensive and where the enemy would be most likely to strike. Given carte blanche, Bevan set to work and in March gave a presentation to Clemenceau, Lloyd George, Churchill, Foch, Haig, Pershing and all the other French and British Army commanders. As it turned out, he got the Order of Battle correct to within three divisions and the point of attack to within ten miles. By any account, this appreciation was an extraordinary achievement and won him the enduring respect of Churchill. Come 1939, all this appeared to have been forgotten; Bevan's first post was with MI5 on censorship matters, then after a stint as a Brigade intelligence officer in Norway,[24] he was sent to the Home Guard to lecture them on security. Adamant that he would not be spending the rest of the war vegetating in a backwater staff job, Bevan decided to pull some strings including his brother-in-law General Harold Alexander, Sir Charles Hambro, the head of SOE, a great friend and the author Dennis Wheatley, the RAF member of LCS, another close friend. Before long, his name was circulating in the corridors of Whitehall and a position was found for him in the Joint Planning Office of the Chiefs of Staff.

His arrival at the LCS coincided with a revised charter for the Controlling Officer:

1   To prepare deception plans on a world-wide basis with the object of causing the enemy to waste his military resources.

2   To co-ordinate deception plans prepared by Commands at home and abroad.

3   To ensure that cover plans prepared by ISSB fit with the general framework of strategic deception.

4   To watch over the execution by the Service ministries, Commands and other organizations and departments, of approved deception plans which you have prepared.

5   To control the support of deception schemes originated by Commanders-in-Chief, by such means as leakage and propaganda.

6   Your work is not limited to strategic deception alone but is to include any matter calculated to mystify or mislead the enemy whenever military advantage may so be gained.

⚓

Six months after Fleming arrived in India, Sir Ronald Wingate, Bt., who had been advising the Chiefs of Staff on the organization of deception measures, joined the LCS as the Army member of the operations sub-section with responsibility for India and South-East Asia. Twenty years older than Fleming, he brought with him an encyclopaedic knowledge of India and the Middle East acquired over thirty years of foreign service. After completing his studies at Oxford including learning

Arabic, Urdu and Persian, Wingate began his Indian Civil Service career as an Assistant Commissioner in Punjab, still 'Kipling's India' where 'the Army, and so the Englishmen, were everywhere'. After promotion to ADC and assistant private secretary to the governor, he left for war in June 1917 as the assistant political officer to the Mesopotamian Expeditionary Force. Arriving in Basra, he viewed the Tigris a 'desolate and uninviting region' in enemy-occupied territory which somehow the British had to administer. With a number of Arabists seconded to Middle East Forces from the Levant Consular Service and Sudan Political Service, Wingate found himself in distinguished company.

At the head of the political mission was Sir Percy Cox – 'Cokkus' to the Arabs and Persians. He had been more than twenty years in Arab countries in the Gulf. He spoke Arabic and Persian, and was a brilliant, if enigmatic, diplomat whose long and rather crooked nose created both alarm and respect … Then there was Arnold Wilson, his deputy [with] a huge head, burning eyes and a personality so overpowering that in conference it was difficult to realize there was anyone else in the room. Another political officer was Lieutenant Colonel Gerard Leachman of the Sussex Regiment who, easily passing for a Bedouin with his dark looks and camel riding expertise, 'ruled the Western desert and the Anaizeh tribe' … Major Ely Banister Soane – once of the Imperial Bank of Persia – who had wandered in disguise through Kurdistan as a seller of cheese,[25] spoke five dialects of Kurdish and Persian. His exploits, along with his half a dozen Kurdish desperadoes, on the Karun would fill a volume.[26] Finally, there was Gertrude Bell, scholar, intrepid traveller, polished Arabist with a unique knowledge of Arab personalities and tribes from Damascus to the borders of Persia, and the only woman officer in the Army.[27]

Sent to the ancient holy city of Najaf with its 40,000 inhabitants, Wingate set up his HQ in a caravanserai outside the city walls on the Kufa road. Here 'we dealt out a rough and ready sort of justice. We kept the peace; we collected some revenue.' Then British troops left and after leave in England, although due to return to Mesopotamia, in 1919, the thirty-year-old Wingate was appointed agent and consul at Muscat and Oman, a country in a state of turmoil due to a long-standing power struggle between the Imamate of Oman and the Sultan of Oman. So, as Wingate put it,

My brief was a simple one … it was that something must be done which would relieve us of the responsibility of maintaining a strong armed force at great expense,[28] and with a high casualty rate, to protect a Sultan against whom almost the whole of his subjects were in rebellion, in an area which for us at that moment appeared to have no strategic, political or economic importance.

He skilfully negotiated 'an agreement between the Sultan and his subjects' – the Treaty of Sib – that led to an unprecedented thirty years of peace in the interior of Oman. In January 1923 he was ordered back to Oman to serve as consul a second time. All was well except the town of Sur had refused to remit its custom dues. Having devised a cunning plan to cut off its water supply, Wingate despatched the Levy Corps to implement it. Surprise was absolute, not a shot was fired and two days later £10,000 worth of Maria Theresa dollars were handed over.

In between his two postings to Muscat and Oman, Wingate had been sent as assistant political officer to the resident in Kashmir. He recalled:

To reach Poonch one travelled by car from Rawalpindi some hundred miles up the Jhelum valley road, to a tiny village called Uri where there was a rest-house. From there, one struck out on foot across the mountains over the Haji Pir pass, more than 9,000 feet high, and descended to the little capital of Poonch itself. The journeys took two days. Isolation was complete.[29]

When this post was abolished, Wingate spent time in Srinagar including visiting the Monastery of Hemis, the city of Leh and the valley of the Shoyk on the other side of the 18,000 feet Khardong Pass before returning to India in September 1924 as secretary to the agent to the Governor General of Rajputana, the greatest of the congeries of Indian States under an agent. In 1927, Wingate moved to the same position in Baluchistan and then was appointed the deputy commissioner and political agent in Quetta and Pishin, a district which included a long stretch of the Afghan frontier. Wingate would later call his years in Quetta,[30] 'the happiest time that [he] spent in India', and greatly enjoyed the autonomy and respect he was granted there. While serving in Quetta, Wingate established a new water supply in the city and frequently became involved in matters relating to security and criminal justice.

In 1930, Wingate received a year's leave from India, during which he travelled around Europe. On his return to Baluchistan in 1931, he became the political agent in Sibi, but after only a few months he was appointed the Deputy Secretary of the Foreign and Political Department of the Indian government. As India was in the middle of reforms aimed at eventual independence, the result of the report of the Simon Commission, his first job was to help integrate the princely states into federation with the rest of India in preparation for independence. A particular challenge in the process involved determining how many representatives each of the states would have in the Constituent Assembly of India. Wingate proposed 'a scheme based upon permutations and combinations of the number of guns which were fired to salute the categories of Indian princes'. The idea was acclaimed 'as a stroke of genius' and adopted by the government.

In May 1935, when on a year's leave in Vichy, he heard of the terrible earthquake and cutting short his leave by six months, returned to Quetta where he found most of his Indian friends and acquaintances in the city had been killed; 'Quetta itself was flat on the ground.' As the Revenue Commissioner in Baluchistan, he also acted as agent for the governor general, and like many officers of the Indian Civil Service, he supported Indian self-rule, and began to see the end of British India as inevitable. As such, Wingate decided in 1936 that he would leave India once his term as Revenue Commissioner ended. In November 1937, he was offered the position of Minister to Nepal but instead took two years of leave that he had accumulated, planning to retire at its conclusion.

Wingate spent the next year travelling throughout Europe, and in early 1939 he rented a flat on the Chelsea Embankment, where he planned to live with his wife. He spent his time exploring London and soon began planning to stand for Parliament as the member for his constituency was planning to retire. On the outbreak of war, the sitting member decided not to retire, and Wingate abandoned his hopes at politics, deciding that he would 'have been quite useless as a Member of Parliament' anyway. Snapped up by the Ministry of Economic Warfare, he was made head of the Blacklist Department, then recruited by Hugh Dalton for No.20 Military Mission, the Free French Force Operation MENACE to seize Dakar. By New Year 1941, he found himself attached to the West African Governors' Conference, charged with organizing British West Africa for the war effort. Then, sponsored by General 'Pug' Ismay, whom he knew of old in Mesopotamia and India, Wingate joined the planning staff of the Chiefs of Staff.

Ronald Wingate was in some respects a mirror image of Fleming. Both liked shooting, stalking, fishing and winter sports and both were inveterate travellers. Indeed it was surprising that the paths of the two men had not crossed before the war. Yet these similarities were superficial. Wingate was an extrovert, a diplomatic schmoozer and artful facilitator and fixer whereas Fleming was at heart a creative artist with a flair for invention. Furthermore, unlike Fleming, Wingate was ambitious and this was to define their relationship as the war unfolded.

Fleming's direct reporting line was to Brigadier Bill Cawthorn, the Australian-born Director of Military Intelligence at GHQ India. The son of an English commercial traveller, Bill Cawthorn was born in Melbourne in 1896. After graduating from school, he started his working life as a schoolteacher but after the outbreak of the First World War, in February 1915, he joined the Australian Imperial Force as a private soldier. Arriving at Gallipoli in September, he was promoted to regimental sergeant major and then commissioned that November. When his battalion was transferred to France in March 1916, he suffered a severe shrapnel wound to his abdomen and had to be evacuated to England. Promoted to captain in May 1917, he rejoined his unit in France and on the conclusion of the war, was commissioned in the Indian Army. In the 1920s he served with the 16th Punjab Regiment, saw active service on the North-West Frontier (1930–5) and was later a Staff Officer at the War Office in London. In 1939 Cawthorn took charge of the Middle East Intelligence Centre in Cairo which had been set up to coordinate and collate intelligence from existing sources for both GHQ Middle East and the Joint Intelligence Committee in London. A political poisoned chalice, the centre found itself up against the Foreign Office and SIS who were determined to box it in. Their antics in no way deterred Cawthorn who started his own political intelligence wing. Two years later he became Director of Military Intelligence at GHQ India and from October 1943, as an acting major general, he held the additional post of Deputy Director of Intelligence, SEAC.

With Clarke as his muse, Bevan as his gatekeeper, Wingate as his sounding board and Cawthorn as his mentor, in his new role as head of GSI (d), Fleming was able to spread his wings and let his imagination take flight. Cawthorn was particularly empathetic towards Fleming and the strong working and personal relationship that developed between them underpinned the creativity and dynamic expansion and execution of Britain's Far East deception plans.

Chapter 7

Burmese capers and haversack ruses

General Wavell left Cairo on 7 July 1941 to take up his new appointment as Commander-In-Chief India. He was accompanied by his ADC, twenty-three-year-old Sandy Reid Scott of the 11th Hussars who sported a black eyepatch as a result of having lost his left eye in the Western Desert the previous year. When he arrived in Simla, he immediately got to grips with the pressing issues facing his new command which included Iraq and Iran. Deception had long been a favourite stratagem of his in the Middle East but it was not until the Japanese attack on Burma that an opportunity presented itself at the end of April 1942. By now, British forces were withdrawing into India and within days the remnants of the Army in Burma would be gone.

When Fleming reached Delhi on 17 March, he initially stayed as a guest of Wavell while he found an office and set up his fledgling organization known as GSI (d). Reid Scott found him 'a charming chap' who 'does not talk about himself … the only author and traveller and thinker that I know who does not strike one as curious and have a lot of eccentric habits'.[1] He could not have arrived at a worse time. Eighteen months later, Field Marshal Wavell submitted his Despatch[2] to the Secretary of State for War[3] about the situation he faced in March 1942.

When Rangoon fell, in March 1942, it was obvious that the whole of Burma might be occupied by the Japanese and that India itself and Ceylon lay under imminent threat of invasion.

The forces available for defence at this time were dangerously weak. The Eastern Fleet had only one modernized battleship immediately available and that the fleet as a whole was in no position to dispute with the Japanese fleet command of the Bay of Bengal or of the waters around Ceylon. There were only one British and six Indian divisions available for the defence of the whole of India and Ceylon, apart from forces for the defence of the NW Frontier and for internal security, both of which were well below the strength estimated as necessary for those commitments. No single one of these divisions was complete in ancillary troops or fully equipped or adequately trained. Three of them had two brigades only.

The number of anti-aircraft guns (heavy or light) to defend Calcutta (India's largest city), her most important war industries and other vital points, which were or were soon likely to be within effective bombing range, was less than 150, against an estimated total requirement of some 1,500.

The Air Force available for the commitments of defending India and Ceylon and of supporting the army in Burma was similarly inadequate, as was the number of airfields. For the defence of Calcutta one fighter squadron was available with eight serviceable Mohawks. Fifty Hurricanes were delivered to Ceylon in March, and the three fighter squadrons allocated to the defence of the island were equipped during March, just in time to meet the enemy air raids in April.

The remaining air force available (two fighter squadrons and one light bomber squadron) was allotted to Upper Burma, where the greater part of it was destroyed by enemy attack at Magwe on 21 and 22 March. The remnants were withdrawn to India to re-form for its defence.

The airfields in Eastern India were quite inadequate and the warning system was only in a rudimentary stage.

… This was India's most dangerous hour; our Eastern Fleet was powerless to protect Ceylon or Eastern India; our air strength was negligible; and it was becoming increasingly obvious that our small tired force in Burma was unlikely to be able to hold the enemy, while the absence of communications between Assam and Upper Burma made it impossible to reinforce it.

After a visit to Burma with Wavell and Alexander, Fleming flew to Chungking on 4 April[4] to have a look around and renew old acquaintances from his journalist days, including General Cheng K'ai-Min, the KMT Director of Military Intelligence. Then he flew down to Trincomalee in Ceylon to arrange a 'cover' for Operation IRONCLAD-STREAMLINE JANE, the invasion of Madagascar. This was the last engagement between British and Vichy French forces and critical to securing the sea lanes of the Western Indian Ocean by denying the island to Japanese submarines. The British 29th Infantry Brigade and No. 5 Commando landed on 5 May 1942 and after a protracted engagement the garrison surrendered in November.

With Fleming now in post, Wavell concocted a plan to deceive the Japanese as to both the strength and intentions of the British in India, the desired outcome being to bring the Japanese advance to a halt. A great admirer of General Allenby on whose staff he had been in Palestine,[5] Wavell decided to use the 'haversack ruse' which Allenby had played in the run up to the third battle of Gaza in 1917. He called it ERROR.

Major Richard Meinertzhagen, Allenby's Intelligence Officer, had tried to send false information through the use of 'lost documents' near the Turkish front lines but none of the drops had succeeded. So he then decided to plant the documents himself, and he compiled a false Staff Officer's notebook to suggest that the Beersheba movements [of British troops] were only a feint and that D-Day for the attack on Gaza would be some weeks later than the date actually set for the offensive. The notebook along with orders and staff papers was placed in a haversack together with £20 in notes – a tidy sum in those days – to give the impression that the loss was not intentional. He also included fictitious personal letters, one from his wife reporting the birth of their son and another from a disgruntled officer complaining about poor British plans. Finally, he added some information on British codes to enable the Turkish-German radio intercept unit to decode additional British wireless traffic.[6]

Now came the tricky business of planting the haversack. Riding out into no-man's land, Meinertzhagen succeeded in getting himself spotted by a Turkish patrol and when they gave chase, he pretended to be wounded and dropped his rifle, water bottle and haversack which he had previously smeared with blood from a cut on his horse. He rode off, then stopped to check that the patrol had picked up the haversack and continued back to his own lines. The next day, a strong reconnaissance party went forward from the British front lines seemingly to conduct an urgent search for the lost haversack. In a final flourish of coded wireless traffic which he knew the enemy could break, he included a message that an officer named Meinertzhagen was to report to GHQ for an inquiry into the loss of a haversack containing important information.

The contents of the haversack did indeed reach the German General von Kressenstein, who, after examining them personally, felt 'inclined strongly to believe in their authenticity'.[7] The overall effect of the deception plan was to reinforce in von Kressenstein's mind that Gaza was the intended target of the British offensive and it succeeded in the overall goal of achieving surprise and sowing confusion in the enemy's defensive response. However, it was not the contents of the haversack alone that had pulled off the successful deception for Meinertzhagen already had in place a comprehensive intelligence network that enabled him to track and if necessary fine-tune his operations. This, coupled with good security – only Meinertzhagen, Allenby and three senior staff officers knew about the ruse – and a detailed knowledge of the Turkish-German intelligence system, its methods, agents and limitations, ensured the best chance for success.

Operation ERROR was hatched by Wavell and Fleming; the latter carried it out with the assistance of Sandy Reid Scott who noted in his diary:

The idea was that the Chief had just paid a hurried last-minute visit to the Burma front and had had a car accident, the car skidding too fast round a corner and then the Japs being close enough upon our heels we had been obliged to evacuate the car in a hurry and leave behind most of his kit including his letter case containing a lot of faked information actually written by the Chief; for instance there were 'Notes for Alexander' saying how there were going to be two armies in Burma, how large our air strength was becoming and also about a new secret weapon! Perhaps that would make the Japs windy.[8]

Fleming and Reid Scott first took the plan to General Alexander in Myitkyina for his approval. With the withdrawal to Kalewa already ordered, Alexander had no desire to conduct a protracted defence round Mandalay and gave his instant assent to ERROR, pointing out that the Ava Bridge was due to be blown in the very near future. Their next stop was to see General Cowan commanding 17th Division and put him in the picture.

To his amazement and delight, Fleming ran into Mike Calvert, who after his adventures in Kent and Sussex with Fleming, had been posted by SOE to Australia to set up a Special Training School there in October 1940. After working closely with the former explorer Freddie Spencer Chapman who ran the field craft course, Calvert had been sent to Burma as Chief Instructor of the Bush Warfare School at Maymyo; contrary to its name, the task of the school was to train officers and NCOs to lead guerrillas in the plains of China. After the Japanese invasion, Calvert, now Commandant, found himself in command of 'a scratch battalion of odds and sods, including several lunatics and deserters',[9] defending the Gortiek viaduct thirty miles to the East of Maymyo. From there his 'commandos' fought a pugnacious withdrawal, barely breaking contact with the advancing Japanese. In a village near the Ava Bridge, his column literally bumped into Fleming and Reid Scott in their Ford V8 who immediately recruited him and Private Williams of the Welch regiment to help them execute their audacious deception.

The problem was how to convincingly wreck the car and get away safely from the advancing Japanese patrols. Furthermore, if captured in flagrante, they needed a good cover story, hence enter Williams as the staff car driver. An additional planning factor was that the bridge was due to be blown at 20.00 hours: they would have to cross it to get as near as they could to the Japanese and then return in time or be faced with the prospect of swimming the swiftly flowing muddy Irrawaddy River.

In a notebook in pencilled manuscript, Fleming recorded the progress of ERROR:

29 April 1942
Left Delhi in the Lockheed with Sandy and a Colonel Reynolds (from G) at 08.30 hours. Second breakfast at Allahabad whence I sent off a signal about a forgotten document. Landed Dera Drum soon after 12.00 hours local time. Our Blenheim[10] was said (on paper) to take us all to Shwebo. We waited for it until 16.00 hours, when it finally turned up; but by then it was too late to start. An almost exact repetition of the RAF balls up last time. A long wait mitigated by Anthony Powell's *What became of Waring?* Dined and slept heavily at the Great Eastern after a sticky swim.

30 April 1942

Writing this in the back of a Blenheim which at the moment is hedge-hopping. Turned out that we were landing on the deserted airfield at Shewbo. N. Chancellor[11] and a sensible US colonel told us that Alex, Stilwell and Lo[12] were all here. Sunshine was rising from behind some trees where the bazaar was obliterated yesterday by 27 bombers. Everyone seemed a little dry in the mouth and absent-minded. We unloaded some parcels of RAF comforts and drove to General Alexander's bungalow, then down to Operations where I unfolded ERROR to Alex, Winterton[13] and George. The latter seemed quite enthusiastic but the two generals, though approving, had too much urgent business of their own to be really interested. Got hold of Michael, who liked the idea, and a suitable car. It looked like being too late for the Mandalay scheme, so decided to try it at Ava which was [reported] due to go up at 19.00 hours. Set off rather late with Michael, Sandy and a good driver called Williams who had been one of fifteen Commando prisoners who were lined up to be bayonetted. Williams and the Company Sergeant Major broke and ran for it and swam the Irrawaddy, the latter with several bayonet wounds. I asked Williams why he thought the Japs did this and he said he thought it was to keep up the fighting spirit of their troops. Drove about x miles through Oudan to Sagaing. A few wretched Indian refugees and a lot of Chinese troops [96 Division?] drifting back in fairly good order. Officers young and relatively smart; some with field glasses and map cases. No longer elderly opium addicts being carried in chairs. Reached HQ 17th Division on river front at Sagaing just before 19.00 hours. General Cowan[14] most sympathetic and sensible. Withdrawal of 63 Brigade across the Ava to be completed by 20.00 hours. Bridge to be blown not later than midnight. Situation in other respects favourable. Nipped across bridge so as to make the most of the last hour of daylight. Gurkhas doing a timed withdrawal like clockwork, silent and alert. Found a spot about 400 yards from the bridge. Michael made some rather feeble skid marks and we drove the Ford over the embankment. It plummeted down, crossed a bullock cart track and then down again into a water-like depression where it remained the right way up with the engine still self-righteously running.[15] (Something was burning in the middle distance.) Highly unsensational. We laughed and followed it up. Arranged contents of boot, punctured one front tyre and let wind out of another, inflicted minor internal damage (not very logically). An armoured car appeared down the road and we wondered whether it was a Jap. (Whole thing reminded me very much of that other bridge over the Alyakmon, North of Servia.)[16] Withdrew over the bridge, bumping over planks where the charge was laid, at 20.00 hours as it was getting dark. We had been lucky to get the job done in the nick of time and I don't think it was done too badly but it all felt rather tame. Got some food at Divisional HQ, where poor old Freeman-Taylor[17] turned up, grumbling in a rather wet way. Also General Soong of 38th Division and well liked. After dinner we wandered down across the foreshore of caked mud, above which the Chinese had dug themselves in quickly and neatly and sat by the river waiting for the bridge to go up. Very still hot night. From a village on the further bank dogs were barking and men and women were calling and talking excitedly. A Chinese listening patrol of two young men told me the Japanese were there but all they could tell me for certain was that strangers of some sort had arrived. After a bit things were quiet again. Bridge blown at 23.20 hours, after which 17th Division moved out. We slept among many mosquitoes in their HQ, a big stripped bungalow. When it got light next day I found a copy of Punch by my bed with a feeble article signed Peter Fleming. We made some Horlicks and Ovaltine and took the jeep to the bridge. Chinese guarding it had nothing to report. Two spans cut clean. Shells were bursting one to two miles away on the other side. Nobody to be seen on the further bridgehead. A hot cloudy morning. Would have liked to stay and watch developments but Sandy had to catch the plane, if any, so we started back at 08.00 hours.[18]

Fleming later wrote to Celia that 'Burma was the third withdrawal I have been in on and they all smelt the same: a bad smell, charged with suspense, apprehension, waste and a sort of galloping decay. Burnt villages, foundered cars, half-eaten meals, typewriters and valises and army forms and the smelly carcasses of animals, hopeless overdriven refugees, alarms and rumours.'[19]

In an appendix to his official report, Fleming set out a rigorous methodology to assess the success or failure of ERROR. It was an unforgiving examination of whether they had made a difference and typified the innate uncertainties involved in measuring deception operations:

Did it work?
General

1. **The success of this operation is dependent on the answers to the following questions:-**
(a) did the enemy find the documents?

(b) did they reach his Intelligence?

(c) did his Intelligence see through either:

    (i)   the matter planted?

    (ii) the manner of its planting?

2. **Did the enemy find the documents?**
This can almost certainly be answered in the affirmative. The car was left (see diagram at Appendix B) close to the main road at a point where the first

Japanese troops to arrive were virtually bound to halt pending a reconnaissance of, and after that repairs to, the Ava Bridge. The car was the only object of interest in an empty and deserted countryside. Its contents are most unlikely to have been interfered with by either Chinese troops or Burmese civilians before the arrival of the Japanese, which almost certainly took place during 1 May.

3. Did the documents reach the Japanese Intelligence?

This question cannot be answered with any degree of confidence. All that can be said is that the chances of (so to speak) the dog being allowed to see the rabbit were about as good as they could have been. This was due to the following factors:

(a) the discovery was almost certainly made, not by two or three private soldiers on their own, but by a party of men in full view of the road, whence they were probably being watched by the remainder of their own unit or by another unit.

(b) the discovery was almost certainly made during a halt.

(c) officers must have been in the immediate vicinity and may easily have been among those who made the discovery.

It thus seems that the chances of the documents being either pocketed, jettisoned, or otherwise denied to the enemy's Intelligence by his own troops are – though they cannot be dismissed – reasonably small.

4. Did the enemy see through the documents?

More than 80 per cent of the documents, personal and official, were genuine; the important minority of fakes were carefully concocted and, being mostly couched in allusive or otherwise slightly indefinite terms, were almost if not quite proof against definitive exposure. In other words the forgeries, though they included suggestions which may be disbelieved by the enemy, contained no statement of fact which he can disprove. In the circumstances it is considered that the documents were in themselves so persuasive that the enemy, though he may not accept all their implications in full, cannot afford to leave out of his calculations the general trend of the information thus conveyed to him.

5. Did the enemy see through the ruse itself?

(a) Sherlock Holmes, had he been promptly on the spot, could without difficulty have deduced from the skid-marks and other indications that there was something fishy about the supposed accident. But it is safe to assume that, long before his Japanese equivalent could have reached the Ava Bridge, large numbers of Dr. Watsons had decisively prejudiced all chances of reconstructing the crime.

(b) the ruse suggested that General Wavell was in the Sagaing area on 29 or 30 April. General Wavell was in fact in Delhi. By the time the Japanese get around to checking up on General Wavell's movements (if it occurs to them to do so) it is safe to assume that at least a fortnight will have elapsed; and however good their espionage in Delhi, it is:

(i) difficult to believe that they can prove he was not in Burma on the dates in question.

(ii) impossible to believe that they can receive the proof within less than a month of finding the documents.

And even then his presence in Burma was only suggested; to prove that this suggestion was false is a very different thing from proving that the documents are forgeries.

Conclusions

6. On the basis of the foregoing appreciation it would seem that the operation had a better than 50 per cent chance of success.

7. The appreciation is however seriously vitiated in that it makes no allowance for the completely unexpected, a recurrent factor both in war and in the Japanese character. In view of this omission I am inclined to reduce our chances of success to 30 per cent.

8. Assuming that the more or less mechanical processes envisaged in (1) (a) and (b) above went smoothly, the greatest danger to the project is to be apprehended from the impact of a sophisticated and sceptical mind at an early stage. The worst thing we could come up against would be a German liaison officer at Japanese HQ in Burma who was familiar with the story of Meinertzhagen's haversack. A great deal will depend on at what stage and on what level suspicions are first aroused.

Peter Fleming
6 May 1942

In a hand-written comment at the end of this section of Fleming's report, Wavell wrote:

I had always realized this danger, and after Fleming had gone, thought I had made a bad mistake in including in the exhibits a paper which connected me with the writing of Allenby's life, but it was too late to recall it. I think the above estimate is pretty well correct. Any harm done if the Jap decides it was a plant? I don't think so. A.W. 13 May 1942.

⌇

In a letter of 24 August 1944 to Wavell,[20] Fleming passed on the gist of a conversation he had had with General Cheng Kai-min, the Chinese Director of Military Intelligence.

TOP SECRET: Operation ERROR[21]

Cheng Kai-min was closely cross-examined regarding alleged Japanese reactions to this operation. From his account it appeared that during the first Burma campaign the Japanese had captured important documents indicating that India's defensive potential was greater than had been supposed and that Tokyo had asked certain Chinese agents, employed by the Japanese but controlled by the Chinese, whether they were in a position to verify (or disprove) the contents of these documents by carrying out espionage work against India. The agents, on Cheng Kai-min's instructions, replied that such an assignment would take such a long time that it would be hardly worthwhile; they added that their information tended to confirm the fact that our strength in India was considerable. The agents did not see the documents and Cheng Kai-min appeared to have no detailed information as to the manner or place of their capture.

I do not consider that this story constitutes proof that ERROR was successful, though it does suggest that it may have been successful. It is difficult to think of any other documents which the Japanese could have captured in Burma and which would have persuaded and even hinted to them that our forces in India were strong. Cheng Kai-min certainly accepts his own account of Japanese reactions as definite proof that we executed an ambitious stratagem with complete success and made several flattering references to it at later stages of our conversation. It will thus be seen that ERROR either:

(a) Deceived the Japanese and achieved its object; or

(b) Deceived the Chinese and served a useful purpose.

Wavell replied:[22]

My dear Peter,

Many thanks for the note on ERROR. I hope it all puzzled the Japanese. When I am old and garrulous and blimping I shall probably tell a story of how I tricked the Japs and saved India from invasion!

Yours,

Wavell

❧

As the tempo for special operations increased in India and SEAC, the RAF responded by forming Special Duty squadrons. By late 1944, 357 Squadron consisting of long-range Liberators, Hudsons and a flight of C-47 Dakotas was providing 'moonlight' services for all the clandestine agencies, including SIS,[23] SOE[24] and, of course, D. Division [GSI (d)].[25]

On a late afternoon in December 1944 Squadron Leader Terence O'Brien, who commanded the Dakota flight of 357 Squadron, remembered[26] sitting 'on the white pillared veranda of the mess, all serene as we relaxed in the soft light of the setting sun, glasses tinkling with ice … the dark cloud-shaped bulges of the mango trees were set against a transparent organdie sky, with just the single fleck of a late homing vulture sliding slowly down the cloudless horizon …' when a jeep came hurtling down the track and ground to a halt in a thick mist of pallid dust. A Lieutenant from D. Division [GSI (d)] alighted, clutching 'a curious leather object' which turned out to be a combined map case and overnight bag belonging to a brigadier. Inside the map case were several marked-up maps with three memos identifying the brigadier as well as having useful notes on the markings. The overnight bag contained a red-banded cap, pyjamas, shaving kit and a half-empty tube of toothpaste. The idea was to convince the Japanese that a clumsy or drunk brigadier had accidentally dropped it from an observation flight.

O'Brien took the case with him on his next night mission that involved dropping a single SIS agent near the Salween River. The Dropping Zone was on a road near a village south of Bhamo where a large number of Japanese were billeted. After dropping the case from about twenty feet on a treeless stretch between paddy fields, the aircrew saw it lying on a pallid strip just outside the village. When he asked Fleming some months later if the ruse had succeeded, he put it in the 'remote possibility' category.

On another occasion, Fleming arrived at the airfield in Jessore with a haversack for O'Brien to deliver on a road near Moulmein. This time it was more complicated as Fleming needed the haversack to end up near an opened parachute. He wanted the Japanese to find the two items close to one another and make the assumption that the agent had either dropped it accidentally or had to run for his life on landing. The problem was how to effect the opening of the parachute's canopy without the weight of a body. Having already given some thought to the matter, Fleming came up with the idea of using a block of ice.

The advantages of this solution were that by the time the Japanese found the chute and haversack in the morning, the ice would have melted; however, the disadvantages were how to stop the ice melting in the course of a six-hour flight and how to prevent the floor of the aircraft from becoming slippery. The prospect of the despatcher tumbling out of the door of the aircraft as he skidded on the thawed ice filled the crew with alarm. So instead of ice, O'Brien experimented by chucking an opened, rolled-up parachute along with the haversack out of the door of the aircraft fifty feet above the airfield and found it worked perfectly. The drop went ahead and the chute convincingly draped itself over a banana tree with the haversack landing on the road beside it.

Another variety of the haversack ruse dreamt up by Fleming was a dead carrier pigeon. After taking delivery of the bird in a brown paper bag, O'Brien took off on an SIS sortie to drop a team blind in the mountains along the Chinese border. The pigeon's message contained a frequency for a non-existent agent and D. Division [GSI (d)] hoped the Japanese would then make contact. The SIS drop was aborted as the terrain turned out to be solid jungle but the dead bird fluttered down from fifty feet towards a little white pagoda in the Sittang valley. After a ten-hour flight, O'Brien noted that 'all we had done was to drop a dead pigeon'! The SIS conducting officer subsequently filed a complaint against D. Division [GSI (d)].

Crashes behind enemy lines offered opportunities for planting deception material if acted quickly on. In May 1945, D. Division [GSI (d)] asked O'Brien to deliver a haversack to the crash site of a P-38 of the US 10th Air Force in the Karen Hills. Inside were about fifty ordinary blue aerogrammes, elastic-banded into several packets, each with a slip giving a unit address. They were English stamped and postmarked and all from different hands and different typewriters. The purpose of the ruse was to reinforce the story about the attack of Fourteenth Army directed at Moulmein. After completing a supply drop to HYENA,[27] the aircrew fortunately found a gap in the clouds and were able to identify the crash site in a paddy field 'with the tail plane section of the aircraft rising like a monument'.

Although not on the Mediterranean top secret distribution list, Fleming would have probably heard about Operation MINCEMEAT, part of the overall deception plan BARCLAY to persuade the Germans that the Allies were planning to invade Greece and Corsica rather than Sicily in the summer of 1943, when he attended the TRIDENT conference in May 1943. The corpse of a 'Major William Martin, Royal Marines', ostensibly a Combined Operations staff officer, was pushed off the side of a British submarine off the coast of Spain and duly washed ashore. Attached to the major's wrist was a briefcase full of top secret documents, all carefully crafted to convince the Abwehr of his bona fides. Much of this story had been subsequently made famous as 'the man who never was' but in terms of deception methodology it came under the category of 'the haversack ruse'.

In his final report,[28] Fleming wrote up Operation FATHEAD, D. Division's version of MINCEMEAT, in his customary tongue-in-cheek style:

The object of this operation was to provide the Japanese Commander in Akyab with a wireless set, cipher and questionnaire and thus enable him to open up a new channel of the BRASS type. With this object in view, the corpse of a Bengali Hindu complete with all the accessories proper to an agent and accompanied by a notional Burmese companion and two containers was dropped by parachute on the Japanese lines of communication about thirty miles South of Akyab on night 16/17 November 1943.

Operation FATHEAD was planned as early as the beginning of July 1943 but, surprising as it may seem in a country of 400,000,000 odd inhabitants and in the middle of a major famine, it proved extraordinarily difficult to procure a corpse and for this reason the operation had to be continually postponed. On 11 November 1943, an officer of D. Division was detailed to fly to Calcutta, procure a body and carry out the operation and was instructed not to return until he had done so. There then began a five-day hunt round the slums, backstreets, morgues, mortuaries, police stations and hospitals of Calcutta until a body was found. The police, who had promised to supply a body on demand, failed to fulfil their promise when the moment came. The Surgeon-General was charming but hampered by red tape. The morgues and mortuaries yielded their grisly stock for inspection but the only suitable body – a rickshaw pusher in private life – was claimed by his relatives. Early morning excursions round the streets with the trucks which collected the bodies of famine victims from the pavements were also of no avail as these were all either too emaciated or in too advanced a stage of decomposition to serve our purpose.

Time was getting short as the full moon period was coming to an end. The aircraft detailed for the operation was at readiness daily. As a last resort, recourse was had to the army medical authorities at Fort William and two hours later in a thicket at the back of an Indian General Hospital a full colonel in the IAMC might have been seen helping to man-handle the naked body of an Indian out of an ambulance into the back of a 15 cwt. truck.

In a garage in Alipore the body was washed, dressed in native clothes and strapped into overalls, parachute and helmet. Exhaustive tests had previously been carried out with the parachute by the Air Landing School at Chaklala and it had been carefully packed with the rigging lines crossed so that it would open partially, but not sufficiently to break a man's fall effectively. Various odd items such as cigarettes, matches, a wallet, train tickets and small change were inserted in the pockets of his clothes; all the properties were carefully wiped and the corpse's fingerprints were placed convincingly on all polished surfaces. Rubber gloves were worn the whole time the corpse was being valeted.

At 00.40 hours on 17 November 1943, the plane carrying the corpse and D. Division's representative took off from Dum Dum airfield and headed South East, towards Akyab. The night was fine and clear but the flight, which was otherwise uneventful, was marred by the stench of decaying flesh which permeated the whole aircraft eventually reaching the pilot's cockpit. A bottle of Eau de Cologne and some cotton masks brought as an afterthought proved most useful. The Dropping Zone was found with difficulty and the corpse and two containers were dropped successfully from 800 feet – the two container parachutes being clearly visible in the moonlight. The corpse's parachute did not open.

Although D. Division's Control station in Calcutta called and listened on FATHEAD's frequencies for six months, nothing was ever heard from the Japanese and no evidence had yet been recovered which would indicate that this operation came anywhere near achieving its object. It is, however, known that the Japanese recovered the corpse and searched vigorously for his notional colleague.

In his memoir of flying Special Duty missions in the Far East, *The Moonlight War: The Story of Clandestine Operations in Southeast Asia, 1944–5*, Terence O'Brien recalled FATHEAD as

one of D Division's more macabre capers ... those of us who know about it on the squadron always referred to it afterwards simply as Operation CORPSE. The pilot was Jack Churchill and I heard him being introduced one night in the mess with the words: 'He did the corpse job.' It made him sound like a grave-robber, particularly as it was spoken in such a confidential tone.

The Squadron's version of the 'drop' is recounted by O'Brien:

Churchill entered the fuselage first that night, just as the conducting officer stepped back from his latest adjustment of the tent-fly covering. Churchill happened to bang the side of the door with his parachute and this rocked the body slightly; he glanced towards it uneasily and was horrified to see an arm become dislodged out of the covering. It flopped down and started swinging in slow pendulum. He turned away quickly from the sight, shutting it out of mind as he hurried forward to his seat, and, like the Coleridge man who knew a frightful fiend was following him along the lonely road, he never turned around to look back again that night ...

The Dropping Zone was in an area near Toungoo where the Japanese were reported to be present in strength, but there was no fixed installation which might call for heavy Anti-Aircraft protection so they had nothing to worry on that score. The actual site was a triangular patch of paddy beside a well-used spur road that branched off from the main valley road to a large village less than a mile away. It was reasonable to assume that with so many Japanese in the area they would discover quickly, if not actually observe themselves, that a drop had taken place, particularly as Churchill planned to dither about the area for a few minutes like a pilot unsure if he were over the correct site. I have heard that a flare, or Verey light, was fired for the same purpose, but am not sure about this; such flagrant advertising might have evoked suspicion.

They were not worried at D. Division [GSI (d)] about the possibility of a local villager stealing the package. After all that fanfare leading up to the drop it was most unlikely that anyone would dare risk such a theft. The thief would risk not only his own life but those of his fellow villagers whom the Japanese would go on executing in continuous sacrifice until the missing package was recovered. Anyway, a radio transmitter was of no more use to a Burmese villager than was the dead body.

The RAF component of operation FATHEAD went more or less according to plan. Churchill found the Dropping Zone without difficulty and after pottering about noisily for five minutes, ensuring his activities were being attended to, and perhaps sending down that fiery signal, he dropped the radio package and saw the parachute land safely on the paddy fields. He then made a wide leisurely circuit to give his despatcher and the conducting officer time to get the body on the slide.

When he finally made the run however, the despatcher came up beside him, just as he was about to give the green light, and reported that they were not yet ready; he asked Churchill to roam about for a few minutes so they could get organised. It appeared that in handling the body on the slide the bush jacket had been pulled open, and the conducting officer was insistent that the corpse must go out 'properly dressed'.

So Churchill circled the village and the forest area where the Japanese were thought to have their depot, while the two behind him in the fuselage pulled their dead parachutist back up the slide and buttoned up his bush jacket properly again for departure. Then they moved him carefully back on to the slide, with the broken clip attached to the holding twine of his parachute, and told Churchill they were ready. He circled into position, made the low run-in, the green light flashed, and FATHEAD was finally launched.

When Churchill returned that night from his eight-hour flight in the carbolicised aircraft, he and the conducting officer reported that the drop had gone exactly as planned. D. Division [GSI (d)] were delighted. On the off-chance that the Japanese had been drawn to the paddy field immediately, they set up a listening watch the very next morning.

Nothing was heard for over a month. The decision was then taken to drop another W/T set, together with copies of the original signals instructions, to make it appear that FATHEAD's controllers had concluded that the original set had been damaged on landing. This time round there was no special aircraft available for D. Division [GSI (d)], so it had to beg for space on another clandestine mission.

Force 136 was helpful, as usual. They were happy to allow D. Division to include their package as a small diversion drop on sortie planned for BADGER in the next moon period. It was duly delivered from 600 feet on a brilliantly clear night and it fell perfectly in the first tow of paddy fields beside the road, the parachute settling wide like a huge mushroom. It could not fail to be noticed by anyone passing along that well-trodden road, even by nocturnal travellers.

By this time D. Division [GSI (d)] were so anxious for reassurance that a Liberator flying out to Siam the following night, on a track that took it close by the area, was asked to divert and check the site. The pilot did so, identifying it without any doubt, and reported that the paddy fields were absolutely clean. Had there been a parachute on the ground it certainly would have been visible. It must have been collected, and would surely by that time have been in the hands of the Japanese.

But the blockheads would not use the thing. It was infuriating. D. Division [GSI (d)] were in despair at such professional incompetence. How could you conduct any sort of intelligent espionage operation with people who did not understand the simplest principles of the game? Every night at 10.30 hours and every day at 11.30 hours the operator in Calcutta kept listening out for a response, but never a bleep came from the decoy. Weeks passed, the excuses for the silence became muted, hopes became fainter. On the squadron we heard nothing more of FATHEAD.

O'Brien ended his account of FATHEAD with the pithy observation that 'the European "man who never was" did apparently achieve an important deceit of the enemy. Not so our man in Burma. He remained true to his nature throughout. In the hierarchy of nonentity our man was far superior – he not only never was, he also never did.'

Chapter 8
Global strategists and stratagems

The war in the Pacific and South East Asia was first and foremost an American war. Although both the United States and Great Britain had been on the receiving end of repeated Japanese intimidation before Pearl Harbor – in 1937 the Americans lost a gunboat, the USS *Panay*, on the Yangtze River and the British Ambassador, Sir Hugh Knatchbull-Hugesson, was shot in the bottom when a Japanese fighter strafed his car – the American stance towards China had been markedly more overtly supportive in contrast to the British. After the horror of a full-scale invasion by the Japanese army was unleashed on China in 1937, American public opinion was incensed by images and reports of the fall of Nanking with its gruesome mass killings and rape of civilians. However, President Roosevelt did not invoke the 1937 Neutrality Act on the grounds that neither party had formally declared war. Instead the US Treasury quietly purchased 62 million ounces of silver at 45 cents per ounce from the Chinese in July and another 50 million ounces at the same price in November, thus enabling the KMT to buy American supplies which duly reached China in British 'bottoms'.

In June 1940 Chiang Kai-shek's brother-in-law, T.V. Soong, visited Washington to ask for arms and credits. The result was two loans totalling $200 million,[1] one for currency stabilization ($50 million) and the other for the purchase of food, petrol, trucks, small arms and aircraft, the latter destined for retired US Army flier Major Claire Chennault, who had been on the Chinese payroll since 1937 as their air force adviser. Once the Lend-Lease bill had been signed off by President Roosevelt in March 1941, the Secretary of War agreed that the Chinese could begin their rearmament with $50 million of Lend-Lease funds and that $23 million worth would come from US army stockpiles or current production. By late spring an additional $100 million of Lend-Lease funds was allocated, giving the Chinese enough money on paper to upgrade its fighting divisions and create a modern air force.[2]

Britain, with a far smaller cheque book, had been in a somewhat weaker position. Financially it had done its best. In 1939, British banks under a Treasury guarantee provided half of a £10 million currency stabilization fund to thwart Japanese attempts to undermine the Chinese currency[3] and a further £5 million was added to the fund in December 1940 and a £5 million credit for use in the sterling area granted in June 1941. In 1942, the Government made available a loan of £50 million. This turned out to fall well short of Chinese expectations; Madame Chiang Kai-shek told the *New York Times* in April 1942, 'We cannot see why the West, with its vaunted prescience, could not see that each passing hour gave Japan added opportunity to prepare to strike more deadly blows while the powers contented themselves with fortifying their positions with paper bullets.' For the West, read Britain.

The seizure of all Japanese assets and credits in the United States in July 1941, the last and the most significant of a series of trade embargos and restrictions, marked what the historian J.F.C. Fuller categorized as 'a declaration of economic war, and, in consequence, it was the actual opening of the struggle'.[4] By the time Japan attacked Pearl Harbor in December 1941, her 'choice was between two evils – both gigantic. She decided to follow the one she considered the lesser – war rather than economic ruin.' It was almost as if the Americans had goaded the Japanese into war, for as the historian H.P. Willmott pointed out, 'unlike Germany in the Second World War, Japan never had any realistic prospect of not being defeated in the war it initiated … the Pacific war from its start was for Japan sometime akin to a national *kamikaze* effort'. With the veneer of its dubious neutrality now peeled back, the United States determined on the destruction of Japan, with or without the help of the European colonial powers.

A central strand in its strategy was to continue its policy of keeping China militarily afloat, for as long as it stayed in the war, hundreds of thousands of Japanese soldiers would be tied down on the Asian mainland instead of being used to fight on other fronts (see Table 1). China still had about 3,820,000 men under arms. Of these, 2,920,000 were formed into 246 divisions classed by the

Country	Dec 1942 / Mar 1943	Aug 1943	Aug 1945
Manchuria (Kwantung)	13	15	11
China	22	25	25
Burma	2	6	10
Malaya, Borneo, Sumatra	3	1	10
Total	40	47	56

Table 1 Deployment of Japanese Infantry Divisions in the Far East: China and Manchuria devoured most of them.

Source: John Ellis, *The World War II Databook* (London: Aurum Press, 1993)

Chinese as 'front-line' troops, plus forty-four 'brigades'. In rear areas there were another seventy divisions and three brigades. Except for the Generalissimo's personal troops, estimated at about thirty divisions, the loyalties of China's troops tended to lie with their war area commanders, in effect regional warlords in another guise.

In order to do this, it was crucial to keep supplies flowing along 'the Burma Road' into China. Having previously lost his ports to the Japanese and hence access to the Pacific sea lanes, Chiang Kai-shek had ordered a road to be built between Kunming and Lashio in Burma. The 681-mile highway was built by tens of thousands of Chinese and Burmese labourers in a year and a half, and opened to traffic in mid-1939. Supplies were shipped by sea to Rangoon, then by rail to Lashio and finally by road to Kunming. Then on 8 March 1942, Rangoon fell to the Japanese and the Allies had no option other than to develop a high altitude aerial supply route between Assam in India and Yunnan Province in south-western China. Flying over some of the most inaccessible and inhospitable country on earth and through year-round extreme weather conditions, American pilots called it the 'Hump'. Yet it was the same road about which Robert Thompson wrote 'the Burma Road itself was only the end of a longer road ... made of money ... with which China could pay for supplies. That longer road traced back to the Treasury Department in Washington.'[5]

Although Great Britain and the United States were pursuing the same strategic goal of ultimately defeating Japan, Burma, Malaya and Hong Kong were still very much British possessions in the eyes of Winston Churchill, who had no intention of presiding over the dissolution of the British Empire. With the British financial and business establishment standing squarely behind him, Churchill saw the *status quo ante bellum* as a primary British war aim, with India, Malaya and Burma remaining colonies. Not so the Americans, who later jokingly referred to SEAC as 'Save England's Asian Colonies'.

President Roosevelt had an altogether rather different vision of Asia in the post-war world. He believed that the European empires in the Far East were archaic and that their colonies would soon be independent countries, a view shared by the American liberal intelligentsia[6] and big business. He also wanted China treated as an equal Allied partner in the war against Japan in the hope that it would develop into a great power, friendly to the West. In the case of Burma, Thaddeus Holt points out that 'the Americans were interested in liberating Burma only so as to open an overland supply line to China. They were distinctly not in the region to aid the British to recover their imperial possessions.'[7] For their underlying strategy was to arm and train a sufficiently large army for Chiang Kai-shek to drive to the sea in South China and then swing north, opening up airfields along the way for US long-range B-29 bombers to launch attacks on Japan.

The United States did of course have its own colonial possession in the South West Pacific, the Philippines. Taken from Spain in 1898 and incorporated as American territory under President McKinley's Proclamation of Benevolent Assimilation, Washington had deftly distanced itself from the European 'imperialists' by passing an act in 1935 giving the Philippines a ten-year 'transitional period' to full independence. As far as Roosevelt was concerned, this set the bar for others to aspire to.

Burying their differences for the time being, in December 1941 Britain and America formally recognized the imperative of creating a unified command to coordinate the war at the highest level. However, first the Americans had to reorganize their own disparate command structure into the US Joint Chiefs of Staff (JCS) committee, which was formally inaugurated in February 1942, its first members being General George Marshall, US Army Chief of Staff, Admirals Harold Stark and Ernest King, US Navy, and Lieutenant General 'Hap' Arnold, US Army Air Forces. In July 1942, President Roosevelt appointed Admiral William Leahy as his political and military representative and Chief of Staff of the JCS committee for, unlike the British Chiefs of Staff committee, which was integrated into the British Cabinet system, the US version was responsible primarily to the President of the United States as Commander-in-Chief of the US Armed Forces.

In the course of this reorganization, the Anglo-American Combined Chiefs of Staff Committee was established in Washington DC, the British being represented by Field Marshal Sir John Dill together with a team of deputies from the London-based Chiefs of Staff. In the course of the war, there would be over 200 meetings[8] of the Combined Chiefs of Staff and at 89 of them the British Chiefs of Staff themselves were present. Topics of discussion included theatres of war, proposed operations, various strategic plans, movement of forces, a range of logistical issues and strategic deception. It was their deliberations and directives that were to dictate the line Fleming took in his deception operations against Japan.

⋘

As early as April 1942, Wavell adopted Sun Tzu's dictum that 'attack is the secret of defence; defence is the planning of an attack'. In regular contact with Churchill by telegram, he began to plan a counter-offensive with his senior staff officers against the triumphant Japanese. In a paper of 17 September 1942 called Operation FANTASTICAL, he wrote that he wanted 'to create a spirit everywhere from GHQ downwards of determination to get as far into Burma this winter as possible, to recapture the whole of Burma without a day's delay that can be avoided, to be profoundly dissatisfied with our present programme and to be determined to exceed it'.

Fantasy quickly mutated into reality and in consultation with General Stilwell, US commander China-Burma-India, and the Generalissimo, plans were drawn up to advance by land forces into Upper Burma (Operation RAVENOUS) and by a seaborne and land expedition into Lower Burma (Operation CANNIBAL). The prize for Wavell was the capture of Akyab since it would deprive the Japanese of their advanced all-weather refuelling base for air raids on Calcutta and present him with a platform to harass Japanese communications in Central Burma.

Unfortunately, 29 Brigade amphibious assault force remained fully occupied in Madagascar, so Wavell had to abandon the seaborne element of the plan and commit solely to a land advance to the tip of the Mayu peninsula from where Akyab could be attacked at short range. After weeks of delay, Operation CANNIBAL finally started on 17 December and lasted through to mid-May 1943 by which time the British had been forced to return to their original start line. The first Arakan campaign had to all extents and purposes failed but at least it had provided an insight into the enemy's methods and revealed the defects in the training and organization of British forces.

Concurrent with the Arakan advance, Wavell had authorized Major Orde Wingate, his former irregular warfare officer in Ethiopia, to form 77 Indian Infantry Brigade, a long-range penetration force later known as the Chindits. The Brigade moved to Imphal in January 1943 and despite a change of mind by the Chinese not to advance to Mandalay, Wavell gave the green light to Wingate and his two groups of Chindits set off in February to harass the Japanese deep behind enemy lines. What an adventure it was and by the first week of June, over 2,000 men of the 3,000-strong force who had crossed the Chindwin had managed to return to their lines. While no discernible strategic impact resulted from LONGCLOTH and little damage had been inflicted on the enemy, like many of Wavell's 'investments', the medium-term return proved immensely valuable. Important lessons about air supply and support had been learnt and astute public relations turned the expedition into a resounding success, more than offsetting the dismal result of the Arakan campaign. The British and Indian forces had proved themselves jungle fighters to be reckoned with. An unintended consequence of LONGCLOTH was the Japanese reaction; rather than remain on their vulnerable over-extended front line on the Chindwin River, they decided to head west and seize the mountain stronghold of Imphal where they planned to consolidate their position. This decision later transpired to be their nemesis.

It was in the context of a lacklustre land advance in Arakan and Wingate's risky expedition into Northern Burma that plans were hatched at the SYMBOL Conference in Casablanca in January 1943 for the recapture of Rangoon. At a meeting in Delhi in February attended by Field Marshal Sir John Dill, Wavell, General Arnold of the US Army Air Force, General Somervell, head of the American Service of Supply, and General Stilwell, Operation ANAKIM evolved. For the Americans, their primary objective was to keep China in the war and that meant improving existing and opening up new supply routes. Scheduled for 15 November 1943, Phase One stipulated that ten Chinese divisions would advance from Western Yunnan towards Mandalay; additional Chinese troops would move from Ledo to Myitkyina; and three British divisions would cross into Burma from Assam and head towards Pakokku and Mandalay. In December, Phase Two envisaged the capture by seaborne assault of all airfields on the South Arakan coast, Taungup and Prome and Bassein, all the while containing enemy forces while the British and Chinese continued their advance into Upper Burma. Finally, in Phase Three, in January 1944 a direct seaborne assault would be launched against Rangoon. Everyone at the meeting recognized that this ambitious plan depended on substantial Allied reinforcements of maritime assets such as capital ships and landing craft and air assets such as fighters and medium-range bombers. The Combined Chiefs of Staff further stipulated that operations in the Pacific and Far East 'must be kept within such limits as will not, in their opinion, jeopardize the capacity of the United Nations to take advantage of any favourable opportunity that may present itself for the decisive defeat of Germany in 1943'.[9]

With a July cut-off date imposed by the Combined Chiefs of Staff, Fleming was immediately put to work to prepare a strategic deception plan. The first plan KINKAJOU/WALLABY proved controversial as it included 'manipulation of the United Nations and neutral Press'.

In May 1943, Fleming and Bill Cawthorn departed India for Washington DC, where they were members of the British delegation to the TRIDENT conference. En route, they looked up Dudley Clarke in Cairo and, once in London, the two men held a meeting with MI5 to coordinate the handling of double agents. During Fleming's previous visit in September and October 1942 to meet the LCS team, he had been able to fit in the occasional excursion to Merrimoles and a chance to see Celia; this time he managed to squeeze in a night and was delighted to see his four-year-old son Nichol, 'merry and friendly and rather nice-looking'.[10] Then, joined by Sir Ronald Wingate, Fleming and Cawthorn embarked on the *Queen Mary* along with the prime minister and his entourage for the voyage to America.

Over the fourteen-day conference, Churchill and Roosevelt confirmed Operation HUSKY, the invasion of Sicily, and the date of 1 May 1944 – definitive in the US view, provisional in the British – for the landing of twenty-nine divisions in France; but the question whether the conquest of Sicily should be followed, as the British proposed, by an invasion of Italy was left unsettled. The war against Japan took second stage: Wavell's paper on the difficulties of modern armies fighting in the Burmese jungle environment kept expectations under control although it encouraged Churchill to think about amphibious adventures in the Eastern Indian Ocean as an alternative course of action.

In a side-bar meeting with the American Joint Security Control, the British deception trio augmented by Major Michael Bratby from the British Army Joint Staff Mission in Washington were locked in discussion for ten days as to who would control deception in the Far East. From the beginning, the British were at a disadvantage for on an organizational level, GSI (d) had no formal contacts with its American allies in the South West Pacific or indeed further east. As far as the US Navy (Admiral Chester Nimitz) and South West Pacific Command (General Douglas MacArthur) were concerned, their theatres of war in the Far East were their private fiefdoms and they would run their own deception programmes with minimal interference from either Joint Security Control in Washington or the LCS in London.

Lieutenant Colonel Ambrose Trappes-Lomax, a senior SOE officer based in Australia, provides a fascinating insight into the mindset of MacArthur's South West Pacific Command in his post-war report on Special Operations Australia. Not afraid to mince his words, he was scathing about 'the ill will and incompetence' of GHQ South West Pacific Command,

> the only Allied Supreme HQ which was in no way allied. It was purely American. Such diplomatic qualities as a broadminded and urban outlook, tolerance and sense of compromise are rare outside a few carefully selected and highly trained public servants and statesmen. Military commanders and staff officers are in general somewhat nationalistic, narrow and bigoted ... the average American [officer] sees such qualities of tolerance and compromise only as forms of trickery and as such, signs of fundamental weakness.

Britain's good intentions (trade, self-determination of peoples, etc.) were suspected,

> for the South West Pacific Area was a theatre of war in which politics played a more important part than strategy in setting priorities. The Americans sought not only victory but full credit for it. They also determined on a huge diversion to reoccupy the Philippines and on no other diversion. The average American staff officer was thoroughly suspicious of special operations and had grave suspicions of British 'intrigue'.[11]

A charm offensive led by Fleming for a British-designed 'Machinery for Deception of Japan' coupled to putative British-American Deception Planning and Implementation Staffs failed to find favour with the Americans, who were naturally confident in their own abilities as the senior partner in the war against Japan. For Fleming, always the political realist, the outcome was hardly surprising and it was a welcome aside to discover that his brother Ian was also at the conference as a representative of the Director of Naval Intelligence. The two had agreed to meet in New York but a last-minute change of plans prevented Ian from coming, so Fleming took Joan Bright, his old colleague from MIR, to a Broadway musical instead.

For the first time, a General Deception Plan for the War against Japan was drawn up and endorsed by the Combined Chiefs of Staff. Its two principal thrusts were that the Japanese were to be encouraged to keep as many troops in their home islands by threatening air attacks from carriers and from air bases in China. Second, the enemy were to be deceived as to the timing and sequence of actual operations rather than by any specific cover plan.

The plan was a derivative of the US Joint Security Control Strategic Plan for the Defeat of Japan which had been drawn up by the Joint Staff Planners and approved on 8 May 1943.[12] The priority for the United Nations[13] was the defeat of Germany. Until that came about, pressure on Japan was to be maintained, the initiative retained and a position of readiness for a full-scale offensive against Japan by the United Nations attained. In the 'indeterminate period' between, the plan was structured in six phases. Phase One provided for the continuation and augmentation of existing undertakings in and from China, the recapture of Burma by British forces assisted by US and Chinese forces and the opening of a line of communications to the Celebes Sea by the US Navy. The next phase tasked the British to open the Strait of Malacca and to compel wide dispersion of enemy forces while the Americans recaptured the Philippines and the Chinese prepared to capture Hong Kong. During Phase Three, it was envisaged that the British would continue their operations to open the Strait of Malacca while the Americans secured control of the northern part of the South China Sea and assisted the Chinese in the capture of Hong Kong. The last three phases focused on an overwhelming air offensive against Japan from bases in Japanese-occupied China secured by Chinese forces assisted by Britain and America, cumulating in a US-led land invasion of Japan.

'Control of the Seas' was added as a rider to this strategic plan. 'Since control of the seas in the Western Pacific by the United Nations may force the unconditional surrender of Japan before invasion and even before Japan is subjected to an intensive air offensive, every means to gain this control will be undertaken by the United States.'

Reading between the lines, it was obvious to Fleming that the chances of SEAC mounting a seaborne assault were remote since it was clear that the Mediterranean and OVERLORD (the invasion of Northern France) would account for the majority of landing craft and that the US Pacific Fleet would have none to spare as well.[14] It was equally apparent that the Americans had no interest in seeing the post-war return of the Dutch to the NEI or of the French to Indo-China; indeed, the recapture of British colonial Burma only had a strategic value in that it would enhance the supply routes for US war materials to China.[15]

Furthermore, the capture of the British Crown colony of Hong Kong had been tellingly allocated by the Americans to the Chinese.

Nevertheless, the General Deception Plan for the War against Japan required the newly established SEAC to deflect Japanese attention away from Burma. Consequently, Fleming drew up RAMSHORN which disguised the feint attacks on the Andaman Islands (Operation BUCCANEER) and later Sumatra (Operation CULVERIN) as actual operations.

ANAKIM meanwhile had come to nought. By early autumn, due to insurmountable deficiencies in equipment and landing craft, which were all allocated to the Mediterranean theatre at the time, and American doubts about the chances of success for the assault on Rangoon,[16] the Chiefs of Staff had postponed and all but abandoned ANAKIM. In his final Despatch covering 1 January to 20 June 1943 when he was replaced as C-in-C Indian Army by General Auchinleck, Wavell qualified his admiration for the general strategy of the War Cabinet with this one exception: 'During the Arakan and Chindit operations, I received neither encouragement nor help nor understanding of the difficulties, only criticism for the failure of a bold attempt to engage the enemy with inadequate resources, in hazardous circumstances.'

The departure of Wavell and the creation of SEAC combined to make Fleming's modus operandi infinitely more complicated for the command relationships within SEAC were of the greatest complexity. There were now three geographic theatres and one operational, representing the interests of three nations and their three services, all operating in the same area. SEAC was an Anglo-American command which included Burma, Ceylon, Sumatra and Malaya, but not India. India was under India Command (Auchinleck), with responsibilities towards the Middle East, where Indian divisions were fighting, as well as to the Far East. The Generalissimo's theatre was China. The American operational theatre, China-Burma-India, operated across all three geographic areas. It was not subordinate to SEAC.

The Chinese Army in India, commanded by Stilwell, was based on India Command and was to fight in SEAC's area under SEAC command. The US Fourteenth Air Force was based in China, supplied from India, and formally under the command of the Generalissimo. Although SEAC was given logistical support by India Command, the latter's administration, defence and internal security were under Auchinleck, who in turn was responsible to the Government of India. As the representative of the War Cabinet and as Viceroy of India, Field Marshal Wavell was the arbiter between India Command and SEAC, but each could appeal his decision to the British Chiefs of Staff. As an exercise in political compromise, this Byzantine command structure was far from perfect. The historian Louis Allen dubbed it 'a Lewis Carroll absurdity'.[17]

Fleming and Wavell remained close. *Other Men's Flowers*, Wavell's anthology of poems, had been nurtured by Fleming from the beginning. At first it received a frosty reception from Daniel George, literary adviser to the publishers Jonathan Cape, followed by a humiliating letter of rejection in which the general's choice was described as 'familiar school recitations advancing in close formation'. The situation was retrieved only after Fleming lobbied his friend and publisher, Rupert Hart-Davis, who reproved the publisher by telling him his letter was 'tantamount to a sock on the jaw' to a shy man who had delivered 'the complete bones of a tremendously saleable book'. Publication followed this intervention in March 1944 and proved a shrewd decision; it has rarely been out of print and Cape has sold over 130,000 copies. The historian Ronald Lewin, who had worked for Cape before the war, observed that

> generals tend to win their reputations at the cost of other men's lives. By an anomaly unique in military history, Wavell's own reputation has reached its widest range – certainly in the English-speaking world – not because of his prowess as a soldier or a proconsul, but because of his identification with a small miscellany containing a selection of other men's verses.

In his obituary of Wavell in *The Spectator* of 26 May 1950, Fleming penned a perspicacious and affectionate portrait of the great scholar soldier: in this extract the similarity and empathy between the two men in character is engaging:

Immense, patient strength – perhaps that is the quality in Lord Wavell which seems, now that he is dead, the most important part of his character. With it went gentleness, and wisdom, and a remarkable humility. His one eye looked quizzically rather than sardonically upon the world, and he retained a certain innocence of spirit, the uprightness – almost of a small boy who does not yet know that there are alternatives to uprightness. He was shy and reserved, and his reserve was a handicap in public life. He was, for instance, seldom understood and almost always undervalued by Americans, who found it incomprehensible that so legendary a figure should be so little concerned to underwrite the legend with some sort of panache; and he could not command that extra impulse of affability or effusiveness which is so useful a lubricant when dealing with Orientals.

Behind his taciturn manner, and the drawl which often held an unnecessary note of diffidence, and that speculative but too easily disinterested eye, there was a vivid apprehension of beauty, a boyish sense of humour and a quiet capacity for enjoying life. Perhaps the nearest approach to self-revelation which he allowed himself was the marginal comments in his anthology, *Other Men's Flowers*; and the man who emerges from these brief but charming asides is very different from the monolithic figure which he was sometimes apt to cut in public. Feeling as well as style came out in some of his orders of the day, and the latent warmth of his personality expressed itself in innumerable unobtrusive acts of kindness. He had, moreover, a sort of sunniness – again somehow recalling, to me at any rate, a little boy – which would break out in off moments. As we all trotted back to breakfast from a long scrambling gallop over the unlovely plains round Delhi, a sound not readily distinguishable from a giggle would emanate from the august figure on the big bay. 'Did I ever tell you,' he would begin, 'about the Russian admiral?' And as he told us the anecdote (which was invariably very funny and revealed him as something of a connoisseur of the ridiculous in human nature), the mask which could look so grim would become full of glee, and one suddenly saw in the bay's rider a sort of eternal youthfulness. He was a very lovable character.

An aside to the story of his championing of Wavell's anthology, Fleming also took Philip Mason under his literary wing. A senior Indian civil servant, Mason had been accidentally shot while out shooting jungle cock and very nearly blinded. Fleming befriended him in Delhi and persuaded him to take up squash again. After a shaky start, Mason 'soon discovered that it was possible to play quite reasonably again'. In the course of their friendship, Fleming was instrumental in bringing Mason's book *Call the Next Witness* to the attention of Jonathan Cape, thereby triggering the start of a long and successful literary career which resulted in the publication of over twenty books under the name of Philip Mason and Philip Woodruff.

❧

Working on the assumptions of Plan CHAMPION, a modified version of Operation ANAKIM, Fleming's 12 July 1943 cover plan for India Command operations in 1943–4 was code-named RAMSHORN. Sir Michael Howard points out that

> unknown to Fleming, the decisions taken at the TRIDENT conference were still surrounded by so much uncertainty that they provided a very unsure basis for any kind of planning. Political disagreements with the Americans and the Chinese, logistical difficulties and the doubtful availability of forces from the European theatre made it uncertain from the beginning whether the agreed operations would take place at all, and if so on what scale.[18]

In commenting on Fleming's proposals for the Chiefs of Staff, Bevan suggested that in view of the fluid state of Allied plans[19] it would not be wise to draw attention to the Andaman Islands or Sumatra. It might be 'better to give the impression that Allied forces based in India were incapable of mounting any operations, owing to lack of naval and amphibious forces, the low morale and poor state of training of land forces.' So on 6 August 1943 the Chiefs of Staff concluded that it would be unwise to draw up any cover plans at all.

୶

At the first Quebec conference (QUADRANT), held between 17 and 24 August 1943, Churchill and Roosevelt – Stalin could not attend for military reasons – agreed that OVERLORD would commence on 1 May 1944 and that operations against Japan would be intensified in order to exhaust Japanese resources, cut their communications lines, and secure forward bases from which the Japanese mainland could be attacked. Subsequently a new American plan for General Direction for Deception Measures against Japan 1943–4 was drawn up on 17 September 1943. It was to provide the template for all future plans.

CONSIDERATIONS

General

In the war in the Pacific the initiative heretofore possessed by the Japanese is now much restricted. Though they are still capable of offensive moves, particularly in China and from Manchuria, the initiative in the Pacific Ocean has passed to the United Nations. Japan sees her air and naval strength under continual attrition, though her forces and their morale remain strong. Japan is aware that from now on she must be prepared for attacks from many directions. Her air and naval forces must be shifted, therefore, from one area to another, and her ground forces must remain disposed in sufficient strength to meet successfully the assaulting ground strength of the United Nations brought to bear in any one area.

Central and North Pacific

Since the Japanese forces have been eliminated from the Aleutians, Japan is faced with the difficulty of not being able to watch our actions in the North Pacific without the use of considerable naval and air strength in the Kuriles and the ocean area to the eastward. Japan is cognizant of the logistical difficulties of an attack on Paramushiru and probably realises that with the experience of Kiska before us, we will not move into the northern Kuriles until we are assured that we are in sufficient strength to maintain our forces against Japanese thrusts, or to continue the offensive from the Kuriles towards Japan.

In the Central Pacific, Japan must feel that the time of US action nears. The Nipponese are probably assured that operations in the South-west Pacific cannot continue to move forward much farther until the flank of the line of communications is secured.

South and South-west Pacific

Japan appreciates that the major share of our forces is concentrated in this area for the purpose of ejecting the Japanese therefrom.

South-eastern Asia, India and China
Though the Japanese were able to stop the United Nations advance into Burma during the past dry season, they probably realise that because of the desire to retain China as an ally and to build up in China for air operations against the Japanese mainland, the United Nations will again launch offensive operations this year. This area becomes, in a sense, more immediately vital to Japanese outer defences than the New Guinea area, since it is a route, similar to those through the Central Pacific and Northern Pacific, which permits the United Nations to come within striking distance of the Japanese homeland. It is reasonable for the Japanese to expect that operations in the South-west or Central Pacific will be timed by the United Nations to assist operations against Burma, thus forcing them either to weaken their air defence everywhere or to concentrate it at the expense of other fronts.

SPECIFIC OBJECTIVES

For purposes of deception planning and implementation, sections of the Pacific-Asiatic area lend themselves to the three groupings under which they are considered below. Detailed deception plans will be prepared by the Commander in Chief, Pacific Ocean Areas, Commander in Chief South-west Pacific Area and Supreme Commander, South-East Asia Command to accomplish the objectives set forth below. Such plans will be submitted with operational plans and in addition at such other times as may be deemed appropriate. Objectives for each theatre should be as follows:

(1) Central and North Pacific:

(a) To contain maximum Japanese forces in the homeland.

(b) To draw Japanese air and naval strength into the Kuriles, except at the time of an operation in that area.

(2) South-West Pacific:

(a) To induce the Japanese to withdraw mobile strength at the time of initiation of certain operations.

(b) To draw Japanese strength into various parts of the Area when operations are being launched in Burma, the Gilberts, the Marshalls and the Carolines.

(3) South-eastern Asia Command, India and China:

To cause the Japanese to believe that after 1 January 1944, no large scale operations will occur in Burma during the 1943–4 dry season.

∾

On 23 October 1943, Churchill issued his directive to Mountbatten as Supreme Commander SEAC:

1   Your attention is drawn to the decisions of the Combined Chiefs of Staff, QUADRANT, which were approved by the President of the United States and by me on behalf of the War Cabinet. Pursuant to these decisions and acting in harmony with them, you will take up your appointment as Supreme Allied Commander, South-East Asia, provided for in my memorandum and, within the limits of your command as defined therein, you will conduct all operations against Japan. You will be responsible to the British Chiefs of Staff, who are authorized by Combined Chiefs of Staff to exercise jurisdiction over all matters pertaining to operations and will be the channel through which all directives will be issued to you.

2   Your prime duty is to engage the Japanese as closely and continuously as possible in order by attrition to consume and wear down the enemy's forces, especially his air forces, thus making our superiority tell and forcing the enemy to divert his forces from the Pacific theatre – and secondly, but of equal consequence, to maintain and broaden our contacts with China, both by the air route and by establishing direct contact through Northern Burma inter alia by suitably organised, air-supplied ground forces of the greatest possible strength.

3   You will utilise to the full the advantage of the sea power and air power, which will be at your disposal, by seizing some point or points which (a) induce a powerful reaction from the enemy, and (b) give several options for a stroke on your part in the light of the enemy's aforesaid reaction. For this purpose, in making your proposals for amphibious operations in 1944, you will select the point of attack which seems best calculated to yield the above conditions, and will execute the operation approved. You will also prepare plans for the second phase of your campaign in 1944 contingent upon the reaction extorted from the enemy.

4   At least four weeks before your first major amphibious operation you will be furnished by His Majesty's Government with a battle fleet.

5   You will proceed to form, as resources come to hand, a combined striking force or circus which will be available as the foundation of whatever amphibious descent is eventually chosen.

6   You will, at the earliest moment, report your plans, dates and requirements, bearing in mind the advantages of speed.

Although Mountbatten and Ronald Wingate had circulated CULVERIN at the QUADRANT conference, the Americans had paid scant attention to it for their objectives were exclusive of the Indian Ocean. Churchill, on the other hand, was obsessed with it and Field Marshal Alanbrooke, the CIGS and Chairman of the Chiefs of Staff Committee, despaired of 'this ghastly Alice-in-Wonderland situation' brought about by the prime minister's 'defective strategic thinking'.[20] New variants were drawn up including an option to seize the remote island of Simalur off the coast of Simeulue Island. Soon a force had been assembled – on paper – of nearly 190,000 men, 260 ships, 850 landing craft and dozens of fighter and bomber squadrons. For Mountbatten, Churchill's grandiose schemes, however preposterous, chimed with his naval and combined operations background and accordingly he dealt the cards out to his planners. One can only speculate as to whether Fleming realized that the pack had been doctored by none other than the prime minister.

After the SEXTANT Conference held in Cairo between 22 and 26 November 1943 during which Churchill, Roosevelt and Chiang Kai-shek scoped Allied policy towards Japan and its position in a post-war Asia, the US Joint Staff Planners were 'of the opinion that the existing directive concerning deception measures against Japan, requires revision in order to bring it into line with current intelligence and with our agreed strategy' and thus produced a revised plan on 17 February 1944 which took the Combined Chiefs of Staff three months to sign off. It was still far from set in stone.

The main change was their assessment that the initiative in the Pacific had passed to the United Nations:

Japan sees her air and naval strength under continual attrition, though her forces and their morale remain strong. Japan is aware that from now on she must be prepared for attacks from many directions. Her air and naval forces must be shifted, therefore, from one area to another, and her ground forces must remain disposed in sufficient strength to meet successfully the assaulting ground strength of the United Nations brought to bear in any one area.

In regard to the CBI and SEA commands, the planners noted that

though the Japanese were able to stop the United Nations advance into Burma during the 1942–3 dry season, they probably realize that because of the desire to retain China as an ally and to build up in China for air operations against the Japanese mainland, the United Nations will again carry out offensive operations this year. This area becomes, in a sense, more immediately vital to Japanese outer defences than the New Guinea area. It is reasonable for the Japanese to expect that operations in the Southwest or Central Pacific will be timed by the United Nations to assist operations against Burma, thus forcing them either to weaken their air defence everywhere or to concentrate it at the expense of other fronts. However, the Japanese, realizing the threat of an Allied advance into Burma, have substantially reinforced that area. The deployment of their forces is generally defensive but the launching of a limited offensive by the Japanese to disrupt Allied plans is a possibility.

The deception objectives allocated to SEAC were to cause the Japanese to believe that amphibious operations will take place in the Indian Ocean area prior to the 1944 monsoon and to retain or build up their forces in Malaya and Sumatra through September 1944.

⊰

As it transpired, none of these deception measures mattered much for the British since very few offensive operations took place in SEAC in 1944. Operation CULVERIN, the planned seaborne assault on Sumatra, never materialized[21] and a seaborne attack on Rangoon, Operation DRACULA, was postponed, once again due to lack of landing craft. As Fleming had postulated from the beginning, since neither amphibious nor naval forces could be made available on a sufficient scale for such attacks to succeed until Germany and Italy had been knocked out of the war, the whole concept was a non-starter.

Nevertheless, the rigmarole of deception planning continued uninterrupted. On 19 June 1944, Horder circulated from Kandy Plan MULLINER[22] an outline strategic deception plan for the coming monsoon months. Drawn up by D. Division [GSI (d)], all that was required was the approval of the Combined Chiefs of Staff for 'extra-theatre aspects of the plan' before implementation.

Its objectives were laudable, namely to continue during the monsoon to threaten operations designed to contain Japanese ground and air forces in sectors of the Western perimeter outside Burma (preferably malarial areas) and to represent the increased flights over the Hump as a temporary spurt, mainly for Chinese (as opposed to USAAF) purposes. However the storyline left much to be desired for it depended on the incredulity of the Japanese to buy into the idea of a non-stop programme brought about by 'the development of new technical devices … which will make landing operations possible in monsoon conditions' and 'the revelation, by an eighty-five-year-old Buddhist mystic in Ceylon that there will be no monsoon this year, or at least a much milder one than usual. Mountbatten sets much store by the meteorological prophecy of this man, who has so far been surprisingly borne out by the facts and by professional records over the past fifty years.'

Against this background, the Japanese were to be drip-fed with a number of false stories ranging from seaborne assaults on the Andamans and Nicobars, guerrilla landings along the coast from South Burma round to Palembang, assistance to MacArthur in the long-awaited attack on Timor, a secret embassy to Admiral Decoux[23] in French Indo-China for the use of an airfield and fuelling facilities for heavy bombers in the autumn, and the obliteration of the town of Akyab and all Japanese positions between it and the Maungdaw-Buthidaung road by a four-day air assault of 2,000 heavy bombers diverted from the Western Front for the purpose. This air attack would include the use of flamethrowers mounted on low-flying aircraft.

For the plan to work, D. Division [GSI (d)] would require the continuance of Photographic Reconnaissance flights over the Western SEAC perimeter from Andamans to Palembang including the Kra Isthmus and, if possible by using very long range aircraft, Singapore; naval bombardment, carrier strikes and commando raids against selected targets in the same area; build-up of a Naval W/T link between Australia and Ceylon and simulation of Task Force preparing to sail from Fremantle at prescribed times; and feint patrol activity by IV Corps down Tamu-Tiddim road, in support of above.

No such approval was forthcoming and, like so many other SEAC deception plans, Plan MULLINER was shelved. From the start, Fleming told Bevan he considered chances of operating this 'slightly fantastic plan' during the monsoon 'extremely slight without damage to channels'.[24] He had never been happy with the inclusion of the meteorological ruminations of the Indian holy man and took delight in pointing out the absurdity of the story to Horder and the SEAC planners that the monsoon, which predictably had arrived at the beginning of May, showed no sign whatever of letting up.

In his study of British naval planning in the war against Japan,[25] the historian H.P. Willmott considered that

> between August 1943 and August 1944 the British planning effort ... was plagued by distractions, confusion, and fundamental policy differences. Indeed, in this year, it proved impossible for the British high command to settle national policy for the war against Japan. In effect, the only British decisions were formal cancellation of options that had passed by default ... The fact that Churchill and the Chiefs of Staff could not decide between the conflicting claims of the Indian Ocean and the Pacific theatres lay at the heart of British difficulties.

Willmott identified the national demarcation of duties agreed by the combined planners at QUADRANT as the root cause for it

> had the effect of diverting British planning attention into a political and strategic cul-de-sac at a time when there was, very briefly, an opportunity to develop a combined Anglo-American approach to the war against Japan, and with it the possibility of a real British contribution to the war in the Pacific. In the event the British high command ... was condemned to months of futile

argument about options in Southeast Asia that were ever less relevant with the quickening of the American advances into the western Pacific.

❧

It was only after the ARGONAUT conference in Yalta in February 1945, when Stalin agreed to enter the war against Japan, that a clear operational object materialized for SEAC, namely the invasion of Malaya (Operation ZIPPER). In a new General Directive For Deception Measures Against Japan dated 25 May 1945, the US Chiefs of Staff summarized that Japan had been forced on to the strategic defensive; and – except on the Asiatic mainland – the initiative had for some time been in Allied hands. In their consideration, Japan could not hope 'to counter all courses of action within the capabilities of the Allies. The tactical restrictions imposed upon her by Allied successes severely limit her ability to redispose her forces, and make her particularly vulnerable to well-conceived deception.' The new set of deception objectives was designed to induce the Japanese not to deploy ground forces from the Chinese mainland to Japan proper; to disperse their forces in Japan, with emphasis on the defence of northern Honshu and Hokkaido; to commit all available naval and air forces against Allied naval and air strikes on the homeland prior to any invasion; and to misinterpret Allied intentions concerned operations in Borneo, Malaya, China and the Kuriles.

The story was to present to the Japanese an Allied strategy based on an appreciation that a direct assault against the Japanese homeland would be extremely costly and might result in failure. A naval blockade and a long period of saturation air bombardment, similar to that employed against Germany, would first have to be undertaken in order to sever communications, reduce military strength and destroy war industries. This saturation air bombardment would require additional bases close to Japan, including a build-up in the Aleutians in preparation for operations against Hokkaido. Even if successful, a direct assault probably would not terminate the war, as the Japanese Government undoubtedly would have a plan for withdrawal to the Asiatic mainland for a continuation of the struggle. As to Russian intentions, should she enter the war when the Neutrality Pact expired in April 1946, the encirclement of Japan would be furthered. In respect of China, maximum effort would be expended in giving sufficient aid to keep her in the war, including landings from the Pacific on the China coast as early as possible. Finally, although the liberation of British, French and Dutch territories was secondary to the defeat of Japan, political and economic pressures required their liberation as rapidly as possible.

Therefore, the Japanese should be led to believe that the Allies were going to seize additional bases for their saturation air bombardment of Japan; launch an amphibious assault against Formosa in late summer of 1945 preliminary to landings on the China coast and an amphibious assault from the Philippines against French Indo-China in the late autumn of 1945, coordinated with an overland assault by Chinese forces; continue their build-up in the Aleutians in preparation for operations against Hokkaido during the early autumn of 1945 to gain additional nearby air and sea bases; accelerate supply to China to enable the Generalissimo to intensify his activities in the interior of China, with the objective of drawing Japanese strength away from areas of Allied landings on the China coast; launch an assault on northern Sumatra from India in the late autumn of 1945; and advance into the Yellow Sea in the winter of 1945–6 to secure bases for air and inland operations.

From this magisterial overview of a war that encompassed nearly half the area of the planet, the task that trickled down to Fleming came as a pleasant surprise for now at least he had something concrete to work on. He came up with Plan SCEPTICAL that promoted the idea that Allied attacks against Singapore through the Strait of Malacca from bases in Sumatra and Java and overland and airborne assaults against Thailand would take place prior to any invasion of Malaya. The abrupt termination of hostilities in August 1945 denied Fleming history's verdict on the success or failure of his plan.

Chapter 9
Dining with Chinese dragons

MIR had nearly sent Fleming to China in 1939 but was overruled by the Foreign Office. However, his ideas of British military assistance to the Chinese had remained in circulation and in February 1941, Major General L.E. Dennys,[1] Military Attaché in Chungking, entered into discussions with Chiang Kai-shek and General Ho Yaozhu. These discussions ended with a proposal from Dennys to set up an elite guerrilla force, under command of the Chinese but officered and equipped by the British, to attack Japanese lines of communication. The Chinese responded favourably and Detachment 204 was born; the Chinese agreed to raise six battalions and the British to provide officers[2] and other ranks skilled in demolitions. Training began almost immediately at the Special Training School at Maymyo in Burma, with volunteers from Australian and British units. Under the watchful eye of Fleming's friend from XII Corps Observation Unit, Major Mike Calvert, students learnt the art of 'blowing things up' and how to fight and survive behind enemy lines. In London, news of this thoroughly alarmed the Foreign Office, which immediately sent word that under no circumstances could British personnel fight alongside the Chinese until war had been officially declared between England and Japan.

It was the ambassador, Sir Archibald Clark Kerr, who ingeniously found a way around this impasse by suggesting that non-British Europeans should be used to man a China Commando Group, with Britain paying the costs of their expenses and all equipment and materials. Operation ANTIPODES was a neat solution and warmly welcomed by Chiang Kai-shek, who asked General Tai Li, his secret service chief,[3] to implement it on the Chinese side. Choosing to use a long spoon to sup with the British, Tai Li delegated the task to a subordinate, General Zhou Weilong,[4] and in August 1941 the project got under way, the British being represented by Jardine Matheson's John Keswick, who arrived in Chungking in December as head of the Ministry of Economic Warfare, a cover name for SOE.

Keswick understood the politics from the start. He told the War Office that 'the scheme can be worked in such a way that it is of defensive benefit to British interests without prejudicing in any way our political relations with Japan and I see no reason why it should when organized through the Chinese'.

The man chosen to head up the Commando Group was a Dane called Erik Nyholm, a contractor and an agent for the Madsen Arms Company.[5] After a brief period of preparation in Malaya, the group moved to Lashio in Burma and began training the Chinese recruits who started to arrive from October onwards. All went well until, following the Japanese attack on Pearl Harbor, Keswick told Tai Li that SOE, who had all along been the real sponsors of the group, intended to take it over and that from now on he would be in charge. This was construed by the Chinese as contrary to the spirit if not the letter of Dennys' and Clark Kerr's original proposal, for Chiang Kai-shek had agreed that the Commando Group should be a self-contained unit within General Zhou's Chinese Special Operations Section. From here on, suspicion ranked over trust.

Nevertheless, Keswick took over and by April 1942 a considerable amount of stores including explosives had been stockpiled at Kweiyang under Nyholm's supervision. Contact was made with Chinese resistance forces in several provinces, not all loyal members of the KMT, apparently without General Zhou's knowledge.[6] When Keswick merged the remnants of Major Kendall's Hong Kong Z Force with the Commando Group, it immediately led to rumours that they were to be used to recapture Hong Kong, where of course the Jardine Matheson head office was. It was therefore not surprising when Zhou instructed Nyholm to hand over all of his war stores on 20 March 1942 and even less when Chiang refused to meet Keswick. The démarche which Clark Kerr received on 4 April referred to 'bad reports' of the Commando Group and 'improper dealings' with provincial governors.

It was clear to Keswick that these accusations of intrigue were merely the excuse to disband the Commando Group, not the reason. The Chinese had hoped they could sit back and 'wait while the Allies blasted Japan from the map' but

> the disasters which had befallen the Allies gave rise first to a sense of keen disappointment followed by a feeling of resentment, particularly strong against the British who are blamed for the loss of Singapore and Hong Kong.[7] The vitally important failure of the Americans at Pearl Harbor is largely overlooked … The Chinese government has no intention in present circumstances of undertaking any offensive operations against Japan nor of actively stirring up trouble against the Japanese … [so] the dissolution of the Commando Group on orders from General Chiang Kai-shek is not surprising.

He had harsh words for General Zhou who was 'inefficient, jealous and unaccustomed to dealing with foreigners' and for the 'complete incompetence' of his organization. Nevertheless, an important lesson had been learnt, namely 'that China in her present mood will not allow foreigners to play with her guerrillas, she will take any equipment we like to give and will hang on to it for her own use in her own time and until the Far Eastern situation changes we cannot expect anything better for this "octopus" ally'.

Meanwhile, Mission 204, which had been sitting at Maymyo, was finally loaded into trucks at Lashio and driven over the Hump to Kunming where they were transferred to Chinese army lorries, finally reaching the Guerrilla School at Liu Chiu Ping outside Kiyang after twenty-five days on the road. Here, after a welcoming reception hosted by General Li Mo-an to toasts of 'together we will dismay Japanese imperialism with lead bullets', they began training with the Chinese battalions, and on 20 April 1942 orders were received to make their way by rail and foot to Kweiyang in Kweichow Province and from there by truck back to Lashio to commence guerrilla operations in Burma. The mission set out on 2 May, only to be recalled and told by Brigadier Bruce and Sir Frederick Eggleston, the Australian Minister in Chungking, that they would be operating in northern Kiangsi as originally planned. So the force went by rail to Hengyang and then by river sampans to Kuantu where they disembarked and unloaded their stores. From here, with a baggage train of eighty coolies, they set off in heavy rain to the area west of Nanchang-Kiukiang railway and after a miserable and unproductive four months, with most men suffering at one time or other from malaria or dysentery, the three 204 Mission contingents moved back to Kunming during October and November. They had never once been allowed by the Chinese to attack the Japanese.

Back in India, as the Australian contingent prepared to embark for home, Colonel Miller, 2 i/c of 204 Mission, read aloud a cable from Wavell: 'On leaving my command I wish to convey to you, your officers and men, my sincere thanks and congratulations on your gallant work carried out under the most trying circumstances and difficult conditions. Good luck to you all.' To those on parade it resonated with the truth.

∾

On 4 April 1942, Fleming set off by jeep to Lashio and from there by Dakota across the Hump to Chungking. This flight in and out of Chungking was the first of many. Years later, in one of his *Spectator* 'Strix' articles,[8] Fleming vividly described the impression of flying into Chungking:

In the winter, before the Tibetan snows had melted and swollen the Yangtse, you landed on a sandbank in mid-stream, below the level of the lowest houses in this rat-coloured city. Chungking clings to the escarpments on which it is built at an angle steeper than is to be found in any Cornish fishing village, and on the opposite side of the river its suburbs are disposed among the little jagged, tufted, willow-pattern mountains which cover so much of Szechwan. Night was generally falling when the Dakota slid past the half-seen hilltops for its run-in down the tortuous river gorge. Its headlights made an endless silver tunnel in the slanting rain, but at last, far ahead, one saw the foreshortened ribbon of illumination which marked the airstrip on the long sandbank. The city was blacked out (for this was wartime), but if you looked out of the window you could see the lights of cars moving along unseen streets above you, and not very far away. A few seconds later, as the Dakota wheeled at the end of the runway and taxied back towards a cluster of matting sheds which would vanish when the river began to rise, you were actually a shade nearer sea level than any of the several million inhabitants on which you had descended from the air.

If not exactly 'an old China hand', Fleming was extraordinarily well acquainted with the country as a result of his four journeys there before the war. In 1931 he had gone to China as a secretary of Chatham House to attend a conference in Shanghai organized by the Institute of Pacific Relations.[9] On arrival, he stayed with the Keswick bothers, Tony[10] and John, who ran the great Jardine Matheson Far East trading, financial and industrial conglomerate which before the Second World War employed over 100,000 workers in textile mills, factories and go-downs and boasted a fleet of over thirty merchant and passenger ships.

A visit to Peking was followed by two weeks on a boat in Swatow as the guest of Archie Rose, a director of British American Tobacco in China. The author Graham Greene remembered being interviewed by him:

the appearance of a senior army officer, perhaps a brigadier, in plain clothes. He was correctly dressed in dark capitalist uniform, with a well-tied bow tie, a well-groomed moustache; he had the politeness of a man speaking to his equal in age and position. He would have made a good Intelligence officer, and I have little doubt now that he belonged, however distantly, to the Secret Service. A man in his position, recruiting and controlling men for the Chinese hinterland, could hardly have escaped contact with the 'old firm.'[11]

Two years later, Fleming was back in the Far East, this time as a *Times* special correspondent to cover the Japanese occupation in Manchuria. After a brief and dangerous foray into the field with an anti-bandit column in the Fushun area, he stayed with Harold and Nancy Caccia in Peking before moving to Shanghai where once again he was the guest of the Keswicks. It was at this point that he managed to secure an interview with Chiang Kai-shek in Kuling and obtained a laissez-passer to the Chinese nationalists' front line at Nanfeng from where he observed the Communists' defensive positions.[12]

Good judgement tinged with a little luck in hindsight secured for Fleming *persona grata* status for this is what he wrote of the Generalissimo in *One's Company*:

> He came into the room quietly, and stood quite still, looking at us. He wore a dark blue gown and carried in one hand a scroll, evidently part of the agenda of his conference. He was of rather more than average height, and unexpectedly slim. His complexion was dark, the cheek-bones high and prominent, and he had a jutting, forceful lower lip like a Habsburg's. His eyes were the most remarkable thing about him. They were large, handsome and very keen – almost aggressive. His glances had a thrusting and compelling quality which is very rare in China, where eyes are mostly negative and non-committal, if not actually evasive … it was obvious that Chiang Kai-shek enjoyed the sound of his own voice far less than most politicians, in China and elsewhere. He was not the usual type of glib and rather impressive propaganda-monger; he did not cultivate salesmanship … Here was a man with a presence, with that something incalculable to him to which the herd instinctively defers. He was strong and silent by nature, not by artifice … He may not be a great statesman, or a very great soldier; events may prove that the best that can be said of him is that he has been the effective head of the best government China has had since the revolution – a government, incidentally, which is older by several years than any now holding office in the West. But at any rate Chiang Kai-shek has something to him. He is a personality in his own right. He is not only not a mediocrity or a wind-bag, but he could never look like one. That, I think, entitles him to a certain singularity among modern political leaders.

After his epic journey from China to India on foot with the Swiss adventurer Kini Maillart, he returned in February 1938 as a fully accredited *Times* war correspondent to report on the war with Japan. Following trips to Hankow, Chungking, the front line, and Canton during which he twice interviewed Chiang Kai-shek, he reached Tokyo in June in time to interview the Japanese foreign minister. By now Fleming was one of the best informed and best connected British journalists in China.

At the time of his first visit as head of GSI (d), the Allied military situation in Burma had imploded. The Chinese Expeditionary Force, which had been originally sent into Burma in early 1942 to protect US Lend-Lease supplies coming into China via the 'Burma Road',[13] had split in two when the British-Indian army withdrew back into India in May. General Stilwell, the overall Theatre Commander for Chinese forces, escaped to India's Assam Province with General Kan Li-chu's VI Army[14] and elements of Major-General Ma Wei-chi's LXVI Army where they then formed the nucleus of Northern Combat Area Command, code-named 'X' Force. With direct access to British logistics and American training, it was later able to field four divisions, equipped to modern standards.[15] The rest of the Expeditionary Force, comprised mainly of remnants of General Tu Yu-ming's V Army, retreated back across the Salween to China's Yunnan Province, where it was designated 'Y' Force. From then on, it depended on whatever supplies the Americans could fly over the Hump.

❧

The genesis of PURPLE WHALES lay in Fleming's first wartime visit to Chungking in April 1942. The city was teeming with refugees as Sir Berkeley Gage, the First Secretary, describes in his autobiography, *A Marvellous Party*:

> Chungking, originally a provincial outpost, had … become a vast overcrowded collection of hovels built over open sewers, the stench of which permeated the whole place. Thousands of refugees had crowded into it from the cities of occupied China. The climate was foul – in winter dank and chilly under a seemingly endless, clammy cloud cover, in summer under the sun, intolerably hot and humid with temporary relief occasionally from gigantic thunder and electrical storms which sometimes shot off sparks that could burn small holes in furniture and even cause painful burns to the body. There were no such alleviations as air conditioners; one was lucky to find the occasional fan. Moreover, the rat population was about five times that of the human, huge rats galloping across the flimsy boards of our reconstructed dwelling places sounding almost as if they were stampeding Mongolian ponies! They throve on soap, amongst other things, a rare and much prized commodity in Chungking; to preserve a supply, it was necessary to perch individual tablets on places inaccessible to rats, such as small horizontal platforms jutting out high up on the wall.

While in the embassy, he happened to read the proceedings of a high-level but ineffective inter-Allied conference which at the time was held weekly in Chungking. The records of these meetings were kept, verbatim, by an American secretariat. It struck Fleming that 'the verbatim records of a discussion' had peculiar attractions to a forger bent on deception. He correctly sensed that the 'verbatim medium' enabled the forger to avoid over definitively committing himself to facts and figures which could be ultimately disproved, yet at the same time allowed him to convey a vivid impression of the nature of a forthcoming operation. When subsequent events proved the impression to be misleading, any re-examination of the document would reveal no detailed evidence to support its lack of authenticity. When he floated the idea to the LCS in London, he enthusiastically cabled 'what we want is not red herrings but purple whales'!

Integral to his plan was the co-operation and support of Chiang Kai-shek and his senior military staff, one of whom, Lieutenant General Cheng Kai-min (aka Zheng Jiemin), Tai Li's right-hand man and later the Generalissimo's Director of Military Intelligence, was later to become a staunch friend. Cheng had been in Hong Kong in December 1941 when the Japanese attacked it and then in Singapore at Wavell's request to train Chinese guerrilla cadres. Unimpressed by the dismal performance of the British military, he reported to Chiang that, in his opinion, it was a lack of willingness to fight that lay behind the disastrous British defeats in South East Asia.[16]

On 15 April C-in-C India asked London for its reaction to PURPLE WHALES. The reply came that the Controlling Officer, Colonel Oliver Stanley, was 'much impressed' and was taking it up immediately with the Chiefs of Staff. On 27 April, with the proviso that 'the kind of material required is high-class strategic gossip rather than detailed information', the Chiefs of Staff Committee approved the idea.[17] At the beginning of May, Fleming asked for a sixty days' time lag rather than six weeks and requested both Churchill's and Roosevelt's signatures on the document in order to get high level Chinese cooperation.

For Stanley, this was a step too far. He told Brigadier Hollis, the Secretary of the Chiefs of Staff Committee, that

> the proposal to have the fake appreciation signed by the Prime Minister and counter-signed by the President of the United States and then handed to the Generalissimo of China, is rather grandiose. I see insuperable difficulties in the ensuing explanations and considerable danger to security, if the field is widened to take in both the USA and China. Besides, I think it is quite wrong that such high personalities should be openly and formally associated with a scheme of this kind. It would be preferable to accept a reduction in the chances of success by running the scheme on a lower level.

In a neat hand at the end of the typed memo, Stanley penned 'better a tame whale than an unmanageable Leviathan!!'[18] The Chiefs of Staff Committee agreed with him but approved the dummy appreciation as a basis for deception as originally put forward by the Controlling Officer and invited him to proceed as planned.

Filed on 10 May, LCS's first cut of 'an appreciation of situation for July next' read:

ONE

a British in position to establish second front on Continent on scale of approx. ten divisions, including five armoured any time after early July. No decision yet taken. This will depend on developments on Russian front.

b Idea of offensive in Libya this year abandoned, owing to land and air forces now being transferred from Middle East to India. Greater part of future convoys now earmarked for India and role in Middle East will be purely defensive.

c	Americans consider attack on New Caledonia, Samoa and Fiji most probable and have strengthened land and air garrisons these islands accordingly. For example, two divisions and 100 aircraft have gone or are en route to Fiji. Preparation of fleet base in this area to enable Pacific fleet to assist in their defence if necessary now complete.

d	As a result of Pound-King agreement and extensive damage to *Scharnhorst* and *Greisenau* economy of force effected in Atlantic. Pacific fleet now strong enough to enable combined operation to be launched against Japanese mandated islands which will be used as advanced base for pressure on Japan's sea communications. Expedition to be ready by mid-July and to be launched on first certain information that substantial portion of Japanese fleet is east of Singapore. By mid-July Eastern fleet also considerably strengthened.

e	Recent air raid on Tokyo experimental. As a result of lessons learned methods have been radically altered and raids on much heavier scale by other means will now be developed, both on Japan and Formosa.

TWO
You are in best position to decide on disposition and intentions regarding land and air forces in India-Burma area, bearing in mind transfer of forces from Middle East and that most, if not all, of W.S. convoys will also go to India.

On 15 May Fleming proposed a new plan as the time lag was again too short and suggested that the C-in-C India summoned in early June a secret conference in Delhi including representatives of General MacArthur, General Stilwell, GHQ Middle East and the NEI. The verbatim minutes would then go to Chungking and reach Tokyo in mid-August.

After confirming to London on 3 June that the Generalissimo had approved PURPLE WHALES in principle, Fleming received a long telegram from London:

1	... Our objective persuade Japanese not repeat not to attempt further territorial conquest. Should like them to believe that:

a	The only hope of retaining gains to date is devoting all resources to consolidation while United Nations still occupied with Germany in West.

b	That further dispersal of their forces would expose them to risk of losing all conquered territories next year when they will be facing full might of United Nations alone owing to Germany's collapse winter 1942–1943.

2 There are no genuine peace gestures at present. Imaginary ones would lack plausibility and be dangerous and to invent some might prejudice belief in following.

3 We want Japan to believe:

a Germany's defeat inevitable before early September 1943 but other factors make it most probable this will occur much earlier.

b This para which will give for Great Britain of tonnage of bombs dropped, houses destroyed and casualties for given period with comparable projected estimate for Germany will follow shortly in separate telegram.

c Bombing and blockade will progressively reduce German production. US able to go full speed ahead owing to immunity from bombing. Even in Britain German Air Force no longer dare attack inland targets from fear of losses and are reduced to blitzing non-military objectives in cathedral cities near coast.

d United Nations objectives in aircraft and tank production now achieved.

e Total defeat U-boat campaign now only matter of time. Germany started war with 57 submarines, now has 300. In spite of great increase in U-boat fleet British sinkings have gone down steadily. U-boats which at start of war operated in coastal waters of British Isles have been driven to operate further and further afield. The North Sea and Western Approaches are clear of them. On American entry into war, sinkings on East Coast of America were heavy, but since introduction of convoy system sinkings have declined in this area. U-boats are now having to operate in South Atlantic and Caribbean. Most of original fully trained Commanding Officers have been eliminated.

f Timoshenko's early spring offensive succeeded in throwing German preparations for offensive in South Russia out of gear. It is now most unlikely that Germans will succeed in forcing Russia out of the war. With thought of their homeland being nightly blitzed into ruins German army will be in no state to face second winter of stalemate in Russia. By autumn very rapid deterioration of morale will set in.

g Discontent, sabotage and acts such as assassination of Heydrich increasingly daily in occupied territories. These will multiply to a marked extent and require even greater Axis forces to control. Unless Germany can feed starving Europe next winter local revolt fostered by British agents will blaze into widespread revolution. German third line troops now trying to hold down 200 million people and this cannot be done indefinitely. Starvation will beget desperation.

   h Possibility of split between Axis partners.

   i Japanese Asia for Asiatics policy causing great resentment in Germany. Seizure of Tsing-Tap regarded as most serious blow to Germany's post-war commerce. Feeling intensified by Japanese confiscation of Dutch, now German held, assets in East Indies. Good grounds for believing that if Germany was not at war with Britain in the West should wish to make common cause with her to protect white interests in Far East. In event of peace in West, Germany may yet wish to join United Nations against Japanese with object of acquiring her share of Far Eastern markets.

   ii Italy already realises her folly in backing wrong horse and anxious to lay off bet by some individual gain before collapse of Axis. Hence probable Italian assault on Corsica or Nice regardless of Germany's wishes and split leading to separate peace overtures from Italy in autumn.

i Above factors taken in conjunction go to show that Germany's position will be most precarious by autumn 1942 and that even if she does not ask for terms then she will be compelled to do so through the strain imposed by another winter in the early summer of 1943. In any event as soon as Germany sees the end approaching she will certainly sell out on her Asiatic ally. Germany's defeat will be followed by immediate concentration of entire United Nations resources against Japan.

In a typical imaginative flourish, Fleming suggested that after the United Nations had established a continental bridgehead, large amounts of US reinforcements should be conveyed by fast ocean liners direct from the United States. This was dismissed with a curt 'your line considered impracticable and implausible'.

In his last critique of the plan to London, Fleming wrote on 18 June:

ONE
Fully agree confirmatory counteraction needs very delicate handling. Strongly in favour of avoiding all counteraction in recognised whispering galleries like Ankara, Lisbon. Am not using Kabul.

TWO
All items sent by you have been incorporated. Following local items added:

   a Hint that Russia has agreed long-term project for development route Urumqi-Lanzhou. This does not compromise Kuibyshev as dialogue ambiguously worded so that route and government concern might be Tibetan.

b Statement that Bofors guns being flown into China with implication that India has Anti-Aircraft guns to spare.

c British post-occupational intelligence system in Burma and other lost territories highly developed and well equipped with W/T. This ties up with fairly elaborate broadcasting ruse which starts next week.

THREE

Following local and other themes repeated:

a Existence of DUMBOFORCE strength unspecified but contains some heavy armour.

b Fairly large airborne forces in India.

c V bombs in connection with Midway.

FOUR

Proceedings of conference were marked by undercurrent of Sino-British friction but true and/or unfavourable items are a major deficiency in completed document.

FIVE

It seemed to us that bulk of your material was more suitable intimidation than deception. As paras 3 C, D and E were unsupported by clues calculated to intrigue if not convince enemy intelligence they have little value.

The time-lag problem continued to bedevil the operation. In the penultimate draft with a timeline of 'Delhi 31 May', reference was made to a German reprisal bombing raid on Canterbury which had taken place on the night of 31 May,[19] a few hours after the so-called Delhi conference had ended. Spotted by a keen-eyed intelligence officer, this wrinkle was quickly ironed out but another gremlin lay in wait. After arriving in Chungking with the document on 22 June, Fleming was informed that an intercepted Japanese radio message had reported that Major General Davidson, one of the leading actors in Fleming's script, had been received by the Viceroy in Delhi on 30 May. Since this perfectly true statement had been published in the Court Circular, he saw no option other than to move the 'conference' to 30 May which resulted in a delay of four days while the paperwork was amended and retyped in Delhi.

The final document of the fake verbatim record of the Inter-Allied conference included these eight main points:[20]

1 There was no likelihood of Britain suffering a defeat in North Africa.

2 The presence of airborne troops in India was hinted at.

3 Reference was made to the preparation of a naval base either at Fiji or New Caledonia.

4 A proposed operation against an unspecified target in the Pacific was hinted at.

5 Reference was made to further air raids on Japan.

6 Reference was made to an efficient secret Intelligence Service run by the British in Burma and Indo-China.

7 It was stated that a force of not less than ten British Divisions with the necessary shipping would be ready to leave the UK to open a second front any time after the first week of July, but that a decision on whether the second front would be opened would depend on the progress of the war in Russia.

8 A brief strategical appreciation of the general situation by the Director of Military Intelligence, who attended the conference during his visit to India, giving the information that despite the territorial gains the defeat of Germany in 1942 was probable and by the early summer of 1943 inevitable. Great stress was laid on the value of the bombing offensive and on the deterioration of living conditions in occupied Europe.

In its entirety, the document read like the script of a radio play but with a real-life cast of characters (See ANNEX). It was a star-studded Allied line-up, featuring General Sir Alan Hartley, Deputy C-in-C India; Lieutenant-General Lewis Brereton, Commander US 10th Air Force in India; General Lo Cho-ying, Commander Chinese Expeditionary Force (Burma); General Joe Stilwell, US Commander China-Burma-India; and Major General Francis Davidson, Director Military Intelligence (British Army).

The transfer of the document to Chungking and its onward transmission is described in a series of pithy telegrams:

7 July – From Fleming (with British Military Mission in Chungking) to C-in-C India: Document leaves Chungking 7 July. Generalissimo 100 per cent cooperative. Every reason believe Tai Li stage managing should guarantee successful delivery. Chinese who have been exceptionally quick to appreciate broad purpose and minor details this stratagem appears ready for further whaling operation. Suggest these must be genuinely Anglo-American in conception and might usefully be based on visit to Chungking by some prominent and ultimately indiscreet American.

7 August – For LCS from Fleming: PURPLE WHALES fetched 10,000 Chinese dollars on 27 July. Vendor reports purchaser appeared to think a lot of it. TOO Nil.[21]

7 August – From Bevan at LCS to Fleming: Well done. May Jonahs reverse bible story. A dainty dish.

27 August – To LCS from Fleming: From info now available it appears purchaser was important member of Jeeves Special Service office in South China. Vendor estimates manual reached highest military quarters one week after transaction. Office referred to deals with military political intelligence. TOO Nil.

From inception to delivery, PURPLE WHALES had taken just over fifteen weeks. Along its passage, permissions had been obtained from the Chiefs of Staff, the LCS and through them the Americans, the C-in-C India and the Generalissimo. On occasions, events had overtaken its accuracy, requiring last minute re-editing. Given these lofty bureaucratic hurdles and last-minute glitches, Fleming had every right to be pleased with the progress of his new highly prized product and its distribution channel.

Chapter 10
Total Intelligence: a common sense approach

It was while he was in Chungking in July 1942 that Fleming wrote a typically thoughtful and perspicacious paper called 'Total Intelligence'. At one level it is a scathing critique of Britain's inability or perhaps disinclination to recognize Local General Knowledge as a valuable Intelligence currency and a highly critical analysis of the process of Intelligence collection to date, in both war and peace. The use of a fictitious Ruritania as an example of a country in need of an urgent Intelligence appraisal softens the attack but point-scoring punches are still landed on the Intelligence agencies, including SIS.

At another level it is a reaction against what Professor Richard Aldrich describes as the notorious politics of expanding wartime secret service:

> Many organisations competed over new and ill-defined responsibilities. By 1939, secret and semi-secret service encompassed a broad inter-related spectrum of activities including propaganda, deception, escape and evasion, and economic warfare, as well as the more traditional forms of sabotage and espionage … That their activities depended upon secrecy offered a strong inducement to avoid consultation or collaboration. Operations were inevitably less secure if they had been discussed in detail by five interested departments in three different countries.[1]

But Fleming was a realist and as such was not advocating a root and branch reform of British Intelligence. As a creative thinker, he proposed that a new organization – Imperial Information – should be set up in peacetime with the remit of collating information from as wide a universe as possible, in particular engaging with banking, industry and commerce. Such an approach would solve the problems that had confronted Britain at the outbreak of war.

TOTAL INTELLIGENCE

INTRODUCTORY

1 Good Intelligence is essential to the successful prosecution of war.

2 The so-called World War of 1914–1918 showed that, although military operations cannot cover the whole world, Intelligence is called upon to do so.

3 In Total War, such as broke out in 1939, Intelligence is called upon to cover, not only – as in 1914–1918 – the whole world, but also virtually every aspect of the life of the human community. Its net must be flung as wide as before; but it needs a finer mesh. Today the demand for specialised military, naval or economic information is just as great as it was last time; but the demand for what may be called Local General Knowledge is:

(a) greater;

(b) liable to be made at much shorter notice.

As far as can be foreseen, similar conditions are likely to prevail in any future war.

4 By way of illustration, who could have foreseen in September 1939 that among the problems which our Intelligence would have to tackle – and tackle as a matter of urgency – within the next three years would be:

(a) the feasibility of operating a supply route across Tibet;

(b) the geological composition of the Madagascar beaches;

(c) caste as a factor in dealing with Indian air-raid casualties at Rangoon?

5 These are perhaps over-abstruse examples of the kind of question which Intelligence finds itself called upon to answer. But they may serve to illustrate the point that, of the information which is essential to the conduct of a modern war, a very large part comes under the category of Local General Knowledge and lies for practical purposes outside the scope of our Intelligence organisation, even when this had been expanded and developed in the light of two and a half years of war experience.

6 The importance attached by our enemies to the collection and collation of Local General Knowledge during peace-time is well known; and the advantages they have derived from this process have been made painfully obvious to us. Contrast, by way of example,

(a) the maps of Hong Kong, with lines of advance and fire-tasks printed on them, which were issued to junior Japanese Commanders before the operations against that Colony;

with

(b) the few scrappy, Baedekerish sheets of typescript with which (if indeed with anything at all) our Force Commanders were provided in Norway.

Similar contrasts could be multiplied.

7 None of the Axis Powers, nor even all three of them together, had the opportunities for collecting Intelligence in peace-time which were open to the British Empire. We owned more of the world than they did; and in those parts which we did not own, our shipping and our commerce had often a predominant and always a strong position. Most of the interests were in the hands of shrewd and responsible men.

8 These men, moreover, did collect Intelligence. Much of it was automatically collated by their head offices; most of the rest of it remained in their heads and could have been collated if – like our enemies – we had taken the trouble to do so. These men did not think of it as Intelligence (which they associated with foreign countesses, invisible ink and omniscient colonels in Whitehall); and it was in fact no more than that Local General Knowledge whose value the Germans and the Japanese were so quick to recognise – which of the new roads were passable for cars, how far the branch line was double-tracked, who was reliable and who could be bribed, and so on.

9 Thus it came about that the outbreak of war found the British, as a congeries of private individuals and private enterprises, in possession of a vast body of information, of whose value in war they were unaware and to which their General Staff had, and has, no prompt and convenient means of access. This state of affairs must in no circumstances be allowed to recur.

THE EXISTING SYSTEM

10 Before suggesting a remedy, it is pertinent to examine the way things work at present.

11 There is no such thing as a British Intelligence Service. In war, as in peace, the responsibility for collecting Intelligence is shared, competed for, or neglected (as the case may be) by the Intelligence staffs or directorates of a number of different ministries. The majority of these staffs or directorates exist in peace-time, but in a very greatly reduced form. The following (war-time) list is believed to be approximately complete:

Admiralty	Ministry of Economic Warfare
War Office	SOE
Air Ministry	Political Warfare Executive
Foreign Office	BBC (Monitoring)
India Office	SIS

This list covers the Whitehall area only, omits all reference to bodies concerned with scientific or specialised research, does not take into account Intelligence activities carried on by the Dominions Governments, and leaves out the often excellent Intelligence services organised by Allied Governments temporarily based in the United Kingdom.

12 Nobody in his senses would be so rash, so impractical, or so ignorant of the British character as to suggest that all or most of these organisations should be combined under a unified control; it is, in fact, inconceivable that any serious attempt at amalgamation would work. It would, on the other hand, seem to be only common sense that all should have access – as it were to a reference library – to a common pool of General Knowledge. This would avoid much duplication of effort and waste of time, and would result in the production of fuller and more up-to-date information. Before considering the lines on which such a pool of General Knowledge might be constituted, let us see what happens in practice when Imperial Intelligence swings into action.

HOW IT WORKS

13 In the autumn of 1940 Britain had been at war for a year when her Government decides, for reasons which need not concern us here, that it is urgently necessary to seize the neutral Ruritanian port of San Adolfo and its hinterland. The War Cabinet directs the Chiefs of Staff to plan this operation, and the Chiefs of Staff direct the Joint Intelligence Committee to prepare an appreciation of the problems involved.

14 It is generally the unforeseen which happens in war. San Adolfo is not one of those features (like the Khyber Pass, the Trans-Siberian Railway, or the Monastir Gap) which are automatically the cynosures of military eyes. Ruritania (like so many of our battlefields) is the last place in the world where we expected to have to fight. It is not unfair to say that our Intelligence knows, off-hand, very little about the port of San Adolfo and even less about its hinterland.

15 From what immediately available sources can this slender knowledge be supplemented in a hurry? The following are among the first that suggest themselves and are avidly consulted:

(a) Whitaker's Almanack for 1940.

(b) The Ruritanian Yearbook for 1938 (its publisher went bankrupt in 1939 and no later edition exists).

(c) HBM Minister at Zenda's Annual Report for last year. This deals largely with political, cultural and fiscal matters.

(d) The Service Departments' Handbooks on the Ruritanian Army, Navy and Air Force.

(e) HBM's Consul at San Adolfo. His periodical reports, when exhumed, have some value, but he himself is a Ruritanian and cannot with safety be put in the picture or even alarmed by a questionnaire with operational implications.

(f) SIS reports. Examination of these reveals that the only references to San Adolfo made during the last two years concern an ex-mistress of an ex-Minister of Agriculture who resides in the port and is (wrongly) suspected of being a Soviet agent.

16 As far as Local General Knowledge goes – and this is the type of Intelligence which is likely to influence more than any other the success or failure of our operations – the first two or three days of urgent research produce very little indeed. The Admiralty's charts are good; the War Office maps are bad (though this is not suspected at the time). The Admiralty is well posted on matters of coastal defence and port facilities; and MEW contributes some useful information (largely duplicated by the War Office) about the capacity of the railway which serves the hinterland. The Air Ministry knows a good deal about the three air-fields in the area.

17 After a week, in short, a considerable body of useful Intelligence has been sifted and collated. Time wasted and effort duplicated have been in excess, but perhaps not far in excess, of what is inevitable in any British bureaucratic machine. The worst things about this information are:

(a) the political, military and other facts which have been established, and

(b) the things which our forces will in fact want to know when they get to San Adolfo – things like where the Garrison Commander spends his weekends, and how many entrances there are to the power station, and the fact that a path was made last year leading down the cliff from the 18th green to the bathing beach.

18 This information – Local General Knowledge – is available in the United Kingdom, and most of it resides in, or can be obtained through, individuals or offices in London. Some attempt is naturally made to obtain some of it.

19 It is, however, a weakness of our Intelligence – and particularly of its Service branches, who are sometimes pardonably deficient in knowledge of the world – that they fail to appreciate this fact: the people who know a country best (from the point of view of producing practical and detailed Intelligence about it) are hardly even the people whose names are known to the public in connexion with that country. It is these latter who are generally called in first; and much time is wasted by all concerned before Intelligence realise that what they wanted was not the ex-Ambassador, or the famous traveller, or the folk-lore specialist, but rather the ex-harbour-master, or the man who ran a pulp-mill there, or even the experienced commercial traveller.

20 By the end of the first week of planning for the San Adolfo operations contact has been established – in the pursuit of Local General Knowledge – with the following:

(a) Miss Pink, authoress of *Ruritanian Rampage*: six weeks in the country: anxious to help: easy to take out to lunch: quite useless.

(b) Mr White, archaeologist: spent five years in a marsh 490 miles north-west of San Adolfo: anxious to help: would like to go back to his marsh: might just as well do so.

(c) Professor Scarlett, sociologist, author of 'Ruritania Irridenta, The White Guard in Zenda' (illustrated pamphlet dealing with atrocities), &c.: many years in the country: took part in triumphal entry to San Adolfo in 1904, expelled from SA 1912, re-entered 1922, freedom of city 1925, burnt in effigy 1930, would like to go back there: has no recollection of town being on the railway: anxious to help, but would insist on serving with the Ruritanian forces: worse than useless.

21 As the days (which are always precious in war) go by, the first flight of 'experts' is rejected and fades out of the picture, or at any rate into the background, where for several weeks the more pertinacious roam Whitehall with bundles of galley-proofs, snapshots, proclamations or poisoned arrows under their arms, still anxious to help. They are succeeded (generally after the Force has sailed) by some at any rate of the men who really do know. Let us follow the fortunes of one of these, a Mr Brown, who was until six months ago the agent in San Adolfo of Messrs Green & Co., importers and exporters, and who possesses a vast and valuable store of Local General Knowledge. What in practice are the processes involved in picking Mr Brown's brains?

22 The odds are that it is the Naval Intelligence Division who first hear of Mr Brown's existence through his head office in the City, with whom MEW are in contact. Mr Brown, who has retired and lives in Scotland, is summoned to London. He comes, a discreet and rather important patriot, takes a room in a hotel and calls at the Admiralty.

23 San Adolfo being a port, the NID by this time

(a) know quite a lot about it;

(b) know with reasonable exactness what further information they require.

Flattered and impressed by his business-like interrogation, Mr Brown is passed over to the War Office, who have expressed interest.

24 MI42 (b) is the section that deals with Ruritania and they detain Mr Brown much longer than the NID did. The reasons are:

(a) they have to bother about the hinterland as well as the port;

(b) they suspect that there are a great many things that they ought to know and do not know; but

(c) they do not know – with a few exceptions – what those things are or may be.

25 So there is a good deal of conversation of a general nature, and no great military gains are registered before Mr Brown is packed off to the Air Ministry, at the Air Ministry's request.

26 The Air Ministry has gone out to an early lunch. Mr Brown comes back after lunch. He is by now very good at filling up temporary passes and does not in the least mind being treated as if he were an anarchist. The Air Ministry has meanwhile gone out to a meeting. When he comes back at 4.00 he quickly finds that Mr Brown's local knowledge meets no RAF requirements, so after some general conversation he sends Mr Brown over to see the Combined Operations people.

27 We need not follow this expert's progress further. He has still to see SOE (in a bar: 'Ask for Mr Partridge'), the Force 'G' staff, 'I' staff and 'Q' staff, and to vet with an officer from OS the special leech-proof boots which are being made not very secretly by Lillywhite's. After it all he may, on current form, get a job with SOE (lieutenant colonel's pay) as Political Adviser to the Free Ruritanian Special Training Centre at Melton Mowbray. More likely he will return to Scotland having wasted a lot of time and money and no longer so inclined either to patriotism or to discretion as when he came south. His knowledge and experience were a military asset which, having discovered it by accident and much too late, Intelligence exploited in an amateurish and redundant way.

THE REMEDY

28 The Ruritanian operations were never, of course, carried out. (Nor, incidentally, is the foregoing outline of 'I's approach to them based on any specific project.) It may be objected that this outline is unfair to current practice, that the machinery has been vastly improved since 1940, that today the processes are far more swift and sure.

29 It would indeed be disgraceful if this were not the case. But it is not the purpose of this paper to advocate reforms which could or should be

effected during the course of the present war, for even after three years of war experience no amount of reorganisation of our Intelligence can offset or conceal the fact that in peace-time we left undone that which we ought to have done – and that which our enemies did. In these notes war-time weaknesses are described only in order to illustrate the need for peace-time strength.

30 Faulty in some respects though our Intelligence organisation is, it is at least an organisation, and a very large one at that. But, like the Beanstalk in the pantomime as soon as the Giant is dead, it will shrink very rapidly when the war is over. And quite right, too. In peace-time a large professional Intelligence service may be necessary to a country like Russia, whose citizens are permitted to cross her frontiers only in small numbers and on the business of the State. To the British Empire a large professional Intelligence service is wholly unnecessary, if her rulers will only take the trouble to canalize and tap the flow of unofficial information which in peace-time pours automatically into London and other centres from all over the world.

31 This cannot possibly be done (nor should it be attempted) by our peace-time Intelligence organisation. The whole business should have outwardly nothing, and in fact as little as possible, to do with Intelligence. What is necessary is to make

(a) the process of supplying Local General Knowledge to the State a British habit, and

(b) the repository of the information supplied a British institution.

This should not prove as difficult as perhaps it sounds.

THE METHOD

32 The repository or clearing-house should be a public corporation, with the same sort of status as the BBC or the LPTB, but with more independence of State control than the former. It might be called IMPERIAL INFORMATION. It should undertake no propaganda. It should have no connexion at all with the Ministry of Information (if still in existence). By its peace-time charter its terms of reference would be to collate and make available to British subjects information about the world at large, with particular reference to the Empire.

33 Before considering the machinery necessary to enable it to fulfil this function, let us examine the role of this institution in war. Supposing IMPERIAL INFORMATION had been established before this war, how would it have facilitated our projected operations against the Ruritanian port of San Adolfo and its hinterland in 1940?

34 Briefly, it would have had the following good effects:

(a) it would have saved our Intelligence a lot of time;

(b) it would have forestalled much duplication of effort;

(c) it would have provided a fully and more accurate body of Local General Knowledge than was in fact made available to the Force Commander;

(d) it would have lessened, if not eliminated, the risks to security which are generally implicit in the pursuit by the Service Departments of Local General Knowledge

It would, in fact, have served the useful purpose of an up-to-date reference library available to all branches of the Intelligence; and something more besides.

35 How and why was IMPERIAL INFORMATION able to do this? In a word, because it knew the form, or at least had ready access to it. It knew, for example, the disabilities of Miss Pink, the dangers of Professor Scarlett and the complete irrelevance of Mr White the archaeologist. If it did not know of the valuable Mr Brown, it did know of his head office and of the probability that they would have a local expert on tap. It saved the GSO3 (junior Staff Officer) in MI42 (b),[2] and his opposite numbers in the other two Services, most of the time they wasted thumbing through Whitaker and the Ruritanian Yearbook. It had a list of British subjects resident up-country, a town plan of San Adolfo from a tourist folder, a calendar of saints' days and other public holidays, the name and address of the British engineer who completed the railway after the last revolution and several other useful things besides. In a word, it provided promptly, in a compendious form and under reasonable conditions of security, a great deal of Local General Knowledge, most of which

(a) lay outside the scope of our peace-time Intelligence organisation;

(b) though available in the UK, would never – or only tardily – have come the way of our war-time Intelligence for lack of a recognised central clearing-house.

36 We have seen how an institution of the type envisaged might – and should – function in war. How is it going to be brought into being in peace – and moreover in the early, semi-bankrupt days of peace?

37 The end of each successive war finds the British people convinced that never again will the defences of the Empire be allowed to deteriorate to the dangerous and deplorable extent that they did 'last time'. Hitherto this conviction has proved invariably fallacious. It does, however, seem possible that the shocks sustained by us during the present war have been rude enough to be in this respect salutary, and that we shall in fact maintain in being armed forces sufficient to overawe or counter future threats to whatever are judged our vital interests.

38 The first step, therefore, towards the establishment of something on the lines of IMPERIAL INFORMATION is for our rulers to realise three facts which, though far from obscure, are not by the nature of things likely to obtrude themselves when we are settling down to Peace. They are:

(a) it is no good maintaining armed forces unless they are able to carry out successful military operations;

(b) it is seldom, if ever, possible to carry out successful military operations without adequate Intelligence;

(c) our vital interests, our possible enemies, and thus our potential military and naval commitments, are so diverse and far-flung that adequate Intelligence for a modern war can hardly be provided by even the largest professional Intelligence organisation in peace-time.

39 Persuaded of these facts and (it is hoped) impressed by the example of our enemies, those charged with the destinies of the British Empire can hardly refuse to admit, at any rate in principle, that some organisation on the lines indicated in this paper would be valuable if not essential.

40 Having got this far, how is IMPERIAL INFORMATION (or something like it) to be brought into being?

41 The detailed planning of its genesis is beyond the powers of the present writer. But the conception as a whole has one asset, which, though of an ideological nature, may have considerable practical value. It is the widespread contemporary thirst for General Knowledge; and in this context it is reinforced by a guilty feeling – almost equally widespread through probably more ephemeral – that as a nation we have neglected and are almost wholly ignorant of our Empire and our outlying interests.

42 The mainstay, clearly, of any central clearing-house for unofficial information will be its relations with subsidiary clearing-houses – the great banking, shipping and commercial concerns, or whatever replaces them. As these interests re-establish themselves in a semi-chaotic world, it will be natural and constructive for IMPERIAL INFORMATION (if it can be got going in time) both to provide them with, and to ask them for, information.

43 In addition, however, to its high-level contacts IMPERIAL INFORMATION should lose no opportunity of gaining the confidence and affection of the upper and middle-class public, from whom the majority of its unofficial 'agents' will be drawn. This it can best do, in the first instance, by exploiting the thirst for General Knowledge referred to above. The fantastic popularity and great potential influence of the 'Brains' Trust' in England and of similar broadcast programmes in North America seem unlikely to represent only a passing craze. IMPERIAL INFORMATION, by taking over all such features on the BBC, would find itself a national institution almost overnight. For purposes partly of propaganda and partly of making contacts, it should comprise a highly efficient General Knowledge section, on the lines of Selfridge's Information Bureau or *The Times* Intelligence Department. It should have the best reference library and run the best travel agency in London. It should have plenty of character, and as little as possible to do with the Civil Service.

44 In exactly what form these random suggestions might be developed in practice does not greatly matter as far as this paper is concerned. The target aimed at should be the creation of a repository and clearing-house for the vast fund of Local General Knowledge which resides within the British Empire. The primary, but unacknowledged, purpose of collecting this information would be to have it readily available in case of war. The secondary object would be to make the information, and the machinery collecting it, serve as many useful purposes as possible in time of peace. The pattern, status, and expense of the project are unimportant compared with the end it is designed to achieve. For until somebody or something achieves that end there will be a major (but remediable) weakness in the post-war defences of the Empire.

In reality, the overall picture was not as bleak as Fleming portrayed it. SOE recruited a number of prominent businessmen and bankers to assist them in undermining the enemy on a political, economic and financial level. Colin Mackenzie, who ran SOE in India, went out of his way to recruit men from British Far East trading companies and Burmese timber concerns; within their collective experience was a vast repository of Fleming's Local General Knowledge. Margaret Hasluk, who had spent the 1920s and 1930s engaged on ethnographic research in the Balkans, counselled SOE missions before they were dropped into Albania. However, he was correct in identifying the need to centralize this knowledge so that it could be accessed by competing and complementary Intelligence agencies, hence avoiding duplication of effort and territorial attempts to withhold information.

Chapter 11

Wheeling and dealing in information

Fleming wanted to keep the market buoyant by 'interim sales' of most secret and very high-grade material of a genuine nature which could be slightly doctored or emasculated. It should be taken to Chungking by 'a prominent personality not noted for guile or associated with propaganda'.[1] Bevan signalled back that reactions were favourable but 'no concrete plans likely for some weeks'.

On 18 August, he asked ISSB in London for new material by the 25th as there was 'a favourable opportunity' transmitting it through PURPLE WHALES channels. The reply came back on 28 August:

The following fictitious meeting in Moscow was approved for PURPLE WHALES channels:

1 Moscow meeting complete success and full agreement reached regarding interlocking operations. Confident Russians can hold Caucasus long enough to enable adequate reinforcements from UK to reach Persia was established. Consequently, it would be unnecessary to send other than very minor reinforcements from India to Persia.

2 As regards second front in 1942 it was stated that the Americans and British were doing everything within their power to comply with Stalin's requests, and planning for operations against Norway was being accelerated.

3 India is to concentrate on giving increased help to China. Large American reinforcements have been ordered to India for this purpose.

4 There was considerable divergence of opinion on Naval subjects of which the Russians seem to understand nothing. They did not realise the tremendous British effort in Russian and other convoys.

5 The split in ME Command does not apply to air. Tedder will continue as AOC-C. in both theatres.

6 The new Persia-Iraq command will eventually establish HQ in Baghdad but for some time administrative problems will make it necessary for this HQ to remain in Cairo where it is now forming.

7 Attitude of Iraqi PM most satisfactory and interview between HM Minister at Kabul and Afghan PM on 7 August satisfactory.

The courier of these fictitious meeting notes was to be Major General Dennys, the head of 204 British Military Mission in Chungking, who had been in Delhi.

❧

Meanwhile, Fleming had started discussions with LCS to the effect that the sequel to PURPLE WHALES should emanate out of Washington.

Plan FLOUNDERS then evolved and on 8 October, Fleming sent an outline to Bevan:

1 The Pacific War Council is becoming increasingly aware of its own futility. There is friction and distrust between its members and the Governments they represent. Dr T.V. Soong, in particular, considers that China is getting a raw deal and loses no opportunity of bringing pressure to bear on her Allies. There are differences between America and Australia in connection with SW Pacific.

2 But the main grievance of the Council as a whole is that since Dieppe (when one of its members committed a blatant indiscretion) it has been kept in the dark about operations and strategy. Complaints on this score, supported by a certain amount of Chinese blackmail, result in a meeting being convened at which a representative of the Joint Chiefs of Staff circulates a paper outlining, and presides over a discussion of, the operational intentions of the United Nations during 1943–1944.

3 The meeting is not altogether harmonious. The British anticipating trouble, have arranged for a verbatim report to be kept; and a copy of this is airmailed to Sir Horace Seymour in Chungking where it is likely to serve as a useful check on Chinese attempts to garble their version of the proceedings (e.g.) exaggerating the scope of the undertakings which Dr Soong was able to extract from us.

4 The record is diffuse throughout and acrimonious in parts. Like PURPLE WHALES, it is however largely non-committal, operational plans generally alluded to by their code-names and (where they are not) a strong element of ambiguity or uncertainty being always present. The document as a whole will convey:

a) A deplorable picture of inter-allied relations on the Pacific War Council.

b) A plausibly exaggerated picture of our military and industrial potential.

c) As much in the way of definite strategical diversion as the chiefs of Staff can be persuaded to devise.

d) A number of 'bogeys', in the shape of veiled and undecipherable references to plans, weapons, documents, organizations etc., which might mean practically anything at all, do in fact mean nothing. And always have a disturbing effect on the Japanese.

5 If this project is approved decisions should be taken as soon as possible on the following points:

a) What do we want the Japanese to believe?

b) When can this deception most usefully be practised on them?

c) When a) and b) have been decided, how is the actual forging to be done?

6 It would increase our chances of success if the completed document could be brought to Chungking by the safe hand of a prominent personality. For this particular scenario, Sir Alexander Cadogan would fit the bill adequately.

Cadogan was a good choice since not only was he the Permanent Under-Secretary for Foreign Affairs but he had also been His Majesty's Envoy Extraordinary and Minister Plenipotentiary at Peking between 1934 and 1936 and knew the Generalissimo and his close lieutenants well. Fleming was aiming high.

The problem was that, although the Americans fully realized the importance of FLOUNDERS and were anxious to help, there was no momentum in Washington. This was a result of the US policy of devolving both policy and implementation to theatre commanders: in this case it was General Stilwell who had come out against the whole idea. On 21 October, the British Army Joint Staff Mission in Washington suggested that 'an ideal arrangement would be for Wavell to see Stilwell (during his current visit to Delhi) and sell him on the whole principles of which at present he has no knowledge'.

Wavell and Stilwell did indeed meet that month but no word reached Washington of the outcome. On 12 November, the Staff Mission in Washington sent Bevan a copy of the US Order of Battle in the Middle East but with the proviso it could only be used after consultation with Generals Eisenhower and Andrews.[2] Fleming as usual was phlegmatic about 'these far-off projects largely based on imponderables'. Writing to Bevan on 17 November, he opined that it is useless to force the growth of these high-level gambits until there is some high-level strategy to go through them, and there is not likely to be, I imagine, for some time … Whitehall reacts to leading questions about our intentions in the Pacific in much the same rather distrait manner as an inexperienced traveller during a rough Channel crossing reacts to questions about customs formalities.

In early December news reached D. Division [G.S.I (d)] that a paper on FLOUNDERS was being prepared by the Joint Security Control for the Joint Staff planners. However, Stilwell had yet to agree to the use of the names of any American units or formations in the FLOUNDERS product. As 1942 came to a close, Bevan attended a deception strategy meeting chaired by Captain Dyer USN at the War Department in Washington. He reminded the meeting that the principal objective at the moment was to keep the PURPLE WHALES channel open and to do so it was essential that items of true information were provided from time to time. The Americans were in complete agreement with the concept but cautioned that the scheme needed to be sold both to General MacArthur and Admiral Halsey on the grounds that theatre commanders had to know the detailed mechanics of the proposed channel.

Throughout January 1943 requests for information and permissions passed to and from London and Washington. The British Army Joint Staff Mission in Washington viewed the American deception organization as being 'in a complete muddle' and had come to a halt as far as FLOUNDERS was concerned. Nothing had changed by March and finally on 24 April permission was given to use the following information:

1 In mid-January Japanese sank US submarines GRAMPUS and AMBERJACK in Mandated Islands area.[3]
2 Both had successful careers having accounted for much enemy shipping.
3 At the same time two large merchant ships were sunk.
4 Announcement will be made to press of loss of submarines by Navy Department in mid-May.

In June, further material was approved by the Americans:

1 US submarine TRITON was sunk near Truk on 15 March.
2 This submarine had lain in wait for many days near the naval base and had inflicted serious casualties on the enemy before being sunk.
3 News of sinking will probably not be released to press.
4 US battleship badly damaged by enemy submarine in Bismarck Sea area recently. This ship reached port safely.

On 14 June, the *Washington Post* carried an article 'Two US subs missing and believed lost in action against enemy'. The Navy Cross citations for the two captains were used to demonstrate how successful they had been.

In early December 1942, Fleming's office approached London with the idea of a dummy telegram, codename BARONESS, from the Foreign Secretary to Sir Horace Seymour in Chungking which had supposedly been compromised and was likely to reach Japanese intelligence.

Object
1   To weaken the confidences of Germany and Japan in Italy.
2   To indicate that we hope to reduce Italy into submission by bombing and are delaying our next operational step.

Assumptions
Any information obtained by the Japanese would, no doubt, be passed to the Germans and possibly even to the Italians.

Story
A Foreign Office telegram from Eden to Seymour would indicate:
1   Signs of a general decline in Italian morale.
2   Rumours of discontent amongst Italian troops in the Balkans.
3   Spanish Foreign Minister being increasingly outspoken.
4   Possible abdication of King of Italy in favour of the Prince of Piedmont.

In addition, in order to make the telegram plausible, a second or even a third subject should be introduced, based possibly on one of the following:

1   Eden's visit to the US in connection with a supply of landing craft for European operations.
2   Increasing reluctance of neutrals in granting credit to Germany.

Treatment
The Foreign Office telegram would be compromised in Chungking and should this take place sometime in the first half of May it should reach the Japanese in about three weeks or a month later.

By 24 April 1943, the final text of the telegram had been hammered out between the Foreign Office, LCS and India. Bevan cabled Fleming:

Following additional information may be used in your talks with the Generalissimo if you think it is really necessary:

1   We have definite evidence that Italian morale both civil and military has received a further setback as a result of Tunisian reverses and bombing of Italian objectives. Further deterioration is considered certain as our bombing offensive against Italy increases this summer.

2   There are rumours of discontent among Italian troops of all ranks in the Balkans provoked especially by news of devastation and of Rommel's treatment of Italian troops in North Africa. Indeed there appears to have been talk of a second 'March on Rome' being overdue.

3   It is reported that there is the possibility of the abdication of the King of Italy in favour of the Prince of Piedmont and of the formation of a new government.

4   Though we do not necessarily take all this at its face value we have good grounds for thinking that Italian government is taking an increasingly realistic view.

5   Spanish Minister for Foreign Affairs is becoming more outspoken in his interviews with HM Ambassador. I do not believe that he is influenced only by the desire that Spain may play some considerable part in world affairs.

Fleming then intervened at the last minute, expressing a reluctance to use the material through PURPLE WHALES since he felt that the counteraction value was negligible 'unless Japanese diplomatic and consular personal in Italy are all either crass or negligent or both'. His preference was to pass it through high diplomatic channels in Kabul. LCS professed itself to be 'befogged' by his position and wondered how exactly they could help him for surely if they gave the Japanese some accurate operational information which had recently become history and therefore of no strategic value, the Japanese would smell a rat. Furthermore, they pointed out that Fleming was not in a position to judge the merits of the statement on Italy or the reactions of the Spanish Government. A terse telegram followed on 1 May, informing Fleming that 'we do not repeat not wish you to test in Kabul and in view of your reluctance to use PURPLE CHANNELS we have decided to operate elsewhere'. After a telephone call between LCS and Fleming when he explained that all he needed was a hard fact or two since that is 'what the Japs like, not mere appreciations', a new draft was prepared.

In August, the Military Intelligence Directorate in India obtained a copy of an alleged telegram from T.V. Soong to Chiang Kai-shek which had been forwarded from the Japanese consul in Kwangchow Bay to the Japanese Ambassador in Hanoi. The contents ranged from the participation of the Russians in the war against Japan, especially the provision of a Siberian airbase, the post-war future of Korea to the training of Chinese naval cadets and return of air graduates. The conclusion reached by Fleming was straightforward: 'the Chinese are in the PURPLE WHALES business on their own' and 'will attempt strategical counteraction based on QUEBEC conference'. Rating the situation dangerous, he asked for QUEBEC material dealing with Russian and Anglo-American arrangements regarding Siberian bases and stated that he was leaving for China shortly. Both Bevan and SIS in London agreed with Fleming's analysis but the Americans[4] felt it was unsafe to provide him with such material for an interim sale. However, the development of a general scenario of the war against Japan by the Combined Chiefs of Staff and Mountbatten was scheduled for mid-September and they were happy that reference was made to this forthcoming event.

Sensing delay, and 'judging by local talent and machinery available and by performance during last three months, Washington are incapable of producing a comprehensive adequate scenario', Fleming suggested that LCS produced the scenario themselves and sent it to Washington for approval or modification. In particular, he flagged that any reference of the matter to Stilwell would have an adverse effect on all parties concerned 'except Japanese'! On 3 September, Bevan met Major General George Strong, US Army Deputy Chief of Staff for Intelligence, in London and was dismayed to learn that no progress had been made in Washington to improve Joint Security Control. Like Fleming, he despaired about the hopeless set-up in Washington. Of more concern was the looming problem of who would control SEAC. Strong had made it quite clear that he controlled the Pacific and China theatres and that the issue of who ran deception at SEAC was undecided. Until it was resolved, PURPLE WHALES was on hold.

Meanwhile, LCS stuck to its knitting and produced this scenario on 9 September:

WAR AGAINST GERMANY
The British Chiefs of Staff reported on the present situation from Army, Navy and Air points of view. Discussion in the main turned on:

a) The stepping up of the bomber offensive against Germany.

b) The invasion of Italy with the object of knocking her out of the war.

c) Strategy and other operations in 1944.

Decisions were taken in regard to a) and b). Considerable optimism prevailed and both British and Americans agreed on the need to exploit recent successes. Though the German army was still fighting well it was generally felt that the entire German war machine was very severely strained and that the Allies must be ready to take advantage of any eventuality in any quarter.

As regards an invasion across the Channel from the UK it was considered that an assault was out of the question in view of the strength of the coastal defences, and so long as any appreciable German Army or Air Force reserves remained in close reserve.

WAR AGAINST JAPAN
This was the main reason for the conference.

Main strategy. It was considered extremely disappointing that in spite of endless discussions no major decisions were made in regard to the main strategy to be adopted. So long as Germany remains undefeated it was felt that no large-scale Anglo-American effort could be carried out in the Far East. In these circumstances it was decided that the best plan would be to conduct a war of attrition against the Japanese and probe the outer perimeter of their defences at as many places as possible, with a view to finding the weakest spots which could at a later date be exploited. For this purpose, bases in North and West Australia are being developed.

A further conference on main strategy is timed to take place during the next few months.

China. American and British views differed as to the best method of supporting the Chinese forces. The Americans were of the opinion that this support should be given forthwith as a first priority, but the British envisaged many difficulties in this connection. It was, however, decided to continue to give maximum air support and supplies by air, though the extent of the Allied effort would be unavoidably limited due to administrative difficulties.

Russian Front. The Americans were most anxious to approach the Russian Government to negotiate the lease of Russian bases. They considered that this was the best means to effect an early defeat of Japan. The British, on the other hand, pointed out that the Russians were very fully occupied with the German Army and, for obvious political reasons, it would be most unwise to approach Stalin at the present juncture. While the desirability of the lease of these bases was agreed by both British and Americans, it was finally agreed that no approach to the Russians should be made at present.

Tactics. Brigadier Wingate attended the conference and very much impressed both British and American senior officers with regards to his conception of tactics to be employed against the Japanese.

Fleming had arrived in Chungking in late September 1943 and cabled India and London that although suspicions about the Chinese running their own PURPLE WHALES were confirmed, there was no cause for alarm. After all, the Chinese military potential was well known to the Japanese, so they had few marketable secrets of their own. He had met with Ho Ying-chin, the Minister of War, who had been most friendly and had reacted favourably to Fleming's suggestion that there should be a British Liaison Officer in Chungking to co-ordinate deception efforts. Fleming also met Tai Li's No.2 who was responsible for transmission. In a frank exchange, he told him the details of the Chinese operations and how customers had swallowed everything they gave them and constantly asked for more. Fleming came away determined to do everything possible to develop and establish indirect control over the Chinese channels.

A first thought was to suggest to LCS that an approach to the Russians for PURPLE WHALES material would be sensible given that 'we know that the Chinese are relying entirely on their imagination to satisfy their customers' natural curiosity about Russian intentions, dispositions etc.'. The end result would be that these inventions would eventually be revealed as such and thus discredit valuable counteraction sources. If the Russians supplied material, they would ensure that Chinese efforts conformed to their requirements. Since the Russian Military Attaché in Chungking, Colonel Roshchin, would be visiting Delhi shortly, time was of the essence.

When Mountbatten arrived in Delhi to take up his new role of SACSEA on 7 October 1943,[5] mindful of Churchill's directive 'to maintain and broaden our contacts with China', he flew up to Chungking[6] to meet the Generalissimo on 18/19 October. One of the topics raised was the sharing and co-ordination of intelligence[7] and the following February, he wrote him a personal letter outlining proposals to improve co-ordination and co-operation:

My dear Mr President,

You will doubtless recall Lord Wavell's personal letter to you dated 16 June 1942, in which he placed before you specific suggestions for measures calculated to mislead our common enemy. You were good enough then to express your approval of these proposals; and you will in all probability recollect the success which has attended certain joint efforts in deception which we have since carried out from Chungking.

As the struggle against Japan rises to its climax, so do the chances for effective use of the weapon of deception increase. The growing strength of the United Nations, the unwieldy rise of the enemy's perimeter and the inadequacy of his reserves to guard against all contingencies are today undoubtedly making him more and more sensitive to hints of impending Allied operations. Our own experience in India and Burma strongly suggests that he can without too much difficulty be persuaded by special deception methods to dispose his forces in such a way as materially to assist our own operations.

The deception field is thus ready for tilling and it was with this appreciation in mind and with a view to the closer co-operation of our two commands, that a British Liaison Officer (Major S.C.F. Pierson of GSI (d)) was posted in October 1943 to Chungking after consultation with General Ho Ying-chin.[8]

It has, however, to be admitted that progress towards a state of complete co-ordination and co-operation in Sino-British deception efforts has up to now been disappointingly slow; and that Major Pierson's presence in Chungking has so far had little influence on events. I have latterly been increasingly conscious of this unsatisfactory state of affairs; the more so since the need for action becomes daily more imperative. It was for this reason that (as Your Excellency may recollect) General Carton De Wiart approached you a few weeks ago on behalf of Major Pierson asking for guidance towards a speedier realisation of our common interests in the deception field.

You were good enough to direct that Major Pierson work in future through General Ho Ying-chin. I have taken advantage of the pause brought about by the latter's temporary absence from Chungking to call Major Pierson to New Delhi for consultation and to draw up for your approval concrete proposals for the future closer collaboration of the Chinese and SEAC deception staffs. These proposals which are attached at Appendix A to this letter, make for strong mutual support. They are, incidentally, largely based on a conversation which Lieutenant Colonel Fleming (who is in charge of SEAC deception work) had some months ago with General Cheng Kai-min in Chungking. The latter very able officer has, it is understood, been actively concerned in the implementation of the limited operations which have so far been initiated in China from the British side; and it is believed that he is thus well qualified to express the Chinese view.

May I ask for your support and co-operation on this matter? The proposals speak for themselves and their merits or otherwise will be quickly apparent to you. It is, however, worth stressing once again the importance (which you have already been pleased to recognize) of strategical deception work and the brilliant results which have been obtained from it in many theatres of the war. The opportunities now offered for the misdirection of Japanese strategy and the exploitation of Japanese 'nerves' through Chinese channels are so great that I myself feel that we should not lose a moment in setting up an effective organization to make the most of them.

Yours very sincerely,

Mountbatten

The proposals attached to the letter covered both New Delhi and Chungking (GSI (d) had by now been formally rebranded by SEAC as D. Division):

In New Delhi

1 A suitably qualified Chinese officer be attached to D. Division, SEAC.

2 This officer to have an office in D. Division under Lieutenant Colonel Fleming and to be:

   a Kept fully informed of the progress and results of all operations carried out from New Delhi.

   b Kept in the picture as regards future projects.

   c Given every opportunity of seeing all activities of D. Division, including W/T contacts with the enemy.

   d Given a watching brief over all the Interservices Technical Bureau research and development work.

   e Permitted to work with Forward Observation Squadrons (Deception Units) in the field and on training.

3 He will keep Delhi posted as regards the general outline of Chinese plans and the objects aimed at and will make recommendations regarding the development of deception methods in Chungking in the light of his experience in India.

In Chungking

1 Major S.C.F. Pierson to be attached to the Chinese section carrying out deception work.

2 This officer to be accommodated in the office of the general concerned and to be:

   a Provided with an interpreter and translator.

   b Kept fully informed of the progress and results of all deception operations carried out from Chungking.

   c Allowed to see something of Chinese organization and methods.

   d Kept in the picture as regards future projects.

3 He will keep Chungking posted as regards the general outline of New Delhi plans and the objects aimed at.

4 He will be allowed to put forward again his proposals for a W/T contact with the Japanese.

5 He will be prepared at all times to make suggestions and give explanations in the light of his knowledge of New Delhi's activities.

One result of this overture percolated down to D. Division in May. Fleming signalled Mountbatten that

Pierson reports about face on part of [Chiang's] Director of Military Intelligence, General Cheng Kai-min, [who] expressed keen desire to pay early liaison visit to 'Fleming's Director of Military Intelligence' and asked if Fleming could fix. General suggested necessary procedure would be for Mountbatten to signal General De Wiart suggesting visit by general for purpose of mutual understanding and closer co-operation in Intelligence matters. De Wiart would show signal to Ho Yeng-chin who would authorize visit. General is extremely keen to what seems a most sensible idea and Pierson has said he is sure I can arrange it. One result of visit would thus be to materially strengthen D. Division's hand in China. Have asked Pierson to confirm that Cheng Kai-min wants to see both India and SEAC Directors of Intelligence. Pierson's message implies that he does and in view of India Command's Chinese interests and experience joint SEAC/India/China Conference would seem to be called for. General Cawthorn welcomes idea in principle subject to Major General Lamplough[9] (Director of Intelligence SEAC) who may care to mention matter to P. Division since clandestine organizations probably have numerous outstanding accounts to settle with Cheng Kai-min … Can throw no light on motives behind unexpected uncharacteristic breach in PURPLE WHALES deadlock which has prevailed for last nine months. It may well have inter-allied 'political' angle. It is in any case of direct benefit to D. Division and may be capable of exploitation in overall SEAC interest.

An ULTRA intercept of 18 July 1944 of a signal from the Japanese Consul-General in Canton to Tokyo showed that the Chinese channel, identified as 'G.H.', had indirectly passed on particulars about Anglo-American forces in India to the Military Committee in Chungking which had met on 20 May. He had purloined the message from the Chinese Liaison Officer at HQ SEAC. Recognizing that the information was 'a little out of date', the consul stated that he had fixed up direct communication with 'G.H.'. Within a week, another ULTRA intercept revealed that the Chinese channel was active again. In a signal to the Japanese Ambassador in Moscow, the Japanese Minister of Foreign Affairs explained how he had received a telegram from 'G.H.' in Chungking about the visit of Vice-President Wallace[10] to Chiang Kai-shek and the military conference which followed. The details were as follows:

The US wants Chungking to lift the blockade of Chukoo [?], to provide military funds, provisions etc. and to get the Communist armies to operate against Japan.

The following decisions were reached with regard to the future political and military strategy in the Far East:

1 America's request for leasing of air bases in Siberia shall be acceded to by Soviet Russia before a state of war arises between that country and Japan.

2 If American forces land in the Kuriles, the Soviets will at the same time attack Japan.

3 Although China reserves her rights in respect of the recovery of the lost territory of Manchuria, Dairen must remain a free port.

4 The USSR will absolutely not interfere in the internal affairs of China.

5 The Kuriles and the whole of Sachalin to be administered by the Soviet Union (after the war).

6 Great Britain, America, the USSR and China to form the nucleus of an International Peace Organization after the war.

7 The United States shall increase her material assistance to Chiang Kai-shek and will help in the building up of China's industries after the war.

Further telegrams were intercepted in October and November between Canton and the Japanese Embassy in Rangoon which dealt with information planted by D. Division and between Canton and Saigon in April 1945. In every case, Fleming noted, it had not been necessary to describe the source, codenamed INK, nor make any assessment of his trustworthiness. It could therefore be assumed that 'G.H.' was well known to Japanese intelligence circles; indeed this was confirmed by General Cheng Kai-min who said the source had enjoyed the confidence of the Japanese since 1937. Fleming therefore concluded that it would appear that the Japanese controlling staff in Canton and their superiors in Tokyo (a) attached importance to the intelligence supplied by 'G.H.' and (b) were not disposed to doubt the agent's bona fides.[11]

Both the British Far East Combined Bureau (working under the aegis of Bletchley Park) and the US Navy had contributed to breaking the Japanese Naval JN 25 series of codes – some of the most impenetrable of the war. Commander Harold Kenworthy, who with the help of the Metropolitan Police wireless staff, built the 'J' machine, which in 1935 made the first mechanically aided breach in Japanese codes and Captain John Tiltman broke the Japanese Operational Code. The British also intercepted both low-level Japanese 'Consular Y' traffic and high-grade Japanese diplomatic ciphers before the outbreak of hostilities. After the Japanese invasion of South East Asia, British codebreakers relocated to New Delhi (the Wireless Experimental Station for the Army and RAF) and Colombo where the British Far East Combined Bureau concentrated on naval intelligence. In the course of the war, a SIGINT sharing agreement – BRUSA – was reached between the two allies although the majority of intercepts were 'owned' and thus distributed by the Americans whose resources were infinitely larger. The main Japanese army cipher was never broken. Fleming would have had access to much of the material pertaining to the Far East, including relevant German traffic intercepted and decoded by Bletchley Park.

The PURPLE WHALES impasse with the Americans continued. In April 1944, the British Army Joint Staff Mission in Washington suggested going direct to Major General Bissell[12] since Strong would not approach the Joint Security Control. Although Wingate viewed this as 'quite insane', Bissell came back with the idea that a conference of Dominion Premiers would provide a suitable background to release material on South West Pacific command. To that end, he asked the Joint Security Control to develop a story. Typically, the Joint Security Control then asked SEAC to write it since PURPLE WHALES was a SEAC channel and submit it to them for approval. Reading between the lines, the British Army Joint Staff Mission in Washington surmised that this was hardly surprising since the Joint Security Control was 'incapable of drafting any such document'. The end of this game of musical chairs was a note from Bissell to the effect that LCS should ask Fleming, 'who presumably controls the channels in question', to prepare from time to time an outline of such material as he would like to feed to these channels.

By August, an exasperated Fleming signalled the War Office (and Bletchley Park) that Bissell had passed through Delhi before he himself had returned from London and had not contacted D. Division. He thought it was possible that Bissell had met with Pierson in Chungking. However, he had no further information about Stilwell and CBI theatre and no confirmation had been received about PURPLE WHALES.

Aside from the frustrations with the Americans, sales of PURPLE WHALES material continued and on 10 November, Fleming was pleased to report the success of P/W 2, a forged letter from a senior official of the Burmah Shell Company in India to the Chungking representative of the Asiatic Petroleum Company. It dealt in some detail with matters arising out of plans for the rehabilitation of oilfields in the SEAC area. The intelligence deductions which could be made from it were that the Combined Chiefs of Staff had on 14 August 1944 decided to switch Mountbatten's main offensive effort from his original objectives in Burma to the Netherlands' East Indies and particularly Sumatra. P/W 2 was sent from Delhi to Chungking and then transmitted by the Chinese Director of Military Intelligence, General Cheng Kai-min, to a Japanese intelligence officer in Macao. ULTRA intercepts followed its trail to the War Ministry in Tokyo who passed it to the Foreign Office who in turn sent it to the Japanese ambassador in Rangoon.

A sketchbook, purporting to be the property of a war artist working for the Public Relations Directorate and containing SEAC Dummy Order of Battle information portrayed in drawings of senior officers and divisional signs, was introduced through Chungking channels and reportedly reached the Japanese High Command in Tokyo.

When an order came through from a PURPLE WHALES customer in January 1945 for information about an American landing in South China, Fleming pointed out since the going rate had increased from 50,000 to 200,000 Chinese dollars for such material, surely this was a classic demonstration of the need for effective inter-theatre co-ordination and he hoped that the Joint Security Control would make a play with it. Unfortunately, Anglo-American turf wars resurfaced when General Wedermeyer, who had been appointed Allied commander in the Chinese theatre, began to take steps to control all deception plans. To Fleming's wry amusement he had started by asking for copies of the letter of Pierson's appointment. Then, by a stroke of luck, London picked up a *Daily Telegraph* news story that Mr Stimson, the US Secretary of State for War, had declared at his press conference that 'the next Asiatic campaign will be on the China Coast'. Surely the Americans would now play ball.

Further corroboration was supplied by an ULTRA intercept stating that the Japanese had picked up from the Chinese Naval Attaché in Washington that the Deputy Chief of the Far Eastern Bureau of the State Department had stated that Chinese proficient in the dialects of Kwantung, Fukien and 'Kungchuan' were being recruited to assist in the mainland landings. On 1 April, the British Army Joint Staff Mission in Washington identified that this material had been planted by the US Navy without any recourse to the Joint Security Control. In mid-April, another request came in from the PURPLE WHALES customer for American intentions about landings in China. This time Fleming predicted that the channel will 'almost certainly be blown if we stall again since the Japanese are quite convinced that landings will take place'.

Suddenly after six months of inactivity by the Joint Security Control, a message was received from their Liaison Officer with Wedermeyer that the landing question should be played as follows: 'Owing to situation in Europe and heavy opposition in Iwo Jima and Okinawa any contemplated landings on Formosa or China pending postponed.' Sir Ronald Wingate expressed amazement since the message itself seemed likely to allay Japanese suspicions of any early attack on China, 'which seems fairly extraordinary in view of the circumstances'. Without the imprimatur of the Joint Security Control, D. Division were uneasy about using it. A terse telegram to the British Army Joint Staff Mission in Washington followed: 'Consider further action unprofitable, therefore inadvisable.' Mild consternation followed when a *Reuters* report out of Chungking on 5 May quoted Wedermeyer as saying 'American-trained Chinese ground forces will be ready to support Allied landing on China coast'.

Fleming merely reflected that as the policy was wrong anyhow, why worry.

Chapter 12
Building the organization

When he first arrived in Delhi, Fleming had stayed at Wavell's house. The field marshal found him 'an attractive person' and 'full of ideas'. Duff Hart-Davis observed that 'he discovered in Wavell a man whom he immediately liked and respected, and who, moreover, shared many of his own characteristics: deeply modest, diffident about his own abilities yet of great moral strength, widely read, taciturn to a degree that many people found disconcerting ... he and Peter were thus naturally tuned to each other's wavelength'. By July, Fleming had moved into a bungalow with Dr Charles Macneil, Wavell's physician, and Robin Ridgway, private secretary to General Auchinleck.[1]

In one of his first letters home, Fleming told Celia, 'I have just got a very efficient secretary called Miss Noad or Noade or Node or possibly Knowed. She is said to have a temper but seems mild enough.'[2] This lady or in Indian Defence Department speak 'Woman clerk grade "B"' was the first of a series of new appointments in D. Division. On 2 June 1942, the Chief of the General Staff's office sanctioned the creation of six staff officer posts and two intelligence officer posts. Fleming was suspicious and told Celia, 'having been single-handed and not a day off since I got here, my pathetic little branch is now what they call being put on a proper basis, with a full colonel (Hutton) on top and a Naval officer and an RAF officer and all sorts of trimmings'.[3] Miss Noad remained in charge of the office despite her tendency to use a 36 grenade to hammer nails into the wall.

Fleming's suspicion of imported elderly staff officers proved correct and within a day he was writing to Celia that 'Hutton doesn't really see the point ... chiefly because his mind doesn't and never will work in the right sort of way for this sort of job'.[4] It took until November to move Hutton 'up one' and a new colonel (Lawrence Smith) was posted in, 'an elderly officer who doesn't look to me as if he will last long'.[5] The RAF officer proved equally unsuitable. Known throughout the Malay peninsula as the 'Witless Wonder', Wing Commander Lynedoch Wanless O'Gowan, late of His Majesty's Secret Service, provoked Fleming to 'wish I could sack all these colonels and wing commanders and get a couple of sensible young ensigns (second lieutenants) who would see the point and do some work' for 'it is a little on the fatuous side shoving in two idle and ineffective old men of nearly sixty to do a job like this'.[6]

On 16 August 1942, the office was relocated. 'We moved in this morning, by bullock cart, in pouring rain,' he wrote to Celia. 'We are now twice as far from the main building as we were before and that was far enough. This greatly increases the difficulty of getting anything done at all and involves endless sweating round corridors and waiting for people who want to see us but have always become immersed in something else by the time we get over there. The premises themselves you have often seen before in films of Devil's Island. Most of the windows are high up on the walls so that people cannot look in and see what we are doing. Some are at normal level and protected by flaccid-looking bars. You can't see anything out of them except another row of barred windows. The floor is uneven. There are no electric light bulbs. It is physically impossible for anyone to find our telephone number and indeed it is only by the veriest fluke that we have been able to do so ourselves.'[7]

The difficulties in starting up any new organization in India in wartime conditions were considerable. The distances were enormous, recruitment competitive (with SIS and various Indian intelligence agencies) and transport, be it vehicles or aircraft, hard to come by. As SOE's Colonel Bickham Sweet-Escott drolly recalled, 'this far flung but loosely-knit empire was connected, if that is the word, by a telephone network on which it was almost impossible to have any coherent conversation, even if you and the man at the other end remembered the elaborate code system you were supposed to use ... because of the innumerable exchanges through which the land line passed'. Little wonder that GSI (d) shared a 'rather spiritualistic telephone with a brigadier and full colonel who do totally different jobs next door'.[8]

After a month's leave in England that autumn, Fleming returned to India and tetchily confided in Celia that

> we are having a very bad spell in D. Division. The colonel and the wing commander sit around like a couple of effigies doing absolutely nothing at all. I mean really literally nothing. This does not fail to make the section look pretty silly from outside and thus further queers our chances of getting the sensible chaps, let alone the oafs and demi-oafs who abound, to take an interest in our abstruse and unfamiliar racket. It isn't so hot inside our section either. The two girls, who are loyal and hard-working and invaluable little creatures (Miss Noad has left for Calcutta) resent the colonel's idleness and futility and will sooner or later drift off into some other section where the atmosphere is less Chekovian ... Short of learning ventriloquism one has to do all the talking (at meetings) oneself (with frequent pseudo-obsequious asides, like 'As I think you decided the other day, Colonel') and thus gets the reputation of

flat-catching, bumping and boring, talking out of turn and generally confirming the Indian Army's worst suspicions.[9]

All this was to change for Fleming had got wind of a fellow Grenadier officer who had just passed out of the Staff College at Quetta. Peter Thorne, the younger son of General Sir Andrew Thorne, had served with the 3rd Battalion Grenadier Guards in France and been wounded in the neck by mortar shrapnel during a battle near Comines on the Ypres Canal. Evacuated at Dunkirk, he rejoined his battalion in June and then was posted to 2 Division as a junior staff officer. In April 1942 the Division sailed for Madagascar as reserve to 5 Division but by the time they reached Cape Town, the pro-German Vichy authorities had surrendered the island and so they were sent on to India to be trained in jungle warfare. At this stage, the Army decided to send him to Staff College at Quetta for a six-months war course. On passing out and faced with the prospect of life of Staff duties at HQ Eastern Army, a position far from the war, Thorne was delighted to receive a telegram from Fleming offering him a job at GHQ (India). He did not know him personally but, well acquainted with his reputation as an author and explorer, had no hesitation in accepting the offer.

In March 1943 when Thorne arrived, D. Division was in 'a new and slightly cooler office'[10] in the main Army HQ complex next to the office of the Director of Military Intelligence, Brigadier Bill Cawthorn. Miss Noad had retired to Calcutta and Smith and O'Gowan, 'the two rather flaccid spanners in the works', had been moved on. Smith had been replaced by a Colonel Meiklejohn of the Poona Horse who lasted for just five days and his successor, 'a useless Gurkha called Tyne was gone in two shakes of a brigadier's arse'.[11] Apart from Fleming, the office now consisted of Gordon Rennie, a South African in the Black Watch, Major Frankie Wilson and two secretaries, Joan Wavell, the C-in-C's youngest daughter, and her friend, the 'small equestrienne' Bobby Marsden. Neither took shorthand.[12]

The new RAF officer was Wing Commander Mervyn Horner, the son of Baron 'Tommy' Horner, a physician to the Royal family. The Winchester and Cambridge-educated Horner was the closest to Fleming in age and his background as a publisher at the small house of Duckworths and a gifted musician[13] provided him with Clarke's creative credentials.

The Navy was represented by Commander Alan Robertson-Macdonald RN, at age forty-eight the old man of the group. As a retired officer, he had rejoined the navy in August 1939 and spent three years with the Naval Intelligence Division (HMS *President*). He joined D. Division on 1 December 1942 and remained with it until March 1945 when he was replaced by Lieutenant Commander the 8th Earl of Antrim ('Ran') RNVR who had previously been with Combined Operations and played a key role in devising dummy harbours and landing-craft hides.

Major 'Frankie' A.H. Wilson was in charge of Tactical Deception. Commissioned in August 1922, he had joined his battalion, the 2nd Royal Scots Fusiliers,[14] in India, first at Barrackpore and then Sialkot in the Punjab from where he spent a year in Landi Kotal on the Khyber Pass. As a fellow young officer recalled, 'There was tremendous *esprit de corps* and robust competition between companies in work and sport … off duty it was a gay and colourful life.' Wilson was noted as 'a boxing devotee'. In 1931 the battalion moved to Shanghai in China where tasks included six-week anti-piracy patrols on the Yangtze River. On return to England in 1932, garrison life at Catterick and then Aldershot must have seemed mundane in the extreme compared to India: Wilson, by now a captain, transferred[15] to the Indian Army in February 1936 and joined the 19th King George's Own Lancers with whom he roamed around Baltistan and Ladakh after ibex. He went on to command the 44th Cavalry 'who were immediately thereafter disbanded as an armoured unit and remustered, much to their surprise, as ratings in the Royal Indian Navy'.[16] He joined the staff of the Military Intelligence Directorate in May 1943. Fleming later recalled that 'I first met him drinking brandy in the French Commission in Shanghai … But beyond the barrack square – on which there are no pitfalls into which Wilson, mounted, dismounted or mechanized, has not fallen heavily in his day – culture has always beckoned and Wilson has always followed, stopping short only at sculpture'. The two of them collaborated on a book for five-year-old Nichol Fleming – *Mike the Muckshufter* – with Fleming writing the text and Wilson drawing the pictures, 'in *bashas* or even in slit trenches in the Arakan'. On one occasion, when they were cruising up the Irrawaddy on a ML, they fought 'a brisk and successful action in the course of which a two-inch mortar bomb near-missed the artist and holed our aft magazine'.[17]

D. Division's Tactical Deception arm suffered from two major disadvantages. One was the apparent inability of the Japanese radio intercept services to read much of the battlefield traffic – real or false – that was transmitted, or make much sense of it if they did. The other was the absence of Japanese air reconnaissance, which made visual deception pointless except in immediate contact with the enemy, and even then the thickly wooded terrain of Burma gave little opportunity for the camouflage experts. It was only when the air-portable sonic and pyrotechnic equipment came on stream that D. Division's Sonic Warfare Units had the capability of simulating a battle on almost any scale, lasting if necessary for hours.[18]

Fleming noted in his final report that

display, and its complement camouflage, were early abandoned by GSI (d) as an unessential and uneconomical aid to strategic deception in SEAC. This attitude towards display was engendered firstly by the nature of the terrain which rendered enemy observation of any form of display difficult, and secondly by the almost complete lack of enemy air reconnaissance.

Plate 1 Peter (L) and Ian (R) Fleming as boys. © Kate and Lucy Fleming.

Plate 2 Fleming the traveller. © Kate and Lucy Fleming.

Plate 3 En route from Tartary: Kini Maillart and Fleming. © Kate and Lucy Fleming.

Plate 8 (a) Fleming as OC 12 Corps Observation Unit. © Kate and Lucy Fleming.

Plate 8 (b) The Garth. © Coleshill Auxiliary Research Team (CART).

Plate 9 The Thorne family at war (Peter Thorne is second from the left, back row). © Lady Anne Thorne.

Plate 10 Retreat from Greece.

Plate 11 Mongolian cavalry in Russia. Courtesy Bibliothèque nationale de France.

Plate 12 Chungking.

Plate 13 FM Lord Wavell. © The Black Watch Museum.

Plate 14 FM Sir Claude Auchinleck C-in-C India.

Plate 15 Col. Johnny Bevan MC.

Plate 16 Brig. Dudley Clarke by Patrick Phillips. Courtesy Imperial War Museum.

Plate 17 Sir Reginald Wingate, Bt.

Plate 18 Maj. Lucas Ralli. © John Ralli.

Plate 19 Andre Bicat. © Tina Bicat.

Plate 20 Maj. Peter Thorne in India. © Lady Anne Thorne.

Plate 21 Lt. Col. Frankie Wilson.

Plate 22 London Controlling Section.

Plate 23 Trident Conference (Washington). Courtesy of the Franklin D. Roosevelt Presidential Library and Museum.

Plate 24 Sextant Conference (Cairo).

Plate 25 Quadrant Conference (Quebec). Courtesy of the National Film Board of Canada.

Plate 26 Argonaut Conference (Yalta).

Plate 27 Mountbatten arrives at Koggala air base.

Plate 28 Gen. Slim.

Plate 29 Brig. Mike Calvert. Courtesy Imperial War Museum.

The use of dummies and mock-ups in a tactical role was not, however, ignored, and, had the scale of enemy air reconnaissance increased as SEAC forces emerged from the jungle into the plains of Siam or French Indo-China, display could perhaps have been introduced as an element of strategic deception.[19]

Lieutenant Colonel D.J.C. Wiseman, the official historian of sonic warfare, broadly agreed with Fleming.[20] 'The Japanese was slow and frequently completely negative in his reactions to visual intelligence. He was more insensitive to threats and less responsive to our moves than was the German. He himself tended to make a plan and go ahead with it with little regards to our reactions'.

Earlier, in February 1942, Andre Bicat, the artist and sculptor,[21] accompanied by a small group of other artists including the architect Michael Powell and the painter Philip Suffolk had arrived in Kirkee near Poona to teach the Indian army the art of camouflage. They had previously been at the Royal Engineers' Camouflage Development and Training Centre at Farnham Castle which had been set up by the War Office in 1940 and staffed by such luminaries from the art and fashion world such as Oliver Messel, Roland Penrose, Edward Seago, Victor Stiebel and Julian Trevelyan.[22] Here, garbed in unfamiliar battledress, they had learnt to apply their artistic skills to visual deception on the battlefield.

Given the cold shoulder in India by several senior officers, Bicat, armed with a briefcase to pass himself off as a staff officer, blagged his way into Wavell's office and, after tabling his complaint of unwarranted obstruction to this most ardent and sympathetic practitioner of deception, emerged with a piece of paper on which was written 'Give Bicat what he wants. A.W.'. Around the same time, he convinced Major General Cawthorn that he could produce 500 dummy tanks to augment the five real ones currently available to defend India. The result of this successful lobbying was the establishment of the Camouflage Development Wing housed in the bandsmen's quarters on the Viceregal Estate in New Delhi.[23] Furthermore, to Bicat's relief, they reported directly to the Director of Military Intelligence. One of his first orders came from Colin Mackenzie, the head of SOE in the Far East, who had asked for 'Ghost or Spook-like effects' to use in Arakan. He recommended a luminous paint produced by Dr Jordan of the Paint Research Station Teddington!

Fleming liked him from the beginning, writing to Celia in August 1942 that

I have a certain amount to do with a splendid fellow called Andre Bicat, a designer who has worked from G. Miller and Ashley Dukes[24] and used to do the chorus girls' dresses at the Prince of Wales [theatre]. He is now a Sapper and produces dummy objects of various kinds, indeed of any kind, the most unlikely the better he is pleased.[25]

Bicat and his team got off to a good start. On 14 August 1943, General Sir Claude Auchinleck, C-in-C India, wrote to him:

Just a line to thank you for this morning's entertainment! I can only say that I was extremely encouraged and inspired by all I saw – and heard!

I will do all I can to ensure that such ingenuity, keenness and resource is not wasted, so if you feel frustrated – come and see me!

P.S. I was much cheered by the cheerful friendly spirit which obviously permeates your crowd. That is the way to get a move on!

Another letter followed on 10 December, this time from Cawthorn, to record that 'both the C-in-C and the SEAC were very pleased with the demonstration yesterday and I have been asked to express appreciation of the work you and your unit put in to make it the success it was'.[26]

The problem for Bicat and his Special Duties Section[27] was that the employment of visual deception devices was extremely limited in a jungle environment where air reconnaissance was usually rendered ineffective by the dense canopy of trees. In his official history of Visual and Sonic Warfare,[28] Lieutenant Colonel D.J.C. Wiseman wrote that 'there was no call for large-scale visual deception on the lines of that practised in the Middle Eastern or European theatres. There was not, therefore, the same requirement for the numerous visual devices developed for those theatres, and no camouflage units were formed.' Indeed, at Mountbatten's HQ, there was not even a camouflage Staff Officer.

In December 1943,[29] Bicat wrote to Colin Mackenzie to inform him that the C-in-C had approved the reorganization of the section as an Interservices Technical Bureau (ITB) serving all forces and clandestine organizations based in India:

In addition to my present workshop, I propose to set up a small factory outside Delhi which can produce special devices on a limited scale when either security or time does not permit the use of normal channels, and when necessary to make modifications to equipment to meet climatic and other contingencies … I am very anxious to recruit technical personnel on the engineering and explosives side, and I would ask you to consider whether any of your Home stations would care to throw up technical officers for employment with us … I hope this new organization will prove of considerable use to you.

In early February 1944, under the auspices of Lieutenant General Sir Kenneth Loch, the Master-General of Ordnance, India, a meeting chaired by Major General Cawthorn established the terms of references of the newly created ITB:

1 Collation and reproduction of enemy and other documents, passes and certificates, and items of connected equipment needed in connection with certain aspects of special operations, deception schemes etc.[30]

2 Design and where necessary production of all deception equipment.

3 Design and where necessary production of all MI9 devices.

4 Design of camouflage of particular items for special operations.

5 Production of enemy uniforms and personal equipment.

6 Adaptation of design of pyrotechnics for deception purposes.

7 Holding of special deception stores.

8 Distribution and delivery of special deception stores.

9 Instructions in assembling and handling of special deceptions stores.

From now on, Bicat reported to Loch at GHQ India; D. Division remained a prized customer and loyal friend. Among his many achievements, Bicat developed a device for ageing forged banknotes by tumbling them around in a barrel full of oil and ball bearings. On one occasion, when demonstrating a pyrotechnic device to a visiting senior officer, Bicat's trousers caught fire and he had to remove them to stamp out the flames. Far from criticizing him, the senior officer's inspection report concluded that 'much good work is done here'.

After the war, Bicat mentioned to his family that he had endured a fifteen-course banquet in Chungking and at one stage had gone on a long journey carrying metal plates for printing fake currency. Adding these stories together, it is most likely that he had been involved in SOE's Operation GRENVILLE, which involved the printing and distribution of forged Japanese military currency. Indeed, in January 1945, the De La Rue company lent DITB three hand plating machines.[31] The attractions for SOE were obvious in that forged notes would both serve to devalue the military yen banknotes issued by the Japanese in occupied territories and at the same time bankroll SOE and its resistance activities.[32] In a note dated 7 July 1944,[33] SOE's Far East currency position included counterfeit Japanese/ Burman and Malayan notes, NEI Guilder notes, and genuine Siamese Tical notes from existing plates. They had ceased production in London of Chinese Central Reserve Bank 'Nanking' 10 Yuan notes and the plates had been sent to the OSS in America. Not everything went to plan. A signal intercept revealed that the Japanese had spotted a counterfeit Malayan Yen note as there was no smoke coming out of the ship's funnel and the note was a tenth of an inch longer than the genuine one.

The arrival of twenty-four-year-old Major Lucas Ralli,[34] Royal Signals, in the summer of 1944 proved a godsend to the technical side of D. Division's W/T operations. Educated at Eton, where he operated an illegal wireless set with great skill, and at New College, Oxford, where along with Martin Ryle, a future

Astronomer Royal, he founded the University Wireless Club, Ralli had started his wartime service as OC 6th Armoured Division Signals in November 1940. After a two-year posting to HQ Southern Command as Staff Officer Wireless, he demanded a more dangerous assignment and was sent off to India[35] to join Wingate's staff for Operation LONGCLOTH, the First Chindit Expedition. His main claim to fame on this occasion was to give Wingate a glass of neat gin in mistake for water.[36]

Responsible for wireless links[37] between Wingate's HQ and Chindit columns in enemy territory, Ralli went on to play an active part in Operation THURSDAY, the Second Chindit Expedition, when he was mentioned in despatches for his part in organizing the communications for the recovery of 111 Brigade. From a temporary base on the upper Brahmaputra River in northern Assam, two Sunderland flying boats took off and landed on Lake Indawgyi where, over the course of six sorties, a total of 240 wounded and sick British, Gurkha and West African troops were loaded aboard and flown back through thick clouds and vicious monsoon rainstorms. After recovering from a virulent bout of malaria, he was then posted to work with Fleming. His special project was to increase the range of the W/T sets of captured spies.[38]

Other late joiners included Major S.C.F. Pierson (Emergency Commission Indian Army) as Liaison Officer for the Division in Chungking in October 1943. He is fondly remembered by his alma mater, St Stephen's College Delhi:

Colonel S.C.F. Pierson, a jockey from the Calcutta racecourse rose to the post of lecturer in English in College. When he was a Senior Member at the High Table, he would sometimes feel his stomach turning at the thought of the hot and greasy curry for dinner and his unofficial Grace would be as follows: 'Oh God, we don't want to be rude, but must we eat this bloody food?'

In 1944 Major A.G. 'Johnnie' Johnson transferred from A Force, bringing with him links to surplus A Force deception channels.

⊰ঔ

After occupying two temporary and rather unsatisfactory billets, in October 1943 Fleming moved into the bungalow of Major Dick Costobadie and Peter Marriott,[39] the Adjutant of the Viceroy's (Mounted) Bodyguard. Now joined by Thorne, the 'three Peters' lived comfortably, their time off spent riding, duck-flighting and bathing in the Viceroy's pool. When Marriott left to go off to war, they moved as 'paying guests' into the bungalow of Jack and Kate Tweed. As Commandant of the Bodyguard, his house was considerably larger and here they remained until the war end.

Ralph Arnold, the popular novelist,[40] who had been posted to GHQ India as a public relations officer, wrote about his time in Delhi with candour and charm:

Life in Delhi, in fact, was completely unwarlike and entirely artificial. It was neatly, but probably much too cruelly, summed up by an anonymous poet:

STICKING IT OUT AT THE CECIL

Fighting the Nazis from Delhi,
Fighting the Japs from Kashmir,
Exiled from England we felt you should know
The way that we're taking it here.

Sticking it out at the Cecil,[41]
Doing our bit for the war,
Going through hell at Maiden's Hotel
Where they stop serving lunch after four.

Sticking it out at the Cecil
For the sake of the land we adore,
But never you worry, though continents shake,
Whatever befalls our morale will not break,
Provided that Wenger's don't run out of steak.
Doing our bit for the war.

Tightening our belts at Niroula's,[42]
Taking it all on the chin,
For the sake of the nation we suffer privation,
Just look at the shortage of gin.

We frequently feel that in England
They don't know the straits that we're in,
The way that we've cried at the newsreels we've seen,
(They bring it so near if you see what I mean)
And only eight bearers instead of sixteen!
Taking it all on the chin.

Roughing it at the Imperial,
Proving we're sound to the core,
We take BOR's[43] for rides in our cars,
Which is secretly rather a bore.

Doing our bit in Old Delhi,
Gad! but it's grim at the Grand,
The beer that they sell makes some men unwell,
But we're proud to see what they can stand.

> Fighting for freedom in India,
> The Freedom from want and from fear,
> Fighting like hell, for all we love well,
> That's why we rushed to get here!

People certainly worked hard enough all day, but the war seemed a long way off, and they played pretty hard all night. Old Delhi hands at parties either took you into a corner and tearfully told you all about their complicated matrimonial troubles, or played a peculiar game in which two people stood facing each other, full glasses of champagne balanced on their heads. Thus poised, they chanted this song:

> Have you seen the Sampan Man
> The Sampan Man
> The Sampan Man?
> Have you seen the Sampan Man
> Who lives in Shanghai Harbour?
> Yes, I've seen the Sampan Man
> The Sampan Man
> The Sampan Man ...

And so on until one or both of the glasses crashed to the ground amid roars of jolly laughter.

Some weeks after my arrival, on returning one evening to my tent, I found Peter Fleming waiting for me. He had been actively engaged in several clandestine operations since his days with Auxiliary Units in XXII Corps; and he was now directing some equally secret enterprise for SEAC.

'You can't,' he told me, 'go on living in this horrid little tent.'

I told him, with truth, that I was very happy in my tent. Dil [his Indian servant] had bought me a reading lamp with pink silk lampshade – I was pursued all through the war by billets, by pink silk lampshades – and I enjoyed the evening tent parties, where we sat round a log fire. After everyone else had gone away, I liked lying in bed watching the reflections of the flames flickering on the tent roof. The man in the tent next to mine had bought a monkey for 10 rupees. I was secretly envious and was thinking of making a similar purchase.

'I like my tent,' I repeated.

'Nonsense,' Peter said. 'there's no virtue in being uncomfortable when it isn't necessary ...'

I must move out of my tent, Peter assured me, and come and make a fourth at No. 10.

I tried to stick my toes in. It was unlikely, I argued, that the third Peter would want another paying guest. But of course, in the end, I went – to Dil's enormous satisfaction. He snobbishly approved of the bungalow, and had always felt that it was infra dig for his sahib to inhabit a tent. I was very glad that I did make the move.

The bungalow was extremely comfortable and bursting with servants. It had a garden full of English flowers, which were in bud one day, in full bloom the next, and dead on the third. Then they were miraculously replaced. Each of the three Peters had a horse. On Sunday afternoons we bathed in the Viceroy's swimming pool. The Peters used to go out shooting and bring back duck and other game; and then we would have a dinner party. A whole string of interesting people came, including General Wingate. Wingate had already marched his columns into Jap-held Burma and was now preparing for a larger-scale fly-in. At dinner he produced a black squashy Bible from his tunic pocket and read us long extracts from the Book of Revelations, passages which, he claimed, had a direct bearing on the campaign in South-East Asia. With his beard, his hypnotic eyes and his droning voice he put me strangely in mind of a minor prophet.

Christmas came and went. On Christmas morning Dil read me a message from his granddaughter, aged five; and the sweeper presented me with a garland of marigolds. There were more garlands waiting for us in the office, offered by the Indian clerks. 'Some wretched fellow tried to put a lot of filthy flowers round my neck,' the brigadier reported crossly. The Supreme Allied Commander came round the mess while we were eating our turkey and plum pudding. In the evening I went to church. It seemed an odd sort of Christmas.

Wavell's successor as C-in-C India in June 1943 was Sir Claude Auchinleck, who had been fired by Churchill as C-in-C Middle East the previous year. For Fleming, this change played well for D. Division since Wavell, his mentor and sponsor, remained on in India as the Viceroy and the new C-in-C, as a professional soldier, was sympathetic to the cause of deception. In addition, and of equal importance to Fleming, who was slowly and painstakingly building up his deception organization, Auchinleck knew India. He had been commissioned in the Indian Army; he spoke Punjabi; he had served on operations in the subcontinent between the wars; he had chaired the Chatfield Report which formed the basis of the modernization and expansion of the Indian Army; and he had previously been C-in-C India in 1941. Furthermore, the recently created position of Supreme Allied Commander South East Asia which superimposed a new command structure on British operations in the Far East was also temporarily filled by Auchinleck. So when he took over, it was business as usual for GSI (d). Fleming wrote to Celia in early October that

> all the big shots are in town, trying to find out how they are expected to regroup themselves under El Supremo. I hope somebody manages to get rid of Stilwell, who is a foolish and inept old man, very anti-British. I don't imagine the new set-up will affect me very much; I expect we shall plod on with a foot in either grave.[44]

How wrong he was.

All changed when Vice Admiral Lord Louis Mountbatten arrived in Delhi following his official appointment as Supreme Allied Commander that August.[45] Here was 'Prince Rupert of the Rhine', according to Philip Mason, the Secretary to the Chiefs of Staff Committee in India, 'bursting into the deliberation of a parochial church council considering whether they could afford to rehang the bells'.[46] Gone was Fleming's cosy relationship with Wavell and Bill Cawthorn with its accompanying freedom of action mandate. Although he was impressed by Mountbatten who struck him as 'incisive and full of ideas' and he found 'the newcomers very refreshing', he was wary that 'on a high level they are apt to be a little too openly contemptuous and impatient of everything that has been done here'.[47] Within a month, he concluded that 'for all their early and stimulating promise, [SEAC] are a bad bet and will remain one for some time.' Bemoaning the fact that 'you can't fight the Japanese with glamour and gadgets', he found it hard 'to take the first act of the current production of Cinderella as seriously as I should'. By the end of 1943, 'SEAC continue to make no sense at all and I am fast becoming known and loathed as a regular little pest and destructive critic.'[48]

A new HQ and Command structure was created and GSI (d), now rebranded D. Division, found itself absorbed into the burgeoning leviathan of SEAC, 'inter-allied, inter-service, all talking, all singing'.[49] Fleming reported to the newly created post of Director of Intelligence (SEAC) and to the deputy Chief of Staff, SEAC. From now on, all deception plans and operations were to be scrutinized by P. Division,[50] a new umbrella organization designed by Mountbatten with the help of the OSS General Donovan to control and coordinate the myriad of competing Allied clandestine services in South East Asia and China. Presided over by the affable Captain Gerald Garnons-Williams RN,[51] P. Division worked as a commission rather than a committee, on one level liaising extensively across SEAC and later South West Pacific Area Command, and on another level dealing with day-to-day administrative issues and allocating scarce resources to competing agencies.[52]

As a former Director of Combined Operations, Mountbatten was convinced that the future of British offensive operations against the Japanese in South

East Asia lay in amphibious operations. To this end, as early as 14 November 1943, he determined to move his HQ from Delhi to Kandy in Ceylon and set 17 March 1944 as the completion date.[53] Fleming was unimpressed. First, with his access via LCS to strategic intelligence and planning about the war against Germany, he was profoundly cynical about Mountbatten's ideas. Given the Allies' binding commitments in the Mediterranean and north-west Europe, where were sufficient numbers of landing craft going to come from? What capital ships would the Admiralty be able to make available? Secondly, it was clear to Fleming that the immediate threat lay in Burma and that was where D. Division would be primarily engaged in a land war. Thirdly, the intricate web of D. Division's channels was managed out of Delhi. Finally, D. Division's old direct report, the Directorate of Military Intelligence India, and its main customer, Fourteenth Army, not to mention its main office including D Force, were all based in northern India. So on all counts, it was nonsensical to up sticks and move 1,500 miles in the wrong direction.

As the architect of the disastrous Dieppe Raid of 19 August 1942, Mountbatten had upset the British Intelligence community by bypassing its main deception agencies when he decided to go ahead with Operation JUBILEE after the original raid, Operation RUTTER, had been cancelled on 7 July 1942. Unbeknown to him, the British Double Cross operation was feeding titbits of RUTTER to the Germans through their captured Abwehr agents. Furthermore, he chose not to consult SIS or SOE, both of which had agents on the ground. As Colonel John Hughes-Wilson[54] put it,

> the point is that the whole of Britain's exceptional intelligence-collection armoury was needed to mount a successful operation of Dieppe's scale. It was available and perfectly capable of answering all the questions. But if Mountbatten asked for the full Joint Intelligence Committee support package for Dieppe, he knew that the Committee would alert the Cabinet office and the Chiefs of Staff to his scheme to remount the raid, and they might stop him.[55] So, by bypassing the Chiefs of Staff, Mountbatten was forced to bypass the intelligence agencies … This failure to use the full intelligence resources was to cause needless casualties.

The fact that the senior British Army officer in the UK at the time, General Sir Archibald Nye, the Vice Chief of the Imperial General Staff, did not know about the raid shows how successful Mountbatten was in concealing his intentions from his own masters.

March 1944 came and went with no sign of D. Division moving to Kandy. When Fleming went to SACSEA's Operational HQ in April 1944, he described it as 'a cross between a *fête champêtre* and a Colonial Exhibition set in a tropical but still genteel version of the Isle of Wight'.[56] Philip Mason, who like GSI (d) had also been rebranded as Head of Conference Secretariat SEAC, found that

> the dreamlike artificiality of the Peradeniya Gardens … made it hard to believe our activities had much bearing on human affairs. In Delhi we had seemed much closer to wounds and battle … To remember the realities of blood and death was more difficult in Kandy, where the spotless white uniforms and gay three-cornered hats of the Wren officers flitted between the tree ferns and the orchid house, where Noel Coward came and sang to us, where the atmosphere of a large-scale *fête champêtre* could never quite be banished.[57]

On 23 May, Air Vice-Marshal John Whitworth-Jones, the Assistant Deputy Chief of Staff at SEAC, wrote a sharp memo to Fleming. Already a bête noire of D. Division whom Fleming had described to Celia as 'a cross between Napoleon and a giant gooseberry and easily the most vicious of all my boobies',[58] Whitworth-Jones reminded him that, given D. Division had been officially formed within HQ.SEAC in March 1944, 'the present state of the organization [of D. Division] and its general status is not what was envisaged in the plan which was approved by the Supreme Allied Commander. I feel that the time has now come for the whole situation regarding D. Division to be reviewed.'[59] Since Fleming was due in London in June for an LCS conference, Whitworth-Jones suggested that the meeting should take place on 30 May and that Mountbatten should chair it. Due to the unavailability of the participants, it never took place. By the end of August, tempers had frayed.

Fleming had requested on 27 August for the move to Kandy of the main HQ of D. Division to be postponed:

> The Division will seize up during move which at present timed when maximum activity will be required from us … Switch over from direct to remote control of India-based channels extremely tricky business at best of times… am strongly averse to incurring risks and temporary loss of efficiency involved at this important juncture. Most anxious to conform to the Supreme Allied Commander's wishes in this matter but foresee serious operational disadvantages in adhering to programme. Grateful for early decision. No difficulty in providing planning echelon from Delhi to Calcutta, Imphal etc. at short notice.

Whitworth-Jones refused to budge, insisting that Fleming relocated to Kandy by 1 October – 'your failure to develop Policy and Plans Section D. Division this HQ is now placing us in an embarrassing position … Please signal a firm assurance that you will effect your transfer to Supreme Allied Commander's HQ.'[60] Fleming was not the only recalcitrant. Colonel Leo Steveni, the Director of SIS in India, was equally reluctant to move his Delhi and Calcutta stations to Kandy. It was only after he had been replaced in mid-1944 by Brigadier Philip Bowden-Smith that SIS completed its move to Kandy during October. SOE, by far the largest British clandestine organization in South East Asia, held out until December when Colin Mackenzie reluctantly moved his Meerut HQ to Ceylon.

Fleming, uncharacteristically, was almost at his wit's end. In a letter to Celia, he mused that 'the trouble with my nominal boss in Kandy ... time and effort are wasted and it makes me feel sad to be under someone who has absolutely no idea of what one does and how and why one does it.'[61] He signalled Horder, who was now established in Kandy as Policy and Plans HQ D. Division, to tell Whitworth-Jones that

> I cannot comply with orders [if it meant moving his main HQ to Kandy] unless you are prepared to accept full responsibility for effect on enemy with whom we are now in continuous contact and to whom, by 1 October, we shall presumably be transmitting deception plans at high pressure. Extremely sorry to appear difficult but request you realise D. Division like all deception staffs serves two masters. A rocket to D. Division from Kandy hurts nobody of importance. A rocket to D. Division from Tokyo can have repercussions on our forward troops.[62]

Unswayed by this argument, Whitworth-Jones continued to chase Fleming. On 2 September, he signalled him that 'policy decisions in your field must be taken in Kandy in very near future. It is only here that real and fictional operations can be linked. Therefore would you visit Kandy during week commencing 3 September to discuss urgent outstanding problems. We will take this opportunity to clear up the question of the move.'[63] A series of muddled meeting arrangements then followed, with Fleming missing and incurring the displeasure of Mountbatten at Comilla on 8 September, having been advised there was no place for him in the entourage on the Supreme Allied Commander's tour of the front line and Simla. In any case, Fleming himself was engaged in meetings with Eleventh Army Group and also had to fly up to Chungking to meet with the Soviet Ambassador who was anxious to see him. The outcome of this trying tussle was a win for D. Division: its main HQ remained in situ in Delhi with a small Advanced HQ attached to Mountbatten's staff in Kandy, a Tactical HQ in Calcutta and Liaison Officers with key front-line formations.

In the meantime, Captain G.A. Garnons-Williams,[64] the commander of P. Division, had met with General MacArthur in Brisbane on 19 August 1944. Unlike Colin Mackenzie, the head of SOE's Force 136 in the Far East, Garnons-Williams had excellent relations with the Americans, in particular General 'Wild Bill' Donovan's OSS. Notoriously possessive of his own turf and with a dislike of Special Forces of all shades and complexions, MacArthur surprised the P. Division chief by requesting the assistance of SEAC in helping him formulate and execute deception plans in the South West Pacific Area theatre. While emphasizing that any such plans would need to conform to Admiral Nimitz's Pacific Area strategy, he recognized that the SEAC theatre and China provided the best 'switch board' for deception operations and therefore proposed to send two US Deception Liaison officers to Kandy. He also suggested that SEAC Deception Officers should go to Brisbane to assist in the organization of his deception staff.[65]

This offer was warmly greeted by D. Division who knew only too well the difficulties of communicating with and sharing information with the Americans and their system of devolving deception strategy and measures to their Theatre Force Commanders. Fleming responded, 'the sooner, the better'. However, he qualified this enthusiasm by urging any such mission to include an officer who had a detailed knowledge of the military realities of South West Pacific Area; in other words, a staff officer from the rarefied political environment of Washington would be next to useless. He went on to urge Mountbatten to seek high level assistance from London in following up this overture from the Americans. The result of his initiative was relayed to General Pownall, the Chief of Staff at SEAC, by General Ismay in London:[66]

At the request of Dickie Mountbatten and on a suggestion made by Peter Fleming, we are sending out Colonel Wingate, Deputy Controlling Officer to Colonel Bevan, for a short visit to SEAC so that you can be put as completely as possible in the general deception picture and so that the best possible co-operation may be secured between the LCS and D. Division, SEAC.

The present position is complicated by the fact that Washington has not yet issued an overall deception policy for the war against Japan, and have apparently not yet established deception staffs, as we know them, within American theatres in the Far East. It is just possible that both these questions may be settled while Wingate is with you, in which case his visit should be very opportune.

It will, in any case, be helpful to the LCS, who are anxious to gain a more intimate knowledge of the deception problems within SEAC and to render D. Division every possible assistance. Wingate knows India and the East very well and his numerous contacts with Indian institutions, including the Delhi Intelligence Bureau (DIB), should be helpful. He also knows the whole story of the deception side of OVERLORD and could spill it to a very limited audience. Though the Japanese problem is no doubt somewhat different, the experience gained in Europe during the last few years may be of some value.

Ronald Wingate duly set off on his tour of the Far East in November 1944 and in his post-tour debrief he pointed out that 'we cannot have one man running Policy and Plans at Supreme Allied Commander's HQ and, at the same time, looking after the executive elements in the field'. He therefore proposed a separation of these roles and, having endorsed Fleming as the ideal commander of 'D' force, undertook to come up with the name of a suitable candidate to head up the Policy and Plans Division in Kandy. This was music to the ears of Whitworth-Jones, who saw it as a triumphant result in his long-running battle against Fleming's obstinacy in refusing to move to Kandy. Fleming himself was delighted, writing to Celia that 'Old Ronald Wingate's visit is a great success. I think it will make a lot of difference to us; he is a shrewd old boy.'[67]

In London, Bevan was equally delighted and wrote to Mountbatten in February 1945 that he was hoping to release Wingate for a further six to nine months as chief staff officer to D. Division in Kandy. His frustration with the Americans was palpable for there had been no follow-up to the Garnons-Williams meeting with MacArthur the previous autumn. It was time to try again, pointing out to South West Pacific Command that SEAC deception plans could well compromise real SWPA operations if there was no close co-operation between the two and, furthermore, D. Division had secret channels to the Japanese which could be used for SWPA deception plans. Bevan felt that Mountbatten himself had the best chance of persuading MacArthur when they next met in April or May and that a staff officer such as Wingate, who knew about deception matters and who could go over details with SWPA staff, should accompany him.[68]

Meanwhile, in January 1945, D. Division was reorganized[69] under the oversight of General 'Boy' Browning, a fellow Grenadier officer of Fleming, who had arrived as Chief of Staff SEAC in December 1944. In effect, it was split into two components with D. Division, now purely a policy and plans unit, forming an integral part of the Supreme Commander's HQ and responsible for preparation and co-ordination of SEAC deception plans as well as liaison with LCS, Joint Security Control and deception staffs of other theatres.

The rump of D. Division together with D Force became Force 456, a new 'Command Unit', and was responsible for the implementation of approved deception plans. It retained control of all special channels and the all-important role of advising Force and formation commanders through officers attached to their HQs on the preparation of local deception plans and the deployment of deception units and equipment in the field. In his inimitable way, Fleming explained to Celia that 'thanks to Ronald Wingate's sage advice, we are going to be reorganized and they are going to have a lovely shop window in Kandy … and my show is going to become Force Something or Other, which will leave me much freer to play with the Japanese.'[70]

The new head of the restructured D. Division turned out to be none other than Ronald Wingate who was appointed Colonel General Staff, D. Division at Mountbatten's HQ in March 1945 after his work in the European Theatre had come to an end. It was a good choice for his strengths as an experienced diplomat and civil servant[71] and his familiarity with the art of strategic deception complemented Fleming's ingenuity and expertise in dreaming up and executing complex tactical deception plans. Furthermore, the two men knew each other well having worked together within the LCS orbit.

To an outside observer, the reorganization could appear to have resulted in the demotion of Fleming, a construction that found favour with several senior officers in the corridors of Mountbatten's sprawling HQ in Kandy. For however well protected he was in India by Wavell as Viceroy and Auchinleck as C-in-C, Fleming's refusal to comply with the Supreme Allied Commander's instructions to move his main HQ to Kandy, and his frequent forays to the front line in Arakan had combined to give him a certain notoriety in Kandy. What is now clear is that it was Fleming himself who had cleverly finessed a solution to the problem of being over-extended. Oblivious to any sleight, inferred or intended, his agenda remained constant, namely to bring to bear the sophisticated deception apparatus, which he had so painstakingly assembled and fine-tuned over the last three years, on the concluding phases of the war with Japan. For the next eighteen months, there was everything to play for, from the invasion and recapture of Malaya and Singapore to the eviction of Japanese troops from Thailand, French Indo-China, the Dutch East Indies, not to mention Operation OLYMPIC, the planned invasion of the main islands of Japan herself.

Wingate thoroughly enjoyed his new role as titular head and roving ambassador of D. Division. It took him back to his early adventures in the Middle East and India. 'I wish I had the pen of Peter Fleming,' he wrote,[72]

and could write of the odd journeys I made, hitch-hiking in aeroplanes in wartime … flying around Karachi aerodrome for hours in a York, because the wheels would not come down, doing sick-making aerobatics in the high heavens in a final successful attempt to make them come down; bouncing off the runway at Colombo in a small plane, which was hit by a squall and only saved by the skill of the Indian pilot. Flying over the Hump in a C2 packed with American troops – we all had to wear parachutes, why I cannot think, as in no circumstances could they have been of any use to us. We struck a monsoon storm on the way and went up to 18,000 feet without oxygen. Everyone was green and sick, and when we reached Kunming … we could not see a thing owing to the fog. Round and round the pilot flew in an effort to exhaust our petrol, and finally we landed in a field packed with aircraft, pulling up a few inches from a big bomber.

It was a lot more exciting than his previous sedentary life in the LCS's office at Storey's Gate in London.

Chapter 13

Sleight of hand in the order of battle

The principal task allocated by Fleming to Major Peter Thorne was Strategic Deception and specifically to exaggerate the Allied Order of Battle, initially to deter the Japanese from attacking India and, later, to convince them that Britain had sufficient forces to launch overland or seaborne attacks long before it actually had enough landing craft or properly trained assault troops available. Thorne wrote that

> in this context a notional Order of Battle meant the one we wanted the Japanese to accept as genuine. It was composed of both bogus and real units and formations. One could, for instance, have a notional Army Corps consisting of one real and two bogus divisions, with some of their constituent brigades and battalions being real or in the process of formation, but with the majority being non-existent though plausible sounding. The fact that Japanese Intelligence had a good picture of the 1941/42 Order of Battle of the Army in India, but only guesswork about how the Army was going to expand to make good its losses, gave D. Division ample opportunity to create a whole shoal of bogus units.[1]

Sir Ronald Wingate saw the Order of Battle as central to deception:

> The weapon of deception is of very little use unless the side using it has the initiative, or wishes to take the initiative. The maxim of concentration of all available forces at the decisive point implies that you intend to attack the enemy, and the other side of the medal is that he should be induced to move as much of his forces as possible away from the decisive point which you wish to attack. That he will not do so entirely may be taken for granted, but any weakening of his resistance at the point which you intend to attack will

be a contribution to your success. The plans of opposing commanders are always based upon their appreciation of the other side's 'order of battle'. Where exactly are his formations? What is their composition and strength? Deception is based on producing in the mind of the enemy's intelligence a precise but false picture of our own order of battle designed to make him conclude that the main threat, or in any case a strong threat, which he must provide against, is due somewhere other than our intended objective.[2]

There was a peculiar Indian slant on the subterfuge employed since entirely new units could be formed from groups hitherto considered unsuitable by the British who traditionally had a penchant for the martial races of North West India, the Sikhs, Rajputanis, Punjabis and so on. Thorne gives as examples the Mahar Regiment from a Maharatta sub-cast and the Chamars from the Sikh sweeper class. Given a sprinkling of good officers and NCOs, they proved themselves in battle to be quite as good as the average Sikh battalion drawn from the higher castes. In addition, the princely states like Hyderabad and Kashmir made some of their home service battalions, normally only employed in quasi-police duties, available for use overseas. Hence the risk of a newly identified unit or formation being recognized by the Japanese as bogus – and thus 'blowing' an agent reporting its existence – was never very great, always provided D. Division was duly economical with lies. In fact, Japanese Intelligence was extremely credulous about new identifications, even by the standards of other intelligence staffs. As early as November 1943 captured enemy documents showed they had estimated the Allied strength in India and South East Asia at nearly fifty-two divisions. In fact 72 per cent of these formations were the creation of D. Division.

On 21 December 1944, an uncharacteristically excited Fleming sent a report to LCS and the Directors of Intelligence in Delhi and Kandy. Bletchley Park had intercepted and decoded a telegram giving Tokyo's estimate of the Allied Order of Battle in various theatres in reply to a request from the Japanese Military Attaché in Berlin[3] for 'exchange intelligence' to give to the Germans.[4] As at 26 November 1944, the Japanese had identified nine infantry divisions (2nd, 6th, 20th, 32nd, 33rd, 34th, 60th, 64th and 70th), one armoured division, the 26th, and one airborne division, the 3rd. So what were the facts behind these eleven divisions the Japanese had located in India?

There were in fact only two divisions in India, 2nd and 36th Infantry Divisions, the latter consisting of only two brigades. D. Division had created nine notional Divisions – 2nd, 21st, 32nd, 33rd, 36th, 64th and 70th Infantry Divisions, 26th Armoured Division and 3rd Airborne Division. The discrepancies between the details of Tokyo's estimate and D. Division's notional Order of Battle could be explained by 6th Infantry Division being the same as the factual 70th Infantry Division which had been disbanded; 20th Infantry Division had been conflated with the notional 21st Infantry Division; and Tokyo had probably confused the

34th Infantry Division, a notional formation in the Mediterranean area, with the notional 34th Indian Division.

Fleming concluded that 'even after allowing a reasonable measure of success to deception activities, Imperial HQ's margin of error, amounting to over 500%, seems wider than would be expected from a modern General Staff, and it is difficult to resist the conclusion that their Intelligence Staff Duties are, on occasion, erratic.'

～

Since June 1943, D. Division had been using a London-controlled channel called SUNRISE[5] to feed information to the Japanese Military Attaché in Stockholm, who in turn would pass it to Tokyo and would invariably share it with his German opposite numbers in Sweden as well. It was highly rated as an intercept of May 1943 demonstrated: 'To judge from these reports the reliability of the London intelligence is comparatively high. Accordingly, please obtain all available intelligence from this source in future.'[6] A steady stream of TRUE/FALSE stories were sent through SUNRISE until October 1944, when an alarmed Bevan called a temporary halt.

Writing to Fleming on 11 October 1944, Bevan expressed his misgivings not just about the SUNRISE material but about the whole inflated SEAC Order of Battle deception strategy.

> I can well understand your questioning the right of LCS to tamper with SUNRISE material dealing with SEAC Order of Battle. I will try and explain the position as we see it.

> LCS is responsible for co-ordination of plans as between SEAC and Washington. Through nobody's fault SEAC has to all intents and purposes had no main operational plan during the last year. Without such a plan it is extremely difficult, if not impossible, to know how best to treat the strength, Order of Battle and dispositions of Allied land, sea and air forces. Originally, of course, your plan was to discourage Japanese invasion of India and exaggeration of Allied forces in India was the natural corollary. However, I have not yet seen any Order of Battle plan with an operational objective approved by SEAC. When therefore I notice false information on this subject being passed to the enemy, I can only assume that it is in implementation of some general deception policy or plan of which I have no knowledge. (I wrote to you in February and March but so far have had no reply.)

> The last thing in the world I want to do is to stick spokes into your Order of Battle wheel, but I must know what your plan is and its object, otherwise you may for all I know be doing things which run counter to other Japanese theatres.

> During the last year the Japanese have apparently increased their divisions in Burma from four to ten. To what extent D. Division is responsible I do not

know, nor do I know whether such reinforcements are desirable from the Supreme Commander's standpoint. In view of DRACULA [planned seaborne invasion of Rangoon] and CAPITAL [planned reconquest of northern and central Burma] I don't imagine these extra divisions are very welcome, though I dare say that SEAC may have taken the view that no deception plan could ever prevent reinforcement of Burma to some extent, especially in view of the Japs' crazy idea of our strength.

I hope the above will give you a broad picture of the situation from our standpoint. As soon as we know the object of your approved operational or Order of Battle plans, then implementation through SUNRISE, or any other channel, becomes a purely routine matter. If on the other hand you start exaggerating, minimising or juggling with your forces without apparent relation to any approved plan, it is, I think, reasonable enough for us to enquire what it's all about since such action is liable to influence Japanese dispositions in other theatres. As you know, a great deal has been done in Europe during the last few years on Order of Battle deception, but this has invariably been based on an Order of Battle plan with an operational objective approved by the theatre commander. Curiously enough, exaggeration of forces has invariably been the policy followed up to now, but it is worthwhile remembering that both 'A' Force and 'Ops. B' are now furiously trying to reduce their build-up in accordance with new policy. Exaggeration is therefore by no means always the right answer.

On the assumption that SEAC's inflated Order of Battle was responsible for forcing the Japanese to increase their troop dispositions in Burma, Bevan was indeed right to be concerned and to fire a shot across Fleming's bows. As it turned out, his letter crossed in the post with one from Fleming dated 23 September. It began on a conciliatory note:

I don't feel at all strongly about any of the individual cuts which you have made in the (I'm afraid) haphazard and inchoate mass of material we have been sending you, but I'm not altogether happy about the principles involved in making the cuts.

Then, after explaining how SUNRISE was only one (although 'a jolly good one') of a multitude of channels used by SEAC, Fleming gets to the nub of the matter:

What it boils down to (I suggest) is that, when misgivings arise on Order of Battle or other strategical issues, LCS will have to close its eyes, cross its fingers and rely on the judgement of D. Division. Now that what may be called the THIN ICE AGE is drawing to a close and a firm Deception plan is in sight,

I hope that misgivings will arise but rarely; and when they do I suggest that I should be asked by signal to explain and justify the particular items involved.

The only important point at issue in the material under reference is the old and vexed question of whether or not SEAC should build up an airborne threat pending a final decision on strategy. When I was in London I explained verbally why this build-up was practically the only firm plank in my policy during the interim period; and in this context you may be reassured by the following extracts from the 'Cover Plan and Deception' paras of Fourteenth Army's plan for CAPITAL, which were written without reference to D. Division on 23 June 1944:

31 It is to be anticipated that the Japanese will be fully alive to the probability of airborne and air-transported operations into Burma and that we shall achieve tactical surprise only by deception in the size of our forces, their objectives and the time of the operations.

32 We recommend that the cover plan should therefore provide for an airborne and air-transported force of the size the Japanese believe us to possess, and that its objective should be in the area Prome-Rangoon. It should also provide for an amphibious force aimed at objectives between Taungup and Rangoon, including major naval demonstrations using carrier-borne aircraft.

I am sorry to have gone into this matter at such wearisome length but it does seem to me potentially important for the future … and I hope you won't think that I'm being difficult or muttering to myself about apron-strings and remote control.

I'm very sorry not to have kept you well posted in this matter. The trouble has been:

a) That I haven't hitherto felt it was worthwhile or indeed fair to clutter up your files with a mass of intricate and exotic information.

b) That the information is <u>so</u> intricate and <u>so</u> exotic that most of it would have meant nothing to anyone unfamiliar with this theatre.
… Sorry to have been so prolix.

Bevan had not been copied in on a 9 October letter which Fleming wrote to Brigadiers General Staff at Army and Corps level on the subject of the Dummy Order of Battle.[7] It demonstrated that Fleming was totally in touch with the realities of the uses and abuses of a dummy Order of Battle on the ground in the context of the South East Asia battleground. He laid out his impressive inventory of bogus formations and counselled commanders on how best to use them to their advantage.

1   Over the past three years the Japanese High Command, with the co-operation of D. Division, have built up a somewhat erroneous estimate of our Order of Battle in India/SEA Commands. Their margin of error, until recently slightly in excess of 100 per cent, is likely to increase further over the coming months and may do so sharply after the defeat of Germany.

2   Plan FLABBERGAST calls for the mounting of certain large-scale seaborne and airborne operations.[8] After forces have been allotted for these operations, from within D. Division's resources, there still remains a sizeable (though imaginary) army for employment in support of the operations of Eleventh Army group. The dummy Order of Battle requirements of the DRACULA[9] Force Commander will, when they are known, be met by resources released for other theatres. The total notional (notional – either imaginary, or real but not operational) ground forces controlled by D. Division in this theatre are in the order of:

    a   Armoured

       i   British – one Division and two independent Brigades

       ii   Indian – two Divisions

    b   Infantry

       i   British – four Divisions

       ii   Indian – nine Divisions

    c   Airborne

       i   British – one Division

       ii   Indian – one Division

       iii African – one Division

    d   Special Service Troops

       i   British – two Brigades

Total: Twenty equivalent Divisions

3   Experience has shown that the mere existence of these forces in our back areas has little influence on Japanese Intelligence HQ and none on the mind of Commander Burma Area Army, who in March 1944 set out with three Divisions to conquer a sub-continent which Tokyo had told him was garrisoned by fifty plus (divisions).

4   It is accordingly felt that a proportion of our notional forces could be more usefully employed as tactical rather than as strategical reserves and that, if sub-allotted to Corps, their minatory or diversionary value

should be capable of exploitation at the expense of (e.g.) Japanese Divisional Commanders, who may be inclined to take a more realistic view of the odds against them than do the staffs in Rangoon and Tokyo. A suggested allocation of D. Division formations is shown in Appendix A.

5 It is suggested that these formations should be regarded as Corps reserves to be used by the Corps Commander (who will in every case have the assistance of a D. Division staff officer) in support of local deception plans. It is emphasised that all such plans must be submitted for approval and co-ordination through the D. Division Staff Officer attached to Corps HQ, to Advanced Section D. Division at Fourteenth Army HQ, who – should the plan have other than purely local implications from an Order of Battle point of view – will refer it to the D. Division Staff officer attached to Eleventh Army HQ for a decision by the Head of D. Division. Experience on other theatres has proved conclusively that some procedure on these lines, cumbrous though it may appear, is essential owing to the delicate and complex structure of a Dummy Order of Battle.

6 It is further emphasized that the threat to security involved in committing notional formations to forward areas is not negligible and that the compromise of one such formation may impair or even destroy the enemy's faith, not only in other formations, but in the sources from which he has derived his intelligence about them. The need to protect these sources is vital in the interest of future operations and it is requested that Commanders should take all possible security measures to safeguard the military reputation of the formations allotted to them.

7 It is suggested that the tentative allocations proposed could usefully serve as a basis for discussion between the senior officer of Corps Staffs and the D. Division officers who are now in the process of joining Corps HQs …

8 The following points with regards to notional formations are perhaps worth pointing out:

   a The allotment of notional forces to a formation does not increase its strength in the eyes of the enemy until such time as the enemy is informed of the transaction. The release of this information can be timed to conform with a plan.

   b Notional formations committed to forward areas can, if the situation requires it,

      i   Be transferred to other sectors.

      ii Be withdrawn into reserve.

    iii Be disbanded.

    iv Mutiny (in case of native troops).

    v Be otherwise disposed of.

  c The allotment of notional airborne forces to a formation with an airborne role would naturally not be revealed to the enemy until after the assault phase of the fly-in, after which the notional forces can be used for build-up or diversionary purposes.

9 In accordance with practice in other theatres the normal method of disseminating proposals of the kind contained in this paper would be through D. Division officers at the HQs concerned. Owing to a temporary shortage of staff in this Division this procedure cannot be adopted at this stage and addressees are asked to excuse the somewhat eccentric staff duties which have been resorted to in the present instance with a view to avoiding delay.

∾

Fleming's conclusion as to how successful D. Division's Order of Battle Deception activities were is tempered by his poor assessment of Japanese competence:

> Relatively meagre though Mountbatten's resources in manpower were when he took over command, the imaginary forces of which he simultaneously assumed control were both numerous and well-found. In November 1943, captured documents proved that Imperial HQ estimated the strength of Allied forces in SEAC and India Commands at 51¾ divisions. Part of this exaggeration was the result of spontaneous self-deception by the Japanese General Staff, but a considerable proportion (72 per cent) of it can be ascribed to D. Division's efforts to build up the dummy Order of Battle which is an essential background to all strategic deception. As time went on, D. Division's share in Tokyo's fantastic misconception of our strength increased; and when hostilities ceased, despite the withdrawal of the Chinese divisions of the Northern Combat Area Command, the forces believed by the Japanese to be poised for a series of rapid blows against their western perimeter included some six Army Corps and one Airborne Corps, each comprising three or more divisions and supported by a large reserve of trained formations.

> But here again, though D. Division succeeded in completely misleading the enemy about the strength and composition of the forces in SEAC, they were up against the low standard of training and thick wits which hampered them in other directions. All the available evidence goes to show that the

Japanese Command, both in the field and on a high level, had only the most rudimentary grasp of the technique involved in assessing their opponent's Order of Battle.[10] In D. Division's experience the Japanese were virtually incapable of assimilating any Order of Battle Intelligence which dealt with identifications below a divisional level. They could not, for instance, be relied upon to identify a division from one of its component brigades even when they knew its composition; and it was a waste of time to give them information about battalions or regiments, since, although they were glad to get it, they were unable to make any deductions from it.

Chapter 14

The conjurors take to the field

The business of strategic deception resided in the highest echelons of wartime governments and their Chiefs of Staff. For commanders of front-line formations and units, where every yard of territory regained was paid for in lives and expenditure of scant resources, tactical deception became an integral part of operational planning and execution. In a pamphlet dated December 1943, senior commanders were given basic guidelines on deception. Although unsigned, the pamphlet has all the hallmarks of Dudley Clarke and his A Force team.

DEFINITION
Tactical deception can be defined as the deliberate misleading of the enemy force within a Theatre of Operations. In order to make the enemy DO SOMETHING which will assist our operations in that Theatre.

METHOD
The deception plan should aim at feeding the enemy with pieces of information which he imagines he has obtained for himself without our knowledge, which pieces of information, when fitted together by him, will make up the deception STORY. The story should be so framed that it will make the enemy DO what is required in the OBJECT.

TYPES OF DECEPTION
Tactical deception can be divided into two types.

1   Deception which is employed to further a definite operational plan.

2   Deception, which does not form part of any particular operational plan, but is aimed at minimising casualties to both men and material in either the forward or rear areas.

RESPONSIBILITY FOR PLANNING

At the present moment tactical deception is planned and co-ordinated at the Main Headquarters of a Theatre of Operations by a specialist staff who operate under the Commander in Chief. This small staff will normally work under the orders of the Chief of the General Staff, but will work in the closest co-operation with Operations and Intelligence.

PLANNING

A deception plan designed to cover a particular operation should be based on the outline operational plan. It is necessary for the outline deception plan to be agreed to directly after the production of the outline operational plan and before the issue of the detailed plan, as the deception plan may contain various requirements which the final operational plan will have to include. It therefore follows that the officer responsible for the production of the deception plan should be kept fully informed during all stages of planning.

OBJECTS

The object of a deception plan, as already stated, is to make the enemy DO SOMETHING to assist the operational plan. For instance, if a Commander wishes to attack a Point A and hold only at B, he might set his deception planner the following object:

'To reduce to the minimum the enemy forces disposed against A' or, should the enemy forces already be favourably disposed, 'to retain the enemy forces at present disposed against B'.

In framing the object, the Commander should never require the planner to make the enemy THINK SOMETHING. The reactions of the enemy to this THOUGHT may not in fact assist the operational plan. It should be left to the deception planner, whose task it is to study enemy reactions, to decide what the enemy should know, in order to obtain the object, which must be to make the enemy DO SOMETHING.

RESOURCES AVAILABLE TO ACHIEVE THE OBJECT

Moves of formations and units which form part of the operational plan

It is often possible to employ the actual move of formations, etc., which moves form part of the operational plan, to assist the deception plan. For instance, if a force is moving from A to attack B, it is often of assistance to allow the enemy to observe the move as far as point C, but thereafter take the maximum precautions to prevent him observing the further move to Point B, whilst by various methods, the move is indicated to Point X. The interest of the enemy will already have been aroused by the time the formations, etc., reach Point C and he will be prepared to receive either visual or other indications that the force has arrived at the final false destination, Point X, provided there is sufficient genuine operational reason for its arrival there.

Moves designed solely to assist the deception plan

It may be necessary in order to build up the story, to move formations and units for the sole purpose of assisting the deception plan. With this course, as few people as possible should be aware that these moves do not form part of normal operational plans.

Dummy equipment

It is possible to indicate to the enemy, both through his air, and to a degree his ground reconnaissance, and at times through his agents, the location of imaginary formations and units in any particular area by the employment of dummy equipment. The production of dummy equipment such as tanks, vehicles, landing craft, etc., is the responsibility of both 'camouflage' and certain special organizations. Dummy equipment is available to a greater or lesser degree in all Theatres of Operations.

When dummy equipment is used to indicate the presence of formations, units, etc., it is necessary that as much real activity as possible should exist in those areas. For instance, if it is intended to indicate a brigade in an area, then that area should be protected by real anti-aircraft guns and there should be a certain amount of real movement by men and motor transport to create a dust, cookhouse fires, etc. It may also be necessary to create a certain amount of signals traffic.

Signals

The enemy obtains information as to our intention, etc., from our signal traffic. It therefore follows that it is possible to feed the enemy with false information by way of this traffic. The framing of dummy messages requires great care and should always be done in full consultation with Intelligence and Signals. Whenever possible, dummy messages should be supported by either real or dummy indications.

Reconnaissance

The following types of reconnaissance may be employed to mislead the enemy.

- Ground reconnaissance for staging areas, for taking over or for reinforcing parts of the front, etc.
- Patrol activity to gain information of areas of notional attacks
- Air reconnaissance

Where possible these recces should be supported by signal traffic.

Artillery registration and bombing
Artillery registration and preparatory bombing of an area will give an indication
to the enemy which will support the deception plan.

Administrative preparations
The administrative preparations before an operation probably disclose the
extent and direction of that operation to a greater degree than any other factor.
These preparations include the creation of ammunition dumps, the movement
of convoys and the mass of signal traffic which usually passes prior to the
operation. It therefore follows that if dummy dumps and false administrative
traffic are created, the enemy may be misled as to our intentions.

The implementation of an Army-level tactical deception plan constituted
a major undertaking. For example, in the timetable for Fourteenth Army's
tactical deception plan on the Thazi-Taunggyi-Loilem road in support of factual
operations, D-Day was scheduled for 25/26 March 1945. Detailed deception
activities started five days before and included a range of ruses from diversionary
photo reconnaissance flights, simulated parachute and notional supply drops to
feint operations by SOE teams behind enemy lines. Once the factual operation
was under way, the deception plan was to continue for a further eight days,
building in intensity with more dummy parachute drops accompanied by a full
orchestra of pyrotechnic devices. For the planning staff, such plans necessitated
liaising with a host of players including East Asia Command, SOE, Political
Warfare Division, Allied Land Forces South East Asia, OSS, 10th Airforce and of
course D. Division itself.

In a November 1943 discussion paper, Fleming argued for the creation of a
special force within D. Division to facilitate Diversionary Operations. He had
concluded that while the Army had adequate battlefield deception capabilities in
support of overland operations, there was no equivalent naval capability. Given
that the Japanese perimeter in SEAC followed the coastline from Thailand to
Akyab on the Bay of Bengal, this surely was a serious oversight. Likewise, the
lack of any specialist RAF capability inhibited the ability of field commanders to
stage deception/diversionary operations on the enemy's flanks and in his rear.
Once again, Fleming was challenging, albeit in a thoroughly constructive way,
the endemic complacency that characterized much of the military administration
in India.

1   The importance of diversionary operations by small forces of all three services is very great in this theatre. The reasons for this are too obvious to elaborate.

2   Diversions – as opposed to demonstrations in strength or subsidiary operations against secondary objectives which are capable of having a diversionary effect – will normally require forces of the following broad categories:

   a   Fighting forces – that is to say troops, naval units or a/c equipped and trained or small-scale offensive operations.

   b   Specialist forces, who, covered by the above, will deploy and operate various forms of deceptive equipment which, in the fifth year of war, has reached an advanced stage of development and deserves to be taken seriously.

3   It is suggested that consideration should be given to the formation (when resources become available) of a small but as far as possible self-contained force of all three services (herein after called D Force) to train for and execute diversionary operations. This force would:

   a   Be under the direct command of SEAC, detachments being sub-allocated as required to Force Commanders for specific operations;

   b   Be under Naval command and probably predominantly naval in composition and outlook;

   c   Have a small staff of its own (including officers to deal with planning and research).

4   In regard to naval elements the present situation is that the Army in this theatre have taken the lead in preparing for diversionary and deceptive operations. Specifically, the following Army units capable of furthering the deception of the enemy in the field already exist:

   a   Special Duties Section …

   b   303 Independent Brigade …

   c   Two Light Scout Car Companies …

5   No corresponding Naval or RAF units have been allotted to or trained in diversionary activities.

6   This emphasis would appear to be wrong in so far as it devotes our main diversionary preparations to overland operations. This was for obvious reasons a sound policy in the Middle East but bears little relation to either realities or possibilities in this theatre, where 90 per cent of the worthwhile diversionary opportunities require the employment of either sea or airborne forces and equipment.

7   For instance, the use of mule or jeep-borne Camouflage B equipment
     with slow-moving, heavily-spied-on forces advancing into Burma can at
     best achieve only a tactical and very temporary effect. Communications
     are such that no very startling operational noises can plausibly be made;
     and in order to make a plausible noise (e.g. a mule column in bivouac at
     A) you need the best part of a mule column at A to carry the equipment
     to make the noise.

8   To sum up, the most effective diversions will in general be operations
     conducted against or at the enemy's rear or flanks; and in this theatre
     the enemy's rear and flanks are not normally accessible – except on a
     purely tactical level – to other than sea or airborne forces. The exception
     is the case of the Long Range Penetration forces; but the amount of
     deceptive equipment which these forces can carry either on the march
     or (if the equipment is supplied by air) from the dropping area to the
     scene of operations is severely limited.

9   It would seem to follow that a high proportion of our deceptive
     equipment will, or should be, used by or in conjunction with naval or air
     forces.

10   Sideshows and gadgets are expensive hobbies and sometimes tie up
     personnel and equipment who would be better employed in a more
     orthodox role. At the same time the formation of D Force would have the
     following advantages:

     a   It would ensure that such diversionary operations as were required
          in support of an operational plan were carried out effectively. In
          the absence of a D Force it is a natural tendency for Commanders
          to grudge, and in the event to stint, the forces which a plan calls
          upon them to detach for purely diversionary operations (e.g.
          Photographic Reconnaissance Unit, bombing, beach recces,
          raids etc., undertaken against objectives other than the real one).
          In the event of an unforeseen shortage or unexpected casualties
          these operations, regardless of their potential importance which is
          sometimes very great, will generally be the first to suffer.

     b   It would substantially reduce the gap between the Backroom Boys
          and the Japanese by enabling special equipment to be tested and
          trained realistically on an inter-service basis. Our experience with the
          Special Duties Section has shown the importance of this. At present
          the career of a new device tends to be rapid and successful up to
          the 'first demonstration' phase but slow and haphazard thereafter
          i.e. during the phases when it should be undergoing operational
          tests, used on training, having scales for its issue worked out,

and generally so to speak winning its place on the G.1098.[1] The inevitable results of this are:

i That devices are not tested as quickly and fully as they should be, particularly in such matters as packing, waterproofing, length of delayed action fuse likely to be required on operations, etc.

ii With the exception of 303 Independent Brigade virtually no troops in the Command ever see, let alone train with, the relatively small but increasing supply of devices which are now available

11 An example of what is meant in the preceding paragraph has been provided by the development of BRUNYATES (dummy parachutist) and their accessories. A great deal of practical and imaginary work has been done on the 'bodies' themselves, and it seems generally agreed that these devices will be required on operations. But no serious tests on the requisite scale have been carried out because of the difficulty of getting aircraft for this purpose and the improbability of the aircraft, when available, being a type likely to be used on dummy dropping operations. This need for adequate tests as opposed to occasional staged demonstrations, was well illustrated in the ME when we sent a specimen PINTAIL to A Force who are the deception staff in that theatre. They handed it over to the local 'Backroom Boys' to copy in large quantities for use on Operation HUSKY. (Note: The Special Duties Section design, which is foolproof, was modified. Lack of adequate supervision of native labour, and lack of tests which would have discovered defects, resulted in faulty construction, the destruction of one of our aircraft and a general and unavoidable loss of confidence in PINTAILS and deception devices generally).

12 A further factor in favour of D Force is what may be called the question of outlook. Officers and men join the fighting services with the idea of killing the enemy, not of fooling him, and they are in general slow to see the operational connection between the two processes. Take the following examples:

a The crew of a motor torpedo boat detailed, late in the day, to transport a Camouflage B unit to the scene of a diversionary operation.

b Commando personnel detailed to simulate a beach recce of an objective which they probably deduce from the text of their orders and other internal evidence we are not going to attack.

c The crew of an aircraft detailed to carry out a dummy supply drop at a point where they know there are no Allied troops.

13 The natural tendency will in each case be for the personnel to be less keen on these particular operations than they would be on 'real' operations of which they can see the point. This is likely (though of course not certain) to be the attitude of the Commanders and staffs controlling them and will have its effect on the operational personnel. This will affect adversely the degree of efficiency with which the operations are carried out.

14 They will moreover tend to do their jobs less well than personnel specifically trained for diversionary and deceptive operations, imbued with a belief in their operational importance, accustomed to handling or working with the handlers of deceptive equipment; and briefed by a D Force staff.

15 D Force on the other hand would – as specialists generally are – be extremely keen on deceptive operations and resolute in carrying them out. Their training would ensure that the operations were carried out with the maximum possible efficiency and (where necessary) with imagination and ingenuity. They would get the best out of their special equipment and improve it as a result of experience gained both on training and operations. This experience would also enable their staff to give practical advice to SEAC's planners on the possibilities (and impossibilities) in the diversionary field.

16 It is accepted that the creation of D Force would raise a number of problems, few of which can be solved in the near future, but it is suggested that the idea is sound and should be considered at this stage.

Although his argument, supported by Cawthorn and Mountbatten, was well received by the Army Commanders and to a lesser extent by the RAF and Navy, Fleming was right to be conservative in his expectations of when D Force would become a reality. A SEAC stock check of Deception units in January 1944[2] showed D. Division and its Special Duties Section (shortly to become the Inter-Services Technical Bureau), No.2 Light Scout Car in Jubbulpore, No.303 Indian Brigade, consisting of a depot and six observation squadrons, and a number of Combined Operations Scout Units allocated to India but still in the UK. It was from these components that Fleming planned to construct D Force but it was only in October 1944 that 303 Independent Brigade formed up in Barrackpore to be renamed and inspected as D Force.

X Force or 303 Independent Armoured Brigade (65, 66 and 67 Cavalry) had started life as a deception unit in the Middle East under the auspices of 'A' Force for the deployment of mobile and static dummies, and then been transferred from Persia Afghanistan Iraq Command to India during 1943.

Based in Karachi and under command of D. Division, it was reorganized into six squadrons and tasked with deception of all kinds in the field and behind the enemy lines. Now called 303 Indian Brigade and its sub-units Observation Squadrons (Nos. 51–58) it was sent forward to the Imphal and Arakan fronts in December and January where it participated in numerous actions throughout the fighting season.

Mountbatten took the initiative to create his own naval special force comprised of Combined Operations Pilotage Parties for beach reconnaissance and a RM detachment and three SBS Groups for coastal raids and river crossings. Known as the Small Operations Group (SOG),[3] while command was vested in C-in-C Eastern Fleet, SACSEA retained policy and operational control, and like D. Division, all operational plans had to be cleared by P. Division. In SACSEA's Operational Directive No.14, it was made clear that 'personnel of SOG will not be qualified to work as agents' which must have given Fleming some comfort. That said, 'providing diversions' was one of the tasks allocated to them.

꒰

Another element of D Force was 4 and 5 Light Scout Car Companies with No.1 Field Park in support, which had arrived at Jubbelpore in India in December 1943. Originally formed in Scotland[4] in August 1942, these units trained and equipped for sonic warfare were expert in reproducing a range of sounds from tanks advancing and lagering, landing craft advancing inshore in waves and landing troops to the clearing of jungle by bulldozers and soft-skinned vehicles moving around the front lines. These noises would then be broadcast in the vicinity of the enemy's front line to simulate factual activity. The heavy Scout Cars used in Europe were unsuitable for jungle conditions, so the Light Scout Car Companies reorganized their loads onto jeeps and mules. The latter proved unworkable as the two 3 feet by 3 feet by 2 feet speakers weighed 180 lbs each, so the load-carrying configuration which was finally adopted was two jeeps and one lightweight trailer on which the speakers were mounted. An American-made Onan generator which weighed in at over 300 lbs was transported in one of the jeeps. However, confronted with bad terrain and almost non-existent communications, it was to prove difficult to deploy the jeep-borne equipment under satisfactory conditions.

When, in September 1944, Captain Robertson-Macdonald, Fleming's Naval Liaison Officer, visited Major Llwellyn's No. 1 Field Park at Cocanada,[5] he found a unit of six officers and twenty other ranks with a remarkable collection of exotic vehicles: two Recording vans, two Dark Room Developing vans, two Editing vans for cutting sound tracks, two storage vans, one Dynamo lorry, one refrigerator van and two personnel trucks. He noted, while it still belonged to GHQ India, there needed to be a plan in regard to making future recordings to avoid duplication with those provided direct from the UK.

The main customer for sonic deception was Combined Operations who had been tasked to operate along the Burmese seaboard. In a wish list[6] submitted to GSI (d) in July 1944, Colonel D.W. Price, Head of Combined Operations Division SEAC, asked for sounds of 'paddling, splashing of paddles in water, scraping of boat bottoms on the shore, footsteps on coral or shingle, cracking of twigs and dried seaweed etc., whispers, orders given in low voice' to imitate a night-time reconnaissance mission. For commando raids, his requirement was less stealth and more noise,

> ships engines in reverse, anchor cable running through hawse pipes, winches, landing craft engines revving up, kedge anchor dropped with splash into water, loud creak of bow ramps being lowered, orders given in a whisper or loud voice e.g. 'Stop engines', much crunching of sand and shingle, occasional clink of weapons, sharp challenge, a struggle, small arms fire (first from enemy side, then from both sides), fire from support craft (light machine gun and mortar fire), demolition charges going off.

The idea was simple, namely to confuse and keep the enemy off balance and in a constant state of jitters. In response to these sounds, he would be tricked into opening fire thereby revealing his own position and hopefully filing an erroneous report to his superiors the next day. Over time, he could even be persuaded to reinforce what he thought was a vulnerable point.

If the concept was straightforward, the execution was fraught with difficulties and it was as to how best to mitigate them that Fleming and his team now turned their attention.

∽

On the advice of GSI (d), 303 Indian Brigade and the Light Scout Car Companies were reorganized into a combined British and Indian unit known as D Force, consisting of a Force HQ, a Depot Company and three British and five Indian Companies.[7] The British Companies each had a strength of fifty all ranks, and were equipped with sonic (POPLIN) equipment and with various pyrotechnical and other devices which had been designed and produced locally; the Indian Companies had a strength of thirty-six all ranks and were equipped with pyrotechnic devices only. All Companies were trained as fighting units and proved well able to look after themselves in action. The Depot Company was responsible for training and supplying reinforcements and deception stores for Companies in the field.

D Force was commanded by Lieutenant Colonel P.E.X. Turnbull, MC,[8] who had his HQ and Depot at Barasat, near Calcutta. During periods out of action, Companies were brought back to the Depot for refitting, leave and general rehabilitation.

Companies of D Force were attached at one time or another to virtually all the divisions in Fourteenth Army and XV Independent Corps and gave a distinguished account of themselves both in the bitter fighting, including numerous rearguard actions, in the Arakan and Minopur areas in 1944, and in the successful advance through Burma in the following year. Honours and awards earned by and recommended for the personnel of those small units up to October 1945[9] included a Victoria Cross for twenty-one-year-old Lieutenant Claud Raymond of the Royal Engineers. His citation read:

In Burma, on the afternoon of 21 March 1945, Lieutenant Raymond was second-in-charge of a small patrol, which was acting in conjunction with a larger detachment of a special force, whose objective was to obtain information and create a diversion in the area of Taungup, by attacking and destroying isolated enemy posts some forty miles in advance of an Indian Infantry Brigade, pushing down the road from Letpan to Taungup.

The patrol was landed on the south bank of the Thinganet Chaung, an area known to be held by numerous enemy strong points and gun positions, and marched about five miles inland. As they were nearing the village of Talaku and moving across an open stretch of ground, they were heavily fired on from the slopes of a jungle-covered hill by a strongly entrenched enemy detachment.

Lieutenant Raymond immediately charged in the direction of the fire. As he began to climb the hill he was wounded in the right shoulder, but he ignored this wound and continued up the slope firing his rifle from the hip. He had advanced only a few yards further, when a Japanese threw a grenade which burst in his face and most severely wounded him. He fell, but almost immediately picked himself up again, and, in spite of loss of blood from his wounds, which later were to prove fatal, he still continued on, leading his section under intense fire. He was hit yet a third time, his wrist being shattered by what appeared to have been an explosive bullet. In spite of this third wound, he never wavered but carried on into the enemy position itself and, in the sharp action which followed, was largely responsible for the killing of two Japanese and the wounding of a third.

The remaining Japanese then fled in panic into the jungle, thus leaving the position in our hands, together with much equipment.

The position itself was strongly fortified by foxholes and small bunkers and would have proved extremely formidable had not the attack been pressed home with great determination under the courageous leadership of Lieutenant Raymond.

Several other men were wounded during the action and Lieutenant Raymond refused all treatment until they had been attended to, insisting despite the gravity of his injuries, on walking back towards the landing craft in case the delay in treating his wounds and carrying him should endanger the withdrawal of the patrol.

It was not until he had walked nearly a mile that he collapsed and had to allow himself to be carried on an improvised stretcher. Even then he was continually encouraging the other wounded by giving the thumbs up sign and thus undoubtedly helping them to keep cheerful and minimise the extent of their injuries until the landing craft was reached. Soon after he died of his wounds.

The outstanding gallantry, remarkable endurance and fortitude of Lieutenant Raymond, which refused to allow him to collapse, although mortally wounded, was an inspiration to everyone and a major factor in the capture of the strong point. His self-sacrifice in refusing attention to his wounds undoubtedly saved the patrol, by allowing it to withdraw in time before the Japanese could bring up fresh forces from neighbouring positions for a counter-attack.

As Lieutenant Raymond's citation demonstrates, D Force operations were equally as dangerous as those of any other front-line unit. Here is a digest of an operation[10] carried out on the night of 24/25 January 1945 by a D Force party under the command of Lieutenant Colonel Turnbull. The intention was to obtain information of enemy strength and dispositions in the general area of Yanbauk Chaung by inducing the Japanese to open fire. The plan was to lay on an offshore sonic demonstration opposite the Japanese defences between 04.10 hours and 04.55 hours while a shore party would land around the same time and advance inland to lay 'effects'. The force sailed without incident but at 03.20 hours, forty-five minutes before moonset, an enemy gun opened up and surprise was lost. Turnbull, therefore, decided against landing the shore party. In a carefully choreographed display, various sonic-equipped launches criss-crossed the coastal waters, playing the sound of landing craft heading northwards while three rafts with twinkling lights were cast off. The yield was most satisfactory. By carefully observing gun flashes, D Force and Naval observers identified enemy artillery positions and recorded the state of alertness of their coastal defences.

Another example is a D Force operation[11] in February 1945 to 'attract the attention of the Japanese troops in the area between Yebok and the upper reaches of the An Chaung during the initial stages of 25th Indian Division's operations against the road Kangaw- Taungup'. Two companies, 52 and 58, embarked on a British Y Class minesweeper and two Motor Launches and almost immediately ran into heavy weather. Their Landing Support Craft signalled she was in trouble and after attempts to take her in tow failed, she was sunk by friendly gunfire. This incident wasted five hours of daylight and by the time the force landed in a dense mangrove swamp it was dark. By 03.00 hours they finally established a firm base in a small village. Throughout the day, recce patrols sighted small parties of Japanese troops either in sampans or on the riverbank and engaged them whenever possible. Various 'effects' (Verey lights etc.,) were laid and began to explode towards evening, drawing Japanese machine gun fire. At one point they came under fire from a heavy Japanese mortar, a near miss being recorded.

On the night of 16/17 February, sonic equipment was loaded onto Motor Launches and despatched to the Sittwe-Myengu Island area where a D Force contingent was in the process of withdrawing. By playing recordings of Landing Craft under way, the object was to give the Japanese the impression that it was actually moving up the *chaung* to make a further landing. The ruse succeeded and the Japanese remained in their positions for the next three days before moving north to engage with 25th Indian Division. It was the last sonic operation in Arakan and the Sonic companies withdrew to Barasat in early April where they regrouped. Thoughts now turned to the future use of the Sonic companies on land, for example, in Thailand's Chao Phraya valley and Khorat Plateau, rather than amphibious operations and whether they should be deployed at company level in support of platoon operations. It promised to be a very different canvas to their adventures in Arakan.

In addition to D Force, No. 1 Naval Scout Unit (an Admiralty unit trained and equipped to operate POPLIN and BLOSSOM sonic equipment at sea), commanded by Lieutenant Commander H.B. Brassey, RNVR, arrived in the theatre in early 1945. The unit formed part of the East Indies Fleet, but D. Division were sometimes called on to advise on various points in connection with it, and many of the recordings which it required were produced by No. 1 Field Park.

Surprisingly, unlike in North Africa and Europe, fake signals traffic did not play a great part in D. Division's deception activities. Although following the fall of Singapore and the loss of Burma, various Naval and Air Force W/T Deception schemes of strategic significance were operated with a certain degree of success, only a few small-scale W/T Deception plans in support of the Order of Battle, devised by the Signal Security Committee of the Combined Signals Board SEAC and W/T Advisory Committee, India Command, were implemented by D. Division. Fleming identified two reasons for this:

> Firstly, no evidence was ever received, until the last fortnight of the war, that the Japanese Signals Intelligence organization was intercepting, or was in a position to intercept, major Army W/T links on a scale sufficient to jeopardize the success of deception plans implemented without W/T support. Secondly, the specialized resources of personnel and equipment essential to the successful operation of large scale W/T Deception were never made

available to SEAC, and it was felt that the negligible dividends likely to accrue from strategic W/T deception did not justify the very considerable diversion of resources from normal service tasks implicit in its practice in the SEAC theatre.[12]

❧

Of all the curious collection of tactical deception tools assembled by Fleming, airborne pyrotechnics took pride of place. These locally produced deception devices were designed and, for the most part, manufactured by Lieutenant Colonel Andre Bicat's Inter-Services Technical Bureau which had originated as a sub-section of D. Division, working in a small office in the bandsmen's quarters of the Viceroy's estate. It eventually expanded into a large organization controlling several factories, and much of its work, particularly on rifle fire simulators and airborne deception equipment, was recognized by the War Office to be far in advance of similar work undertaken under much more favourable conditions in the UK.

Airborne deception equipment proved the most useful and practical means of deceiving the enemy on the Burma front. The main items were Paragons (dummy paratroopers), Pintails (Verey light signals), Parafexes[13] (rifle fire and grenade simulators), Aquaskits and Aquatails (aquatic Verey light signals). By these means it was possible to put down, in one sortie by a Liberator bomber, equipment which would simulate an engagement on the scale of a platoon-level battle lasting for up to six hours.

In March 1944, Fleming circulated a list of equipment, asking for orders for the campaigning season of 1944/45 as early as possible before large-scale production started. It was an extraordinarily impressive inventory, given the vast distances of supply and distribution in India, not to mention the ups and downs of the labour market. Items included rifle fire, gun flash and exploding grenade simulators, smoke generators, dummy paratroopers and mysterious bamboo spheres containing battle noises. Drawings and pilot models of a comprehensive range of dummies were also on offer, from tanks to aircraft, elephants to mules, artillery pieces to steamrollers, landing craft to lorries. However, in view of the limited use made of them in the past, ITB only met demand on an ad hoc basis.

At a meeting of interested parties chaired by Major General Bill Cawthorn on 28 March, 400,000 Bicat strips, 10,000 airborne effects and 500 Herberts were ordered, more than justifying Fleming's confidence in Bicat and his 'effects'.[14]

At the end of the war, Mountbatten wrote to Auchinleck,[15] asking him to convey his thanks to Bill Cawthorn 'in connection with deception activities'. The 'Auk' passed a copy on to him and Cawthorn wrote to Mountbatten to thank him for the thought which prompted you to write in such appreciative terms about the part the Indian Intelligence Directorate played in the initial development and working of D. Division and ITB. I am afraid it exaggerates my personal share in this, for I was extremely well served by officers such as Peter Fleming and Andre Bicat and those under them. It was they who provided the initial and recurring inspiration – my main task was providing the initial and recurring expenditure and to help in selling their ideas, admittedly at times to unwilling customers!

In turn, Cawthorn passed a copy of his letter to Fleming and Bicat.[16]

Having finally succeeded in creating D Force, the next challenge for Fleming was to persuade commanders to use it correctly.[17] Somewhat late in the day, on 20 March 1945 the Chief of Staff of Allied Land Forces South East Asia circulated a memo to Fourteenth Army, Northern Combat Area Command and XV Indian Corps on the subject of the planning and co-ordination of Deception measures. In essence it was identical to a memo which Fleming had drafted on 27 February.

> Experience in all Allied theatres of war has abundantly proved the need for centralized control of all strategic deception measures and (to a lesser extent) of tactical deception measures designed to further the ends of strategic deception. Failure to observe this principle will almost inevitably lead, at best, to confusion, delay and waste of effort and, at worst, to the miscarriage of deception plans in support of current operations and damage to the extremely delicate deception machinery which will adversely affect the prospects of both current and future operations.
>
> Tactical HQ of D. Division is a small staff modelled on the advanced elements of A Force, the deception staff which serves commanders in the field in the Middle East and Mediterranean theatres. The D. Division officers who are attached to this HQ and to its principal subordinate HQs are intended to perform the following duties:
>
> **(a)** To advise the commander to whom they are attached on tactical and technical deception measures and on the employment of any sub-units of D force which have been allotted to him;
>
> **(b)** To assist in the preparation of deception plans and to ensure that these do not conflict with the requirements of the overall deception plan which D. Division is implementing on behalf of the Supreme Allied Commander and his C-in-Cs;

(c) To ensure that D. Division's deception machinery gives the maximum possible support to commanders' deception plans when these have been approved by the HQ;

(d) To furnish to, and obtain from, the HQs to which they are attached information (especially about our own real, imaginary or supposed Order of Battle) which has a bearing on current or future deception plans.

The Chief of Staff expanded this memo by directing commanders to share 'all communications dealing with deception measures' with D. Division staff officers while emphasizing that 'this procedure in no way limits a commander's control over his own deception plans and requirements, but ensures that his own views and needs are made known to the widely dispersed deception staff sufficiently promptly for them to be reflected in the continuous flow of misinformation which is being passed daily to the enemy'.

Fleming was justifiably proud of the achievements and reputation of D Force. In his final report,[18] he recorded that 'D Force was successful in avoiding the stigma which commanders and staffs of field formations are often inclined to attach to specialist sideshows', and the popularity of the Companies with commanders is not unfairly illustrated by the fact that XXXIV Indian Corps asked for and were allotted no less than six Companies of D Force for Operation ZIPPER (the planned invasion of Malaya).

Chapter 15
Feints and noises off

The Japanese army's advance on Kohima and Imphal in the spring of 1944 had been a costly failure, eventually forcing it to a disastrous retreat. Whereas normally there would have been a lull in the fighting during the monsoon, this time the Allies decided to pursue the retreating enemy. Both Corps of the Fourteenth Army (IV and XXXIII Corps) crossed the River Chindwin in a move that surprised the Japanese as they had not anticipated any such major operations and advanced to the Irrawaddy River. In its middle reaches about 2,000 yards across and dotted with treacherous and shifting sandbars, this great Asian river presented a major obstacle covered by a determined Japanese defence.

Given the numerical superiority (nine Japanese Divisions v. five British Divisions) and the fighting spirit of the Japanese Army in Central Burma, General Slim quickly realized as his forces approached the Irrawaddy that he would need to catch the enemy off balance. His plan was simple yet at the same time devilishly complex. XXXIII Corps would cross the river to the north and west of Mandalay and capture the city; simultaneously, IV Corps would cross to the south and take Meiktila, the main enemy communications hub some ninety miles south of Mandalay. To make this work, he had to time the river crossings of the two different Corps to perfection. If IV Corps appeared on the east bank too soon, the Japanese would move their reserves to Meiktila; but if it crossed too late, the Japanese with their superior numbers would have time to defeat the diversionary attack on Mandalay first and then turn their full attention to IV Corps in Meiktila.

At the heart of the plan lay an ambitious and bold deception strategy. To achieve surprise, Slim wanted the Japanese to believe that both XXXIII Corps and IV Corps were operating to the north and west of Mandalay. Anything happening further south he wanted construed as either diversionary or probing attacks. So a dummy IV Corps HQ was established in the north with fake radio traffic between Corps HQ and Fourteenth Army; the real IV Corps moved south in radio silence and under a protective overhead screen of RAF fighters to deter Japanese reconnaissance.

To convince the Japanese that Mandalay was his main objective, Slim sent 19th Indian Division to cross at Kyankmyaung and Thabeikkyin to the north of the city on the night of 14/15 January. Then on the night of 12/13 February, 20th Division was ordered to cross at Myinmu. Fierce fighting lasted for a full week before the Division managed to establish a bridgehead. The Japanese now faced two bridgeheads over the Irrawaddy, one 45 miles to the north of Mandalay and the other 30 miles to the west. A pincer attack on the city looked imminent which was exactly what Slim intended the Japanese to think.

All the while, Meiktila, the beating heart of the Japanese logistics system in Central Burma, was Slim's real objective. IV Corps took Pauk on 28 January and on 3 February attacked Pakkoku on the west bank of the river. A simulated crossing by 28 East African Brigade at Seikpyu opposite Chauk with the assistance of D Force was completed by 8 February 'with much fanfare and hullabaloo'. The Japanese assumed it was an irregular force trying to distract them from concentrating their forces further north to defeat the impending attack on Mandalay. In almost perfect synchronization with XXXIII Corps to the north, 7th Indian Division secured a bridgehead at Nyaungu on 21 February and 17th Division then passed through them and headed at full speed for Meiktila. Only now did the Japanese realize that they had been caught off balance. By 1 April, they conceded defeat and headed south. By 3 May, Rangoon fell to 26th Indian Division and the campaign in Burma was effectively over. Long after the end of the war, the Japanese remained convinced that IV Corps had been part of the assault on Mandalay.

Designed to achieve virtually complete surprise for IV Corps' crossing of the Irrawaddy and breakthrough to Meiktila, the deception plan was drawn up by Lieutenant General Frank Messervy, commander IV Corps, assisted by the D. Division Staff Officer attached to his HQ and by another D. Division Staff officer at HQ Fourteenth Army, who was in a position to effect the necessary co-ordination among the Army and RAF staffs involved in the forward areas. Supported by special means, extensive tactical W/T measures[1] and also by a large dollop of airborne and audio deception equipment, Plan CLOAK was to be Fleming's battlefield deception 'pièce de résistance'.

On 13 January,[2] after scrutinizing every paragraph in IV Corps deception plan for their thrust to Meiktila, Fleming gave his response. 'Although D. Division can do much to assist ... by negative inference, it will not be possible – owing to the risk of subsequent exposure – to give this deception plan positive support through high-grade channels.' On matters of details, he noted that no large quantities of dummies will be necessary as the requisite impression can be best achieved by emphasis being laid on: first on movement and dust, together with the smoke of camp fires, to attract the air observer's eye in the area required; second on tracks and the clearing of undergrowth, particularly under trees; thirdly on the erection of a few improvised dummy tanks etc, sited to indicate the presence of a larger number under cover.

He also pointed out that 'any drop of airborne deception equipment that is extended over several days will probably be exposed as deception before the real crossing takes place. It is therefore recommended that these diversionary drops should depend on intensity rather than duration for their effect.'

The role of D Force, which had been transferred to 11 Army Group on 29 January 1945, in Messervy's deception plan was explained by Fleming in his final report.[3]

On the evening of 10 February 1945 a drop of dummy parachutists and airborne deception equipment was made at a point east of the Irrawaddy, between Yenangyaung and Pakokku. At the same time, and for some days afterwards, D Force simulated preparations for a crossing of the Irrawaddy in the Pakokku-Pagan area and our intention was to create an impression that airborne forces had been landed in advance of a large scale crossing and thrust towards the oilfields ...

The second phase of Plan CLOAK, the advance by 7th Indian Division and '11th East African Division' down the west bank of the Irrawaddy to the oilfields was then implemented. 18th Indian Division (bogus) was notionally flown from Ranchi to Imphal and transported thence by road to reinforce the Indian and East African Divisions. 18th Indian Division was implemented both by tactical and special means and, with D Force assisting, strong patrolling of the Irrawaddy valley was continued with occasional crossings to the east bank of the river.

By 20 April 1945 20th Indian Division (real) had thrust south-west from the railway axis to Magwe and had cut the Irrawaddy south of Yenangyaung and of the area of operations of the 7th Indian Division, which was, by then, the only factual formation in the river valley north of the oilfields. Implementation of Plan CLOAK was faded out and 18th Indian Division withdrawn to Monywa as 14 Army reserve.

Though not all developments and disposition in the oilfields area could be attributed to Plan CLOAK, deception could claim a high proportion of responsibility ... It is also possible that the strength the Japanese believed we had in the Irrawaddy valley from Pakokku to Yenangyaung discouraged, with, for them, disastrous results, attempts at a large scale eastward withdrawal of 54th Division from the Arakan coast across the Arakan Yomas to the Irrawaddy.

With regard to the airborne deception operation on 10 February 1945, we have concrete evidence from documents and prisoner-of-war statements that it alerted all Japanese posts in the oilfields area and as far afield as Magwe; that a battalion in Yenangyaung was 'stood to' when the drop was reported and a company sent out to investigate. A member of this battalion admitted that his first reaction on hearing of the landing was: 'This is the end.' The Yenangyaung oilfields, when occupied by 7th Indian Division were found to be a veritable fortress with a perimeter of defensive works and, as final evidence of the success of the plan, a Japanese broadcast of 21 February 1945 may be quoted: 'The 11th Division of the enemy's West African forces (later corrected to the East African 11th Division)', the commentator announced, 'were trying to advance to the oilfields area but were routed and driven back.' In point of fact a patrol of 28 East African Brigade had made a diversionary crossing of the Irrawaddy south-west of Chauk and had withdrawn voluntarily.

F.M. Slim was unable to mention D. Division or D Force in his account[4] of Fourteenth Army's crossing of the Irrawaddy River as they were still classified secret, so he attributed the success of the deception to his Corps Commander, General Messervy:

The success of IV Corps' crossing at Pagan was due, first, to the fact that the enemy command was concentrating on the crossings of XXXIII Corps to the north and regarded all riverbank activities from Pakokku southward as mere demonstration. A captured Japanese intelligence officer later explained that they did not believe that there was more than the East African Division in the area, and that it was directed down the west bank to Yenaungyaung. Even when crossings appeared to be threatened, the enemy considered they would not be in force and that if any actual attempts were made they would be at Pakokku and Chauk. They therefore pulled their troops away to meet these threats, leaving only small detachments and the Indian National Army to watch the Nyaungu sector. In fact, as the 7th Division made its crossings, the enemy was hastily marching away to the north and the south from the sites – a happy result brought about by Messervy's able deception measures. He considered 'the feint at a crossing opposite Chauk by 28 East African Brigade was so convincing that it brought prompt and violent retaliation'.

What did the D Force Companies get up to on the front line? Here is a patrol report from 51 Company on the planting of documents and marked map:

These documents and map were planted in the area Chauk Sheet 3. The area at the time was being occupied by a company of 46 King's African Rifles.[5] who were in contact with the enemy. On 10 February, this company was moving from this position and this area seemed to be the best place to do the planting in with some certainty of the enemy coming back and finding the documents. The planting was carried out as follows: the letters, photos and other documents were put inside the pages of a *Men Only*, also the map; this book was then placed under some scrub in the area occupied by the Company officers; also in this area were odd pieces of paper, open bully beef tins etc. and cigarette ends were left lying about. The Company of 46 King's African Rifles left the area and that night the enemy occupied it and the following day one of our patrols visited the area; also the place of planting and found the documents and map had been removed by the enemy. I feel certain that the manner in which the documents were planted would give the enemy no reason for smelling a rat.

Captain Timmis of 57 Company filed a report of their time with 7th Division which they joined on 5 February at Ondaw, to the south-east of Pauk. They were responsible for deception measures from Pakokku to a point opposite Pagan.

On 9 February, Company Commander was asked by Intelligence to get three Burmans across the river south of Pakokku who were being sent across to create the impression that a crossing was to take place in that area by attempting to get information of enemy dispositions on the east bank. Officer Commanding went out with a patrol of 4/14th Punjabs to do this on night of 9/10 February. On arrival at riverbank, no boats could be found and there was a gale blowing. A small raft constructed by the 4/14th Punjab was not thought to be capable of getting across the mile or so of rough water so the Burmans were left close by a village with instructions to get a boat from the villagers the next morning. On 11 February, the remainder of the Company proceeded to Mytche to assist in deception against the Pagan area. They were joined by the detachment that evening. On the following day, 57 Company came under command 1/11th Sikhs (89 Brigade) and recces were made for a deception crossing by Officer Commanding with Battalion commander. On 13 February an urgent call was received from 114 Brigade, so the detachment was sent back. On night 13/14 February the detachment carried out similar operations to the previous occasion plus the making of noise with signal engines and flashing of lights. Fire was definitely drawn on this occasion and answering light flashes were received from the east bank, the reason for which is not known. On both occasions, this detachment went with patrols of 4/14th Punjab and on the second occasion they came under fire from our own troops when returning but no casualties were sustained. On

13 February the remainder of the Company under the Officer Commanding less base details left near Mytche proceeded to join 1/11th Sikhs on the island opposite Pagan in order to take part in a deceptive crossing. The plan was for the Company to cross in the first wave with B Company and on getting ashore to move inland to try and draw any opposition there may have been away from the beachhead. 57 Company eventually set sail in country boats at about 04.45 hours on 14 February and when about two thirds of the way across, encountered heavy enemy rifles and light machine gun fire thought to be mostly from Japanese Indian Forces in view of its inaccuracy with a sprinkling of Japs. Our boatmen, being in the most vulnerable position in the boat, somewhat naturally took cover and the boat drifted for a time. All boats eventually succeeded on returning to the home shore and the total casualties were two Sikh wounded. 57 Company then put down light machine gun fire on enemy seen on the opposite bank … On the evening of 15 February 1/11th Sikhs sent a patrol across further south and we were asked to have effects ready to draw fire from them should they run into trouble. A magnificent raft containing a large basket full of effects, a Herbert, gun flashes and Bren guns were teed up but were not put into operation as the patrol encountered no opposition. Some light machine gun fire was put down on persons seen drawing water on the opposite bank.

⌁

Ralph Arnold, Fleming's fellow lodger at the Bungalow in Delhi, played a small part in Plan CLOAK and in the process had very nearly blown the whole deception plan.

The routine of my daily life at Barrackpore was simple enough. Din brought me a cup of early morning tea, I breakfasted, listened to the All India Radio news broadcast, and then went to the office and began drafting the daily communiqué. At 8.30 I attended 'morning prayers' in the sunk garden that lay between Government House and the river. The latest situation reports were read out and we were generally put in the picture. Then I went back to the office where I finished off the communiqué, which had to be passed by the Operations and Intelligence branches and by our censors before it was sent off. It was in connection with this … that my most ghastly public relations experience occurred.

By January 1945 the Fourteenth Army plan for its breakthrough into central Burma was in full operation. This plan depended largely on a huge piece of deception or bluff … One morning, when these plans were boiling up, I had to go into Calcutta on some piece of business directly after breakfast. I had arranged that someone else should draft the communiqué. I did not get back to Barrackpore until dinner-time, when I asked if everything had gone all right. It had. The communiqué had been written and had been passed by all concerned and sent off. Next morning I was rather late going to breakfast and I came into the mess in the middle of the All India Radio news broadcast. As I was sitting down I heard these words: 'Troops of the Fourteenth Army are pressing forward in the direction of Pakokku.'

In moments of frightful stress, one's heart is supposed to miss a beat and one's blood is supposed to run cold. One can also be rooted to the ground. I suspect that all these things happened to me simultaneously. After a few stunned seconds I uprooted myself, dashed out of the mess, and began running in the direction of my office. I found the previous day's communiqué on the file. As sure as fate it contained the frightful sentence. Arthur Moore, when he had finished his leisurely breakfast and had made his appearance in the office, seemed quite unmoved. He was well used to crises. It was true, wasn't it? In any case Operations and Intelligence had passed the communiqué, so it must be all right. If the Japs noticed it at all they would probably think it was a neat bit of deception on our part. I suspect he was really just as worried as I was.

I hoped that the Commander and his Chief of Staff, to say nothing of the Commander, Fourteenth Army, would take this gaffe as calmly. The telephone rang. Would I go at once to the Chief of Staff. He was not taking it calmly at all; and the Army Commander had already been through to him on the telephone. I spent a nightmare morning, in the course of which I visited Lady Canning's tomb. In moments of stress at Barrackpore I always went there. Lady Canning was the wife of India's first Viceroy. She died in Calcutta in November 1861, and was buried at Barrackpore at dawn next morning. The site chosen for her grave was the raised embankment overlooking the river at the end of Government House garden, reached by a path that ran past my banyan tree hut. There was a stretch of mown grass, and then an ironwork enclosure with scrolls repeating her initials, CC; and finally, inside the enclosure, an ornate Italian marble cross. Augustus Hare gives a most affecting account of her funeral in his *Two Noble Lives*.

At lunchtime the Brigadier General Staff and I took off from the red brick airstrip at Barrackpore to fly to HQ Fourteenth Army in obedience to an irate and peremptory summons. We had a perfectly beastly flight. Crossing the mountain barrier between India and Burma, against the grain of the hills, we flew slap into the middle of an electric storm which tossed the little aircraft about as if it had been a leaf. I thought that the wings would be torn off. I was so desperate that I half hoped that this would happen. Arrived at Fourteenth

Army I was asked what, if anything, could be done to repair the damage. I had expected this question: and the answer I had to give was, 'Nothing.' It was not a very convincing reply. The Brigadier and I flew back to Barrackpore. I heard no more about this appalling indiscretion, and I am still uncertain how it occurred. The word Pakokku, which was certainly written on my heart, and which may still be legible there, made me squirm inwardly every time I heard it mentioned at subsequent 'morning prayers'. I never ceased to be thankful that the Japs did not take advantage of this breach of security … To this day I have a slightly uneasy feeling whenever I listen to a news broadcast. For months I used to breakfast early so as to avoid the ordeal.

Chapter 16
The double agents' impresario

'The Double-Cross System', whereby agents trusted by the enemy were used to feed carefully orchestrated misinformation into his intelligence system, provided a channel of communication to the other side far more continuous and reliable than could be furnished by the normal tactical means of visual or sonic deception, and even the sophisticated measures of radio deception which were an essential component of the whole picture.[1]

In March 1943, John Marriott, the assistant head of MI5's Double Agents Section (B1a),[2] arrived in India at the request of DIB's Director, Sir Dennis Pilcher,[3] to advise on the formation of a special section to handle double agents. As deputy to Lieutenant Colonel Tar Robertson, the head of B1a in London, and also secretary to the multi-agency XX Committee which oversaw double agent operations, Marriott's credentials were impeccable save in one respect. He had never been to India and knew next to nothing about its peculiarities, impediments and handicaps. In his first letter back to Robertson,[4] he refers to Fleming's imminent arrival in London when he assumes the two will meet, although he is peeved that 'the blighter never told me he was going home … and he left Delhi an hour before my return (from Calcutta)'. His initial impression was that

> DIB are not, in my opinion, as matters stand capable of running, to the exclusion of anybody else, all double agents in India. They neither have nor are in a position to get adequate staff for the purpose, while when it comes to the Eastern Front, and indeed all that part of Eastern Bengal and Assam in which, although there is a civil administration, the military nevertheless are in practical control, they simply haven't got the facilities without at every turn having to call upon the Army.

It was a fair assessment.

Marriott also had reservations about D. Division.

> The military, i.e. Peter, are – to an almost absurd extent determined to get some channels somehow somewhere, and they have embarked – and I don't doubt will embark again – on a number of enterprises off their own bat … God forbid that I should get mixed up in the deception world but really the chap I ought to be advising is not the Bureau but Peter … the trouble is, of course, that there is nobody to run the thing apart from him, and he and all his boys are utterly ignorant of the ABC of the work.

But the reality was

> that the sources of supply of likely material are largely out of DIB's control, e.g. if a spy is caught anywhere in the East he goes into military custody. If he is caught anywhere else in India by the police, he may or may not go to a central interrogation establishment. If he does, then he becomes a military asset; if he doesn't, he may find himself anywhere.

Marriott took a swipe at DIB by highlighting what he called its 'nebulousness of ideas' by citing how SILVER, 'the only double agent in their hands, albeit a first-class one, is being run by a Punjab policeman' and his case officer in Delhi had never even met him. He concluded that 'I am determined somehow or other to get all this work under one hat, which I am quite clear ought to be a military one, with Johnstone (of DIB) seconded to Peter.'

A week later, Marriott was still mulling over turning 'the whole thing over to a joint section with the military … since it provides a solution to the problems of manpower, communications and transport, and combines the advantages of enabling DIB to keep an eye on some of Peter's wilder activities with the equal advantage of demonstrating to the military that the Bureau are not missing opportunities.'[5] Yet there remained a professional anxiety about 'the heresy that deception is the first and only objective of the Double Agents Section'. Consequently, he proposed an ambitious plan to expand the remit and resources of DIB and in the process set up Provincial Double Agent Sections. In effect, he was advocating that DIB should create its own B Division complete with the equivalent of Latchmere House (Camp 020), MI5's wartime holding centre where captured enemy agents were interrogated.[6]

After a meeting with Sir Dennis Pilcher, Marriott told Robertson in late May that he had convinced him that the prime reasons for running double agents were:

1   To find out the methods and intentions of the enemy Intelligence Service

2   To provide the enemy with an espionage system under our control which will so satisfy him that he will not attempt to introduce another unknown to us

3   To deceive

Better still, Pilcher rejected 'any ideas of a joint section with the Army (which at one time I had thought was a solution) for reasons with which I entirely agree now that I have seen them in action'. The volte-face was now complete and in a final tilt at Fleming he ended his letter with a reference to agent FATHER whom 'Peter's outfit … would have unquestionably have made a mess of … and what's worse would not have known how to treat the old boy as a person' if they had run him as a double agent.

In a note on double agents and deception dated 6 June 1943, Robertson was more tactful, noting in his introduction that 'it is fully realized that local conditions in India may make some of the experience gained in England inapplicable.' He also recognized that 'the necessity for sending information to the enemy via double agents carries with it the opportunity of sending misinformation with the express intention of deceiving the enemy as to our strategical or our tactical plans; as to troop and convoy movements and a variety of other subjects'. Again treading carefully, he stated 'it would be out of place in this note to dilate at any length on the subject of deception, which is a vast and complicated one. Suffice it to say that experience in the Middle East has shown that the use of double agents as a channel for deception of the enemy is an integral part of the general deception machine.' However, he went on to promote Marriott's plan that, with the limited assistance of the military, DIB should head up an overarching committee with responsibility for policy and message clearance and should also establish a new organization for handling channels and providing case officers. Once adopted, it would mean that the general policy with regard to the running of agents and all deception matters would be left to the Controller of Deception or his deputy. He ended his note with a strong endorsement to replicate the London Reception Centre in India to which all suspected enemy agents would be sent for screening and advocated that the military's Forward Intelligence Centres should each have an experienced Intelligence Branch officer attached. With Pilcher, Robertson and Marriott now in full cry to take control of double agents, Cawthorn and Fleming waited for the right moment to play their cards. Having received a lecture from Robertson in London on their way to the TRIDENT conference, they had a fairly good idea of the nature of the coming turf war.

Judging by his report of 1 September 1943[7] to Sir David Petrie, the head of MI5, Marriott had over-egged his case in stating that '[Cawthorn] and Colonel Fleming asserted claims with regard to the manipulation of double agent channels which went far beyond what was necessary or appropriate for the effective exploitation of double agents'. In a withering critique of D. Division, he asserted that 'with possibly one exception, no member of Colonel Fleming's section had any experience of India or spoke any Indian language. They were equally ill-informed about the simplest details of the internal political situation.' When he officially proposed to entrust the running of double agents to the heads of the DIB in each Province with oversight provided by Regional Committees under the direction of a Central Board in New Delhi, Cawthorn rejected it. Instead he proposed a joint section, headed by Fleming, and answerable to himself and Pilcher. The outcome of these discussions was a compromise brokered by Cawthorn whereby Fleming and Malcolm Johnstone sat down together and thrashed out a modus operandi. DIB went on to provide the case officers for double agents and liaison with the Indian Police; D. Division controlled messaging. It proved to be an efficacious solution that leveraged the respective resources of the two organizations and one that avoided Marriott's cumbersome organizational infrastructure so unsuited for India. Some friction at a personal level inevitably remained. Colonel Bill Magan,[8] the DIB officer who ran SILVER with Johnstone from April 1944 onwards, found Fleming 'an irresponsible, ambitious and irrational man who was always trying to persuade us to pass messages which we believed would "blow" the channel'.[9]

In the course of the war, working closely with DIB and other agencies, D. Division went on to collect an assortment of double agents and whenever possible put them to good use as information channels to the enemy.

The PAWNBROKER party, which was landed on the Kathiawar coast from a Japanese submarine in December 1943, was sponsored by and directly responsible to Subhas Chandra Bose, and consisted of eight men (of varying race – Gujarati, Madrasi, Bengali, Punjabi, Sikh) equipped with four wireless sets. The party planned to set up sub-parties, each consisting of two men and a W/T set, at Benares, Bombay and in the North West Frontier Province, with a head office at Calcutta; contact was to be made with revolutionary and subversive elements throughout India, and information of political and military interest was to be transmitted from the outstations to Calcutta and thence relayed to Bose's HQ at Rangoon.

However, the party was caught soon after landing, and in January 1944, D. Division and DIB drew up a plan to set up W/T stations in Bombay and Calcutta (the latter being the link with Rangoon) and to notionally eliminate the remainder of the party. The first message was transmitted from Calcutta to Rangoon at the end of March and from then on a steady volume of traffic was regularly transmitted. When the Bengal Volunteer Group, which notionally provided the bulk of PAWNBROKER's higher-level information, was shut down in October 1944, there was a hiatus until early 1945 when notional contact with the factual All India Youth League in Bengal provided an excuse for renewed upgrading and from then on PAWNBROKER became one of the highest-grade channels at D. Division's disposal. From the deception angle, PAWNBROKER's most useful work, apart from its share in the progressive build-up of the Dummy Order of Battle, lay in its implementation of Plan STULTIFY, and subsequently, and in an intensified degree, of Plan SCEPTICAL.

A year after the capture of PAWNBROKER, on the night of 13/14 December 1944, the TRAVEL party, consisting of one Bengali and two Sikhs, was put ashore on the Orissa coast from a Japanese submarine. The party, which was also sponsored by and responsible to Subhas Chandra Bose, had been given no political contacts. It was in possession of a W/T set and had orders to take up residence in any large town such as Patna or Calcutta and to collect military, naval and air information (it also had a sabotage role). The party was instructed to come up on air sixty days after landing, and thereafter to transmit information on a regular schedule.

Arrested on landing and handed over to DIB./ D. Division for exploitation, TRAVEL came up for the first time in February 1945, from (notionally) Amritsar. In April, TRAVEL announced its arrival in Howrah, where the set had from the very first been installed. Communication was not consistently good, but after the fall of Rangoon, TRAVEL began to send out a flow of moderate-grade material designed to further Plan SCEPTICAL. Control showed considerable interest in the case. In May they issued orders for one member of the party to proceed to Vizagapatam and send information about that port back to Howrah. Though Bose in June informed TRAVEL of his safe arrival in Bangkok, the case fizzled out as the Japanese military situation in South East Asia deteriorated. Control was last heard calling on 14 July 1945.

Within days of the arrest of TRAVEL, another Bose-sponsored party called TROTTER, comprised of three Madrasis equipped with a W/T set, were landed by a Japanese submarine near the mouth of the Cauvery River and caught almost immediately. Their instructions were to collect naval, military and air information, with one man going to Colombo and one to Trincomalee from where they were to send back information by secret letter to the third member of the party, in Madras, who was to transmit it, together with the information he himself was able to gather in Madras, to Control.

This programme was notionally carried out. The set was installed in Madras and TROTTER after some initial delay sent his first message on 3 April 1945. Control showed immediate interest, responding with a flattering message of congratulation. Thereafter TROTTER began to pass useful naval information but the ineptitude of the Control operators rendered most of the traffic abortive and towards the end of July the case faded out.

In April 1944, a group of eight Indian agents was landed from a Japanese submarine on the Malabar Coast. Like PAWNBROKER, they were sponsored by and responsible to Subhas Chandra Bose. The group was divided into three parties, one party being allotted to each of the three areas Trichinopoly, Madras and Rameswaram. These parties had orders to collect military, naval and air information from their respective areas and to transmit it by W/T to a Control Station which proved to be in the Andaman Islands. They were instructed to begin transmitting by the middle of June.

The arrest of the Trichinopoly party, which occurred very soon after the landing, was much publicized. It was therefore decided that no deception use could be made of this party. The Madras and Rameswaram parties were, however, quickly seized on as potential double agents, the Rameswaram party being moved notionally to Ceylon.

The Madras party was named DOUBTFUL. Coming up for the first time on 15 June 1944, it made early contact with Control and in addition to announcing its own safe arrival in Madras provided a suitable cover story for the notional move to Ceylon of the Rameswaram party. The latter party (AUDREY) experienced some initial delay in establishing itself as a going concern, but eventually came up on 22 August 1944, when it confirmed its presence in Colombo.

Starting out in life with equal chances, DOUBTFUL and AUDREY failed to do equally well. Never anything more than low-grade channel, AUDREY's share in the implementation of specific D. Division plans was confined to the plugging (on an unavoidably low level) of the STULTIFY threat to Northern Sumatra and its successor the SCEPTICAL threat to the Sunda Straits. At the time of the Japanese collapse AUDREY's traffic was being stepped up, and given a longer lease of life she might well have made a greater name for herself.

In contrast, DOUBTFUL developed into a very useful channel. Well placed (he had branches at Madras and Vizagapatam) to assist in the building up of D. Division's Dummy Order of Battle, he was afterwards prominent in the implementation of Plans STULTIFY and SCEPTICAL. He had a special responsibility in connection with Plan SCEPTICAL (Madras and Vizagapatam being key ports for Operation ZIPPER), and at the time of the Japanese collapse had begun to play a vital part in the implementation of D. Division's SLIPPERY threat to the Kra Isthmus.

The BACKHAND case was quite unlike the hapless parties captured on landing. Captain Mohammed Zahiruddin of the Indian Army, who had been cashiered in 1940 for anti-British activities in Singapore, had applied to rejoin the Army after changing his views. After being interviewed by Bill Cawthorn and the C-in-C India, he was offered by DIB to Fleming who arranged for him to be parachuted north of Rangoon on 14 February 1944 with orders to give himself up as soon as he landed, the idea being to run him as a triple agent and penetrate the Indian National Army and the Hikari Kikan, the Japanese Liaison Office to Bose.

Although the Japanese believed his cover story, they initially decided to make propaganda out of his arrival. On 12 October, British monitoring stations picked up a broadcast by the Japanese Overseas Service[10] in English to the effect that 'an Indian Army deserter had joined Bose'. The main body of the story ran that

> Cawthorn, Chief of British Military Intelligence, may be a clever man but he is not clever enough for Major Mohammed Zahiruddin, twenty-eight-year-old Indian patriot who is now fighting in the ranks of the Indian National Army. This young man of the British Indian Army bailed out of a British plane behind Japanese lines in Burma. In February of this year he had volunteered for espionage work in Burma and before starting on his mission he was received by General Auchinleck. After receiving detailed instructions from General Cawthorn, he started to Burma from Dumdum aerodrome near Calcutta. General Cawthorn suggested that he should try and establish contact with the HQ of the Indian National Army in order to elicit otherwise unobtainable information from the Indian National Army authorities. He was to communicate his reports to the British authorities in India and a portable radio transmitter was given to him for this purpose.

The expectation had been that the Japanese would use the W/T set to transmit false information to New Delhi but instead they sent Zahiruddin to join Bose's team in Rangoon where he was put to work giving broadcast talks. With considerable mental dexterity, he initially managed to convey to his British handlers information about the Indian National Army and its relationship with the Japanese but, after a while, Bose became suspicious and had him incarcerated in a prison camp. Released by the British in 1945, he was awarded the MC in February 1946.[11]

Another group of double agents (BATS) under D. Division control worked directly back to the Hikari Kikan[12] and Kempeitai in Rangoon. They were members of a group of seven parties (each of three agents) which the Japanese dropped by parachute in Assam on 21 April 1943. Each party consisted of a leader, a W/T operator and a courier, five of the parties being recruited from Indian NCOs and sepoys who had been taken prisoner in the Malaya and Burma campaigns and had subsequently joined the Indian National Army.[13] The remaining two parties were made up from Indian civilians resident in Malaya. Their orders were to establish themselves in various parts of Bengal and Assam and to send back information about the local military installations, the armed forces and the war situation generally.

The majority of the BATS agents either gave themselves up or were arrested shortly after they landed, and although some absconded and were arrested much later than the others the general impression gathered from their interrogation was, firstly, that the prospect of returning to India was their main incentive in volunteering for espionage work, and, secondly, that few if any of them seriously intended to work for the Japanese. Two of the military parties, OWL and MARMALADE were selected for double agent purposes and were put on the air from Calcutta and Dibrugarh in May, when contact was successfully established. It was subsequently discovered that the standard of education of both parties was low; the operator of the MARMALADE party was unable to write, while the party's standard of Roman Urdu, the language in which they were required to communicate, was so low as to render their messages extremely difficult for an average Indian – let alone a Japanese – to understand.

Both agents started off cautiously, sending low-grade information which, although obviously of no great interest, was consonant with their personalities. OWL (painted in as a one-man show) gathered confidence and gained in status as he proceeded and there is evidence to show that the Hikari Kikan graded the information they received from him as being very reliable, and that they passed it on to all important HQs in South East Asia.

The MARMALADE party did not do so well. Continually having trouble with their set, and always (notionally, but very reasonably) short of funds, the bulk of their traffic consisted of domestic wails; and although Control soothed them from time to time with promises of assistance in the shape of money and a new set, these promises of assistance were never in fact implemented. Even when MARMALADE was moved from Dibrugarh in Assam to Imphal, an operational area, it failed to impress and from D. Division's point of view the case was reckoned a disappointment.

OWL, on the other hand, went from strength to strength in 1945. Having built up during the earlier stages of his career such varied sources of information as a Sikh taxi driver in Calcutta, a Calcutta Bengali keeping a wireless shop and a Royal Indian Navy sailor friend travelling to and from East Indian ports, he was gradually able to supply a steady flow of useful information concerning Order of Battle in India, naval, military and air installations, moves of troops and shipping, civilian morale, rumours and gossip in Calcutta and so on. Communication with Control remained consistently good and, when the time came for the implementation of STULTIFY, OWL was well established and so was able to play a useful part in the proceedings. The highlight of his traffic at this time was probably message No. 301 of 12 January 1945, which stated categorically that the British would cross the Irrawaddy at Chauk (Plan CLOAK) and which evoked a congratulatory flash from Control.

When Rangoon fell, D. Division moved OWL to Rangoon and lost no time in fitting him into the SCEPTICAL pattern. During OWL's short career in Rangoon (he came up for the first time on 9 July) he was able to include in his traffic direct reference to the coming assaults by XXVI Airborne Corps on Bangkok and by Twelfth Army on Moulmein, as well as to point to the Kra Isthmus as SEAC's main post-monsoon objective [Plan SLIPPERY]. OWL was still going strong up to the last days of the war. He holds the distinction, unique among D. Division's channels, of having received (on 17 August, when the war was over) a valedictory pat on the back from his Control in the shape of 'Thanks for the trouble. Goodbye.'

Then there were double agents under actual Japanese control who were exploited by D. Division. BRASS was the codename for a party of three Karen agents consisting of a leader, a W/T operator and a courier who were dropped by SIS near Rangoon in November 1942. When the party came on air, it was evident that they were working under Japanese control and the case was handed over to D. Division to run for deception purposes. The technique used was firstly to convince the Japanese that they were successfully deceiving the British, and secondly, to implement D. Division's own deception plans by means of suitable instructions or questionnaires transmitted to 'our' agent. If, for instance, the current deception plan called (as it invariably did) for an airborne threat to be exerted to a particular area, D. Division would instruct BRASS to send a sub-agent to reconnoitre DZs, himself meanwhile spreading a rumour in Rangoon that there were no airborne divisions in SEAC. The 'spread the rumour' gambit always worked well. Once, in a lean period, the rumour ran: 'The Emperor of Japan is NOT a monkey but he and all his family have short, furry tails of which they are very proud'; this was known to have reduced the Kempeitai to a state of near-apoplexy which lasted for several days.

Considering that the Japanese ran the case for two and a half years (until they evacuated Rangoon) one of its most remarkable features was their apparent failure ever to reassess its status and its value to them. In all, they transmitted a total of 177 messages and received 127 in return, and on numerous occasions took executive action in response to D. Division's messages in such a way as to leave no doubt that they had faith in their bona fides. A captured document emanating from Japanese HQ Burma Area Army describes BRASS, in complimentary but disingenuous terms, as 'our spy who is operating among the enemy (this is our special source of information … and is most secret)'.

During the two and a half years the case was running, four supply drops were made for the party, consisting mainly of clothing, W/T spares, watches, pistols, ammunition and some Rs. 11,000 in Indian and Burmese currency. On one occasion BRASS asked for and got a large stock of remedies for venereal disease, from which, it later transpired, the case officer suffered severely. No attempt was ever made to intercept the aircraft, nor was ground fire encountered; but it is known that a small force of armed Japanese gendarmerie were in attendance on each occasion in case an attempt should be made to land further parties of agents by parachute.

❧

One of the more unusual double agent operations run by D. Division was not of its own making. Operation OATMEAL, a three-man SOE sabotage and observation team commanded by Captain Ibrahim, was inserted by Catalina flying boat off the Perhentian Islands on the west coast of Terengganu, on 31 October 1944. The following day, they were arrested by a Japanese patrol and during the interrogations that followed, the three SOE men, all Malays, managed to convince their captors that they were not trusted by the British and had been given only the vaguest of instructions. Satisfied by their stories, the Japanese told them to get in contact with their HQ over the W/T link (codename VIOLIN). After initial transmission problems, the first message was sent on 13 November. Although the Japanese were in possession of the security check details, Ibrahim still knew the verbal check which had not been written down and was therefore able to alert Calcutta that he was transmitting under duress. The Japanese now began a double-cross operation, taking Ismail round the coastal area of Kelantan and to Kampong Lembah where the Kempeitai had decided to 'base' OATMEAL.

In Ceylon, meanwhile, D. Division were aware that they now had a perfect conduit for feeding the Japanese misinformation.[14] So the OATMEAL party was informed that SEAC was interested in Gong Kedak airfield. A satisfactory answer was received which provided details of Japanese activity on the airfield. However, Kampong Lembah offered little opportunity for the party to report on matters other than political and domestic. Accordingly, on 15 December, they were asked if it was possible to move across the peninsula to the Penang/Butterworth area to obtain military intelligence and then rendezvous with a contact who would be inserted into the area. Before they left, they were asked to send their route. Concerned that they could be compromised if they went by land or rail, the Japanese immediately flew OATMEAL to the west coast and installed them in a house on a hill near Kamunting close to Taiping. On arrival another message came in from D. Division saying that the contact had been delayed and they were to lie low until the spring. Somewhat disappointed by this turn of events, their captors nevertheless continued the deception and 'installed' Zain in the Penang area with Ismail and the W/T operator 'living' in a village on a rubber estate near Jarak where the set was 'kept'.

By May, the Japanese were beginning to get impatient and told Ismail to send a message asking for contacts, and stores and money to be dropped. He explained that this was totally out of order and it would only serve to alert HQ that something was suspicious. His bluff worked and after a dicey moment when one of the team was recognized by an old acquaintance in the street in

Kamunting, D. Division came to the rescue. It had been decided to give the Japanese confirmation of their supposed success in running OATMEAL. This was to be achieved by dropping a second W/T set to the party with instructions to despatch the new set, when it arrived, together with the operator to Singapore where it was to report on troop movements. Any reports indicating movement into the Kra Isthmus and towards Bangkok were to be reported without delay i.e. information that fitted in with Plan SCEPTICAL.

However, owing to the non-availability of Malay personnel in India suitable for training as W/T operators, D. Division told the party that it would have to recruit and train an operator locally. This was manna to the Japanese who immediately began training up one of their own operators in British Morse code. The W/T set and other stores were promised for dropping during the July moon period. In quick succession, DZs were recced, changed and confirmed, dates postponed and drops cancelled. On one occasion, a Japanese officer failed to notice a ten-foot pig trap near the drop zone and fell into it. Finally at 20.45 hours on 7 August, a perfect drop took place on a DZ near Kebun Kopi and the next day all the stores were on display at the Kempeitai HQ in Taiping. Ismail was congratulated in helping to fool the British and urged to keep up the good work. However, on checking, there were a number of deficiencies in the five containers according to the packing list. Where were the money, crystals, signals plan and codes and why was there soap, rice and .22 ammunition which were not on the manifest? Ismail immediately sent a signal informing Ceylon of the errors and an apologetic reply was received, arranging another drop on 19 August. In the event, it was too late since Japan had surrendered by then.

Ismail's immediate concern was that 'the Japs might just bump us off', and regretfully informed his Kempeitai captors that his religion would not permit him to commit hara-kiri with them. Eventually the OATMEAL members were released and made contact with British forces which had landed without opposition in early September.

In his post-operational report of 19 November 1945, Ismail summarized that

> although we were caught, we were determined then to put up some sort of fight and when we decided to collaborate with the Japanese our only aim was to sabotage their time and energy for nothing. We knew that we were running much greater risks by doing that but we were prepared to suffer the consequences if things did not work out well for us. Providence helped us right through and we succeeded in what we set out to do.

For Fleming, the Japanese case officer for OATMEAL had proved an unusually worthy opponent, working to a definite deception plan (details of which D. Division already knew from other sources) in direct contrast to the familiar 'hit or miss' efforts employed by BRASS for instance. At the end of April 1945, they reported that a large number of reinforcements, totalling five divisions, had recently arrived from Japan. They went on to say that two of these divisions had proceeded to Burma and that the remaining three were disposed in Malaya and Thailand. Further messages dealing with troop movements, codenames of formations, locations and movements of VIPs were on the same lines. Fleming rated 'their handling of OATMEAL, though by no means brilliant, was more methodical, imaginative and enterprising than any of their work that we came across in connection with other channels'.

With a good working relationship now in place, MI5 made available to D. Division a number of its channels from India to Germany and hence to the Japanese. These channels were tangential to the main thrust of D. Division's work and suffered from inbuilt delays of up to two months and uncertainties in the timing of onward transmission. The product also had the label of second-hand information attached to it, so its efficacy lacked immediacy like Herbert Farjeon's girl who 'danced with a man, who's danced with a girl, who's danced with the Prince of Wales'. That said, although well aware that sharing intelligence with one's allies could never be taken as given, D. Division felt it could rely on the efficient Germans passing the information on to their Far East ally with a degree of confidence.

Fleming recorded their exploits in his final report:[15]

GLEAM
GLEAM was the codename for a notional letter-writing WRNS working at HQ SEAC in Kandy who corresponded with the Germans in Lisbon in secret ink through a subversive organisation in England. GLEAM was an offshoot of the GARBO network and it was through the offices of MI5 that she was brought into being and placed at the disposal of D. Division.

Her background was that she was recruited by a sub-agent of GARBO's who was connected with a movement known as the Aryan World Movement formed by members of the Welsh Nationalist Party, who were engaged in collecting military information for the Germans in England. GLEAM, the mistress of an Indian member of the group, was acting as secretary until she was called up for service in the WRNS in February 1944. When she had completed her training, which included a course in Hindustani, GLEAM arrived in London in early June to await embarkation orders. Before she sailed she was given instructions in the use of secret ink and the security measures she should take in conducting her work. She was also given £300 to cover whatever expenses she might incur and a questionnaire supplied by the Germans which instructed her:

a) to locate and identify Allied formations in India from Divisions upwards, the arrival and departure of such units, their destinations and whence they came;

b) to report on the locations of naval units and convoy movements;

c) and to report as above on the Allied Air Forces.

GLEAM arrived in Kandy at the beginning of August 1944 where she was posted to the office of Air Vice Marshal Sir Philip Joubert de la Ferte, Deputy Chief of Staff, Information and Civil Affairs, and despatched her first letter to the Germans later the same month. Her letters consisted of two texts, a cover text which was written in the form of a normal chatty letter to a girl at home and a secret text which contained the information which D. Division wished passed to the Germans. For the sake of simplicity a supply of suitable note paper, stamps and envelopes were sent to London and both texts, which were composed in Delhi, were typed separately on ordinary paper and despatched by fast bag to MI5 where they were combined into one – the secret text being written in high-grade invisible ink. Notionally, however, GLEAM wrote cover and secret text all in one in Kandy and sent her letters home by air mail. In this way it was possible for the secret text to be altered or enlarged upon, if necessary, with the minimum amount of trouble. The information despatched by GLEAM was of an unusually high-grade nature and she was congratulated by the Germans both on the contents of the secret text and on the ingenuity of the cover text. This grade of information was made possible by the introduction of five sources in the persons of a naval officer on Mountbatten's planning staff, a Wing Commander in SEAC, a Commander in the American Naval Air Wing, a Staff Colonel in the British Army and an Officer in the Dutch Army. GLEAM was on very friendly terms with several of these officers and was therefore in an excellent position to pick up important information about plans for forthcoming operations and movements of units and formations of all services from their conversation.

During the six months that this channel was in operation GLEAM despatched twelve letters, ten of which were acknowledged by the Germans and there is good reason to believe that the bulk of the information contained therein was passed on to the Japanese, though after some delay. The average time that each letter took in transit from Delhi to Lisbon was approximately six weeks, although it is doubtful whether the material reached the Japanese until a further six weeks at least had elapsed.

In February 1945, there was some reason to believe that the suspicions of the Germans might be aroused by the striking similarity of reports received by them from GLEAM and SILVER and MI5 judged it prudent that she should meet with an accident which would prevent her from writing for a period. An elaborate story was worked out to explain the lapse in her correspondence but this was never put into effect owing to the collapse of the Germans in Europe.

FATHER (with which is incorporated DUCK and RADJA)
FATHER was a Belgian test pilot attached to the RAF who after the fall of France was sent into Britain by the Abwehr to collect technical and operational RAF information. The method of communication arranged by the Abwehr was that they would talk to FATHER by means of wireless code messages which could be picked up by an ordinary commercial receiver; whilst FATHER would correspond with the Abwehr by including messages written in secret ink in otherwise harmless letters despatched to an address in Madrid.

On arriving in Britain, FATHER at once made contact with the authorities and blew his mission. He was thereupon set up as a double agent working under the auspices of MI5. His connection with D. Division begins in July 1943, when owing to the fact that the Germans had begun to ask him technical questions which in his notional role it was implausible for him to answer incorrectly or to ignore, it was decided that he should be sent to India.

Having arrived in India he was placed under the control of Delhi Intelligence Bureau/D. Division. He was factually posted to an RAF squadron at Chittagong, and his first messages from India were contained in letters to Madrid dated 31 August and 1 September 1943.

In September 1943, FATHER was factually transferred to an RAF night-fighter squadron near Calcutta; he remained, however, notionally at Chittagong until November 1943, when he made a notional move to a Spitfire squadron at Alipore in Calcutta. He was now provided with a notional source of information in the shape of an unconsciously indiscreet female friend employed as secretary to the Military Secretary, Eastern Army.

An Indian disadvantage in the case was the fact that FATHER's letters (which could not plausibly be speeded up ahead of ordinary mails) were taking a minimum of two months to reach their Madrid destination. Fortunately the Germans found this a disadvantage too, and in January 1944, information was received in India that they were trying to get a set from Istanbul into Bombay. It was not clear at first for whom this set was intended; but in mid-February the Germans asked FATHER if he could take delivery of 'an object' which was, of course, a W/T set (plus codes, frequencies, etc.). It was eventually collected by FATHER after a long and complicated process (known to D. Division as DUCK) involving much elaborate precaution against any risk of compromise. He came up on air from Calcutta for the first time on 2 August 1944, contact with Control being made on 5 August. Communication was good.

As a flesh-and-blood individual FATHER was inclined to be temperamental, and in October 1944, it was decided that he should be factually sent home. He therefore told Control that his CO was trying (in view of the liberation of Belgium) to get him repatriated; and in November and December he gradually built up as his successor a notional disaffected Indian courier (RADJA) of Strategic Air Force HQ in Calcutta. RADJA took over on 3 January 1945, when FATHER faded out of the case.

RADJA's courier duties carried him to various parts of India, and he was thus able to supply Control with a steady and plausible flow of information. As the situation in Germany worsened he endeavoured to keep the case going by asking Control to give details of his frequencies and codes to Subhas Chandra Bose. Control, however, failed to respond, and with the collapse of Germany in the spring of 1945, the case came to an end.

A review of the FATHER traffic shows that the importance of the case to D. Division increased considerably after the introduction of the W/T set. Up to that time the difficulty of communication satisfactorily by letter with Madrid, plus the fact that SEAC's plans were constantly fluid, precluded any systematic and operationally constructive use being made of FATHER. After August 1944, and especially when STULTIFY emerged as a firm basis for planning, FATHER became far less haphazard, and gradually developed into a high grade channel passing a very considerable volume of significant military, naval and air information. There is evidence to show (a) that the Germans rated the channel high, and (b) that they did on occasion share with their Japanese Allies the information they obtained from it.

'A' Force also gave D. Division access to one of its channels. It proved far from reliable and was prone to fast-changing political ruptures that wrong-footed its messengers.

BULL'S EYE
In April 1943, Major General A.C. Arnold, British Military Attaché in Ankara, offered D. Division through 'A' Force a channel for the passage of medium to high grade misinformation to the Japanese through the medium of a Japanese journalist. It was agreed that 'A' Force should handle the material in Cairo and pass it on to Ankara but before the first batch of items could reach the Japanese the journalist concerned was arrested by the Turks.

In June 1943, D. Division was informed that a channel to the Japanese via the Germans through the Polish Military Attaché was possible and a certain amount of material was passed. However, during August 1943, BULL'S EYE suffered another setback as the Polish Military Attaché stated that he was incapable of passing any further information to the Germans; but at the same time General Arnold intimated that medium grade material was acceptable for experimental purposes.

A month after Italy's capitulation (in September 1943), General Arnold had an interview with the Italian Military Attaché who stated that he would be able to pass information to both the Germans and the Japanese. Meanwhile, the Polish Military Attaché again established contact with the Germans and a considerable amount of BULL'S EYE traffic was passed – this time to the German Naval Attaché.

During the summer of 1944, however, Turkey broke off relations with Germany and interned the staff of the German Embassy in Ankara and as the Germans had nothing organised against this event, the only method remaining was to try to pass low grade rumours through journalists and members of the British colony. When Turkey eventually severed relations with Japan and the Russians refused to allow the Japanese to travel via the Soviet Union, the Spanish Ambassador in Ankara agreed to accept telegrams of a non-military nature from the Japanese Embassies in Madrid and it was hoped that this method might be developed to carry BULL'S EYE traffic but nothing came of it.

In April 1945, Spain broke off relations with Japan with the result that the Japanese, and consequently BULL'S EYE, had no outlet from Ankara for they, like the Germans, had no clandestine links prepared beforehand. BULL'S EYE was therefore closed.

It has never been possible to establish how much, if any, BULL'S EYE material reached either Berlin or Tokyo but it is known that on several occasions it was very well received by the Germans and the Japanese in Ankara. Indeed, the Japanese Military Attaché is stated to have 'jumped four feet in the air' when he received the first information about the new American B32 Dominator strategic bomber via BULL'S EYE. The main difficulty about running this channel was that, knowing little about the background of the various contacts, it was hard to find suitable high grade information which could plausibly have found its way to Ankara and consequently, apart from a few 'hot' items, the traffic was not of a very satisfactory quality. The running of the channel was not made any easier by the signal lack of initiative on the parts of both the Germans and Japanese in failing to establish any clandestine espionage network before they were interned and by their mutual suspicions of each other.

Fleming was philosophical about the outcome, content to fall back on the age-old axiom of nothing ventured, nothing gained.

∽

In the course of the war, other unexpected opportunities came D. Division's way, one of which was the use of HBM Ambassador in Moscow as a channel to the Japanese High Command in Tokyo.

After visiting Moscow, Bevan wrote to Fleming on 20 April 1944:

I am afraid my negotiations were entirely concerned with the war against Germany and I was not allowed to touch on Japanese matters as this was too delicate. While I was there I managed to open a new channel which the Ambassador (Sir Archibald Clark Kerr, former Ambassador in China) himself agreed to operate. It seems likely that anything he might say to the contact in question is likely to go to the Japanese pretty quickly, and possibly also to the Germans. Obviously it would have to be something which was plausible for the Ambassador to know and which would not be too difficult to put across. I have informed 'C' (the head of SIS) about it and in addition told one or two of the most senior officials at the Foreign Office. I have already given the Ambassador two items to pass, but am not yet in a position to say what success, if any, has attended these efforts. You might, however, like to bear this in mind. I have given the channel the code-name of GODSTONE, so if at any time you would like to try it out, perhaps you could send me a signal with this prefix.

My negotiations in Moscow ended up by the Russians agreeing to what we had asked them to do. This was most satisfactory, but on the extent to which they are actually functioning I would not like to express an opinion. I got the impression that they did not pay much serious attention to our sort of work, but that on the other hand played a good deal with dummy tanks, aircraft etc.

Fleming reacted enthusiastically and on 5 May responded that

GODSTONE is of the first interest to us and I will make one or two suggestions by signal when I have thought about it a bit. In the meantime – if it hasn't already occurred to 'C' – it may be of interest for you to note, and presumably point out to the Ambassador, that Jock Balfour's[16] wife's brother, a Lieutenant Colonel van Millingen,[17] works for SIS in Delhi. Letters from him to his sister could theoretically carry a good deal of Far Eastern news and gossip; he could be for the purpose be 'on the staff' or 'something to do with intelligence'. If he is used as a notional sub-source I presume the Balfours would have to be put partly in the picture, in case of a local check-back. Let me know what you think of this random and rather abstruse suggestion.

The next day he sent a signal to Bevan, offering three titbits of 'true' information that had already been passed to SUNRISE:

1   Government of India has succeeded in speeding USA postal service which delivers over land mails to China via Sinkiang,[18] north of Tibet.

2   RAF now reconnoitring air route through Sinkiang to China using new type of four-engine British-built aircraft. This follows establishment of British and American-built Consulates at Tihwa[19] capital of Sinkiang. British Consul's name is Turrell.

3   Considerable stir caused in Chinese and Anglo-American circles in Chungking by concrete signs of rapprochement between the KMT and Chinese Communists. Representatives of Generalissimo are now meeting Reds in Sian-fu and Foreign Correspondents after many unsuccessful efforts are at last being permitted to proceed to Siah-fu to see position for themselves.

LCS did not use this material and also turned down Fleming's 'false' offering of 1 August:

Striking example Empire solidarity presented in India by formation airborne corps of one British, one Indian and one African airborne divisions. Corps is commanded by British General whose staff includes some Indian officers also American technical advisers. Consequent on release of numerous transport aircraft by relief of Imphal and Kohima intensive training is going on apace. The Imperial Airborne Corps is largest airborne formation in military history.

Never a man to take no for an answer, Fleming was back a week later with more material:

1   TRUE: Grounds to believe certain Japanese POWs taken in recent fighting in Imphal area who are suspected of having anti-war or communist sympathies are being given preferential treatment by British.

2   FALSE: Recent visitors to India have reported presence of Japanese anti-war communist party from China who are aiding British in propaganda campaign to encourage subversive movements and tendencies among Japanese troops in Burma.

This elicited a rather laboured response from Ronald Wingate at LCS:

In order to pass messages across, the channel concerned has to arrange a cocktail party or some such function in Moscow in order to meet the source. Functions of this kind in Moscow, however, are scarce and quite an effort is required to bring about the necessary meeting. In these circumstances I feel the material passed should be of a rather more definite character than mentioned in your signal, which really has more of a propaganda smell about it than pure operational deception.

I am sorry to turn down these two proposals of yours, but hope you will appreciate the reason. After all GODSTONE is a man in a very high position and I don't think we can ask him to go to the trouble of passing over material unless it is really worthwhile. Perhaps you feel that the two messages concerned are of importance, in which case I must have failed to appreciate your dark intentions.

GODSTONE was never going to be Fleming's own channel since given Clark-Kerr's importance, both Bevan and Wingate would have acted as intercessors. Hence his investment in time and creativity was restrained and his expectations were never dislocated.

≈

In a note attached to his draft history of D. Division, Fleming recalled that 'in the summer of 1943 an event occurred which was radically to improve the prospects, hitherto bleak, of the deception staff in the Far Eastern theatre.' He was referring to the arrival in Tokyo of the Indian revolutionary leader, Subhas Chandra Bose:

Brilliant, audacious, overweening, shrewd, Bose in the years before the war had left a career of what might be described as calculated turbulence … [he was] above all an activist, to whom Gandhi's doctrine of non-violence appeared futile if not contemptible; and although during most of the decade before the war he was either in gaol or outside India his power of projecting his personality was such that in 1938 he was elected President of the Congress Party, hitherto dominated by Gandhi.

Bose became increasingly vociferous in his anti-British invective, prophesying imminent defeat for Great Britain. When he returned to India from Europe in July 1940, he was immediately arrested and imprisoned. As Fleming correctly noted, 'There was not one of the King-Emperor's subjects on whom the British authorities were less anxious to bestow a martyr's crown; they sent him home under house arrest, and on 17 January 1941, a few days before he was due to stand trial on charges of sedition, Bose, newly bearded and in disguise, absconded.' Ten days later, with the help of a shadowy figure by the name of Bhagat Ram Talwar, he arrived in Kabul. The city was 'little more than a glorified village … The great majority lived in mud houses and for the traveller, particularly a fugitive, there was only the *serai*; a sort of café, where most people ate on the pavements and slept on charpoys or beds in a large communal hall.'[20] For a week he stood in the snow outside the Soviet Embassy who showed no interest. It was only with the help of the Italians who gave him a diplomatic passport under the name of Orlando Mazzotta that he was able to travel to Berlin via the Soviet

Union where he vented his spleen on the British as the voice of Azad Hind ('Free India') radio which was beamed into Central Asia and the Indian subcontinent.

A meeting with Hitler on 27 April 1942 ended with the Führer wishing Bose well on his travel plans and in return Bose described Hitler as 'a Teutonic Fakir of Ipi with whom one could not hold a coherent conversation for more than a few minutes'.[21] Invited by the Japanese to join their triumphal progress through Asia, on 8 February 1943 he sailed from Kiel in a German U-boat and, after transferring to a Japanese submarine in the Indian Ocean, reached Tokyo on 13 June. On the following day he was received by the Japanese Prime Minister, Tojo, and after formalities had been concluded, he installed himself in Rangoon as self-appointed Supreme Commander of the Indian National Army[22] on 25 August 1943, and two months later, when the 'Provisional Government of Free India' was formed, he took the offices of Head of State, Prime Minister and Minister for War and Foreign Affairs.

It was at this point that Fleming became involved.

His friends are always pleased when a man who is rather deaf acquires a hearing-aid; and the arrival of Bose in the Japanese camp was for analogous reasons welcomed by the small Deception Staff in Delhi. They were already – or had been until he left Germany – in touch with Bose through a high-grade channel to the Abwehr, and they had good reason to hope that his quick wits, his dynamic personality and his long experience of under-cover activities would before long widen the front, hitherto disappointingly narrow, on which they were in contact with the enemy's Intelligence; they looked forward, also, to dealing with a sophisticated adversary who could be relied on – as the Japanese could not – to see the point of the information they gave him.[23]

At this stage, 'the shadowy figure of Bhagat Ram Talwar' enters the story. Recruited in Kabul by Karl Rasmuss,[24] a senior Abwehr intelligence officer, to conduct covert activity in India, when Germany invaded Russia in June 1941, Ram, who unknown to the Germans was a communist, offered his services to Mikhail Allakhverdov, the NKVD station chief in Kabul, and kept him posted on his work as the link between the Axis legation in Kabul and Bose sympathizers in India. With Russia and Britain now allies, at a meeting in Moscow on 27 June 1942, Soviet intelligence disclosed Bhagat Ram's status to the British as one of their agents[25] and proposed that they should run him jointly in exchange for the British sharing information about Japanese activity and intentions in Mongolia. DIB officers visited Moscow and after agreeing the details, from October 1942 Bhagat Ram became SILVER, a DIB double agent.

To feed false information to the German Legation in Kabul,[26] DIB concocted the All India Revolutionary Committee, a group of extreme nationalists with headquarters in Delhi, which controlled all revolutionary activity in India. A W/T station, MARY, was set up in Delhi to link the Committee to the German W/T station, OLIVER, in Kabul; later a direct link, TOM was established directly between Delhi and Berlin. In the course of the war, SILVER took a report of the Committee's activity back to Kabul on his five cross-border journeys.

For Fleming and D. Division this offered a chance to feed both strategic deception material and false Order of Battle details into Japanese intelligence with whom the Germans shared information from September 1943 onwards. Then in October the NKVD unexpectedly blew SILVER to the Abwehr during an attempt to induce Rasmuss to defect. Whether the British ever found out remains unknown but it is instructive to note that Rasmuss was given freedom of passage through India when he returned to Germany in 1944.

SILVER's last journey to Kabul in March 1945 featured in D. Division's Weekly Progress Report No. 8.[27] Arriving in the city after eighteen days' transit through the tribal areas, he handed copies of his latest report to the Abwehr W/T operator's Zugenbühler and the German Ambassador, Hans Pilger, before going on to visit Mr Inouye at the Japanese Legation. Later ULTRA intercepts showed that parts of the report had been transmitted to both Berlin and Tokyo. More meetings with both parties followed; Bose tabled six questions through Zugenbühler with two supplementary questions added by Berlin. Of more significance was a directive handed to SILVER by Inouye that purportedly came from Bose, instructing the All India Revolutionary Committee to initiate sabotage against lines of communication in India, to direct propaganda towards engineering a rift between the USSR and the Anglo-Americans, and to keep encouraging the INA and all Indians in their struggle for Indian independence.

During his stay in Kabul, SILVER tried to re-establish his high-level contacts with the Russians but to no avail. Then, armed with the code and W/T plan for ELEPHANT, the long promised direct link to Bose which was scheduled to go on air on 20 May, SILVER left at the end of April and was met by the British outside the tribal areas on 6 May. For his services, the Germans gave him an Iron Cross and paid him nothing; the Japanese paid him Rs 20,000 Afghani and US $4,000. History does not record whether the British rewarded him.

All these channels and agents came together like a bundle of telephone wires when in the autumn of 1944, the Combined Chiefs of Staff directed Mountbatten and General Stilwell to implement Operation CAPITAL, the re-conquest of north and central Burma, including the Arakan coast, Akyab and Ramree Island. Once completed, this would radically improve the flow of war materials to China along the Burma Road thus enabling the US strategy of securing airfields on mainland China from which to launch a bombing offensive against Japan. With the object of making the Japanese concentrate their forces in south-west Burma and to beef up their garrisons in Sumatra, Fleming came up with Plan STULTIFY in November 1944.

STULTIFY envisaged a series of actual and notional operations including seaborne and airborne assaults, all of which were grouped together under the codename KNOCKOUT. Using elements of the bogus Order of Battle so painstakingly built up over the previous two years, backed by dummy W/T traffic, and activating a complex programme of carefully crafted messages sent via 'special means' channels, D. Division went into overdrive. The storyline was simple enough: the main assault would take place in March/April at Prome and then exploitation to Rangoon would follow. Landings in Sumatra were scheduled for April; next stop was Java. Meanwhile the advance by Fourteenth Army into Central Burma would be billed as a secondary thrust.

The emphasis on airborne troops was deliberate for it imposed on the enemy the need to guard with static troops key points such as airfields, major road junctions, railway systems and main road bridges and to keep a reserve to counter-attack any airborne landing. The same criteria applied to seaborne landings and the necessity to keep sufficient troops deployed on manning static coastal defensive positions.

By any yardstick, it was an imaginative and impeccably executed deception operation, yet, as with most previous attempts, there was no evidence to support its efficacy. Once more, the Japanese sitting at the apex of Dudley Clarke's triangle remained impervious to the intelligence fermenting beneath them.

The intricate design of STULTIFY deserves examination as a deception exercise in creativity and audacity. On 22 December 1944, Fleming circulated Plan KNOCKOUT. Its key components were FANG, a notional attack on north-west Sumatra; CLAW, a notional seaborne/airborne assault on Prome/ Taungup/Sandoway prior to exploitation to Rangoon; ROMULUS, real operations in Arakan; CAPITAL, the actual advance in northern and central Burma; and TARZAN, notional airborne drops in support of CAPITAL.

A paragraph was added to the covering letter that 'in the light of future planning and unforeseen eventualities it may be necessary to alter this programme'. Fleming had no illusions that STULTIFY/KNOCKOUT was going to fare any better than its predecessors. For as Professor Sir Michael Howard concluded in his study on British strategic deception in the Second World War, 'the real problem which confronted the British deception staff in India … was that created by its own side; the continuing uncertainty as to what Allied strategic intentions really were.'

The intricacies of disseminating the various messages to support 'the story' were wholly Byzantine in character. Using nearly every channel at his disposal like sections of an orchestra and the Dummy Order of Battle he had so painstakingly created as his musical score, Fleming wrote and conducted a masterful symphony of deceit. In December, using the BULL'S EYE channel in

Ankara and 'gossip in Cairo', information was planted that one brigade of 6th Indian Division[28] was already in India, another brigade with Divisional HQ left for India last week. DOUBTFUL, the Japanese agent under DIB control in Madras, signalled his Control on 1 February that 9th Indian Airborne Division was moving from Secunderabad apparently to Calcutta. His Indian Navy friend reported in March that 'there are many British soldiers in Bombay who train in small boats. He sees many signs of 64th Infantry Division, some of 21st Infantry Division. Also African soldiers with them who wear the sign of a palm tree (83rd West African Division).' The next week, the keen-eyed sailor reported 'many Indian soldiers wearing the sign of a flying eagle (Frontier Armoured Division) with tanks have arrived at Vizagapatam'.

FATHER, the Belgium RAF officer who belonged to MI5, told Berlin on 31 December that 26th Indian Division has gone into reserve with XV Indian Corps in Arakan. It has been replaced in operations by 82nd West African Division. This true information was followed by the false statement on 10 January that 'a Brigade of African Airborne troops is now in Arakan'. As befitted an airman, FATHER kept up the misinformation about airborne forces with snippets on 30 January that 'officers of HQ Airborne Corps have gone through Calcutta to establish an HQ at Comilla'; on 20 February that '9th Indian Airborne Division is now in Eastern Bengal consisting of two brigades. One of these is 6 Gurkha Parachute Brigade which was in Middle East'; on 1 March that 'Airborne Corps now believed to be at Comilla consists of 3rd Airborne Division, 9th Indian Airborne Division and 10th African Airborne Division. Some of the latter are in Arakan. There is another division who practise with them but I know very little about this.'

MI5's other channel, GLEAM, the treacherous Wren based in Calcutta, wrote to GARBO in London that 'XV Indian Corps is carrying out operations in the Arakan. Its commander is General Christisson. It consists of 25th Indian Division, 81st and 82nd West African Divisions with 26th Indian Division in reserve and I think an independent tank brigade.' Her next letter was not so truthful. She had heard from Bill that 'XX Indian Corps is at Bombay and has two British Divisions I think numbers 21 and 64 and one West African Division whose number I am not sure but is eighty something. 103 Commando Brigade and an armoured Division will join them. Believed these forces to do big seaborne operation against Sumatra but not for some time.'

The MARY/TOM W/T link from Delhi to Berlin carried a mix of false and true information since D. Division knew it would be passed on to the Japanese and weighted accordingly. Its log read:

14 December: The Frontier Armoured Division has its HQ at Jubbulpore. It consists of 51 Indian Armoured Brigade[29] and a Brigade of Motorized Infantry. It is training in jungle warfare.

17 December: Some battalions of 16th Indian Division[30] which were in Iraq have arrived back at Quetta. It is believed that this division is to be reformed when units have returned and had leave.

18 December: XV Indian Corps now in Arakan fighting – consists of 25th Indian Division, 26th Indian Division, 81st West African Division and 82nd West African Division.

2 January: 26th Indian Division has been relieved by 82nd West African Division and is no longer fighting but still with XV Indian Corps. A Brigade of West African paratroopers has joined this Corps.

6 January: 6th Indian Division a portion of which has already returned from the Middle East has opened its HQ in Karachi where it will be reformed after all its units have returned.

20 January: The XX Indian Corps at Poona has 64th British Division, 21th British Division, 83rd West African Division and 103 Special Services Brigade. They are training in combined operations.

25 January: It is believed that 32nd (Air Transit) Division now completed training at Jhansi will be moving to East Bengal with 3rd Airborne Division sometime near future.

14 February: HQ Airborne Corps has moved from Gwalior to East Bengal.

21 February: 32nd Indian Armoured Division has moved from Ranchi to Ahmednagar.

26 February: 2nd Indian Division[31] which have been at Chhindwara for many months is moving to Vizagapatam.

4 March: The Frontier Armoured Division is moving from Jubbulpore to Vizagapatam on completion of training.

OWL, known to his control to be a one-man band, nevertheless did his usual best, reporting on 28 December that 'the African troops are a Brigade of 10th African Airborne Division and are going to Arakan'; on 17 February, his friend, Hari Singh (an anti-British taxi driver) 'saw many Gurkha parachute troops on trains in station. They are wearing the sign of 9th Indian Airborne Division and he heard they were going to Comilla'; and in March, OWL upped his game with no less than four reports – 'British soldiers wearing sign of 32nd (Air Transit) Division are in Calcutta', 'Kanshi Ram says many more African parachute troops have joined the other ones. He heard that it was the rest of 10th African Airborne Division', 'Kanshi Ram says that many Indian soldiers with tanks are at Vizagapatam. They have come from Central India. Also other soldiers wearing sign of a pouncing panther (21st Indian Division) are at Vizagapatam. He will try and find out what the signs are for on his next visit' and 'the sign of … is for 32nd (Air Transit) Division. They go in large numbers to aerodrome where they get into and out of big aeroplanes.'

PAWNBROKER proved to be the best at spotting Divisional signs and told Indian National Army HQ in Rangoon in February that 'many Indian soldiers with tanks went to Poona this week. The vehicles and soldiers wore signs of 32nd Indian Armoured Division. They came from Ranchi'; 'the soldiers with tanks have written on shoulders 8 Cavalry and 43 Cavalry. They are all Indians. They have gone to Ahmednagar'; 'many Indian soldiers are going through Calcutta. They are wearing the sign of 9th Indian Airborne Division and are mostly Gurkhas, a lot of whom have blue wings on their breast'; 'the soldiers wearing this sign – blue winged horse on a red background – are parachute and glider troops. They have come from Secunderabad. They are in an Indian Airborne Division. We think number 9'; 'the sign of a black rhinoceros head on a red square is for 32nd Indian Armoured Division'; 'there are many British and African soldiers at Juhu and Besada who train with landing craft. They wear many different signs but hear most of them are from 64th and 21st Divisions. The Africans come from West Africa.' His last message in March even mentioned regiments: 'We see many British soldiers in Calcutta. They have Glosters,[32] Devons[33] and Welch[34] and other names on shoulders and wear sign of 32nd (Air Transit) Division.'

Like the MARY/TOM link to Berlin, Fleming took great care feeding SUNRISE, the channel to the Japanese Military Attaché in Stockholm, with a high-grade mix of True and False information. Its log read:

3rd week December: FALSE General Messervy formerly commanding 7th Indian Division now given command XX Indian Corps. This Corps comprising two British, one African and one armoured Divisions now concentrating at Poona and doing extensive training in combined operations.

3rd week December: TRUE 6th Indian Division formerly with Persia Afghanistan Iraq Command is in process of being returned to India. One brigade has already arrived. FALSE HQ and another leaving shortly and HQ being established at Karachi where division will be reformed on arrival of remaining units. Believe this division will be used as training division.

Last week December: FALSE 32nd (Air Transit) Division has been training at Jhansi as Air Transit Division with other divisions of Imperial Airborne Corps. This division comprised solely of British troops is now in an advanced state of training in airborne operations. Is now moving to … for intensive training in jungle warfare prior to being put under command Airborne Corps for future operations.

First week January: TRUE 26th Indian Division which has been in constant action in the Arakan for many months has been relieved by 82nd West African Division and FALSE put into reserve XV Indian Corps. After leave and rehabilitation believed 26th Indian Division will be trained in combined operations as assault division.

2nd week February: FALSE HQ Imperial Airborne Corps is moving from Gwalior to Eastern Bengal. It is believed that divisions comprising this Corps will be moving to assembly areas in Eastern Bengal during the next few weeks.

2nd week February: FALSE 32nd Indian Armoured Division has again been concentrated at Ranchi and is shortly moving to Bombay where it will come under command of XX Indian Corps and be re-equipped with armoured fighting vehicles.

2nd week March: FALSE The Frontier Armoured Division which has been training near Jubbulpore and TRUE the 21st Indian Division which for many months has been training at Chindwara are FALSE being moved to Vizagapatam where they will both undergo training as follow-up divisions for seaborne operations.

It was no wonder that Fleming was so sensitive to the dangers of interference by higher formations or battlefield commanders with this delicate web of deceit he was trying to weave to ensnare Japanese intelligence.

Chapter 17
Imaginary spies and fantasy networks

When in the middle of June 1942, Wavell ordered Fleming to consider the use of fake broadcast messages to disturb the balance of the enemy's mind, little did he know he was presiding over the birth of HICCOUGHS, a fantasy network of non-existent agents. On 25 June 1942, listeners to All India Radio transmission of news in Burmese heard the announcer, at the end of the morning bulletin, read out an extract from *King Lear*, Act V, Scene iii, and at the end of the evening bulletin a further extract from *Macbeth*. In both cases key words were emphasized. This mumbo jumbo, which in fact gave the Japanese cryptographers the necessary details of the secret cipher Fleming proposed to use, was continued for five days. On the sixth day, the announcer read out: 'RRUTE UIFII UERIE CTTRN' and the first HICCOUGHS message had been transmitted. Similar messages were transmitted by All India Radio, twice daily, until hostilities ceased more than three years later.

The original object of HICCOUGHS was, by trading on the spy fever endemic in the Japanese nation, to create alarm, if not despondency, in the mind of the Japanese Commander in Burma, to make him doubt the security of his base and thus introduce a deterrent factor into the various factors on which he might base a decision to advance on India. The picture which Japanese cryptographers were able gradually to piece together for their Intelligence Staff was one of a network of post-occupational agents whose stations or areas of activity were thinly disguised by code equivalents e.g. MYTCHETT – MYITKYINA. Their numbers fluctuated slightly owing to casualties but averaged about eight. They communicated with Delhi by W/T and occasionally by courier. Their duties included intelligence, sabotage, subversion and political warfare. One of them, in Rangoon, was a woman.

Early in the career of the HICCOUGHS organization, D. Division furnished the Japanese through a channel in China with a high-grade document, which contained, among other and more strategical secret information, explicit references to the strength of its 'stay-behind' network in Burma, and to the excellence of the agents' W/T equipment.

For two years, Fleming and the HICCOUGHS case team attached little importance to this rather tiresome routine commitment since it was so transparently flawed. 'Why,' asked Fleming, 'if our agents could communicate with us by W/T, could we not communicate with them by the same means? Why, if we were forced to broadcast messages to them, did we continue to use a low-grade cipher? How was it that they were all (apparently) able to listen in twice daily at fixed times to receive a message which in most cases only affected one of them? How was it that the Japanese Radio Security Service never obtained the slightest clue to the places and times at which they transmitted their lengthy and invaluable reports? Why, after all this talk about subversion and sabotage, did nothing ever *happen*?'[1]

It was to compensate for this glaring inactivity, that on the night of the 16/17 August 1943, after leading the Japanese to it in the traffic, D. Division dropped a container packed with a quantity of high explosives and accessories, medical supplies, a Japanese uniform, a revolver and ammunition, a long directive in a new cipher, a letter in Burmese to one of the agents from his wife in Simla, and a ribbon of the MBE (Civil Division) for the leader of the organization, with a personal note in General Auchinleck's handwriting. This, in three years, was the only physical clue to the existence of the HICCOUGHS network.

The main deception task allocated to HICCOUGHS was during the last eighteen months of the Burma campaign when it was tasked to hold as many Japanese troops as possible on the south-west coast of Burma thereby preventing them from reinforcing the Arakan or Central Burma front. In this it is considered that partial success was achieved for the greater part of the time considerable numbers of Japanese troops, including one fresh division, were located in lower and south-west Burma. How far this was in fact due to HICCOUGHS itself is impossible to say; but it is certain that the Japanese coastal defences were in a continual state of jitters and that even isolated HICCOUGHS messages from time to time generated a state of alarm out of all proportion to their apparent import.

It was only after the fall of Rangoon and the liberation of Burma that captured documents revealed how seriously the Japanese took HICCOUGHS. Burma Area Army, the Naval Signal Intelligence unit and Kempeitai HQ in Rangoon began to read, and to make a careful study of, the traffic sometime during 1942, and probably from the date of its inception. Decodes were normally distributed within twenty-four hours of the HICCOUGHS transmission and executive action had frequently been ordered in the light of the traffic. With no machinery for the centralized interpretation of HICCOUGHS traffic, HQs far removed from Burma were at liberty to place their own alarmist interpretation on the messages they intercepted. Best of all, HICCOUGHS caused a comparatively large diversion of effort on the part of staff and executive personnel of the Burma Kempeitai who spent a great deal of time and trouble issuing orders about and hunting for non-existent spies which they might otherwise have devoted to more profitable ends.

Another notional espionage network, ANGEL ONE, was based in Thailand. It was concerned mainly with the collection of information but had also a sabotage role which was necessarily limited to reconnaissance and preparations for unspecified future operations. Communication was initially opened with Bangkok only but in May 1944, another notional organization with efficient communications and adequate funds, covering Jumbhorn, Kanchanaburi and Chiengrai, was 'taken over' and transmissions were stepped up accordingly.

The imaginary spies were equipped with W/T sets and transmitted their messages to a control station in India. Control passed its messages to Thailand over All India Radio Thai broadcasts with one message per day transmitted to one or other of the agents. A simple half-Playfair cipher was employed, the keyword being changed each month. A four months' supply of keywords was passed and enciphered with the keyword currently in use, so that once the Japanese had broken the cipher, continuity of translation was ensured.

During January 1945, a supply drop was scheduled to be made to a factual party in Thailand. Included in the drop was a container destined for ANGEL ONE. Arrangements were made for the factual party in the field to bury the container and to inform India of its location. ANGEL ONE, who had already been warned, was then to be instructed to collect the container. However, at the last minute ANGEL ONE was to be informed that as a report had been received that the Japanese were waiting to ambush anyone retrieving the container, no action should be taken. Unfortunately the supply drop never took place with the result that D. Division were unable to instruct ANGEL ONE (i.e. the Japanese) to collect it.

Owing to the fact that for two years after the opening up of ANGEL ONE neither factual Allied operations nor SEAC deception plans directly involved Thailand, the time was spent in building up the agents and increasing the spy fever amongst the Japanese, thus tying up security and counter-espionage personnel. Information from captured documents and other sources later proved that not only had the Japanese broken the code but that the existence of the ANGEL ONE organization, of whose role and geographical distribution they were aware, was the cause of considerable concern to them.

One notional network that never gained traction was COUGHDROP, a party of notional British agents in northern Sumatra, the existence of which was simulated by means of dummy two-way wireless communication from Calcutta operated on the same wavelength as that used for transmissions to BRASS. The object of the plan was to lead the Japanese to believe that SEAC intended to launch an amphibious attack on northern Sumatra.

The party, which consisted of an English leader and W/T operator, a Dutch officer formerly stationed in Sumatra and two native couriers, was notionally landed at the end of December 1944 to collect intelligence about Japanese forces and to reconnoitre suitable landing beaches, airfield sites, etc., in connection with an Allied seaborne invasion. After a month had elapsed, Control came up from Calcutta and went through the rigmarole of trying to make contact with the COUGHDROP party, calling and listening alternately. After contact had been notionally established, to make the traffic realistic a number of messages of purely domestic interest were sent, references were frequently made to IN messages and control occasionally repeated back complete messages to the COUGHDROP party to check whether they had been received correctly, and, of course, to give the Japanese an opportunity of decoding them. Once Rangoon had fallen, it was apparent that the Japanese had not been reading the traffic and the plan was, therefore, operated on a reduced scale until the cessation of hostilities, no evidence having been seen that it had achieved any success whatsoever.

❧

Not everyone was convinced by the efficacy of HICCOUGHS and its ilk. SIS wrote to Fleming on 17 March 1945 that, while they agreed that it was 'a valuable instrument when used in conjunction with your other channels to implement deception plans covering operations in Burma (and possibly Siam and Malaya)', there should be no references either to strategic objects outside of these areas or to the Japanese Order of Battle. They were also critical that HICCOUGHS had 'resulted in tightening up Japanese security precautions, which is a disadvantageous factor which must be weighed in the balance against its advantages from a deception point of view'. In a lecturing tone, they reminded him that 'it has always been one of the rules of war to try and make the enemy believe that he is entirely secure and therefore any tendency to make the enemy tighten up his security must be a bad thing'.

D. Division hit back. Fleming wrote to Bevan on 30 March, that having read SIS's comments on HICCOUGHS, 'it would be a waste of time to comment on the various points … over which I can't really disagree with them … as a less favourable interpretation [of HICCOUGHS] is possible. This of course is frequently the case in intelligence work.'

As to the statement that there were no indications that the Japanese had ever been attacked by spy fever, he questioned the credentials of the author.

I did refer to spy fever as being 'endemic in the Japanese nation' and it is: like bandy legs. I don't pretend to be an authority on the little beasts but I have spent many happy months travelling about the more unlikely parts of Manchuria and thus acquired a fairly wide experience of the national idiosyncrasy on all levels, from Generals Koiso and Doihara down to 'Gumshoe Bill', which was the generic name for one's personal detective. (I grant you I may look a more suspicious character than most, but I'm sure that anyone who has lived in Japan or Japanese-occupied territory would bear me out). Nothing will ever persuade the Japanese that the world isn't full of spies, and jolly good spies too. One of our premises has always been that no amount of jittering will make any material difference to their overall security policy, because it's already based 100 per cent on 'the worst possible case'.

As to the matter of increased security by the Japanese having an unfavourable impact, while he agreed that any tightening up of signal and cipher security must have such an effect, Fleming argued that

the more security precautions they try to take the more they must [in Burma] realise their inadequacy. It's quite impossible for them to ensure the physical security of (e.g.) a Divisional HQ in Burma. They daren't go into buildings for fear of bombing and in the jungle they have to keep widely dispersed for the same reason. They would need, to guard their far-flung perimeter, an astronomical number of sentries; and they can't avoid contact with the natives, for they need guides, labour, food and intelligence. Also jitters breeds distrust of any Indian National Army and Burma Defence personnel who may be attached to them; and they breed the usual delay and confusion consequent of the frequent change of code names, reissuing of passes, etc.

Fleming concluded that HICCOUGHS had 'paid a slightly bigger dividend than SIS appreciate'. Based on an extract from a SEAC Special Intelligence Summary: Japanese Signal Intelligence Organisation (Tokushu Joho Han) submitted by Colonel Sir C.R.W. Lamplough,[2] Bt, DSC, RM, in which a Japanese POW confirmed that the whole Japanese Staff was infested with 'spy fever' most of the time. Ronald Wingate continued D. Division's spirited defence and wrote to Bevan on 1 May 1945, quoting from the SEAC report that 'the Japanese invariably ascribe the leakage of information regarding their Order of Battle to activities of "radio spies," that is local agents equipped with radio sets for transmitting information back to the Allies'.

For Fleming, this was vindication of HICCOUGHS. In a letter to Bevan on 4 May, he tabled the motion that 'may we take it that this organisation now leaves the court without a stain on its character from the security point of view?'

❦

As early as January 1943, D. Division submitted a short paper to LCS[3] on 'The Insertion of Phoney Code Messages in Broadcasts to Japan and Japanese-Occupied Territory'. Although HICCOUGHS was still in its early days, this did not deter Fleming from thinking ahead to the day when he could deploy 'this potent weapon' in Japan proper.

1   For just over six months the All India Radio twice-daily broadcasts in Burmese to Burma have been followed by short messages in a cage-code, the key to which, based on quotations from Shakespeare, has been changed once a month.

2   The picture in the mind of anyone breaking these messages (Code-name HICCOUGHS) has been as follows: the British have a number of agents (at present ten) in different parts of Burma. Some must have been left there when we evacuated, others have taken up their posts since then. These agents report to India by wireless and by courier. Their duties include small-scale sabotage and (probably) assassination. The agent in Rangoon is intermittently in touch with Bangkok by courier.

3   The HICCOUGHS service, owing to improvisation in the initial stages, shortage of staff throughout and lack of supervision by a W/T expert, has been cruder than it need have been. (It has, for instance, been much too regular.) But a certain amount of topicality and realism has been infused by close attention to enemy broadcasts and RAF recce reports, etc., and by personal touches such as a Christmas message from H.E. the C.-in-C., the birth of twins (one has since died) to one agent's wife in India, and so on.

4   The hoax, if it has not been ignored altogether, must have received useful support from a document (PURPLE WHALES), bought by the Japanese in July, which stated on the authority of H.E. the C-in-C., that our intelligence organisation in Burma was extensive and well provided with W/T.

5   No indication has in fact been received that the Japanese are paying the slightest attention to HICCOUGHS.

6   It is however just possible that HICCOUGHS have played a subsidiary part in bringing about the following events:

    (a) the banning in Burma of all listening in to broadcasts other than those from Rangoon and the (attempted) impounding of all radio sets;

    (b) the arrest by the Japanese of Gill,[4] a prominent Indian National Army personality, in December 1942. Two HICCOUGHS messages at the end of October contained references to Gill which implied that he was, or might be, in touch with us. (Gill is now believed to be loyal to us and there is no reason to connect his arrest – he has since been released – with HICCOUGHS.[5])

7 Even if – as is possible – these two clues have no bearing on the usefulness of HICCOUGHS, it is difficult to believe that the Japanese mind is capable of <u>conclusively</u> rejecting the service as spoof; and it is fair to assume that it adds, however infinitesimally, to their anxieties and uncertainties about a country which is already causing them trouble and where they are thin on the ground.

8 The question arises whether it would not be worthwhile initiating a similar service

   (a) to other Japanese occupied territories

   (b) to Japan herself.

9 To be effective – particularly in regard to (b) – such a service should not be handled from India only but should be worked into all the more important British and American broadcasts to Japan. Handled with subtlety, and developed slowly, (e.g. opening up first in Thailand, then to French Indo-China, then to Japan), it might in the long run make a useful contribution to that disturbance of the enemy's mind (never very stable in adversity) which it should be our object to effect.

10 A service of this kind offers opportunities for transmitting leading information or impressions to the enemy. Accordingly, LCS are being asked for their comments.

Although nothing came of this initial proposal, Fleming continued to keep it on the table. An early 1944 Extension of Plan 'HICCOUGHS' was circulated:

1 <u>OBJECT</u>
   To encourage the Japanese to believe in the existence of an extensive American Clandestine Organisation in Metropolitan Japan, and thereby cause the Japanese

   a) to waste their effort in countering this imaginary organisation;

   b) to lose confidence in themselves.

2 <u>CONSIDERATIONS</u>

   a) During the last few months, and especially since the capture of Burma, evidence has accumulated from captured documents, Japanese POW statements and most secret Intelligence, confirmation that the Japanese have wasted very considerable efforts in trying to counter the imaginary British spy organisation simulated by Plan HICCOUGHS.

   Although it is clear from most secret Intelligence that the Japanese suspected that HICCOUGHS might possibly be a ruse, it is equally clear that they did not dare to accept this conclusion and ignore the obvious risks involved. In fact, HICCOUGHS has compelled the enemy to take every precaution and issue numerous instructions to ensure that British spies in Burma were rounded up. Apart from this wastage of effort and the loss of confidence, it also seems that HICCOUGHS has made no small contribution from the deception point of view.

b) Though it would be possible for D. Division, SEAC to extend HICCOUGHS by simulating messages on All India broadcasts to imaginary Allied spies in Metropolitan Japan, it will be more plausible and more advisable if this could be undertaken by the Americans on one of their own broadcast networks.

c) The experience gained by SEAC in the development and execution of Plan HICCOUGHS during the last few years has been considerable. D. Division would be glad to explain to any American officers who might be appointed to develop a similar plan against Metropolitan Japan, the methods which have been adopted in HICCOUGHS and the lessons learnt.

3   CONCLUSION

(a) The extension of Plan HICCOUGHS to cover Metropolitan Japan might make a considerable contribution towards the achievement of the objects mentioned in Para. 1 above.

(b) It would be more desirable if the new plan were operated by the Americas rather than that D. Division should extend HICCOUGHS to cover Metropolitan Japan.

(c) The new plan should not only simulate the existence of an American Clandestine Organisation in Japan by HICCOUGHS methods alone, but other ruses, such as the factual dropping of empty parachutes, pintails and wireless sets should be employed simultaneously.

(d) If Joint Security Control believe that a plan on the above lines is desirable, it is suggested that American officers appointed for the purpose might proceed to D. Division, SEAC, where they could study the methods which have been used in HICCOUGHS and the lessons learnt.

In July 1944, after meeting with Fleming in London, LCS circulated their updated response[6] to GREMLIN.

The objects of Plan GREMLIN would be:-

(a) To cause apprehension and uncertainty in Japanese official circles by causing them to believe that a network of secret agents had been established by the Allies in Japan itself;

(b) To provide (eventually) a channel through which items of strategical deception could be passed to Japanese Imperial Headquarters in support of approved deception plans.

To achieve the objects set out above, the broadcasts would begin with messages to a single 'agent' in Japan. In time the network of agents would be notionally increased. When once it appeared that the Japanese were convinced that the network of agents existed, suitable items of deception would be introduced into the traffic. This type of ruse has proved particularly valuable in support of bombing operations; one of the duties which the 'agents' would normally be expected to perform is to report on bomb damage, and their instructions in regard to this matter can produce misleading impressions with regard to the timing, objectives and general pattern of a bombing offensive. The traffic is of course (as HICCOUGHS has shown) extremely effective in support of either real or imaginary assault landings.

It will be apparent from the above that what is required is for Washington to give approval now to the first stage of the plan, the establishment of a network of notional agents in Metropolitan Japan. The matter has been discussed here with MI5 and SIS, who see no objection from their point of view. Provided, therefore, that OSS do not consider that the proposed plan would interfere in any way with their operations, there would not seem any reason why the first stage should not be initiated at an early date. Unless an objection is lodged, Colonel Fleming proposes to start transmitting in September, as he feels – and we agree – that the longer a channel of this type has to 'play itself in' before it is used for deception, the better it will work.

Once the plan is working (say, by mid-1945), a channel for strategic deception to the Japanese would exist and would be available for all Theatre Commanders who choose to make use of it.

Peter tells us that Col. Hunter knows of the project and considers it would eventually be of considerable value to 14th USAAF and 20th Bomber Command, with whose deception plans he (Hunter) is of course directly concerned.

After the contretemps with SIS over the efficacy of HICCOUGHS from which Fleming emerged ebullient, he lobbied Bevan at LCS in May 1945 about GREMLIN.

This brings me to the question of GREMLIN, a project of whose potential value Ronald [Wingate] is as firmly convinced as I am. The objection to this plan being operated by HQ SEAC has hitherto been the constitutional one that matters relating to the strategical deception of Japan must be cleared with Joint Security Control, who have never shown the slightest sign of being either able or willing to clear GREMLIN, though its eventual object could and ideally should be to provide us with a means of implementing approved strategical deception plans, would – and indeed would have to – start, just as HICCOUGHS did, on a purely 'jitters' basis. More specifically, the first three months (say) broadcast traffic would have nothing to do with strategical deception or with military operations of any kind; its sole object would be to convince the Japanese security authorities that a network of Japanese agents or cells, controlled by us, was carrying on intelligence and subversive activities on the Japanese mainland. During this formative stage GREMLIN would merely be a form of psychological warfare, crude by Sefton Delmer's standards but effective out here – more effective, incidentally, than it would have been when the idea was first mooted three years ago on account of the growing administrative chaos and discontent in Japan. (HQ SEAC, of course, transmits 'straight' Political Warfare[7] broadcasts to Japan.)

After the formative stage, when the notional agents had played themselves in, GREMLIN could be exploited either

(a) in aid of strategical deception plans (if there are any) or

(b) in aid of 'jitters' or

(c) in aid of both.

It could be used, that is, either operationally against the Japanese General Staff or psychologically against the 'will to resist' of the whole Japanese official hierarchy. I am, as you know, convinced that in either role it has great possibilities.

The crux of the matter is that there seems to me (will Ronald [Wingate] please confirm that he agrees by signal to you?) no earthly reason why HQ SEAC should not initiate GREMLIN for 'jitters' purposes without reference to anyone else. Nobody can lose anything by it. If anybody objects strongly, the transmissions can be discontinued with impunity and without difficulty at a moment's notice. If, again, anybody says it is a good idea but nothing to do with D. Division, we can if necessary hand over control to literally any staff or organisation which has access to a suitable transmitter. If anyone wants to coordinate it with anything, this presents no difficulty, since this medium has the maximum of flexibility.

In short, I would like to go ahead with GREMLIN as soon as possible as a purely 'jitters' basis, using cryptic and ambiguous traffic with a high proportion of 'ham-chat' in the initial phases and ensuring all necessary coordination with Political Warfare Division in this theatre. Do you see any possible objection to this, and if so is there any way in which we can help to overcome it from this end? Ronald would of course vet all traffic before it was put on the air.

It seems, incidentally, more than possible to me that we shall sooner or later be called in, just as I believe you were, to attack the Japanese 'will to resist'; and if we are, something on the lines of GREMLIN is the only answer I can think of. I would far prefer to have this answer ready for immediate use in such a contingency than to have to waste several months on the tiresome and intricate business of building up our notional organisation.

LCS and British Army Joint Staff Mission in Washington between them realized that D. Division and SEAC were punching above their weight. The Pacific War was a US war and the business of bringing Japan to her knees belonged to the American-led Operation OLYMPIC. Ronald Wingate recalled that

> the immensity and the detail of the operation were bewildering, at least to us. I can remember some of the figures – seven fleets, 8,000 operational aircraft, 200,000 men landed in the first wave. The imagination boggled. We had planned, I think, for a two-divisional landing with one in the follow-up. Our fighter air was of the order of 200, from two auxiliary carriers, and so on. We in turn explained our modest plans, which till then had seemed almost splendid. When it came to my turn I began: 'After the Lord Mayor's coach comes the municipal dust cart – please regard me as the dust cart.'

So the object and implementation of GREMLIN was modified by LCS.

> It is doubtful if the plan could be plausibly used to implement strategical deception. It is effective in SEAC because it is possible to broadcast to a notional agent 'Establish yourself at Moulmein for the future', 'Report on the defences of Hastings Harbour', and so on, from which the Japanese may draw conclusions as to our intentions. Upon the assumption that a notional allied spy ring had been built up by a HICCOUGHS plan in Japan itself, could such questions be asked? At a very late stage and with the object of achieving a measure of tactical surprise they might be, but the conditions of an assault on a thickly defended area such as the Japanese islands are quite different from those on a thinly defended and vast area such as Burma, Malaya, Netherlands East Indies and so on. So such an object can only be secondary, and should be excluded for the time being, though if machinery is successfully built up, and the Japanese take it seriously, an attempt might be made later to achieve this object if circumstances warrant.

> We are left then with the first object, to create alarm and apprehension in Japan as to the existence of an allied spy ring in Japan. This is a plausible object, but it needs a great deal more working out, and consultation in America with the experts.

The object would then be <u>political</u>. A Japanese committee would have to be notionally created in the USA working for the USA, whose object was to persuade the Japanese people or government to end the war, or to bring a party in Japan into power which would see sense and so save Japan from utter destruction. Such a committee would have its agents in Japan and would question them as to economic and political conditions, prominent individuals and so on. If the Japanese really could be made to believe something on the above lines, then military plans would certainly be affected, and possibly to our advantage.

The build-up would have to be very carefully done. The base would have to be America, and a very careful plan worked out by the American experts on Metropolitan Japan.

CONCLUSIONS

a) GREMLIN can only be worked from America.

b) Its object must be political, to create alarm and apprehension in the Japanese government and High Command in Japan itself as regards the political situation in Japan. Its use in direct furtherance of military plans is doubtful, though such a belief on the part of the Japanese would probably affect their military plans to our advantage by creating a serious security problem at any rate, if not worse.

c) A very careful examination of its plausibility and its possibilities should be made in America.

d) If agreed upon by the Americans, LCS might advise upon its implementation based on experience in SEAC.

e) No implementation to Metropolitan Japan should be done by SEAC.

On 28 August 1944, Fleming cabled Bevan his response. Although he was 'disappointed but not surprised by Washington's attitude to GREMLIN', he remained 'convinced the rejection of the plan means missing important opportunity of contributing to the overthrow of Japan whose deteriorating position provides steadily improving psychological background for success [of the plan]'. He was particularly irritated by the objection to GREMLIN on territorial grounds which seemed 'slightly absurd' for the target as of all counteraction activities was the chairman of Tokyo Joint Intelligence Committee 'whose in-tray we already bombard from long range through SILVER, PURPLE WHALES, SUNRISE etc'. He failed to see why 'we should be debarred from addressing him direct on behalf of Mountbatten who is at least as interested as the other theatre commanders in disturbing the base from which the enemy plans war and dispatches forces against him'. On a positive note, he suggested

Washington should be asked to send suitable officer to me to study project in light of HICCOUGHS and Siamese broadcasts backlog and report on its value by carefully co-ordinated adjunct of overall deception programme. If Americans would run it so much the better. I could if necessary detach officer to act as adviser but see no advantage in doing so until Americans show definite willingness to accept and implement plan.

Although there is no record in writing, Fleming must have also despaired to see his tried and tested 'jitters' strategy elevated to the status of a nationwide political campaign, a clear breach of Dudley Clarke's fundamental distinction between deception and psychological warfare.

Not surprisingly, the stumbling block for the implementation of GREMLIN was the lack of 'definite willingness' on the part of the Americans: without their wholehearted approval it proved a non-runner. In July 1945, Ronald Wingate wrote apologetically to Fleming:

I have to confess failure over Plan GREMLIN. South West Pacific Area were not averse to the Plan itself but they said:

a) 'This Plan affects Washington and Admiral Nimitz far more than it affects us. He can do nothing in Psychological Warfare without the authority of Washington and agreement with Admiral Nimitz. Therefore, we are in no position to give clearance for your implementing Plan GREMLIN, nor would we be in a position to take up Plan GREMLIN from Manila. The whole matter must be cleared with Washington if you wish to go on with it.'

b) The target date of Plan OLYMPIC, in South West Pacific Area's opinion, made it impossible, owing to the time required for build-up, for it to have any effect from the Deception angle.

c) Their contemplated arrangements for Psychological Warfare, target date beginning of August, are to flood with leaflets the area in the Japanese homeland pin-pointed for bombing seven hours before the attack, saying that an attack is coming within seven hours, that the area will be obliterated,[8] and warning the people to get out and get rid of their Government which is subjecting them to this disaster.

South West Pacific Area is of the opinion that the effect on Japanese morale of inculcating spy fever by Plan GREMLIN will be very small compared to their combined method of leaflet dropping, followed by bombing.

2. I suggest that you might discuss the matter with Johnny as to whether, as a result of his meetings in Washington, it might be worth trying to get clearance for initiating GREMLIN on the <u>Deception</u> angle.

I am exceedingly sorry that I failed over this but South West Pacific Area from their point of view were unanswerable.

By now it was too late. On 2 August, Bevan wrote[9] to Colonel H.M. 'Tim' O'Connor of the British Army Joint Staff Mission in Washington:[10]

I feel I should give you an account of what I have been up to since I got back from America. I am afraid it is going to be a story of what I have failed to do rather than what I have actually done ...

Plan GREMLIN
You will remember that we have had considerable correspondence on the above subject. I have now had a long talk to Peter on the subject and have also heard from Ronald who, when visiting Manila, suggested that South West Pacific Area should themselves carry out this plan. They replied, as one would expect, namely, that this was entirely a matter for Washington and they themselves would take no hand in it without Joint Security Control authority.

When I talked to Captain Thurber[11] on the question of causing the Japanese to waste their effort on Metropolitan Japan, he seemed very interested on the subject and I gathered he intended to start the ball rolling by suggesting that the Air Force should drop dummy parachutes and pintails etc. on Metropolitan Japan. Peter and I both feel very strongly that an extension of Plan HICCOUGHS coupled with this dropping of dummy parachutes etc. might have a most disturbing effect on the Japanese mind. I therefore enclose a suggestion on the above lines in the hopes that Thurber may think it worthwhile. If he did, then D. Division would be only too delighted to supply Joint Security Control with information regarding their experience with HICCOUGHS. Undoubtedly, the best plan would be for the Americans to send one or two officers to India to consult D. Division on the subject.

... I rather fancy this will be my last official letter to you. I expect to be getting into civilian clothes at the end of next week or possibly the following week. Please remember me to everyone in Joint Security Control and I hope we may all meet again one fine day. I imagine you, yourself, will be coming back about the middle of August and I shall hope to see you in London. Lastly, thank you a thousand times for all your help while you have represented us in Washington. It has been a terribly uphill task. Nobody could possibly have done it better.

Four days later an American B-29 bomber dropped the first atomic bomb on Hiroshima. After the second bomb fell on Nagasaki on 9 August, Japan sued for peace and surrendered on 15 August. It was the end of GREMLIN and of Fleming's war.

Chapter 18

The bright eye of danger: a chance with the Chindits

Like Clarke and Fleming, Orde Wingate, the architect of the Chindit expeditions, was a student and advocate of deception.

> The Japanese mind is slow but methodical. He is a reasoned, if humourless, student of war in all its phases. He has carefully thought out the answer to all ordinary problems. He has principles which he applies, not over-imaginatively, and he hates a leap in the dark to such an extent that he will do anything rather than take it … On the other hand, when he feels he knows the intention … of his enemy he will fight with the greatest courage and determination to the last round and drop of his blood. The answer is evidently never to let him know the intentions or strength of his enemy but always to present him with a situation which he does not thoroughly understand … Our own methods, as opposed to those of the Japanese, were always to present him with a new situation which he could not analyse …[1]

Major Peter Thorne, Fleming's second-in-command, recalled that he only had 'one real row with Peter'. This was at the time that Operation THURSDAY, Wingate's second Chindit expedition, was being mounted. Up to then, Fleming had often ventured out to the British front lines in Arakan, usually with Frankie Wilson, and occasionally had come under direct and indirect fire. For instance, in January 1943 he had visited HQ 123 Brigade on the front line at Rathedaung where he wrote:

> It's a wonder that two bodies of men should be contending so desperately and at such close quarters for a position which as far as I can see is of little or no value to either … I had some little bamboo rafts made and fixed up a

couple of 4 lb charges of guncotton with a half-hour delay and we slipped them downstream after dark to opposite the Japanese positions.

A week later he went to Buthidaung by sampan and from there to the Donbaik Front 'where we shuffled nervously off to an Indian battalion in the jungle which was having a mildly anxious time'.[2]

This time it was different. He had already been on exercise with Mike Calvert and John Hedley in late October the previous year and it was then that he had hatched his plan to go behind enemy lines with them for 'he smelt the prospect of amusement combined with danger'.[3] Furthermore, he was a great admirer of Orde Wingate. In a letter to Celia, Fleming described how he had great respect for him.

He is dour, tragic, egotistic, ruthless (and therefore often rude but mainly to his equals and superiors), generally right in big things, often wrong in small ones, humorous in a donnish or perhaps a Wykehamist way, quite unsparing of himself, generally right about chaps he knows well but possibly often wrong through over-hastiness about those he doesn't know well, intolerant, impatient, not very good at running a staff, indomitable, ill, and a keen, professional and cunning fighter.[4]

Thorne was powerless to stop him.

I knew he had a vague desire to join Michael Calvert's brigade when the situation at WHITE CITY (the area where his glider borne brigade was to land) became stabilised.

I pointed out that this would be breaking one of the basic rules, that no one on the ULTRA list should risk falling into enemy hands. Four or five days before the launch of the operation he told me he was going in with Calvert's HQ gliders and that I was to keep it a strict secret. To make matters worse, that night I had one of my occasional bouts of second sight and learnt in my dream that Peter had crash-landed. I begged him not to go in with the first wave, but he persisted in his plan and went off to Delhi to join Wingate's force. The day after the operation began I received a coded message from Mike Calvert's HQ to say that the pilot of the plane towing Peter's glider had had to cut the tow rope, owing to turbulence, and that the glider had presumably landed somewhere on the east (i.e. the Japanese) side of the Chindwin.

Duff Hart-Davis confirms the magnitude of the risk Fleming took.

Somehow – perhaps by issuing himself with the necessary order – Peter got himself attached to the headquarters of 77 Brigade and prepared to fly in with its advance party. He certainly had no business to do so; apart from the fact that the excursion was of practically no value to his deception activities, his own head contained a dangerously large amount of high-grade information which, had he been captured, might have been extorted from him by the Japanese.[5]

Oblivious to Thorne's concerns, Fleming left Delhi for Burma on 27 February to join Calvert as he made his final preparations. Two days later, he wrote in his diary:

Lovely camp in a little re-entrant with turf down the middle and friendly sort of jungle climbing up the sides. The sun is setting and the British other ranks are joyfully throwing 69 grenades into the bushes thirty yards away. Shades of street warfare in Battersea. The crows here make a noise rather like the Joyce Grove rooks … Shot well with my Luger and Humfrey's.45 Colt, impressing the British other ranks and dumbfounding myself … Slept on the ground last night without a net, slightly bitten by rather effete mosquitoes. Feeling very cheerful and peaceful and optimistic.[6]

The same day he 'collected a slight, rather serious twenty-year-old Chinese orderly whose proper name was Yeung Man Sun but who was always known as 'Automatic', on account of his orderly and methodical habits'.

Staged from Lalaghat, with D-Day fixed for 5 March, Calvert's 77 Indian Infantry Brigade was to spearhead the landings deep in the Japanese rear. The mission of the advance party was to prepare two airfields to receive the Dakotas which would fly in the main body of Chindit troops. That morning, one of General Philip Cochran's B-25 Mitchells photographed the landing zones. The pictures clearly showed that BROADWAY was clear but PICCADILLY had been blocked by tree trunks. The consensus was that the Japanese had realized its potential as a LZ and had deliberately blocked it.[7]

Wingate and Calvert weighed their options. Of the three planned sites only two were now available; Calvert suggested that his brigade should fly into BROADWAY. He later wrote:

We had taken into account that (third landing site) CHOWRINGHEE was to the east of the Irrawaddy while BROADWAY was west of the river. I told Wingate, 'I don't want to split my brigade either side of the Irrawaddy. I am prepared to take all the brigade into BROADWAY alone and take the consequence of a slower build-up.'

The American C-47 Dakotas normally only towed one glider but due to the need to fly in a force capable of constructing and defending an airstrip as quickly as possible it had been decided that each aircraft should tow two heavily-laden Waco CG-4 gliders. Although a double tow posed no problems for a competent pilot in good weather, many of the pilots were inexperienced and the route across the 6,000 feet Chin mountain ranges bordering the Chindwin River guaranteed a turbulent, unsettled flight. The first wave consisted of 52 gliders towed by 26 Dakotas from 1st Air Commando; another 28 gliders followed in the second wave. At 1812 hours on 5 March eight gliders of the first wave took off, scheduled to arrive at BROADWAY by 2130 hours followed half an hour later by the main body. By 0200 hours Wingate and the others waiting at Lalaghat had heard nothing. All was not well.

Poor reconnaissance had failed to show a number of ditches scarring the field at BROADWAY. Calvert later wrote:

All six of the advance party gliders had landed and the plan had been that we would wheel them off to make way for the next batch, which would in turn be wheeled away and so on. But we had reckoned without the ditches. Three of the six gliders were so badly wrecked that the small force at present on the ground could not shift them. We worked at them furiously but suddenly I heard a shout and looked up. In the bright light of the moon I saw to my horror that the first two of the next batch had cast off [their tows] and were winging their silent way down.[8]

Calvert transmitted the prearranged signal SOYA LINK to stop all flying, but at 0630 hours on 6 March he radioed the code words PORK SAUSAGE to resume flights into BROADWAY. A strip for C-47s was in place that evening, and from then on supplies rapidly built up.[9]

Fleming's glider was number 15P – the fifteenth in the run to PICCADILLY. 'I am co-pilot to a charming and enthusiastic American (Flying Officer Williams),' he wrote in his diary: 'The thing not to do is to press the knob which casts us off. When landing I may in an emergency have to pull a lever called "Spoilers", thus (they say) bringing us down faster. I dare say I shall manage.' With a complement (besides the pilot) of six officers,[10] seven British other ranks, one Indian other rank and one Chinese (Automatic), the glider took its place in the queue for take-off. At 2015 hours, the Dakota tug took off with 15P as the short-tow glider on the port side and her sister glider, 14B, on the long tow to starboard. Unknown to the crew of 15P, the intercom to the tug and sister glider did not work and the 'spoiler' was defective.[11]

From this point Fleming recounts what happened in his report:

The pilot had asked for one man to be detailed to come forward if it proved necessary to trim her, and this man was ordered forward immediately after take-off. It soon, however, became apparent that the glider was not behaving satisfactorily, and at ominously frequent intervals the pilot called 'another man forward' until all the passengers were wedged in a sort of pate immediately behind the pilot's and co-pilot's seats.

From a relatively enviable position in the latter, I (and nobody else) was able to see 14B, the long-tow glider on our starboard quarter. Or rather, I *had* been able to see her, for at an early stage in the flight I realized that she was no longer with us. At this point I made a serious error of judgement in not informing the pilot that 14B had cut, for if I had (he afterwards told me) he would have cut too – owing to the danger of glider 14B's loose tow rope removing our starboard wing – and we should have landed on or near our base at Lalaghat.

My reasons for suppressing this information were (apart from ignorance of its full implications) that the pilot appeared to have quite enough on his mind already and I considered it essential to take no action which might lessen the Brigade Commander's chances of getting at any rate part of his staff into Broadway that night …

Glider 15P reached an altitude of 8,000 ft and proceeded on her way with every sign of reluctance. It had become apparent that the controls … were not working … Spells of relatively smooth flying alternated with mild but disturbing aerobatics, during which the glider shuddered convulsively and the blue lights on the tug see-sawed up, down and sideways across our field of vision. (There was no radio communication between tug and glider.) F/O Williams afterwards told me that he was expecting the tail to come off, and I consider that he showed commendable determination in maintaining his objective in these circumstances …

We crossed the Chindwin at 8,000 feet approximately one hour after take-off. At about 2140 hours 15P had a fit of recalcitrance which culminated in (according to the pilot) an attempt to loop the loop. She banked steeply, causing all loose objects in the cockpit and elsewhere to come adrift. The pilot struck the release mechanism above his head, and we found ourselves diving, fairly steeply and in comparative silence …

For what must have been several minutes we spiralled unsteadily towards a point where a stream bed in a gully splayed out in an irregular patch of white sand. On this restricted and uneven space … Williams put the glider down with extreme skill and a resounding bump which broke open the forepart of the cockpit. Impelled partly by tactical considerations and partly by a sense of self-preservation (for the pilot and I, at the bottom of a groaning and blasphemous pile of soldiery, were now most unfavourably placed), I ordered all ranks to deplane with their arms.[12]

Major Colin Pringle was also full of praise for the pilot: 'Without doubt, all members of the party owed their lives to Flying Officer Williams … whose bravery and expertise in handling his unserviceable glider in flight and on landing was responsible for their survival.'

None of the party was seriously injured, and, having burnt all the ciphers and secret documents, Fleming as the senior Allied officer withdrew his men in a northerly direction. Before setting off, he gave them a pep talk.

If we behaved sensibly we had practically nothing to fear from the Japanese, who were almost certainly in a greater state of alarm and confusion than we were ourselves; that no one was to think of himself as a 'survivor' or an 'evacuee' but rather as a member of an unusually well-found fighting patrol, inserted in the enemy's rearward administrative areas and perfectly capable of seeing off the small parties from L of C (lines of communication) units which were all we were likely to meet at this stage; that we had been damned lucky so far.

The party then climbed a low escarpment and for three hours marched briskly along a little-used path, with two men who had no nails in their boots bringing up the rear. At about 0130 hours they came within earshot, though not within sight, of a village from which emerged 'loud and for the most part petulant voices in Japanese as the local post turned itself out', presumably on receipt of news of the glider's landing. The party moved away towards the south-west until finally, when the moon set at 0330 hours, they halted for the night.

Next day they lay up in a patch of elephant grass and sorted themselves out. They carried eight days' K rations, and Fleming at once put the party on half-rations in case their stay in the jungle should be protracted. Every man was armed with a sub-machine gun, a Sten gun, a .303 rifle or a .30 carbine, as well as with grenades, and the officers also carried pistols. There was plenty of ammunition and a number of compasses. So far so good but the problem was that no one had any precise idea where they were. Fleming reacted in a characteristic way. In his report he wrote:

Our position was on paper complicated, but in practice simplified by the fact that we did not know where we were, and had no map of the area other than the escape maps … Opinions differed as to our flying time east of the Chindwin, and the pilot did not know the course on which we had been flying. It was, however, fairly clear that we were between thirty and fifty miles east of the Chindwin and almost certainly south of the Uyu River.

The only sensible course of action the group decided was to walk back towards India. Fleming had considered striking east, to see if he could find WHITE CITY on foot, and heading north-east in an attempt to join Bernard Fergusson's 16 Brigade in ABERDEEN. But both, he decided, were ruled out by the lack of maps and inadequacy of rations. At least they knew that if they kept going westwards they must eventually reach India.

During their first day they heard nothing, and at 1700 hours Fleming led the recce group off to have a look at the first stage of the night's march. After only half a mile he came cautiously to the edge of a large and apparently oblong space:

While spying this through field glasses I observed a Japanese in an elaborately camouflaged uniform (including a silly sort of hat and as far as I could see, a mask) proceeding across my front at a range of approximately three hundred yards. His gait was one of exaggerated stealth and he was moving so slowly, with what appeared to be a machine carbine at the ready, that at first I assumed he was stalking a deer or buffalo …

I then noticed, on the far side of the clearing, what appeared to be a camouflaged hide and near it the legs of a man whose body was concealed by a bush. I accordingly sent the remainder of the recce group back to the main body, who would by this time be moving up. Meanwhile I had lost the exponent of slow-motion eurhythmics, but on moving forward found him again up a tree, in a *machan,* the base of which appeared to be improvised from some form of metal plate, presumably with a view to protection from small arms fire. He was gazing intently towards the centre of the clearing, and his buttocks offered, at 250 yards, a target which it required the strongest sense of duty to forgo.

I withdrew, picked up the main body and made a short detour to the south-west. It appeared however that the clearing curved, and that we were on the inside of the curve, for very soon we bumped the edge of it again, at a point where another Japanese, in an attitude of exaggerated vigilance, was peering through a loophole in a kind of camouflaged stockade.

This necessitated another slight detour, but this too brought us back to the perimeter immediately behind another sentry crouching in a tunnel-like *basha* and sedulously watching his front. It was now nearly last light. We shifted off and halted for a few minutes. I took the opportunity of pointing out to the party that conditions locally were much more favourable to us than we had supposed. All the evidence available suggested that the local commander was in a state of flap; his troops, who appeared to be thin on the ground, were committed to a static defensive role; he was obviously expecting an airborne landing in the clearing and had made careful arrangements to ambush it; there were bound to be other similar clearings in the area which he would have to watch; he had misappreciated our role and probably exaggerated our strength; and we had the initiative.

By this time the Dakotas had begun to drone overhead on the Broadway run, lending colour to the local commander's (alleged) fears. I do not consider that the above appreciation was far wide of the mark, and it had a noticeable effect on the morale of all ranks (including my own), and the march continued in an atmosphere of discreet truculence.

After proceeding for perhaps a mile and a half and almost bumping a small group of tents in or near which ducks were quacking, we reached, recced and crossed a narrow neck of the clearing which at this point appeared to be unsuitable for glider landings and was watched either not at all or inefficiently.

For the next four days, until 10 March, they marched in a westerly direction through jungle and teak forest, avoiding paths, villages and clearings, and often following dry stream beds which they knew would lead to the main watercourse. They saw few signs of life except an occasional woodcutter. At one point when they stopped on the edge of a large clearing, the Indian member of the party spotted a patrol of fifteen Japanese marching very fast along a path that ran just inside the jungle on the far side of it. The fugitives kept still, and the enemy marched on unaware of their presence. At 2100 hours on 9 March, they arrived at the top of a steep escarpment below which flowed a river. It was the Chindwin.

After some preliminary scrambling down and up the escarpment they reached the riverbank at about nine the following morning and settled in a triangular patch of jungle. The slow-moving river looked about 650 yards wide. The east side, lined by fifty yards of sandy beach, was shallow enough to be waded for the first 150 yards. After that, it was a matter of swimming to the far bank for there were no boats within easy reach. Believing that the far bank was dominated by enemy patrols, Fleming considered that:

There seemed nothing for it but to build a raft, and to this task all ranks addressed themselves with enthusiasm under the ingenious direction of Major Faulkner,[13] the Brigade Medical Officer. Our scope as shipwrights was limited by the fact that we were working in or on the outskirts of a village and only a few yards from the main land line of communication in the area (a path along the riverbank), and cutting or hammering was therefore out of the question.

Fleming was indeed fortunate to have with him thirty-six-year-old Major George Faulkner, MC. A Canadian who had volunteered to join the British Army in August 1939, Faulkner was commissioned in the Argyll and Sutherland Highlanders and served with them at Dunkirk. He then volunteered for service overseas and was with the first Chindit expedition LONGCLOTH as senior medical officer. He developed new techniques in self-diagnosis and encouraged men to administer their own drugs and first aid. In a 1969 lecture to St Mary's Hospital London, Mike Calvert described Faulkner as 'a man of magnificent physique and realistic brilliance' whose report on the first Chindit expedition 'helped revolutionize the attitude throughout the Burma Army to disease and casualty treatment and problems of evacuation'.

This in no way deterred Major Faulkner. All packs (fourteen British, one American) were emptied and repacked with empty water bottles and K rations (which we believed incorrectly to be watertight) at the bottom, the remainder of the contents being stowed on top of this supposedly buoyant foundation. The packs were then divided into three lots of five, each of which was enclosed in a groundsheet … The three floats thus formed were to be lashed together within a framework made of half a dozen lengths of dead bamboo … Two paddles were improvised, and would each be wielded by a non-swimmer seated on the raft. The remainder of the party, sustained where necessary by Mae Wests, would hang on to the bamboo framework and propel the raft swimming … The raft was far too heavy and fragile to be carried down the bank and would have to be assembled in the water after dark.

These novel and pleasantly absorbing tasks were interrupted throughout the day by various alarms, which grew frequent towards evening but were all caused by Burmese passing along the path behind us or along the foreshore immediately below us …

At last light sentries were withdrawn. I gave out my orders and we moved down to the beachhead and took off our trousers and boots. All three floats were placed in the water; all three floated. Tremendous activity ensued among the shipwrights, accompanied by a good deal of splashing and the creaking of bamboos. In a surprisingly short time the raft was assembled, and the arms, clothing and equipment loaded on to it in that order.

At this point it was discovered

(a) that the raft had been aground for some time;

(b) that all the groundsheets were full of water and the packs were waterlogged.

I ordered the raft to be unloaded and dismantled.

Our situation at this stage appeared so unpromising as to be almost comic. Fifteen officers and men, in nothing but their shirts and by this time extremely cold, were engaged in dismantling, by the brilliant light of the moon, a contraption which had hitherto seemed their only hope of escape. For an hour and a half we had been making a good deal of noise in the immediate vicinity of a village, the whole foreshore was plastered with our tracks, our waterlogged packs were too heavy to be carried away, and we were dominated at less than a hundred yards by a steep bank carrying a track on which even an optimist had to admit the probability of patrols.

A former captain of swimming at the Royal Military College Woolwich and a canoe builder when a boy, twenty-five-year-old Major Colin Pringle, Royal Signals,[14] took over as chief shipwright. By lashing in the contents and turning the craft upside down, thereby trapping enough air in it to make it float, he collected the five non-swimmers wearing their Mae Wests and ordered them to hang on to the sides and kick their legs while he steered it across. Halfway across, Signalman Angus swam ahead and was never seen again.[15] Pringle returned to the east bank with Mae Wests and groundsheets for the second party but found the beach deserted. Collecting some weapons and equipment, he swam back and was relieved to discover the rest of the party had managed to cross the river safely and were drying their clothes in front of a large bonfire. The next day, together with another officer, he returned to the east bank to collect the remaining weapons and kit that the swimmers had left behind, in particular their boots. Pringle thus swam the Chindwin five times in the course of a twelve-hour period, mostly at night.

In the morning they redistributed their remaining rations and prepared for another series of clandestine marches. After an unsuccessful search for Signalman Angus's body they set off at 1030 hours, but they had gone hardly a mile when they bumped into an observation post manned by the 9/12 Frontier Force Regiment who directed them south. After two hours, they met a patrol of the 1st Battalion Seaforth Highlanders and were given a warm welcome by Battalion HQ. Jimmy Marks, the Seaforths' Mortar Officer, remembered Fleming standing in a cleared patch among a tangle of sawn-down bamboo looking extraordinarily neat and collected, and worrying less about himself than about finding a comfortable place for the faithful Automatic to sleep.

Summing up the experience in his report, Fleming concluded that the main factor contributing to their escape had been consistently good luck. Apart from this, and 'a certain amount of tactical common sense', he believed that their best ally had been high morale:

All ranks came out full of self-confidence and genuinely anxious to rejoin their brigade in the field, and there is no doubt that practically everybody keenly enjoyed a great many of their experiences after the somewhat alarming first night.

I attribute the high level of morale ... to the doctrine laid down by Brigadier Calvert (Commander, 77 Independent Infantry Brigade) and inculcated by him in training. This doctrine consists in effect in maintaining a sense of proportion with regard to the Japanese, the jungle and other real or supposed hazards which beset a small, isolated detachment in enemy-occupied territory. The feeling of being hunted is an unpleasant one, and personnel who become oppressed by it are liable to act, should a crisis or irksome delay arise, in a foolish and unsoldierly manner. Though I never felt justified in attempting any offensive action, I think we managed to avoid this hunted feeling.

In the last paragraph of his report Fleming generously praised the coolness of several of the officers and other ranks in the party.[16] He did not, of course, mention his own, but several of his fellow survivors did, and they made it clear that without his unshakeable courage and determination their chances of escape would have been infinitely smaller.

It was in a Buchanesque vein that he reiterated his experiences to Celia.

I honestly enjoyed practically the whole of the eight days. At its best it was like an intensely exciting stalk and the only bad bits were when we couldn't sleep at night … What I felt I had to do, practically from the moment the glider cut loose, was to impose my own attitude to the Japanese on fourteen complete strangers – British, American, Canadian, Chinese and Indian.[17]

On 13 March, the party marched twelve miles over a pass in the Naga Hills to the roadhead and from there to Tamu by truck. The following day a Dakota flew them to Imphal where they found Advance HQ Special Force and the Rear HQ of 77 Brigade. After a couple of days, Fleming along with the rest of the 77 Brigade advance party officers were flown into BROADWAY and then to Mike Calvert's WHITE CITY stronghold at Mawlu. Once there, he insisted on driving a jeep out into the jungle so that he could mortar the surrounding Japanese. On 3 April Fleming attended the newly appointed Major General Lentaigne's conference at ABERDEEN with all the Chindit Brigade Commanders[18] after the death of Wingate. After the discussion, Calvert remembered being continually amused by Peter Fleming's 'cryptic and acid summary of the situation'.[19]

By this time, the Japanese High Command had realized that the threat posed by Wingate's Brigades was much more serious than they had first thought and they began to move more troops into the area to dislodge the Chindits from their jungle fortresses. On the evening of 5 April, Fleming took a three-inch mortar and its crew to Mawlu to harass the Japanese who were forming up to attack the airstrip. 'He did so to great effect … [and] diaries captured later … showed that his efforts with the mortar caused consternation and casualties.'[20]

Throughout all this time, Thorne had understandably been in a pickle.

I could only hope for the best, but I told two of Peter's friends, Philip Mason and John Keswick, both very high up in Mountbatten's entourage, what had happened. As Peter often disappeared from Delhi to go to Cairo, Chungking etc., I hoped to keep the matter quiet until he got back. This was not to be. Mountbatten was due to hold one of his meetings with the heads of the clandestine services – MI5, MI6 etc. – so I went along to represent Peter, who always attended. Mountbatten saw me and asked where Peter was. I said he was briefly away from Delhi. Mountbatten asked me when I expected him back, and when I replied, 'I hope fairly soon,' he asked again where he was. I had to say that he had crash-landed somewhere east of the Chindwin. All hell broke loose – 'why hadn't Thorne stopped him going,' etc. – but no one could raise the matter of the risk to ULTRA because some of those present were not aware of its existence. Mountbatten finally earned my gratitude by saying, 'I think Major Thorne was in a very difficult position. Let's turn to the first item on the agenda.' Wonder of wonders, Peter brought his party safely back across the Chindwin, but then compounded his original sin by flying back immediately to WHITE CITY for three or four days with Mike Calvert.

When Fleming finally got back to Delhi on 13 March after hitching a ride with Brigadier Bernard Fergusson in his light aircraft, Mountbatten sent for him, but according to Thorne he was only 'given a mild rocket'. Fleming later told Celia[21] that 'the Supremo was quite reasonable about it and the Auk … downright nice about it. So for that matter was the Viceroy.' In a hilarious sketch, he recalled his meeting with Wavell:

W: Have a bad time?
F: No, Sir; thank you, Sir. Not too bad.
Pause
W: Mph …
F: (trying to make the grade) Had a lot of luck, Sir.
W: I see.
Pause
F: (telling all) As a matter of fact it was rather interesting, Sir.
W: Oh.
F: (piling on the interest) There's an awful lot of room in there, Sir.
W: Room?
F: (practically down to pidgin English) Very big country, Sir, very few Japanese.
W: I see.
Pause

F: I mean, Sir, you could hang about for a long time. With a small party I mean. If you wanted to, of course.

W: Yes, I suppose you could. *Pause*

W: Well …

F: Well, Sir, …

W: Thank you very much for coming and telling me about it, Peter.

F: Not at all, Sir.

Nevertheless, the whole episode did not sit comfortably with the powers that be. At the time, the risks of landing behind enemy lines by glider were considerable and Fleming's voluntary participation highly questionable. In hindsight, he was lucky to be alive and his survival can be attributed to the remarkable airmanship of Williams. On the way back to India, the presence of the immensely experienced Faulkner in the party was also a godsend. Ironically, Fleming always worried whether he had the leadership skills to command men in battle for he was well aware of his inclination to rely on himself rather than others and that his reserve and shyness could be a hindrance in motivating others. While this foray proved any such doubts wrong, it called into question his judgement for the risk of such a high-value intelligence asset falling into enemy hands bore no relation to any contribution that Fleming could have made to Calvert's 77 Brigade in their 'behind enemy lines' operation. Yet he remained unrepentant – 'I hated leaving Mike [Calvert] who I reckon to be as good a fighting commander as you will find anywhere in the world's various services and who likes having me around'[22] – and defiantly flew up to Shaduzup in August to see Major General Joe Lentaigne who had succeeded Wingate.

Chapter 19
Enough of war crimes

During the course of the war against Japan, Allied governments had become increasingly alarmed by reports of ill-treatment of POWs and civilian internees in Japanese-occupied territories. In 1944, the United Nations War Crimes Commission, which included a Far Eastern and Pacific sub-committee, reissued its policy statement of 4 June 1943.[1] It found that although the Imperial Japanese Government had signed the Geneva POW Convention of 1929 (but had not yet ratified it), they had undertaken to observe its terms *mutatis mutandis* in respect of Allied POWs, and as regards food and clothes, to take account of national and racial customs on a basis of reciprocity. However, very shortly after the outbreak of hostilities with Japan it became apparent that both officers and men of the Japanese Imperial Forces were, in their conduct towards POWs, in many cases not governed by the normal dictates of civilized humanity and that, though examples of correct behaviour were not unknown, Japanese treatment of POWs was at best callous and irresponsible and at its frequent worst characterized by a bestial cruelty which had its roots partly in sadism and partly in a racial impulse to humiliate members of white races.

Furthermore, although the Japanese Government was aware of the gross misconduct of the Imperial Forces, 'it was unable if not unwilling to remedy this shameful state of affairs'. Irrespective of the attempts of various Allied Governments to exert moral pressure on the Japanese Government and General Staff by releasing for publication selected items from the growing volume of intelligence regarding the treatment of POWs, all such attempts had failed. Shocking though the revelations were, and deeply though they stirred Allied and neutral opinion, their effective impact on Japanese policy in respect of POWs was negligible. Moreover, they caused widespread distress among the relatives of the POWs.

So in May 1943, the War Crimes Commission was asked by the Combined Chiefs of Staff to formulate a long-term policy which would provide answers to the following questions:

a) Was it possible to influence the Japanese Government to stop the maltreatment of POWs, and to improve the conditions in camps?

b) If so, by what means?

c) If these means included the publication of reliable information regarding atrocities against POWs, how are the feelings of their relatives to be spared?

d) If publication was regarded as either ineffectual or for other reasons undesirable, what use could best be made of the vast and increasing body of intelligence bearing on the treatment of POWs by the Japanese?

In its Progress Report No.7 for the period 1 October to 31 December 1944[2] which was based on intelligence updates from a variety of sources including captured Japanese soldiers, the Commission concluded that 'it is most unlikely that any Japanese Government of the present type can be influenced in the manner desired' and 'that the most suitable means by which to attempt to exploit the scanty opportunities … are strong diplomatic representations made through the normal channels' since 'in the light of experience to date and of the known attitude of militarist circles in Japan, the publication of even the most sensational information regarding atrocities against our POWs will [not] act as a deterrent on Japanese inhumanity'.

In SEAC, plans were drawn up by the newly formed E Group under Lieutenant Colonel R.C. Jackman[3] to rescue the POWs, not just from their captors but from the desperate malnutrition and endemic diseases that threatened their survival; BIRDCAGE, a leaflet information campaign to inform camp inmates of a Japanese surrender and the procedures they should adopt until Allied land forces arrived to liberate them and take the Japanese guard forces into custody, was to be followed by MASTIFF, designed to airdrop medical teams and stores to the camps identified by SOE and other clandestine agencies.

As head of D. Division with access to this dismal picture, on 6 April 1945 Fleming forwarded to LCS his outline plan (BASSINGTON) to pressurize the Japanese government into improving the conditions of Allied POWs.

OBJECT
To improve the treatment by the Japanese of Allied POWs.
METHOD
The object will be attempted by passing to the Japanese Foreign Office and Greater East Asia Ministry a Top Secret document from which the Japanese will draw the following deductions:

a The Governments of the United Nations[4] have collated a very considerable body of evidence about the treatment by the Japanese of our POWs.

b   Most of this evidence is highly discreditable to the Japanese
military authorities and exhibits the Japanese national character in a
dishonourable and indeed repulsive light.

c   Very little of this evidence has so far been published.

d   Our comparative reticence in this context reflects a carefully
considered long-term policy which may be summarised as follows:
The piecemeal publication, in war time, of information regarding
Japanese maltreatment of our POWs serves no useful purpose. It
does not act as an effective deterrent on Japanese inhumanity, it is
extremely distressing to the relatives, and its impact on world opinion
is transitory because so many other horrible things are happening
elsewhere that, as far as atrocities are concerned, world opinion
is punch-drunk. The United Nations policy is accordingly, while
publishing from time to time selected scraps of evidence in order to
maintain public interest in the whole subject, to hold the bulk of the
available information in reserve for use after the defeat of Japan. It
will by that time constitute a 'Black Book' of the most formidable
kind and will serve as the spearhead of a propaganda campaign to
decisively discredit the Japanese nation in the eyes of the civilised
world and thus to prevent or at any rate to delay the resurgence of
Japan as a respectable member of the community of nations.

e   In the interests of justice and fair play, and in order to enhance
the objectivity of the final dossier, cases of good and humane
treatment of POWs are being recorded in as much detail as cases
of the opposite kind. Very little evidence of good treatment is so far
available.

f   Every endeavour is being made to keep our long-term policy secret
and great importance is attached to it.

CONSIDERATIONS
From the evidence available in this theatre, including captured documents
and the narratives of escapees, it would seem that the Japanese are, on
certain of the higher levels, at any rate mildly disturbed by the revelations
which have been made from time to time about their inhumanity towards
POWs. This is a factor in favour of the plan.

The somewhat Machiavellian approach which will be implicit in the document
is (curiously enough) very much in line with what the Japanese expect and
far from the Anglo-Saxon powers and the document is likely to command
complete credulity and to arouse misgivings to a greater or lesser extent. This
is a factor in favour of the plan.

The Foreign Office and the Greater East Asia Ministry, who will be the recipients of the document in Tokyo, are in the matter of treatment of POWs a potential moderating influence. They are aware of the standards by which the civilised world judges these things, and of the terms of the Geneva Convention; they have to handle and answer protests and deal with Red Cross matters; they are propaganda-minded and will be directly concerned with restoring Japan's international prestige after her defeat, which they are coming increasingly to regard as inevitable. Their power vis-a-vis the militarists may not be great but it is not negligible. This is a factor in favour of the plan.

ADVANTAGES
The potential advantages of putting this plan into execution are obvious.

DISADVANTAGES
The main if not the only potential disadvantage is the possibility that the Japanese will attribute our information to an intelligence service operated within the POW camps and either impose additional security measures or inflict reprisals …

RECOMMENDATIONS
It is recommended that:-

    a Plan BASSINGTON should be submitted to Supreme Allied Commander for his approval.

    b D. Division should forward the plan, if approved, to LCS with the request that they should:

        (i) Obtain the views of MI9 on it;

        (ii) If these are favourable, add the necessary touches of local colour and return the finished product to D. Division for transmission to the enemy.

The final draft of Fleming's carefully crafted top secret document was a masterpiece of innuendo, half-open windows and half-shut doors. The plan, slightly amended by LCS, was approved by the Joint Intelligence Committee and both the Foreign Office and the Directorate of Political Warfare declared themselves in favour of it. However, for D. Division and SEAC to go ahead in planting the document, the approval of Washington was essential. Yet again, the differences between the two Allies in the procedure of approving deception plans prevailed and the Joint Security Control insisted that it should be put before the Combined Chiefs of Staff. In a note to General Hollis, Bevan explained that he did not feel that it was a suitable matter for putting before the [British] Chiefs of Staff in the normal manner entailing circulation to Service Ministries. I recommend, therefore, that it could be put before the Chiefs of Staff privately, and I assume that since the Joint Intelligence Committee have already passed it, the Directors of Plans need not be consulted. [After that had taken place] I recommend that the Chiefs of Staff should forward Plan BASSINGTON to Joint Security Control Washington for the approval of the Combined Chiefs of Staff.

Hollis acted quickly. BASSINGTON found favour with the Chiefs of Staff who 'agreed that the plan was well worth trying; it might be of considerable benefit to the prisoners, and in any case could do no harm'.[5] Within three days, Field Marshal Ismay sent the prime minister the following minute.

Japanese Treatment of Allied POWs

The Chiefs of Staff have considered a plan (BASSINGTON), put forward by the Deception staff, with the object of improving the treatment of Allied POWs by the Japanese. The object will be attempted by passing to the Japanese, through special channels, a Top Secret document from which it is hoped they will conclude that the United Nations have collated a considerable amount of evidence about the treatment of their POWs by the Japanese, and that this evidence is highly discreditable to the Japanese though very little of it has so far been published by the Allies.

The reason put forward for Allied reticence in this context is the fact that the world as a whole is already 'punch drunk' with numerous accounts of atrocities. The United Nations policy is therefore to withhold the bulk of the available information in reserve for use after the defeat of Japan. It would then constitute a 'black book' of the most formidable kind to be used to discredit the Japanese nation and prevent, or at any rate delay, the resurgence of Japan as a respectable member of the community of nations.

From the evidence available it appears that the Japanese are already disturbed at the revelations made from time to time of their inhumanity towards POWs and that this plan might arouse considerable misgivings.

The Chiefs of Staff consider that this plan is well worth trying. It should do no harm and might result in improved conditions for our prisoners.

They therefore propose, subject to your approval and to that of the Foreign Secretary to whom I am sending a copy of this minute, to forward the plan to Washington for the approval of the American Chiefs of Staff before it is put into effect.

Churchill approved BASSINGTON and minuted 'Do proceed' on 15 April. Such were the bureaucratic delays on the part of the approving authorities in London and Washington, that Fleming's document was only passed for despatch a few days before the end of the war by which time further unimaginable atrocities against Allied POWs had been committed.[6]

Chapter 20

Home is the hunter

Following the POTSDAM Conference and the ensuing Potsdam Declaration announcing the terms for a Japanese surrender, the Combined Chiefs of Staff issued a Directive to Mountbatten on 26 July 1945. The following extracts show that for SEAC the war was far from over:

1   Your primary task is the opening of the Straits of Malacca at the earliest possible moment. It is also intended that British Commonwealth land forces should take part in the main operations against Japan which have been agreed as the supreme operations in the war; and that operations should continue in the Outer Zone to the extent that forces and resources permit.

2   The eastern boundary of your command will be extended to include Borneo, Java and the Celebes.

3   Such Dominion and Dutch forces as may be operating in your new area will come under your command. They will, however, continue to be based on Australia.

4   The area to the east of your new boundary will be an Australian command under the British Chiefs of Staff.

5   It has been agreed in principle that a British Commonwealth land force of from three to five divisions, and, if possible, a small tactical air force, should take part in the main operations against Japan in the spring of 1946. Units of the British East Indies fleet may also take part.

6   You will be required to provide a proportion of this force together with the assault lift for two divisions.

7   The requirements for the force taking part in the main operations against Japan must have priority over all the other tasks listed below.

8   You will, within the limits of resources available, carry out operations designed to:

   a   Complete the liberation of Malaya

   b   Maintain pressure on the Japanese across the Burma-Siam frontier.

   c   Capture the key areas of Siam

   d   Establish bridgeheads in Java and/or Sumatra to enable the subsequent clearance of these areas to be undertaken in due course

9 You will submit a programme of operations to the British Chiefs of Staff as soon as you are in a position to do so.

10 You will develop Singapore and such other bases as you may require to the extent necessary for operations against the Japanese.

So D. Division and Force 456 were geared up to implement complex deception operations in support of Operation ZIPPER, the invasion of Malaya and Operation MAILFIST, the ensuing plan to retake Singapore, both of which had originally been scheduled for December 1945 and then brought forward to September. In support of these operations, Fleming crafted Plan SCEPTICAL to wrong-foot the Japanese into thinking that an uprising in Thailand would precede them and therefore necessitate a large Japanese garrison of battle-hardened troops to be stationed there. Additional plans were also in place to assist Allied operations in the Dutch East Indies, Indo-China and mainland China, including Hong Kong. Although there were no British ground troops involved in Operation DOWNFALL, the seaborne invasion of Japan planned for October 1945, a Commonwealth Corps was in the process of being formed to take part in Operation CORONET, the follow-up landings on Honshu scheduled for March 1946. Given Fleming's proven leadership and the considerable experience accumulated by all members of his organization, the chances are that D. Division and Force 456 would have acquitted themselves with distinction and added some more 'wins' to their tally.

Eleven days after the POTSDAM Conference, the Allied threat of 'prompt and utter destruction of Japan' became a reality. Following the detonation of two atomic bombs over Nagasaki and Hiroshima, the Japanese capitulated on 15 August 1945. Soon after, Sir Ronald Wingate requested that D. Division and Force 456 be closed down as at 15 October 1945. 'There is no more useful work to be done by the Division and that in fact it would help SIS and other Intelligence branches considerably if they knew they would receive no more policy directives from D. Division.'[1] As early as June 1945, the new Director of Intelligence SEAC, Air Commodore Penney, had written to Assistant Chief of Army Staff in response to the deception plan for Operation ZIPPER that 'I think the time is rapidly approaching if it has not arrived when no notional plan will have any effect on the Japanese'.[2]

Sifting through the old files, Fleming wrote to Celia:

Honestly you know, when I glance through the rubbish I've been wrestling with for the last three and a half years I'm amazed how much sense of proportion I've managed to retain: after reading through the old controversies, complaints, attempts-to-get-a-move-on, insincerities, eyewash, long analyses of things which eventually turned out to be of no importance at all, complaints about pay, about the telephone, about correspondence gone astray, nonsense about security precautions, requests for an electric fan, raspberries, reconciliations, 'Following Personal for Fleming', 'To be opened only by addressee', more complaints about pay, about aeroplanes, about the lavatory, about the American General Staff, about topees and travel allowance and time-saving – you never *saw* so much bumf! After reading about all the muddles and squabbles and changes of plan and hurried flights hither and thither I feel as if I've just woken up from a particularly horrible and arbitrary nightmare. I am glad it is all over. I don't think I ever allowed myself to realize how badly I wanted the war to end.[3]

In March 1945, D. Division had introduced a Weekly Progress Report, edited by Horder, which was circulated to LCS, British Army Joint Staff Mission in Washington, HQ SEAC and the Director of Military Intelligence India. Never more than a few pages long with an annex showing latest deception signals traffic, the report covered 'Comings and Goings' within the division, a short overview of intelligence and an update on plans and channels. After the Japanese surrender, when its use came to an end, Fleming could not resist sending out a final bittersweet edition dated 11 September 1945:

1   With the end of the Japanese war, addressees will have noticed that the above mentioned reports, though much easier to write, have become virtually impossible to read, such information as they contain being of a purely domestic nature and concerned with the imminent disbandment of D. Division and Force 456. No further reports will accordingly be published during the remaining month of our official existence. Should, however, any significant material nearing on our past activities come to hand it will be made available to the LCS, who are requested to give it whatever distribution they consider appropriate.

2   It would be implausible (which for a Deception Staff is a graver charge than the equally applicable one of hypocrisy) to pretend that it is with the slightest feeling of compunction or regret that we bid farewell to our small but far-flung public. 'NIL', which has figured so largely in our recent reports, is our favourite monosyllable, and it would not surprise us to hear that this goes for most of our readers, whose interest in the putative reasons for RHINO's failure to make contact, the date of Major Warde-Aldham's return to Monywa, an ambiguous clue to Japanese strength in

the Nicobar Islands and similar *faits divers* with which we have grappled for three and a half years, must have worn almost as thin as ours.

3   We apologize for the shortcomings – obscurities, typographical errors, misspellings, etc. – which have sometimes been noticeable in our Weekly Progress Reports; but for our part we marvel that there were not more of them, seeing how adverse the administrative conditions under which these reports were written, edited, typed, duplicated, sealed and dispatched by a small staff.

4   Finally, we hope that, for all their failings, these reports did not altogether fail in their main purpose, which was to provide recipients with a first-hand glimpse into the workings of our enemy's mind. The glimpse was seldom more than a fleeting one but it was (or seemed) sometimes suggestive; and we like to think that the dull and inconclusive nature of most of our material, and the fact its accent was mostly on error and doubt and disappointment, was not altogether our fault but was due in part at any rate to the singular but unimpressive character of the Japanese military mind.

He made a bonfire of most of the files and after a fact-finding tour of the Far East that encompassed Burma, Malaya and Vietnam, flew home from Saigon to England in November. Fighting first the Germans and then the Japanese, he had been at war for nearly seven years, five of which had been spent abroad. Yet his extraordinary career and the remarkable contribution he had made with D. Division received paltry recognition in the award of an OBE, the same decoration bestowed on his grandmother in 1918 for running a hospital in her Grosvenor Square house. His senior officers thought highly of him. In a Special Confidential Report dated 16 December 1944, even his old antagonist Air Vice-Marshal John Whitworth-Jones wrote of Fleming: 'An officer gifted with imagination, wit and ingenuity. He possesses mental and physical energy to a high degree. The balance associated with the late thirties has not stifled in this officer a love of adventure usually associated with the early twenties. An outstanding and individualistic officer.' Lieutenant General Sir Henry Pownall added: 'A very remarkable and outstanding officer in his own line. The report sums him up well. His military future should lie in some activity connected with Intelligence.' His subordinates, like Peter Thorne, rated him equally highly as 'an extremely kind, friendly and inspiring employer'.

Fleming did not shy away from self-criticism. In a letter to Celia in August 1944, he reckoned he had

made a certain amount of difference to the Japanese but in this as in all my other jobs I've handicapped myself by, if not putting people's backs up, at least failing to ingratiate myself and win people's confidence. People think

I'm wild, which in a way I am, and even when I'm on my best behaviour it's only too easy to see that I don't really give a damn for practically anyone and people naturally find this galling. I would myself.[4]

Always committed to getting the job done, Fleming undoubtedly compromised his chances of further promotion when he chose to remain in Delhi after Mountbatten moved SEAC to Kandy in Ceylon. His operational rationale was entirely correct. If based in Kandy he would be far from the front lines and his carefully cultivated intelligence 'channels': furthermore, he would be hundreds of miles from his key staff. He was convinced that Mountbatten's 1943 notion of SEAC mounting amphibious assaults and seaborne invasions from Ceylon was 'pie in the sky' for the necessary naval assets were all earmarked for the Mediterranean and north-west Europe: the real war would be fought in the jungles of Burma. By sending others like Horder down to Kandy, he neatly extricated himself from the daily drudge of meetings and attendance at rapidly proliferating committee meetings, for all such activities came under the heading of 'non-productive'. But in the politics of high command, absence from the corridors of power is a mistake for 'out of sight' means 'out of mind'.

Not that Fleming particularly cared for he was not a career soldier and was immensely proud of holding an emergency wartime commission in the Grenadier Guards, a regiment where he had many friends.[5] He wrote to Arthur Penn, the Regimental Adjutant, on 28 May 1942 from the British Legation in Kabul.

Dear Arthur,

It ill becomes a Grenadier to write to his Regimental Adjutant from neutral territory, but it's all right, I am not a deserter and am only here for a few days on some obtuse duty. The field of honour is indeed a long way off and the nearest I have got to a war-like action was scowling at the Italian Minister (a rather small man) in the bazaar on Tuesday. The object of this scrawl (I'm sorry, I can't find the Military Attaché's ink) is to let you know – belatedly I fear – that I was posted to GHQ New Delhi as a Staff Officer in the Intelligence Directorate w.e.f. 17 March 1942 and that communications addressed to GHQ will find me until further notice. I have had two trips to Burma and one to China whither I expect to return in a fortnight or so: though it's becoming rather hard to get there. I heard of but did not see a Grenadier called Grinling in Burma[6]; and Tommy Cooke[7] is in India with the ex-Governor (very Hanoverian) but appears to have reverted to civil life. Jerry Seymour (whom I also haven't seen) is ADCing in Calcutta and is expected to be pining for more active service. Shelley (Lt. Col.) has an 'I' job in GHQ. The Regiment has no permanent representative in China; but I hear that the Third Guards[8] have been stiffened and steadied by the enrolment of a son of the Chinese Finance Minister, the third crookedest man in Asia. Ah well, *à la guerre comme à la guerre*.

Please give my respects to the Lieutenant Colonel and my best love to Tim and Geoffrey Dawson if you see them. I am awfully sorry to have been so slow in reporting my rather snipe-like movements.

Yours ever

Peter Fleming

After meeting in London in May 1943, when Fleming was en route to the TRIDENT conference, Penn took delight in teasing him:

My dear Peter,

I have just been checking the Handbook of the 1st Guards Club,[9] which is in the course of preparation.

You are shown, I observe, as a Major, whereas I could not help noticing the other night the somewhat offensive way you were displaying the badge of rank of a Lieutenant Colonel.

You have now before you a hard choice. Face it, my boy, like a Grenadier. Are you a Lieutenant Colonel? And if so, when, or shall I show you instead under the popular heading 'West End playboy poses as Guardee'. What do I care?

Yours ever

Arthur

Fleming responded by return of post:[10]

My dear Arthur,

In reply to your P/A/23/4 of 10 June 1943 I should like to be shown as a Major General, in rather larger type than the other fellows, but feel this might make for jealousy. So perhaps we had better stick to the facts, which are that I am a Grade One Staff Officer ('I') GHQ India Command, w.e.f. (I think) 1 March 1943 and my recreations are knitting and hashish. Incidentally Peter Thorne is a Staff Officer of similar vintage.

It was particularly nice seeing you the other day. What one misses most Out East is chaps who are able and willing to talk sheer nonsense. It's a terrible deprivation.

Yours ever

Peter

After the war, having been invited to command a TA battalion of Light Infantry, Fleming wrote to the Grenadiers on 23 January 1948:

Dear Colonel[11]

I have been asked several times recently by the OC 6th (TA) Battalion of the Oxfordshire and Buckinghamshire Light Infantry to help him in his rather uphill struggles and I would like to do this if I can. Apart from more general reasons, my youngest brother raised a half-company loyally in 1936–1939 and died as a prisoner of wounds received while serving as Adjutant to the (4th) Battalion, virtually the whole of which was put in the bag at Cassel in 1940.[12] The Battalion' s bad luck has naturally not created a very fertile soil for recruiting in the district and Lieutenant Colonel Ward (the new CO) needs all the local help he can get.

I feel – and have told him – that I cannot very well do anything unless I take an active part myself. I can hardly (for instance) urge the twenty-odd men of military age who work for me to join the TA and go to camp and so on if I do nothing about it myself; and on paper the logical solution would seem for me to resign my commission in the Regiment and join my local TA battalion as a rather elderly Intelligence Officer.

I need not say how much I hate the idea of leaving the Regiment, nor do I know whether it is permissible for me to do so. But it does rather look as if I ought anyway to ask you for your views and advice on the matter, and that is the purpose of this letter. The idea of ceasing to be a Grenadier (even a bad one) is distasteful in the extreme, but looking at things from a less personal point of view it does seem as if, my age and circumstances being what they are, I might be of more use to the country if I did transfer to the Territorials.

Anyhow, I should be awfully grateful if you would tell me what you think I ought to do. I suppose it is possible that other officers of the Regiment have found themselves in a similar dilemma, so there may be a standard procedure for dealing with it.

Yours ever

Peter Fleming

Subsequently and on an entirely amicable basis, he took command of the 6th (TA) Battalion.

In early 1955, Fleming got wind of the Tercentenary Exhibition which the Grenadier Guards were organizing in London. In a typical self-deprecating note, he wrote to Regimental Headquarters that

I see that the Regimental Exhibition will include medals, and I thought it just worth asking whether the organizers would like the loan of a Chinese medal (the Order of the Cloud and Banner) which for some extraordinary reason was awarded to me in the last war. It is a fairly exotic piece of bric-a-brac and, since I do not suppose that many others are held by members of the Regiment, I thought it might be amusing as a curiosity.

His offer was gladly accepted and the 'slightly ridiculous exhibit' duly delivered to London.

∽

Whether he finished his wartime service as a brigadier with a CBE or a colonel with an OBE was but a military nicety in Fleming's war. What drove him was the intellectual challenge to create from scratch a deception organization that could be deployed as an effective weapon of war, be it at the strategical or tactical level. Always cognizant of the delicate nature of constructing and implementing deception plans, he carefully protected his channels by educating his customers, whether C-in-Cs or Corps Commanders, about the theory and practice of deception and, above all, the paramount importance of security. There were, of course, limits to the efficacy of D. Division for, at a level way above Fleming, cooperation and coordination with the Americans proved evasive and indeed at times abrasive. Given the vast canvas on which the Pacific and SE Asian war was fought, including the presence of no fewer than four separate theatre commands (five if India Command is included), and the different post-war political agendas promoted by individual Allied nations, it was of little surprise that no cohesive strategical deception plan was agreed until the final year of the war. Within SEAC itself, the best-laid deception plans were invariably thwarted by events on the other side of the world that devoured the lion's share of maritime assets such as capital ships and landing craft.

Deception operations are notoriously difficult to measure since evidence to prove their impact depends on the actions of the enemy at the time and, in the event of victory, on his written and oral testimony. Furthermore, there is a tendency by all participants to propagandize their deception stratagems as gambits for successfully pulling the wool over the enemy's eyes, making them look smart and the enemy stupid. Typically, Fleming with his sense of the ridiculous and understated style made few such claims about his work.

Although he kept himself fit and worked punishingly hard, at times Fleming felt the lesser man for not being in the front line. His Grenadier contemporaries fought with the British Expeditionary Force in France, with the British and US Armies in North Africa and Italy, and in north-west Europe; many of them were killed or wounded. This explains rather than justifies his numerous excursions to the front line in Arakan and his ill-fated attempt to fly in with Mike Calvert's Brigade on the second Chindit expedition from which he was lucky to escape back to his own lines. Given that he was one of only a handful of officers cleared to read

Top Secret ULTRA traffic in the Far East, his judgement was rightly questioned. However, his superior officers, including Mountbatten, only mildly admonished him for they well knew the value of this energetic free-thinking officer with such verve and flair for deception, who was determined to degrade the Japanese war machine by any subterfuge he could devise. Far from undermining Fleming, the appointment of Ronald Wingate as Head of D. Division in April 1945 served to relieve him of time-consuming international 'office politics' and ensured that he was able to concentrate on bringing the deception weapon he had so fastidiously assembled to bear against an increasingly desperate and dangerous enemy.

Against a background of conflicting demands and 'tangled events', H.P. Willmott concludes that

> the British attempt to settle strategic priorities in the Far East reflected both the strengths and weaknesses of the 'war-by-committee' system: the ability to check misdirected or irresponsible intentions was matched by an inability to come to decisions other than those imposed, more or less, by events. In the final analysis, arguments that reflected conflicting political, strategic and military perspectives counted for little in the shadow cast by American power, and British decisions were those rendered inevitable by immutable factors of time, distance and national frailty.

Sir Michael Howard in his study of *British Intelligence in the Second World War* highlights that although Fleming 'had by 1944 built up an orchestra of deception almost as impressive as that created by Dudley Clarke in Cairo and (MI5's) BIA at home', unlike them he suffered from 'a total absence of any settled Allied strategic intentions in the Far East at all – at least, until the final year of the war'. He identifies

> the real problem which confronted the British deception staff in India … however, was that created by its own side; the continuing uncertainty as to what Allied strategic intentions really were. In default of firm actual plans the best that the deceivers could do, as one of them ruefully put it, was to ensure the enemy remained as confused as they were themselves.

That said, he acknowledges that

> their lasting achievement was to build up in the minds of enemy intelligence a totally erroneous idea of available Allied strength. What mattered in 1945 was not whether the Japanese were expecting to be attacked at one point rather than another. It was that, like the Germans in Europe, they believed their

opponents capable of delivering multiple attacks, and had in consequence to spread their forces so thinly to meet them that the actual assault, when it came, achieved overwhelming local superiority.

Fleming acknowledged this in his end-of-war report:[13]

It must be emphasised that the scope of strategic deception in the SEAC was in no way comparable with the standards attained in the Mediterranean and European theatres. The two main reasons for this are briefly examined in the following paragraphs.

The first reason was a chronic uncertainty as to what operations Supreme Allied Commander South East Asia was in fact going to carry out. This uncertainty arose from factors which were outside the control of this Command, and was an inevitable by-product of the low priority allotted by the Chiefs of Staff to operations in this theatre. Not only was the Supreme Commander invariably short of resources for major operations, but his plans had constantly to be modified in the light of unexpected cuts in his already meagre potential, which were caused by unforeseen developments in other theatres.

The effect of this uncertainty on deception planning was naturally profound and far-reaching. It is impossible, or at least highly dangerous, to attempt to tell a lie until you know what the truth is; and as time went on the frequency with which the notional or feint objectives proposed for the Supreme Allied Commander by D. Division turned out in the end to be his real objectives became something of a standing joke at his HQ ...

The second main reason for the relative ineffectiveness of our attempts to make the Japanese dispose their forces in accordance with our deception plans lay in the failings of the Japanese themselves. There can be no question that the Japanese Intelligence was greatly inferior in all respects to the German and even the Italian Intelligence. The successful deception practised on the Axis military machine in Europe was made possible by the fact that the enemy's Intelligence staffs and services were, though gullible, well organised and reasonably influential. Their reactions were those of civilised and highly trained Europeans, their staff methods and communications were effective and up-to-date, and their appreciations exerted, as is usual in a modern military machine, a preponderant effect upon the decisions of the enemy commanders.

In hindsight, D. Division's plans were too sophisticated and the bait too rich for the Japanese who time and again declined to nibble. Philip Mason, who had served as Secretary to the Chiefs of Staff Committee in India and then Head of Conference Secretariat (SEAC) came to the same conclusion.

He [Fleming] found two serious difficulties. We were ourselves still far from clear what we were meant to do and the Japanese were not particularly interested. They made their own plans and carried them out with rigid and unalterable determination. Deceiving the Germans had been very different; they wanted to know our plans and expected us to try and deceive them. That had been like playing chess with someone not quite so good as oneself; with the Japanese, it was like setting up the chessboard against an adversary whose one idea was to punch you on the nose.[14]

Sir Ronald Wingate attributed the lack of success to poor liaison with the Americans:

What stands out is that had we in South-East Asia ever had a firm real strategic plan, and had it been possible to establish effective liaison with the American theatres of operation in China and the Pacific, (which was not done till June or July when I myself visited General Wedermeyer in China and accompanied Admiral Mountbatten to Manila) deception might have made a very effective contribution to the success of our operation. The Japanese would have swallowed almost anything, and we had good lines to them. Their eyes were fixed in the last year of the war mainly upon the American theatres. We only needed a knowledge of the American plans and intimate co-operation with them and of course a firm plan of our own, to have worked a combined and co-ordinated deception plan on the grand scale which, in spite of the manifold weaknesses of the Japanese staff machine, might have been successful.[15]

Despite the soul-searching, Fleming looks at D. Division's record as a glass half full. In his final report,[16] he concluded that:

Nevertheless, a number of deception plans were drawn up by D. Division in consultation with the Joint Planning Staff and were approved by the Supreme Allied Commander. There is evidence to show that these plans were on the whole successfully put across to the Japanese Intelligence, but there is, on the other hand, insufficient evidence to suggest that they had an important effect on the course of his operations. A possible exception to this generalisation is offered by Plan STULTIFY, in which a strong seaborne and airborne threat was exerted against the Moulmein area. In this case there is a certain amount of evidence which does suggest that the Moulmein threat may have done something to accelerate the withdrawal of the Burma Area Army from the Rangoon area, which our forces reoccupied from the sea with virtually no opposition.

It may also be said that the influence of certain aspects of Plan SCEPTICAL, the final SEAC deception plan, on SOUTHERN Army's dispositions was pronounced if not strictly favourable to the Supreme Allied Commander's impending operations. The plan included a strong airborne threat to Bangkok linked with a somewhat vaguer threat of overland advance from Burma down the Burma-Siam railway to Bangkok. There is abundant evidence to show that these threats were taken in all seriousness by the Japanese HQs both in Bangkok and Saigon, and that they contributed towards the reinforcement of South East Siam by a division from French Indo China. It is also probable that the concentration of Japanese forces in the North Malaya and Lower Kra Isthmus area in the final stage of the war was partly motivated by the threat to the Central Kra Isthmus exerted by Plan SCEPTICAL.

Fleming's perspective on the dropping of the atomic bombs is not recorded but Sir Ronald Wingate was uneasy about it.

America and ourselves were obsessed with the probability of fanatical suicidal Japanese resistance to the last man – just as the Americans continued to believe in fanatical suicidal German resistance in the mythical Bohemian redoubt. But why at the beginning of August 1945 when Japan had no fleet, no air, was trying to surrender, was faced with overwhelming defeat with conventional forces poised for the assault, the atom bomb was dropped and simultaneously Stalin was pressed to declare war on Japan on his outrageous Yalta terms, must forever remain one of the great historical mysteries.[17]

In a quaint farewell to the world of deception, Fleming penned *The Sixth Column: A Singular Tale of Our Times*, which was published by his friend Rupert Hart-Davis in 1951. It was classic Fleming, a gentle parody of the secret services that apologized for its lack of 'high seriousness'. It was based on the premise that since every Briton 'wanted to be well-fed, well-paid, well-housed, well-defended, well-everything else', and he needed to be in touch with his opposite number in Russia to reassure himself that there was no appetite for any war between the two countries. Enter the villains and dupes, be they the KGB in London, a fledgling CND styled as the Peace Guild or a Sixth Column 'composed of cool, level-headed individuals who don't work for any particular cause or believe in any particular doctrine, who don't care whether or not they are rewarded for what they do, who haven't really any special grievance against their own country or any special like for her enemies'. The glue that linked them together was the mysterious Plan D of which 'the object was to accelerate the current deterioration of the British national character with a view to undermining and eventually eliminating British influence in the affairs of the world'.

Having set the scene, Fleming takes potshots with his trusty rook rifle at the ghosts of the Intelligence barons and their acolytes in India and SEAC and out of the trees tumble the fictional A2 (f), B (Coord), DMI, DSSP (Director Special Security Problems), Army Topographical Unit, H2O (so secret that people thought it had something to do with water) and the mysterious Section D2 (d), irreverently known in the corridors of the clandestine world as 'Dust to Dust' (surely a worthy contender for Evelyn Waugh's HOO or Hazardous Offensive Operations).

These fictional organizations correlate to Fleming's actual wartime experiences with GSI (d), D. Division, P. Division, DIB, DITB, Force 136, GS (k), Force 456, D Force, MI5, MI(R), Section D, ISRB, Army Topographical Unit and a host of other 'funnies'. His Director of Military Intelligence, who

> combined flair with organizing ability ... had an invaluable capacity of appearing, when dealing with other branches of the Staff, to regard the duties of his own Directorate as slightly ridiculous. Since this is the light in which the rest of the Staff automatically regard Intelligence anyhow, [his] show of insouciance did much to disarm criticism, and [he] was generally regarded as a very reasonable sort of fellow.

Whether a self-portrait or not, it is a perfect epithet for Fleming's last wartime appointment.

As to Fleming the man, Joan Bright captures him perfectly.

> He was in his way a famous figure, not only because of his early and romantic success as an explorer and writer and his marriage to one of our best actresses, Celia Johnson, but also because he kept his own brand of personality intact and dignified, dealt with all men as equals, and ... used his pen honestly and well, based on logic and spiced with satire.[18]

Wavell found 'courage and kindliness ... the only two qualities that excuse human existence.'[19] Peter Fleming was blessed with both. When his wartime friend Michael Calvert was court-martialled in July 1952 for committing acts of gross indecency with a number of German youths, it was Fleming, together with the Chindit leader Brigadier Bernard Fergusson, who rallied round and raised over £2,000 to provide him with a defence lawyer, Julian Hannay. In the homophobic legal climate of that time, this was an act of true loyalty and staunch friendship.

∾

Unlike her husband's wartime career which had taken place in the shadowy world of secret intelligence, Celia Johnson's public image had burgeoned and she had become a household name for her roles in Noel Coward's patriotic films *In Which We Serve* and *This Happy Breed*. When she was not filming, Celia conscientiously carried out her duties as a Special Constable in Henley and, as chatelaine of Merrimoles, she presided over a houseful of Fleming family children for the duration of the war. Apart from a brief visit in autumn 1942 and one weekend in May 1943, Fleming did not see her until July 1945 when he returned for a brief period of leave. When he finally returned home in November, Celia was expecting their second child, Kate, and was the toast of British cinema audiences for her star part in Noel Coward's new film, *Brief Encounter*.

Demobbed in 1946 aged thirty-nine, Fleming's peripatetic and varied career as a foreign correspondent, best-selling author and senior wartime intelligence officer soon opened several doors in high places. As the new world order unfurled, with his knowledge of and experience in dealing with Russia and China, he was eminently well qualified for a top post in either SIS or MI5. He was also in the running as a future editor of *The Times* and had been offered a safe Tory seat at Henley from which to launch a political career. Instead he decided to settle down to the life of an Oxfordshire squire. For a man of keen intellect and seemingly inexhaustible energy, this surprising decision could be construed as opting out of fulfilling his true potential. But it was altogether more complicated for, in addition to having 'absolutely no conventional ambition',[20] he found himself torn between the introvert and extrovert, the countryside and the city, the wanderer and the home-lover.

In *News from Tartary*, he gives us a clue to the duality of his character.[21]

Kini rode ahead, a familiar silhouette ... Coming back meant less to her than to me, who had, paradoxically, at once more ties and more detachment: a greater capacity to enjoy a life to which at frequent intervals I feel myself a stranger, and at the same time more friends and facilities with which to enjoy it. I wished it was not like this. On the road we had, I think, found much the same kind of happiness in much the same kind of things; and I would have liked the end of the road to have given us both an equal pleasure.

So the decision to turn his back on the traditional avenues to success should be seen as a compromise, erring towards the profound and powerful gravitational forces within him. He quickly settled down, managing his 2,000 acres' estate at Nettlebed with characteristic élan and supporting his county and local community, all the while keeping his literary hand in by filing for *The Times* and *The Spectator*, and reading for Jonathan Cape. In time, he took to writing books again, producing four well-received and eminently readable histories – *Invasion 1940/Operation Sea Lion* (1957), *The Siege at Peking* (1959), *Bayonets to Lhasa* (1961) and *The Fate of Admiral Kolchak* (1963). His turn of phrase was as vivid as ever. In *The Siege at Peking*, he writes 'the Yellow River had inundated hundreds of villages; at one time 150,000 people were squatting, like cormorants on some endless reef, on the breached dykes above swirling waters.' His sense of the ridiculous bubbled over when comparing the demands of the French for Roman Catholic bishops to be ranked *pari passu* with Governor-Generals and Governors in Manchu China. He advises his readers that 'the effect of this measure on Chinese opinion can approximately be gauged by imagining nineteenth-century British reactions to an announcement in the Court Circular that senior witch doctors were to have equal precedence with Lords Lieutenant'.

One literary project he particularly enjoyed was translating André Migot's *Caravane vers Boudhha* into English. A pre-war alpinist of distinction, a doctor, a traveller and explorer, Migot had set off from Indo-China in 1946 to research Buddhism on a journey that took him from Kunming to Langar and then Peking. Fleming admired how 'his extraordinary powers of endurance are matched by his powers of observation' and concluded that 'the end result is an intimate and detailed portrait of a society outwardly primitive and outlandish but based on values and traditions from which the West has much to learn'. Clearly they had a lot in common in character, wit and outlook; at times, so alike is their style of writing, Fleming could well be the author himself. Rupert Hart-Davis published it as *Tibetan Marches* in 1956.

The urge to travel to remote places, which he once described as 'the fascination with complete uncertainty',[22] may have subsided but never wholly left him; he took his godson, Duff Hart-Davis, to Russia in 1957 and daughter Kate to the Republic of Georgia in 1966. But it was the countryside of the British Isles with its many rural delights that continued to captivate him, whether shooting pheasants at Merrimoles on misty late autumn days or grouse on Scottish hillsides in the height of summer. This was the landscape where he found the freedom he so loved, the land of the rook rifle, a place where nature held no truck with his pet hates of cant, red tape and hypocrisy. It was on one such rustic day in August 1971 that he suffered a fatal heart attack while out grouse shooting on the Black Mount overlooking Rannoch Moor in the Scottish Highlands.

He was buried in the churchyard of St. Bartholomew's Nettlebed. As befitted a man of letters, he wrote his own epitaph:

He travelled widely in far places:
Wrote, and was widely read.
Soldiered, saw some of danger's faces,
Came home to Nettlebed.
The squire lies here, his journeys ended –
Dust, and a name on a stone –
Content, amid the lands he tended,
To keep this rendezvous alone.

Despite his many and varied gifts, his penetrating intellect, unbounded energy and zest for life, Fleming was haunted throughout his life by a distrust of the accolades that go with success. People saw it manifested as a rather charming self-deprecation, typical of the upper-class tradition of 'non-swanks', but it was deeper rooted. In summing up his 'three years, three interesting fairly hard journeys … as all great fun' in a BBC *Spoken Word* recording in 1969, he asked himself: 'What good did it do anyone except me and my publisher?' His answer was, typically, 'precious little, probably none at all'.

Writing in *Guerrilla War in Abyssinia* (1943), Bill Allen, a close colleague back in the early days of MIR in the summer of 1939, captures the complexity underlying Fleming's persona: 'Every man has manifold personalities; there is the self which he never knows; the self which he sees himself; the self which he presents to the world; and the self which the world accepts; lastly, the ever-changing self of the future – battered, shorn, remoulded by external events, worked down, destroyed and raised again by the inner experience of the man.'

Annexes

Annex A

The Mir War Establishment as at 3 September 1939

Head (London)
Lieutenant Colonel J.C.F. 'Jo' Holland, DFC, RE

Europe Section
Major E.P. 'Eddie' Combe MC, Royal Scots
Captain J. Walter, TA Reserve
Captain R.M. Greg, Black Watch

Asia and Africa Section
Major N. Crockatt, late Royal Scots, later Brigadier and Head of MI9
Captain R.P. Fleming, Grenadier Guards
Captain W.E.D. Allen, The Lifeguards
Captain Colefax

Engineering Section (MIR (c))
Major M.R. 'Millis' Jefferis, MC, RE, later head of MD1[1] and Major General
Captain R. 'Stuart' Macrae, TA Reserve, later joined Jefferis at MD1
Corporal W. Bidgood

Personnel Section
Captain J.C.P. Brunyate, TA Reserve, formerly a solicitor with Coward Chance

Secretarial section
Miss Joan Bright
Miss L. Wauchope

No.4 Military Mission to Poland
Major General Adrian Carton De Wiart, VC, later British Military Representative to General Chiang Kai-shek.
Lieutenant Colonel Colin Gubbins, RA, later Operational Head (CD) of SOE

Major Peter Wilkinson, Royal Fusiliers, later Sir Peter Wilkinson, FCO
Captain Herbert 'Boy' Lloyd-Johnes, RA (T)

Annex B

Purple Whales 1

The proceedings of the conference commenced at 10.30 hours.

GENERAL HARTLEY:[2] Gentlemen, I must begin with two apologies. The first comes from the Commander-in-Chief who asks me to express his sincere regret that he cannot be here this morning. He is unfortunately laid up for a day or two. As you probably know he injured his back in Singapore, nothing very bad, he had a fall in the black-out. Yesterday he took the afternoon off to go pig-sticking – against the advice of his doctor, I understand – and his horse came down with him and he is out of action of today at any rate.

CAPTAIN VAN DER KUHN: I am very sorry. I hope the injury is not serious.

GENERAL BRERETON:[3] Will you please convey our condolences to General Wavell? I surely am sorry to hear this.

GENERAL HARTLEY: Thank you. The Chief will I know appreciate your sympathy but I do not think there is much wrong with him, I am glad to say. Our second piece of bad luck, for which again I must apologise, is the absence of General Davidson. General Davidson, as perhaps you know, is the Director of Military Intelligence at the War Office and he has just arrived in India on a short tour. We were most anxious that he should attend this meeting, as he naturally has a clearer and more up-to-date picture of the way the war is going than we have out here. He should have reached Delhi last night but unfortunately his plane has been delayed, I do not know what by, the weather looks all right. I gather there is a chance that he will arrive in the course of the morning. If he does, he will be brought straight here from the airport. But I really am very sorry for these two unfortunate hitches.

GENERAL LO: It cannot be helped.

GENERAL HARTLEY: Well, as you probably know, the Commander-in-Chief called this Conference because he felt it would be helpful, particularly after our somewhat disheartening experiences in Burma, if he put before you such information as he has about the progress of the war in general, I mean the future progress, the prospects before the United Nations. In this connection the first thing he would like us to consider is this short paper which Major Coats is distributing. This paper is a short summary, telegraphed to General

Wavell last week by the Chief of Staff in London, of what we intend or hope to do during the coming months. As you will see, the telegram does not go into any great detail. I think it is encouraging myself. It is divided into five points, five paragraphs. I suggest that we consider each in turn. Let us begin with paragraph A.

GENERAL LO: Is there a map?

GENERAL BRERETON: I have a map here, a small one, showing the whole Pacific area.

GENERAL HARTLEY: Thank you. In the meantime, I will send for a larger map.

GENERAL STILWELL:[4] I suggest that it is not necessary to wait for a map of the Pacific before considering Paragraph A.

GENERAL LO. No, it is not necessary.

GENERAL HARTLEY: In view of the somewhat controversial atmosphere which surrounds this question of a so-called Second Front, I should like if I may to call your attention to the last sentence of Paragraph A. There you will see that no final decision as to the despatch of this force has yet been taken.

GENERAL LO: Is that on account of shipping? Perhaps there is uncertainty as to whether you will have sufficient shipping to transport ten divisions. Many British and American ships are being sunk.

GENERAL HARTLEY: The ships are available.

GENERAL STILWELL: If I may, I should like to get this Paragraph A quite clear. As I understand it, the force referred to is already in being. I do not say that it has actually been concentrated, but it exists and it disposes of whatever is necessary for the operation – ships, supporting aircraft, naval covering forces, all that is necessary. Am I right, General?

GENERAL HARTLEY: Yes. I am glad you have raised the point. I should like to make it clear that Paragraph A does not represent a pious aspiration on the part of Great Britain. It means exactly what it says. It is not a question of what we may be able to do in certain contingencies, it is an accurate statement of what we shall be able to do at any time after the first week of July.

GENERAL STILWELL: Thank you, General.

GENERAL LO: These three Armoured Divisions – with what type of tank are they equipped?

GENERAL HARTLEY: We can take it that they have the latest types.

GENERAL LO: Heavy tanks?

GENERAL HARTLEY: Yes, certainly.

GENERAL LO: In Libya last year the latest types of British tanks were too light and their guns were too weak. The German tanks were superior.

GENERAL HARTLEY: I am sorry that I have no precise details but I think you can take it that the whole of this force is provided with and fully trained in the use of the very best British and American equipment.

GENERAL LO: I hope so.

GENERAL HARTLEY: I think I am right in saying that General Yu, your Master General of the Ordnance, inspected an armoured formation equipped with some of our heaviest tanks when he was in India. Perhaps he furnished you with a report on their performance. It was when he visited DUMBO Force.

GENERAL LO: I will look up the report.

CAPTAIN VAN DER KUHN: I would like to ask a question with regard to the last sentence of Paragraph A. There it says that the decision whether or not to make this offensive depends on developments in Russia. What sort of developments, and in what way does it depend on them?

GENERAL BRERETON: I think I see what the Captain means. Broadly speaking, three things may happen in Russia. The Germans may be thrown back; they may be held; or they may break through. In which of these cases will the British launch their offensive?

CAPTAIN VAN DER KUHN: Yes. That was my meaning.

GENERAL HARTLEY: I am afraid I cannot answer that question. I doubt if anyone can answer it at this stage. I certainly cannot, as I say. I can only state my personal belief that this operation will be carried out if there is the slightest prospect of it contributing to a decisive result against Germany.

GENERAL LO: But it may not be carried out at all?

GENERAL HARTLEY: Well, that is of course –

GENERAL STILWELL: It may not be necessary.

CAPTAIN VAN DER KUHN: Unlikely, I think.

GENERAL HARTLEY: It has already been the object of my country to defeat Germany. If this operation will enable us to achieve that object, we shall certainly carry it out.

GENERAL LO: That is rather good news.

CAPTAIN VAN DER KUHN: When the British troops arrive it is my opinion that oppressed peoples in the occupied territories will rebel and carry on guerrilla warfare against the German troops.

GENERAL LO: They will do so in some places, but only if the British are successful in fighting the Germans. If the British are not very successful, the local peoples will not do much on account of the strong oppression.

GENERAL BRERETON: May I suggest, General, that we should now consider Paragraph B?

GENERAL HARTLEY: Has anyone any further questions to ask about the contents of Paragraph A?

GENERAL LO: Will parachute troops be used?

GENERAL HARTLEY: I am afraid I have no information on that point. As to Paragraph B, I do not know exactly when these strategic decisions were taken but I gather that it was about a fortnight ago. It was probably before the British General Staff had a clear indication that this fresh Axis offensive was going to be launched two or three days ago.

CAPTAIN VAN DER KUHN: Have you news of this battle? From the newspapers it is difficult …

GENERAL HARTLEY: It is too early to prophesy. But it does not seem to be going too badly so far.

GENERAL STILWELL: Can you tell us, General, whether the outcome of this major engagement in Libya is likely to, or perhaps I should say is capable of modifying the decision recorded in Paragraph B?

GENERAL HARTLEY: You mean …

GENERAL STILWELL: Supposing for the sake of argument that General Auchinleck beats off this Axis attack and inflicts really considerable damage and losses on the enemy and particularly on his armoured forces. Well now if that happened, General Auchinleck might report to London that he no longer felt tied to the defensive and was in a position to take the offensive with good prospects of success. In that case or in a case like that, might not London reconsider their decision to transfer these fairly considerable land and air forces out here? Or again might they not hold back for the Middle East some of the convoys referred to in this paragraph?

GENERAL HARTLEY: I see what you mean, General. It is not a question, as I think you will appreciate, that I can answer quite definitely. But I am sure that we can take this much for granted: the very important decision in Paragraph B regarding reinforcements and supplies for this part of the Pacific Theatre was not taken lightly. I mean that it was not taken, it cannot have been taken, without due appreciation being given to the probability of an Axis offensive in Libya and without a very careful estimate of the weight of that offensive. It follows, I think, that we can regard our Middle East armies as being for practical purposes self-contained and capable – or perhaps I should say regarded in London as capable – of fulfilling a defensive role (including, of course, counter-attacks) without the reinforcements and supplies earmarked for us out here.

GENERAL LO: Supposing on the other hand that the British are defeated and are driven out of Egypt by General Rommel?

GENERAL HARTLEY: I do not think that is possible.

GENERAL LO: Many British officers did not think it was possible for the Japanese to take Singapore.

GENERAL BRERETON: That's quite true, General Lo. But I do not think there is a close similarity between the two cases. Would it not be better …

GENERAL HARTLEY: Might I suggest, as we have a good many matters to consider, that anyone who has a question which is relevant to the contents of Paragraph B should raise it now?

CAPTAIN VAN DER KUHN: Little is said concerning the exact composition of these reinforcements. Can General Hartley tell us anything on this subject?

GENERAL HARTLEY: I am afraid not. As I told you at the beginning of this meeting, this memorandum deals only with our strategy in its broadest aspect. It does not purport to go into details.

GENERAL STILWELL: It gives no indication whether the reinforcements will include airborne formations.

GENERAL HARTLEY: No, no details.

GENERAL STILWELL: I asked because, although I am not fully in the picture yet, I gather from our people here that MacArthur sets a good deal of store by airborne troops, particularly in relation to some of the islands … I wondered what sort of importance General Wavell attached to them.

GENERAL HARTLEY: A great deal, I know. We are not too badly off here in that respect, you know. But I have no particulars about reinforcements.

CAPTAIN VAN DER KUHN: May I ask what system of co-ordination exists between General Wavell's HQ and General MacArthur's? In Ceylon we seem to know very little from Australia.

GENERAL HARTLEY: There is no system of co-ordination. It is a bad state of affairs. But it is being improved.

CAPTAIN VAN DER KUHN: That is good.

GENERAL HARTLEY: Are there any more questions dealing with Paragraph B? Shall we deal with Paragraph C?

GENERAL BRERETON: I am in a position, as it happens, to add something to the paragraph as it stands. May I go ahead, General?

GENERAL HARTLEY: Please do.

GENERAL BRERETON: Here it reads 'approximately two Divisions and 100 aircraft have gone or are en route to' the islands named. Well, that is now out of date. I heard from our people this morning that the whole of one Division and all combat elements of the second had arrived at their stations by 26 May.

GENERAL LO: Have the aeroplanes arrived also?

GENERAL BRERETON: The telegram I saw did not mention aircraft; but that should not be a difficult move to carry out.

GENERAL LO: To whom does Fiji belong?

CAPTAIN VAN DER KUHN: To the British. New Caledonia to the French.

GENERAL LO: Caledonia is the same word as Scotland?

GENERAL HARTLEY: Yes. But New Caledonia is French.

GENERAL LO: It does not say on which of these three islands the base is being prepared.

GENERAL HARTLEY: No. It merely says 'a base is being prepared in this area' for the Pacific Fleet. I am afraid I am not a naval expert.

GENERAL BRERETON: Nor am I. But it's pretty clear that the defence of these islands is enormously important. If we can't keep the Japs out of them our communications with Australia go up in smoke.

GENERAL HARTLEY: Well, there seems to be a good deal less danger of that happening than there was. Has anyone any further points to raise with regard to this paragraph?

GENERAL LO: No, it is clear.

GENERAL HARTLEY: Now, Paragraph D. This again is largely concerned with naval matters.

GENERAL STILWELL: I should be interested to know, General, just how extensive the damage to those battle cruisers was.

GENERAL HARTLEY: We are not given any details; but it is obvious that the Admiralty consider that they have ceased to be a factor in the Atlantic for the time being.

GENERAL LO: I hope that is the case. Your information about those ships has been sometimes unreliable, has it not?

GENERAL HARTLEY: I am afraid I don't know very much about that.

CAPTAIN VAN DER KUHN: Can you tell us, General, whether this paragraph needs to be modified as a result of the battle in the Coral Sea?

GENERAL HARTLEY: I understand that it does not. We have not been given details of the damage suffered by the American Fleet but I understand that it was not severe.

CAPTAIN VAN DER KUHN: The combined operation referred to can still be carried out?

GENERAL HARTLEY: As far as I know, yes, any time after the middle of July.

GENERAL STILWELL: But not unless the Japanese main fleet is west of Singapore?

GENERAL HARTLEY: It is not clear from this summary whether that is an essential condition. Probably it is, it would obviously be an advantage. Any more questions?

GENERAL LO: I think it is a pity that this paper does not give us more details about these various strategical plans. They seem to be somewhat vague and not clear in some respects. I mean, the paper says that certain operations will take place, if certain other things happen or depending on various circumstances. To my mind it is possible that nothing at all will happen, nothing will be done. That was the case with regard to air support for our troops in Burma.

GENERAL HARTLEY: I am sorry, General, that you find the record of these decisions vague and indefinite. I quite agree with you that at certain points – in Paragraph A for instance, and to a certain extent in the last paragraph we dealt with – the actual execution of these plans is stated to be contingent on outside factors, on what you might call imponderables. But is that not always so in military strategy, particularly when the enemy is very strong and has up till now held the initiative? All I can tell you is what I think I have said before – that these decisions summarised here do represent the intentions of the United Nations in the immediate future. I hope and expect that most of these intentions will be carried out, though they are of course, as you point out, inevitably dependent to a certain extent on circumstances over which we have no control. Does that do anything to allay your misgivings, General?

GENERAL LO: Thank you.

GENERAL HARTLEY: I do not think the final paragraph of this summary need occupy very much of our time. It is no secret that Brigadier Doolittle's raid on Japan, though boldly and successfully carried out, was only in the nature of an experiment or reconnaissance. And of course, valuable lessons were learnt from it, particularly in regard to the two matters mentioned here. But I think we have all known for some time, or at any rate guessed, that future raids on Japan will be rather more serious operations.

GENERAL LO: Again no details are given.

GENERAL STILWELL: You could hardly expect them in a case of this kind, General. This, as I understand it, is a strategical summary, not an operation order.

GENERAL HARTLEY: Well, if there are no further questions, I think that concludes our discussion of this document. Would you all be so kind as to hand me back your copies? Now here is a short note on two points which General Wavell thought would probably be of interest to this meeting. I take it that General Stilwell and General Lo – I take it that you both know about these negotiations; but you've been more or less out of touch in Burma and …

GENERAL STILWELL: I certainly had no idea that they had got on as far as this. Those people are darned cagey.

GENERAL LO: They have not yet decided, I see.

GENERAL STILWELL: Not finally, no.

CAPTAIN VAN DER KUHN: Those are encouraging figures. I should have thought they were perhaps too high. I do not know that part of the world myself but I always understood that conditions were very difficult.

GENERAL HARTLEY: I believe they are. The whole thing is obviously going to take a long time, a very long time.

GENERAL LO: We built the Burma road very quickly.

GENERAL STILWELL: Yes, that was a fine job, but things are different up there.

CAPTAIN VAN DER KUHN: At the Chinese end this organisation is already in being?

GENERAL HARTLEY: That is not quite clear, but it should not take long to create such an organisation. Any more points?

GENERAL BRERETON: I think not, General.

GENERAL HARTLEY: As regards the second point on this paper, I think you will appreciate that we cannot give details. All that is presented here is a general picture. Some of the details we do not want to commit to paper even inside GHQ if we can avoid it. But there have been so many criticisms of our intelligence organisation that C.-in-C. felt it would not be amiss to present this very general summary of what exists or has been set up in occupied territory.

GENERAL STILWELL: I understood you were short of wireless sets, General?

GENERAL HARTLEY: We are, unfortunately.

GENERAL STILWELL: Then how is it that you manage to equip these agents or spies or whatever you call them on such a generous scale? The figure for Burma is remarkable.

GENERAL HARTLEY: Ah, but these sets do not belong to us, they are not Army sets. They are paid for out of special funds by a certain organisation. These people generally manage to get priority in matters of supply. Compared with the Army, they get the things they want very quickly.

CAPTAIN VAN DER KUHN: Are they all Frenchmen, these groups in Indo-China?

GENERAL HARTLEY: I haven't the slightest idea.

(At this point the Director of Military Intelligence at the War Office, Major General Davidson, joined the Conference. After some conversation on a non-official nature, of which General Hartley directed that no record should be kept, proceedings were formally resumed.)

GENERAL HARTLEY: Our time is getting short. I am very glad indeed that the DMI, in spite of his adventures on the way, has reached Delhi in time to take part in this Conference. He left London less than four weeks ago, he has seen the picture of what they are doing in the Middle East, and I am going to ask him to give us a short talk on what the major aspects of the war look like as seen from London, where of course they have much fuller information and are much closer to the big issues than we are over here. Will you carry on, DMI?

GENERAL DAVIDSON: Thank you, Sir. I do not think I can do much better than tell you very briefly what I told General Auchinleck when he asked what we were thinking in London. First, the position in Germany? Desperate? Not quite. But not at all good. Put it like this; Germany's defeat during 1942 is probable. Not merely possible. Probable. Germany's defeat by the early summer of 1943 is inevitable. That is what we think. Why do we think it? Because all the facts, all our information, permit of no other deduction being made.

Russia. In Russia, Hitler has failed once; it was not a disastrous failure. The next one will be. His spring offensive is late. At Kharkhov Timothenko has taken a bad knock, a fairly bad knock at any rate. But he has upset the Boche. Delayed him. Thrown a spanner into his plans, perhaps quite a big spanner. The Russians have got their tails up. They still do not tell us much but we know enough now to realise they cannot be knocked out. They are short of food. They may lose Leningrad or Rostov or even Moscow. I do not think they will but they may. But they cannot be knocked out. I do not know whether Hitler knows this. But I do know that several of his generals do. So do a good many, and an increasing number, of the rank and file. It is still a great army but it's not the army of a year ago. I would not like to answer for it if it's called on to stand a second winter. I will not prophesy but I will bet, and I will bet that the German Army will not stand a second winter. Inside Germany morals are sagging, not cracking. Any day now you will hear of bombing on a scale never equalled before. Nobody likes having several hundred heavy bombers dropping stuff on them. Germans like it even less than we do. It is going to happen to them quite a lot. Morale will continue to sag. These bombs are affecting production. The blockade is not helping them either.

What is on our side of the picture? Production is going up steadily. In tanks and aircraft the objective has been reached; we have ceased to need to expand, though as a matter of fact the Americans are still expanding. What is the Luftwaffe doing about it? Going for Bath and Exeter and so on with a fiddling little force of 20 or 30 bombers. They no longer fly inland. As far as the British Isles themselves are concerned (I am not talking about shipping) the German Air Force has practically ceased to be a factor in the war.

U-boats are a different matter. They have given us a lot of trouble lately. It is a matter of time really. We have got their measure. We shall defeat them utterly in the end; but it takes time. Germany started the war with fifty-seven U-boats. Today she has 300. A big steady increase all the time. What about British shipping losses? A steady decrease all the time. I think that is significant, do you not, Sir?

GENERAL HARTLEY: Most certainly.

GENERAL DAVIDSON: At the beginning of the war we had their submarines in our coastal waters. Where are they now? Much further afield. The North Sea is clear. The western approaches are clear. They have been making a big bag off the east coast of America but now that the Americas have got their convoy system working, sinkings are going down. That situation is in hand. One other thing. In a submarine a tremendous lot depends on the commanding officer. They are getting short of good ones, fully trained ones. It is important, that.

What about the occupied territories in Europe? They are giving trouble. They will give more. Some of what goes on you read in the papers, but only some. The people are getting near starvation; in some places they are actually starving. When you are starving you do not feel resigned, you feel desperate. It is a big job to hold down 200 million people who are beginning to feel desperate. The Germans are tackling that job with third-line troops. It is not a very sound position from their point of view.

I am not going to talk much about Japan: Japan is your pigeon. I will say this: if Japan does not concentrate on consolidating her gains while we are preoccupied in the west, she will be foolish. I have an idea she is just now contemplating certain adventures in the Pacific; I have also got an idea that she will get a bloody nose if she tries them. Whether she realises it or not, she cannot afford to disperse her forces any further. Perhaps it hardly matters what she does. She cannot, no nation can, take what is coming to her when Germany packs up.

GENERAL STILWELL: Can you say something about Italy?

GENERAL DAVIDSON: Italy is now merely one of the occupied territories. She's actually worse off for food than some countries that have been conquered. No peace-feelers yet, but she will take the first chance to rat on Germany. She is quite likely to have a fling at Corsica or Nice before the Axis finally cracks. She wants something to show for it all. The Axis is in a queer state. Germany did not relish that run of big Japanese successes. She is not interested in Asia for the Asiatics. It is the last thing she wants. She is furious at the way Japan is handling Dutch interests in the NEI; you have probably heard about that. We had an interesting account of Falkenhausen's views recently. He looks after Belgium. He used to be head of their Military Mission in China. He was quite witty about the Nips and their Emperor. I have made one bet already. I will make another. If Japan is still at war in 1944 she will have German forces in the field against her before the end of that year. I do not say large forces. They may only be pro-Chinese volunteer formations on the lines of the American Volunteer Group. But they will be there, if we allow them to be, showing the flag of a new Germany to those 400 million customers in whom the Boche has already been keenly interested. I may lose that bet. I do not think I will.

GENERAL HARTLEY: Well, I know I shall be expressing the feeling of this meeting when I say that General Davidson has given us a most interesting and certainly to me refreshing exposition. I am very glad he managed to get here after all. I know you all have questions you will want to ask him, but in ten minutes' time we must adjourn so that I can take you over to see the Viceroy, so I suggest we give the DMI a breather and bring this meeting to an end. Before I do so, are there any points which have not been dealt with that anyone wants to raise?

GENERAL STILWELL: General Lo here has a matter he wants to mention.

GENERAL LO: It is concerning the AA guns and equipment. My government instructed me by telegram to find out whether the experiments of transportation have been carried out.

GENERAL HARTLEY: They have. I read the report two days ago and I will see that you will receive a copy of it this afternoon.

GENERAL LO: Is it possible to fly them?

GENERAL HARTLEY: Yes. It is. Not the 3.7s, unfortunately. We could have given you lots of those but the aircraft can't take them. But the Bofors apparently is quite an easy job – the Americans have been handling it of course and I am bound to say I think they have got the whole business fixed up far more expeditiously than is at all usual in India.

GENERAL LO: Have any been sent?

GENERAL HARTLEY: None, I think, up till two days ago. Perhaps they have started since. I know that the first lot are down on the airfield ready to go.

GENERAL LO: My government will be most pleased to hear this. Please do insist that the guns are sent at the first opportunity.

GENERAL HARTLEY: The orders have already been given. I move that this meeting now adjourns or we shall be late.

(The meeting adjourned.)

Annex C

Staff List – GSI (d) / D. Division / Force 456

Officer commanding GSI (d)
Colonel Peter Fleming

Officers commanding D. Division
Colonel Peter Fleming (from November 1943)
Colonel Sir Ronald Wingate Bt. (from 25 April 1945)

Officer commanding Force 456 (from 25 April 1945)
Colonel Peter Fleming

Policy and Plans HQ SEAC Kandy
Wing Commander The Hon. Mervyn Horder, RAFVR
Lieutenant Commander the Earl of Antrim, RNVR[5]
Captain Saunders

D. Division Rear HQ Delhi
Commander Alan Robertson-Macdonald RN, Eastern Fleet Representative
Major Peter Thorne, Grenadier Guards
Major Lucas J. Ralli, Royal Signals, GSO 2 Wireless Comms
Major A.D.R. Wilson
Captain the Hon. A.J.A. Wavell

Navy Lieutenant Pei, Chinese LO
Operations Section
Lieutenant Colonel A.G. 'Johnnie' Johnson, RA[6]
Major Gordon Rennie
Captain K.L. Campbell (from 12 March 1945)
Captain J.N. Carleton-Stiff, R.Sigs.
Technical Section
Major C.H. Starck, RE
Captain J.A. Gloag, (Z Force from 15 March 1945)
Captain G.T.H. Carter, RE (from 2 April 1945)
Captain D.W. Timmis
Captain Skipworth

Tac HQ Calcutta (Advanced HQ ALFSEA)
Lieutenant Colonel 'Frankie' Wilson, GSO 1
Major J.M. Howson (from 30 March 1945)
Major J.C.W. Napier-Munn, RA
Major R.A. Gwyn, Base Signal Office Calcutta
Squadron Leader J. King[7]
Captain 'Jack' Corbett (US) March 1945
Control Section
Major S.C.F. Pierson, GSO 2

D Force
Force HQ
Lieutenant Colonel P.E.X. Turnbull – Commanding officer
Major E.F.A. 'Ted' Royds – 2 i/c
Major J.C. Gladman[8] – Officer i/c Sonic
Captain K.A.J. Booth – Adjutant
Captain P.R. Hedges – 2 i/c Sonic
Lieutenant M.W. Trennery – i/c Sonic training
Lieutenant B.E. Chambers – i/c Sonic training
Companies
Captain G. Morgan – OC 51 Coy
Lieutenant E.H. Morris, RE – 2 i/c 51 Coy
Captain J.A. Fosbury – OC 52 Coy
Captain C.A.R. Richardson – OC 53 Coy
Lieutenant R.A. Spark - 2 i/c 53 Coy
Captain J.I. Nicolson, KAR Reserve of Officers – OC 54 Coy
Lieutenant R.H. Walton, RA - 2 i/c 54 Coy
Lieutenant G.H. Smith – i/c Sonic 54 Coy
Captain G.W. Boyd – OC 55 Coy
Lieutenant J.D. Taylor - 2 i/c 55 Coy

Captain C.J.C. Lumsden – OC 56 Coy
Lieutenant J.H. Atkinson – i/c Sonic 56 Coy
Captain D.W. Timmis – OC 57 Coy
Captain R.H.D. Norman – OC 58 Coy
Lieutenant B. Raymond - 2 i/c 58 Coy
Lieutenant J.G. Sommerville - i/c Sonic 58 Coy

No.1 Naval Scout Unit
Lieutenant Commander H.B. Brassey, RNVR

ITB
Colonel Reginald Bicat
Chief Clerk: Sergeant Ashley
Major N.P. Dawnay
Major J.A. Denney
Major H.L. Frenkel
Major D.W. Gaylor
Major J.F. Howarth
Major D.K. Kerker
Major J.L. Schofield
Major J.E. Vaughan
Captain H.N. Barker
Captain R. Baxter
Captain A. Forbes
Captain D.H. Pickhard
Captain B.K.H. Richards
Captain E.G. Sperring
Captain A.H.D. Williams

Liaison officers with Army Formations
Eastern Army (1943): Colonel 'Fookiform' Foulkes and Major Frankie Wilson
HQ Fourteenth Army: Major John Warde-Aldham
NCAC: Captain Jack Corbett (US). Appointed February 1945
IV Corps: Major J.M. Howson
XV Corps: Major D. Graham, MC
XXXIII Corps: Major R. Campbell GSO 2

Control Section China Chungking
Major S.C.F. Pierson
Lieutenant Colonel F.G. Bishop

Notes

Chapter 1

1   Duff Hart-Davis, *Peter Fleming* (London: Jonathan Cape, 1974), 18.

2   He was called to the Bar in 1907 but never practised, becoming a partner in Robert Fleming & Co instead.

3   Fleming, audio recording 'The Spoken Word – Travel Writers', August 1969.

4   18 June to 1 November 1932.

5   June to October 1933.

6   A talented cartoonist and accomplished artist, Pettiward was killed in the Dieppe raid on 19 August 1942, leading a troop of No. 4 Commando attacking the German heavy gun battery at Varengeville.

7   Fleming obituary of Pettiward in *The Spectator*.

8   He is often identified with the fictional Professor Challenger in *The Lost World* (1912).

9   Trailed on 17 June 1932 as 'The River of Death – Search for Lost Explorer – The New Expedition to Brazil'.

10 Hart-Davis, *Peter Fleming*, 107.

11 Fleming obituary of Pettiward in *The Spectator*.

12 Martin Stannard, *The Art of Travel: Essays on Travel Writing*, ed. Philip Dodds (Abingdon: Routledge, 1982).

13 Fleming: audio recording 'The Spoken Word – Travel Writers', 9 August 1969.

14 *Steppe* Magazine, 16 May 2012.

15 The other two were 'Suppression of Bandits in Manchuria' (8 July 1933) and 'Antagonisms in China: The Fukien Revolt' (14 December 1933).

16 6th Viscount Gage, Lord-in-Waiting to the King at the time. Christened Henry, he was known as George.

17 Sent by Fleming to London on 13 November 1934 and published by *The Times* on 2, 3, 4 and 8 January 1935.

18 The Gages had gone on to Armenia.

19 Fleming kept a diary between 27 August 1934 and 5 January 1935 which was later published in 1952 by Rupert Hart-Davis as *A Forgotten Journey*.

20 'Benefactions of Japan' 25 March 1935; 'Priests and Politics' 26 March 1935.

21   Under the heading 'Rivalries in Sinkiang', the last three articles – 'A Certain Power',
     'Russia at Work' and 'Soviet Aims' – were published on 16, 17 and 18 December
     1935.

22   RPF had first met Celia in 1929 when she was an aspiring young actress. In 1932,
     they began to go out and were married on 10 December 1935 in Chelsea Old
     Church, London.

23   A despatch from Oman. In 1957, *The Times* sponsored Fleming on 'A Journey
     from Moscow to Crimea' (with his godson Duff Hart-Davis) and, in 1966, also ran 'A
     Journey from Ukraine to Georgia' (with his daughter Kate).

24   Pereira had been one of the first officers to be seconded to the newly formed
     Chinese Regiment in 1899. Fluent in Chinese, he went on to serve as Military
     Attaché in Peking for five years. His diaries were later edited by Sir Francis
     Younghusband and published as *Peking to Lhasa: a Narrative of Journeys in the
     Chinese Empire by the late Brig-Gen George Pereira* (1925).

25   In Book 5 of *The Aeneid*, when the Trojans have left Carthage, the helmsman Palinurus
     advises Aeneas to forestall sailing to Italy and to wait out a terrible storm on Sicily.

26   May 2007.

27   Known in the family as 'Nichol'.

28   Regular Army Reserve of Officers.

29   Hart-Davis, *Peter Fleming*, 213.

Chapter 2

1   A.R.B. Linderman, *Rediscovering Irregular Warfare: Colin Gubbins and the Origins of
     Britain's SOE* (Oklahoma: University of Oklahoma, 2016), 46.

2   HS 8/256.

3   Commissioned in the Grenadier Guards in 1906, in the war of 1914–19 Viscount Gort
     was awarded the VC, DSO and bar, MC and mentioned in despatches eight times.

4   A more specific paper followed on 3 April and was approved by the Chief of the
     Imperial General Staff on 13 April.

5   Hart-Davis, *Peter Fleming*, 215.

6   Joan Bright.

7   His first journey to the Georgian Soviet Republic was during June and July, 1926;
     and the second, to the Georgian districts within the Turkish frontier, during May and
     June 1929.

8   W.E.D. Allen, *Guerrilla War in Abyssinia* (London: Penguin, 1943), 10.

9   Ibid.

10   MIR War Diary.

11   MIR Report No. 2, 8 August 1939.

12   Fleming may have had in mind the Old Etonian adventurer Francis 'One Arm'
     Sutton, MC (1894–1944) who became a major general in the army of the warlord
     Zhang Zuolin in the interwar years.

13 British-American Tobacco, Asiatic Petroleum Company and Imperial Chemical Industries.

14 Accounts of these journeys were published in *The Times*.

15 After nearly eight years in Japanese-occupied China and in the intervening time the father of two children, he finally left Yenan in November 1945 and returned to England where his father, the Master of Balliol College, was now a hereditary peer, an ennoblement which conferred on Hsiao Li the distinction of being Britain's first Chinese peeress when her father-in-law died in 1952.

16 A Chinese province on the southern edge of Mongolia.

17 Croft and Munthe were followed by Whittington-Moe, Scott-Harston and O'Brien Hitching.

Chapter 3

1 TNA: CAB 83/3.

2 HS 8/261.

3 Another mission, KNIFE, consisting of six former members of the now disbanded 5th Battalion Scots Guards led by Lieutenant Colonel Brian Mayfield, sailed for Hardangerfjord but their submarine was damaged by a mine and had to return home.

4 Killed in Normandy in 1944 when serving with the Parachute Regiment.

5 The War Office did receive a message from MIR timed 19.45 hours on 14 April that 'no enemy in or near Namsos. Am stopping all outward telegraph, telephone and road communications. Trying to get pilots. Fleming.'

6 WO106/1916.

7 Fleming's obituary of Carton De Wiart.

8 Sir Adrian Carton De Wiart, *Happy Odyssey* (London: Jonathan Cape, 1950), 166. He uses Fleming's 1945 rank of colonel. At the time he was a captain.

9 MIR War Diary 24 April.

10 Report of Sergeants Berriff and Bryant.

11 De Wiart, *Happy Odyssey*, 171.

12 Leland Stowe, Stockholm correspondent of the *Chicago Times*, had filed a report that Stockholm radio had announced that Captain Fleming had been killed etc.

13 Hart-Davis, *Peter Fleming*, p. 230 and CAB 121/105.

14 In the *Times* obituary of Fleming, the writer states that Fleming remained behind in Norway to organize stay-behind parties and came out via Sweden. There is no documentary evidence to support this and he may have confused him with Malcolm Munthe or Andrew Croft.

15 Fleming's obituary of Carton De Wiart.

16 Letter RPF to CJ 6 October 1944 (Fleming family archives).

Chapter 4

1 As Commanding Officer of the 3rd Battalion, Grenadier Guards, he was awarded the DSO and two bars.

2 In *A Forgotten Journey*, Fleming found him 'very courteous and very able'.

3 Kate Fleming, *Celia Johnson* (London: Weidenfeld & Nicolson, 1991), 82.

4 MIR War Diary.

5 Peter Fleming, 'Bows and Arrows' in *With the Guards to Mexico!* (London: Rupert Hart-Davis, 1957), 149.

6 Donald Lindsay, *Forgotten General: A Life of Andrew Thorne* (Wilby: Michael Russell Publishing, 1987), 140.

7 Peter Fleming, *Invasion 1940* (London: Rupert Hart-Davis, 1957), 270–1.

8 Calvert, *Fighting Mad*.

9 Fleming, *With the Guards to Mexico!*, 152.

10 Ralph Arnold, *A Very Quiet War* (London: Rupert Hart-Davis, 1962), 53.

11 Others included George Scott-Montcrieff, Nigel Oxenden and Billy Beyts.

12 Andrew Croft, *A Talent for Adventure* (Self-Publishing Association), 160.

13 Lindsay, *Forgotten General*, 144.

14 Colonels Holland, Gubbins, Crockatt, Blacker, Mawhood and Brocklehurst; Majors Wilkinson, Kennedy, Davies, Combe, Jefferis, Kenyon; Captains Greg, Greig, Brunyate, Walter, Fleming, Perkins, Macrae, Wilson, Hogg; Sergeant Bidgood and the secretaries.

15 William Mackenzie, *The Secret History of SOE 1940–1945* (London: St Ermin's Press, 2000), 54.

16 Calvert, *Fighting Mad*, 46.

Chapter 5

1 Roderick Bailey, *Target Italy: The Secret War Against Mussolini 1940–1943* (London: Faber & Faber, 2014), 79.

2 Hart-Davis, *Peter Fleming*, 240.

3 Commissioned in 5 RHA (Mercer's troop), Barstow had gone to France with the BEF and was mentioned in despatches for bravery. His father, Sir George Barstow, was a friend of Celia Johnson's family.

4 Bailey, *Target Italy*, 88.

5 Quoted by Kate Fleming in her biography of her mother, Celia Johnson.

6 HS9/1418/6 see MZ/626 dated 1.6.41.

7 HS3/197.

8   A retired major in the Sherwood Foresters, Barbrook had served in the Albanian King Zog's police in the 1920s.

9   General Wavell, C-in-C Middle East.

10 Fleming presumably meant 'W' Force under General Sir Henry Wilson.

11 Actually SO2, the early designator of SOE.

12 Fleming signalled SOE HQ – 'Am holding Monastir Gap'.

13 Forward Defence Line.

14 Delayed action.

15 The hard standing on which rails are laid.

16 The main British Army logistics centre.

17 Leonard Parrington was later captured in Greece.

18 Prince Peter of Greece and Denmark was third in line to the Greek throne. He joined the Royal Guards of Denmark in 1932 for basic military service and was commissioned as a second lieutenant in 1934. He was the BMM's LO to the Greek government.

19 In his book *With the Guards to Mexico!* (1957), Fleming writes that two Greek deserters stole his car at this point.

20 Ibid. 'Do you know how to stop?' we shouted. 'Not yet,' replied Norman, a trifle testily.

21 Ibid. 'The only damage the Luftwaffe did to us was to make a hole in a map somebody had left in the cab.'

22 Standard British light field gun.

23 On the way down to Athens, the YAK Mission took cover in a ditch to avoid German fighter bombers and found themselves next to the C-in-C General Jumbo Wilson!

24 Chief of Staff Operations.

25 Large Greek fishing boats.

26 Fleming was great friends with the Caccias; he was a contemporary of Harold in Mr Slater's house at Eton and on his journeys to China, he often stayed with them in Peking where Caccia had been posted as a diplomat.

27 Assistant naval attaché.

28 Other passengers included Nancy Caccia, her two children and Chinese amah, and family dogs; Doreen Blunt, wife of Colonel Jasper Blunt (the British Military Attaché); Charles Mott-Radclyffe, KRRC, a liaison officer with the British Military Mission to Greece; Communist leader Miltiades Porphyroyennis and André Michelopoulos of the Greek government.

29 WO193/628 SOE Intelligence Reports 20/1/41 to 31/5/44.

30 Peter Fleming's papers, University of Reading.

31 Major Bill Barbrook, SOE Athens.

32 Other rank.

33 Wing Commander Arthur, Viscount Forbes (later the 9th Earl of Granard) – formerly Air Attaché in Bucharest Legation, then head of RAF Intelligence to Air Commodore Sir John D'Albiac, Air Officer commanding RAF Forces Greece.

34 Captain Graham Forrest-Hay, MBE, RAMC, was later taken prisoner by the Germans.

35 Passport Control Officers i.e. MI6.

36 Reading University MS 1391 B/3.

37 *The Spectator* of 26 May 1950.

Chapter 6

1   Joan Bright Astley, *The Inner Circle* (London: Hutchinson, 1971).

2   Out of a total of approximately eighty officers, thirteen were killed or died of wounds, twelve were wounded and two taken prisoner.

3   October 1940–October 1941.

4   Commanding Officers and their key staff were frequently summoned to 'planning conferences'. The 3rd Battalion, for instance, readied itself to invade Sicily (February 1941), Pantellaria (December 1941), the coast of Norway (January 1942) and the Isle of Alderney (May 1942).

5   In the area Thessaly Road – Dashwood Road – Patmore Street – Corunna Road.

6   Personal for CIGS from Wavell IMMEDIATE dated 8 Jan 1942: should be glad of Peter Fleming as early as possible for appointment to my staff. Other requests may follow.

7   It surrendered on 6 May 1942.

8   Samuel Eliot Morison, *The Rising Sun in the Pacific; 1931–April 1942* (London: Oxford University Press, 1948).

9   Dennis Wheatley, *The Deception Planners* (London: Hutchinson, 1980), 21.

10 Section 9 of Military Operations.

11 MI9.

12 Churchill was personally informed of the incident.

13 Leonard Hamilton-Stokes was the head of the SIS station in Madrid.

14 FO 1093/252.

15 *Daily Mail*, 23 May 2013.

16 Major Victor Jones and Captain Mark Ogilvie-Grant plus two specialist officers, Major Jasper Maskelyne and Major E. Titterington.

17 Miss Hopkins ATS.

18 CAB 121/110.

19 Modestly, Clarke does not highlight how brilliantly the plan was executed through multi-channels and a myriad of media, all according to a strict timetable.

20 Wavell.

21 Their deputies were Lieutenant Commander Ewen Montagu RNR (later famous as the author of *The Man Who Never Was*), Flight Lieutenant Tennant and Major Cass of MI5. The secretariat under Major Eddie Combe, MC and bar, was composed of Majors Brunyate, Goudie and Moffat.

22   In November 1942 he became Secretary of State for the Colonies.

23   Wheatley, *The Deception Planners*, 58–9.

24   In a note to General Ismay of 20 May 1942, Oliver Stanley wrote that Bevan 'was closely associated with Fleming' in Norway on deception operations. There is no other collateral documentation to support this. (CAB 121/105).

25   Soane was the author of *To Mesopotamia and Kurdistan in Disguise*, 1912, and *A Short Anthology of Gurani Poetry*, 1921.

26   When the Cairo conference in March 1921 finally decided to abandon the idea of Kurdish autonomy as part of the overall policy of maintaining British control as cheaply as possible, Soane was summarily dismissed.

27   Sir Ronald Wingate, *Not in the Limelight* (London: Hutchinson, 1959), 44.

28   The Bombay Grenadiers.

29   Wingate, *Not in the Limelight*, 109.

30   Ibid.

Chapter 7

1   Malise Reid Scott, *Major Alexander Reid Scott MC: War Diaries, June 1941–August 1942*.

2   Operations in Eastern theatre, based on India, from March 1942 to 31 December 1942.

3   Published in *The London Gazette* on 18 September 1946.

4   Letter RPF to CJ 14 April 1942.

5   Archibald Wavell, *Allenby, A Study in Greatness* (London: Harrap & Co., 1941).

6   Anthony Cave Brown, *Bodyguard of Lies* (New York: Harper & Row, 1975), 280.

7   Cyril Falls and A. F. Becke, eds., *Official History of the War, Military Operations Egypt and Palestine vol. 1* (London: His Majesty's Stationery Office, 1930), 11.

8   Malise Reid Scott, *Major Alexander Reid Scott MC: War Diaries, June 1941–August 1942*.

9   Fleming introduction to Mike Calvert, *Prisoners of Hope* (London: Jonathan Cape, 1952).

10   A twin-engine British light bomber.

11   Captain N. Chancellor, Burma Rifles, ADC to Alex.

12   General Lo Cho-ying of the Chinese Expeditionary Force.

13   Major General Sir John Winterton, KCB, KCMG, CBE, DL. At the time, Chief of Staff to Alex.

14   Major General David Cowan, CB, CBE, DSO & Bar, MC.

15   Reid Scott remembered it ending up 'at the bottom of the 30 ft. cud on all four wheels, with the engine running and completely undamaged!'

16   See Fleming in Greece.

17   Major Richard Freeman-Taylor, Royal Norfolk Regiment.

18 Reading University 1391 B/35.

19 Letter RPF to CJ 5 May 1942 (Fleming family archives).

20 Note on letter by Lord Wavell: 'This refers to a despatch case of mine left behind near Ava Bridge in April 1942, to deceive Japs.'

21 There was a note attached by Wavell to this letter: 'Operation Error! Sandy and Mike Calvert and Peter Fleming. A.P.W. in Delhi. A Ford Mercury was shoved over khud side (in India a deep ravine or chasm). It dropped about 150 feet. (The engine was still running and the lights working!) Our forces had pulled back out of contact from Japs and withdrew over this bridge. Peter Fleming and party went 1 mile the Jap side of the bridge and selected point to shove over car on way back. Intention was also to make Japs think A.P.W. badly smashed up.

Idea of taking phial of fresh blood and sprinkling this in car – was mooted but thought 'too much of a good thing'. (Also too much like haversack ruse. A.P.W.)'

Note by Lady Wavell: 'A photo of EMW put into a wallet for this too.'

22 Letter Wavell to RPF dated 30 August 1944 (Fleming family archive).

23 Known as the Inter-Services Liaison Department in India and SEAC.

24 Known as Force 136 in India.

25 Also 404 OSS, E Group (SIS and MI5), PWD and BAAG.

26 Terence O'Brien, *The Moonlight War: The Story of Clandestine Operations in Southeast Asia, 1944–5* (London: Arrow Books, 1987), 47.

27 A Force 136 mission.

28 CAB 154/99 Fleming final report.

Chapter 8

1 The United States also continued its silver purchases, which gave China $252 million in cash.

2 Although Chennault's American Volunteer Group was not supported by Lend-Lease funds, both the War and Navy Departments released pilots whose terms of service included a generous $500 for every Japanese aircraft they shot down.

3 In addition, in 1939 export credits worth £3 million were granted.

4 J.F.C. Fuller, *The Second World War* (London: Eyre and Spottiswoode, 1948), 128.

5 Robert Thompson, *A Time for War* (Upper Saddle River NJ: Prentice Hall, 1991), 51.

6 Pearl Buck, the best-selling author and Nobel Prize winner and arguably one of the most influential American women of her generation, campaigned for Indian independence throughout the war. She was vehemently opposed to Churchill's promotion of the British Empire and attacked him in the US media on numerous occasions.

7 Thaddeus Holt, *The Deceivers* (London: Weidenfeld & Nicolson, 2004), 395.

8 The first twelve meetings (the ARCADIA Conference) took place between 24 December 1941 and 14 January 1942.

9 CCS 155/1 19 January 1943 Conduct of the War in 1943.

10 Hart-Davis, *Peter Fleming*, 185.

11   US Army Colonel Miers, deputy director of the AIB, was on record as saying that 'there can be no doubt that British [UK] organizations acted against GHQ policy on orders of London'. He further remarked 'we put the brake on things we don't understand'.

12   FDR Library.

13   The original signatories of the 1 January 1942 Declaration of the United Nations were the United States of America, the United Kingdom of Great Britain and Northern Ireland, the Union of Soviet Socialist Republics, China, Australia, Belgium, Canada, Costa Rica, Cuba, Czechoslovakia, Dominican Republic, El Salvador, Greece, Guatemala, Haiti, Honduras, India, Luxembourg, the Netherlands, New Zealand, Nicaragua, Norway, Panama, Poland, Union of South Africa, Yugoslavia.

14   In annex on Amphibious Operations from India, an entry of a list of naval forces to be provided by the British is qualified by a note that reads 'the possibility of conflict of the above deployment with OVERLORD and the South of France Operation must be borne in mind' (Papers and Minutes of the Quadrant Conference p. 339).

15   US projections were to increase the tonnage of supplies per month to China (by air ferry, road and pipelines) from 102,000 tons in November 1943 to 220,000 tons in January 1946 (Papers and Minutes of the Quadrant Conference).

16   FDR Library JCS 297 (10 May 1943) Operations in Burma 1943–4.

17   Louis Allen, *Burma: the Longest War* (London: J.M. Dent and Sons, 1984).

18   Sir M.E. Howard, *British Intelligence in the Second World War: Volume 5, Strategic Deception* (London: HMSO, 1990).

19   'Our main difficulty at the moment is that Allied strategy for the war with Japan is not yet settled. Consequently, there is no broad deception policy and no deception threats are being undertaken in other theatres of the Far East to contain enemy forces'. LCS (43) 13 2 August 1943 Report on Cover Plan RAMSHORN.

20   BROOKE 3.B.XII diary entries 17 and 21 March 1944.

21   The order to halt all preparations was given by 11th Army Group on 26 April 1944.

22   WO 203/5743.

23   Governor General of French Indo-China for the provisional (Vichy) French government during the Second World War.

24   Signal 19 June 1944 HW41/149.

25   H.P. Willmott, *Grave of a Dozen Schemes* (Marlborough: Airlife Publishing, 1996), 19.

Chapter 9

1   Killed in an air crash in China on 14 March 1942, Dennys was replaced by Brigadier J.G. Bruce.

2   204 Military Mission included Colonel Munro-Faure as COS and Lieutenant Colonel Gill-Davies and Captain Ananand as instructors.

3   Tai Li was head of the Military Investigation and Statistics Bureau, known as the *juntong* and abbreviated to either BIS or MSB. In June 1940, Tai Li had flown to Hong Kong in pursuit of Y.C. Wen, the head of OSTR, the Chinese cryptographic centre, who had

gone to the colony for medical tests. British airport police arrested him and held him overnight in jail, a humiliation that coloured his attitude to the British from then on.

4   In charge of sabotage and secret activities in Japanese-occupied areas.

5   His 2 i/c was Hans Tofte aka Tufts.

6   In 1943, Major General Gordon Grimsdale, the British Military Attaché in Chungking, took control of it with a sabotage school at Pihu and officer training establishment at Chiki.

7   In a message to London in April 1942, Keswick wrote that 'it is only here (in Chungking) that one realizes how sad and how bitter is the feeling about Hong Kong where all the Chinese that count had their money, their wives and quite a few of them their sweethearts'.

8   Peter Fleming, *My Aunt's Rhinoceros and Other Reflections* (London: Rupert Hart-Davis, 1956) 17–18.

9   The Institute of Pacific Relations (IPR) was an international NGO established in 1925 to provide a forum for discussion of problems and relations between nations of the Pacific Rim. Most participants were elite members of the business and academic communities in their respective countries. Funding came largely from businesses and philanthropies, especially the Rockefeller Foundation. IPR international headquarters were in Honolulu until the early 1930s when they were moved to New York.

10 William Keswick, known as Tony, was born in Yokohama in 1903. Educated at Winchester and Trinity College Cambridge, he joined Jardine Matheson in Manchuria in 1925 as soon as he came down. At the relatively young age of thirty-one, he became taipan in Hong Kong from 1934 to 1935 and then taipan in Shanghai from 1935 to 1941. Married to the daughter of Sir Francis Lindley, HM Ambassador to Japan 1931–4.

11 Graham Greene, *A Sort of Life* (1971), 148.

12 Peter Fleming, *One's Company* (London: Jonathan Cape, 1934), 225.

13 It ran from the Burmese town of Lashio, which was connected by rail and river to the port of Rangoon.

14 Although called 'Armies', Chinese Armies, like those of the Japanese, were actually Corps in terms of organization. In terms of combat strength, they were only the equivalent of a British Division.

15 The 22nd and 38th Divisions were completely rebuilt in India using British/US stores and US training. A third division (the 30th) was formed in 1943 from reinforcements flown over the 'Hump' from China and a fourth (50th) was also in the process of forming. 'X' Force went on the offensive in February 1944, in conjunction with Wingate's Chindits, Merrill's Marauders and 'Y' Force.

16 Maochun Yu, *The Dragon's War: Allied Operations and the Fate of China, 1937–1947* (Annapolis MD: Naval Institute Press, 2006).

17 Brooke, Pound and Portal.

18 CAB 121/105 Note Stanley/Hollis 8 May 1942.

19 The Baedeker raids on old English historic towns were in response to the British 1,000 bomber raids on Cologne on 30 May.

20 Letter ISSB to Lt Col E.F.B. Cook, Washington, by hand of Major Bratby dated 22 August 1942.

21 Fleming's call sign used in Chungking communications.

Chapter 10

1 Richard Aldrich, *Intelligence and the War against Japan* (Cambridge: Cambridge University Press, 2000), 10.
2 An entirely fictional outfit.

Chapter 11

1 Cypher telegram to War Office from C-in-C India 13 August 1942.
2 Lieutenant General Frank Andrews was at that time based in Cairo as Commander of all US Forces in the Middle East.
3 Under the terms of the Treaty of Versailles, Japanese occupation of former German colonies in Micronesia north of the equator (Marianas, Carolines, Marshall Islands and Palau groups) was formally recognized, and Japan was given a League of Nations Class C mandate.
4 General Strong Washington telegram No.435.
5 He actually took over on 8 November after the defence of India against the Japanese had legally been transferred to his command.
6 15–20 October.
7 WO 203/4821.
8 Chief of Chinese General Staff.
9 Major General Charles Lamplough, RM, DSC, first Director of Intelligence SEAC. In December 1944, he was asked to return to UK by GOC Royal Marines and after his successor Major General W.R.C. Penny, CB, CBE, DSO, MC, was delayed by illness, he was replaced by Air Commodore Pendred who finally arrived in December 1945.
10 US Vice-President Henry Wallace visited China from 18 to 30 June 1944.
11 D. Division letter INK 30 May 1945.
12 In January 1944, Bissell was assigned to the Office of the Assistant Chief of Staff for Intelligence on the War Department General Staff. He was the Army member of Joint Security Control and on the Joint Intelligence Committee and the US Army member of the Combined Intelligence Committee.

Chapter 12

1 Letter RPF to CJ 12 July 1942 (Fleming family archives).
2 Letter RPF to CJ 5 May 1942 (Fleming family archives).
3 Letter RPF to CJ 7 June 1942 (Fleming family archives).
4 Letter RPF to CJ 24 August 1942 (Fleming family archives).
5 Letter RPF to CJ 9 November 1942 (Fleming family archives).
6 Letter RPF to CJ 17 November 1942 (Fleming family archives).

7   Letter RPF to CJ August 1942 (Fleming family archives).

8   Letter RPF to CJ 14 March 1943 (Fleming family archives).

9   Letter RPF to CJ 23 November 1942 (Fleming family archives).

10 Letter RPF to CJ 30 June 1943 (Fleming family archives).

11 Letter RPF to CJ 14 March 1943 (Fleming family archives).

12 Letter RPF to CJ 9 November 1942 (Fleming family archives).

13 He later became a prolific composer.

14 Colonel J.C. Kemp, MC: *The History of the Royal Scots Fusiliers 1919–1959* (Glasgow: Robert Maclehose & Co., 1963), 15–16.

15 If he had stayed with 2nd Battalion, he would most likely have been killed or captured in Belgium when the battalion was surrounded by the German army and surrendered on 27 May 1940.

16 Fleming introduction to Frank Wilson, *Mike the Muckshufter* (London: Jonathan Cape, 1946).

17 Ibid.

18 Peter Thorne, *Reminiscences* (Unpublished memoir), 158.

19 CAB 154/99 Fleming Final Report.

20 The War Office, *Special Weapons and Types of Warfare: Volume III Visual and Sonic Weapons* (London: The War Office, 1953).

21 In the 1930s Bicat had worked extensively as a set designer for the theatre including a New York production of T.S. Eliot's *Murder in the Cathedral* and productions for the Windsor Repertory Theatre and the Mercury Theatre.

22 A similar team had been assembled in the Middle East under the designer Steven Sykes, which included Tony Ayrton, Brian Robb, Robert Medley and John Codner.

23 In reply to a letter of condolence she had received from Bicat after her husband Simon Astley had been killed in a car accident in 1946, Joan Wavell wondered 'what you are up to now that dummy elephants and Foulées fireworks are things of the past' (3 April 1946, Bicat family archives).

24 Playwright and theatre manager 1885–1959.

25 Letter RPF to CJ 23 August 1942 (Fleming family archives).

26 Letter Cawthorn/Bicat, 10 December 1943 (Bicat family archives).

27 Rechristened as such in February 1943.

28 The War Office, *Special Weapons and Types of Warfare*.

29 WO 203/5742.

30 Colonel L.J.C. Wood of SOE agreed to undertake the design and production in Poona of all special containers for food and other stores.

31 In a letter dated 29 August 1945, Colin Mackenzie thanked Bicat for 'the consistently good service you have rendered this Force (136)' and advised him that 'Alec Peterson will be getting in touch with you in regard to certain printing and other equipment which we placed at your disposal' (Bicat family archive).

32 In an internal memo dated 28 November 1942, Colin Mackenzie refers to 'calming the fears (of the Finance Department) and recommending that they agree to the printing of Military Yen notes'.

33 HS1/293.

34 The grandson of Sir Strati Ralli Bt, the head of Ralli Brothers, a global trading company.

35 Ralli appears on the Indian Army List of April 1944 as a 2/Lt (temporary captain) in the Indian Signals Corps.

36 Unattributed press clipping belonging to John Ralli.

37 Brigade Signal Section from The Royal Corp of Signals provided five signallers per column. The signals plan included communications within columns, with other columns and with Wingate's HQ. The link between Wingate's HQ and Corps HQ was via a relay station on a mountain crest in order to obtain the necessary range.

38 Immediately after the Japanese surrender, Ralli was sent by Mountbatten to Tokyo on a counter-intelligence mission which involved him in the interrogation of, among others, Prime Minister Tojo and the head of the Japanese secret police who were incarcerated in Sugamo Prison. His work had become so secret by this stage that the authorities had no record of him when he returned to England for demobilization in May 1946; only when SIS vouched for him was he allowed to go home.

39 He subsequently married Lois Maxwell, the original Miss Moneypenny in the James Bond films.

40 *Death of a Sinner* (1933), *On Secret Service* (1935), *The Kidnapped King* (1937), *Fire on the Seven Peaks* (1938), *Despair and Delight* (1939).

41 A five-star hotel owned by the family of the famous Swiss photographer Robert Holz.

42 A restaurant in the Hotel India, Connaught Place.

43 British Other Ranks as opposed to Officers.

44 Letters RPF to CJ 6 October and 19 December 1943 (Fleming family archives).

45 After two months of hard work by General Pownall, Mountbatten's COS, SEAC officially opened on midnight of 15/16 November 1943.

46 Philip Mason, *A Shaft of Sunlight* (London: Andre Deutsch, 1978), 177.

47 Letters RPF to CJ 3 October 1943 and 6 November 1943 (Fleming family archives).

48 Letter RPF to CJ 27 December 1943 (Fleming family archives).

49 Letter RPF to CJ 12 January 1944 (Fleming family archives).

50 P for Priorities.

51 Garnons-Williams had worked with Dudley Clarke in the early days of the Commandos. Winning a DSO and DSC, with two mentions in despatches, he was very much a fighting sailor rather than staff officer.

52 Aldrich, *Intelligence and the War against Japan*, 182.

53 Mountbatten arrived at the new SEAC HQ in the Peradeniya Botanical Gardens, Kandy, on 16 April 1944.

54 Colonel John Hughes-Wilson, *Military Intelligence Blunders and Cover-Ups* (London: Robinson, 2004), 150.

55 On 12 August 1943, the Chiefs of Staff had given him permission to plan a substitute raid for the abandoned Plan RUTTER but Dieppe was never specified.

56 Letter RPF to CJ 29 April 1944 (Fleming family archives).

57 Mason, *A Shaft of Sunlight*, 181.

58 Letter RPF to CJ 19 December 1943 (Fleming family archives).

59 WO 203/5743.

60 Ibid.

61 Letter RPF to CJ 31 August 1944 (Fleming family archives).

62 Ibid.

63 Ibid.

64 Garnons-Williams was accredited to SIS.

65 p/1247 28 August 1944 From P. Div to SAC, copy D. Div.

66 WO 203/3313.

67 Letter RPF to CJ 20 December 1944 (Fleming family archives).

68 Mountbatten Papers MB1/C22/2.

69 SACSEA to War Office 2 February 1945 WO 203/3313.

70 Letter RPF to CJ 10 January 1945 (Fleming family archives).

71 One of his first actions was to produce Weekly Progress Reports for limited 'top secret' circulation from 24 March 1945 onwards.

72 Wingate, *Not in the Limelight*, 212.

Chapter 13

1 Thorne, *Reminiscences*.

2 Wingate, *Not in the Limelight*, 195.

3 When Fleming was in London in the summer of 1944, he had sight of the intercepted signals traffic of the Japanese Naval Attaché in Berlin. Clearly Tokyo was getting sound and detailed material from a source 'fed with reasonable generosity by Berlin'. Since it was D. Division's job to appreciate the overall efficiency (and hence sales resistance) of the Japanese Intelligence organization, Fleming asked to be included on the distribution list.

4 Fleming compared it with two previous estimates:

Imperial High Command estimate dated 25 November 1943

Infantry Divisions: 6th, 32nd, 33rd, 34th, 42nd, 70th, 'N', 'N' ('N' = not known); *Armoured Divisions:* 'N', 22 Tank Brigade; *Airborne Divisions:* 3rd.

Summary of two estimates issued by Tokyo on 23 June 1944

Infantry Divisions: 2nd, 32nd, 33rd, 70th. In addition, 6th, 34th, 42nd and 60th were 'thought to be in India'; *Armoured Divisions:* 25th, 26th, 254 Independent Armoured Brigade; *Airborne Divisions:* 3rd.

5 CAB 154/25.

6 CX.12678/DL 16/8/43 Maj. F. Foley to Maj. H.L. Petavel, Offices of War Cabinet.

7 WO 203/476.

8 A plan put forward in support of a seaborne assault on Rangoon in September/ October 1944 by inferring that the main Allied thrust was to Malaya via Sumatra.

9 The actual seaborne assault on Rangoon.

10 Fleming recalled that 'one useful medium for the implementation of Order of Battle Deception was a sketchbook purporting to belong to an official war artist and containing a number of sketches of officers and ORs of various nationalities, with their formation signs prominently displayed, and pencilled notes identifying and locating their formations. This was much appreciated by the Japanese, who received it via China, but it is thought to have been a little too difficult for them' (See PURPLE WHALES).

Chapter 14

1 An Army list of costly items such as watches, binoculars and compasses. A Board of Inquiry would be necessary to establish the circumstances of loss and who (usually the soldier) should pay for.

2 WO 203/3436.

3 Defence 2/1747.

4 At Laggan House in Ayrshire under Colonel Cecil Barlow.

5 WO 203/3436. In March 1945, the units moved to Poona.

6 WO 203/5743.

7 WO 172/7192–7200.

8 WO 203/476.

9 Officers – recommended three MCs, one MBE, three Mentions; British other ranks – two MMs, one BEM, four Mentions; VCOs – one MC; Indian other ranks – two MMs, one Mention.

10 WO 203/34.

11 Ibid.

12 CAB 154/99 Fleming final report.

13 Local versions were called BICAT SAUSAGES (grenade simulators) and BICAT CRACKERS (rifle simulators). Each had fifty attached to a length of fuse.

14 He was assisted by Majors Howorth and Vaughan, and Lieutenants Denney, Gaylor and Baxter.

15 Copy of SC5/1967/I dated 1 October 1946, Bicat family archive.

16 Letter Cawthorn dated 8 October 1945, Bicat family archive.

17 WO 203/34.

18 CAB 154/99 Fleming final report.

Chapter 15

1 Operation STENCIL.

2 D. Division 454 to Tac HQ D. Division re HQ IV Corps 944/21/G.1(b) dated 3 Jan
   1945.

3 CAB 154/99 Fleming final report.

4 FM Viscount Slim, *Defeat into Victory* (London: Cooper Square Press, 2000),
   430–1.

5 46th (Tanganyika Territory) Battalion.

Chapter 16

1 Howard, *British Intelligence in the Second World War*, x.

2 Later Head of Counter-Subversion branch (1951) and Head of Personnel (1958).

3 Director, Intelligence Bureau, Home Department, Government of India. The Delhi-
   based Intelligence Bureau was known as DIB.

4 KV 4/332: Marriott to Robertson 3 May 1943.

5 KV 4/332: Marriott to Robertson 10 May 1943.

6 KV 4/332: Marriott to Robertson 18 May 1943.

7 KV 4/332.

8 Magan, an officer in Hodson's Horse, an Indian Cavalry regiment, was seconded to
   DIB as an MLO between it and the DMI. He spent most of the war on intelligence
   duties in Persia. His wife, Maxine, was Cawthorn's secretary. Later Brigadier Magan,
   CBE, Head of E Division MI5.

9 KV 4/197.

10 Karl Melchers reporting from Bangkok.

11 WO 373/100/404.

12 The Hikari Kikan was the Japanese liaison office responsible for Japanese relations
   with the Azad Hind Government.

13 A Burma Civil Affairs officer wrote in his September 1943 appreciation of the First
   Chindit Expedition that 'the Indian National Army has found considerable support
   amongst Indians and Indian POWs from Malaya and Hong Kong but its chief value
   to the Japanese is for propaganda purposes. A few agents have probably got into
   India' (IOR/M/5/84).

14 This triple-cross was masterminded from India by a group of intelligence officers that
   included Colonel Peter Fleming of D. Division.

15 CAB 154/99 Fleming final report.

16 British Minister in Moscow.

17 Colonel Evelyn Van Millingen, formerly manager of the Bombay-Burma Company in
   Bangkok.

18 Xinjiang.

19 Urumchi.

20 Mihir Bose, *Raj, Secrets, Revolution: A Life of Subhas Chandra Bose* (Norwich:
   Grice Chapman Publishing, 2004), 199.

21 Ibid.

22 Roughly 60,000 Indian troops fell into Japanese hands when Singapore surrendered on 15 February 1942, and of these about 25,000 were induced, by a wide variety of motives, to join the 'Indian National Army'.

23 RPF draft chapter Reading University MS 1391 B/45–6.

24 TNA KV 2/2463 Oswald Rudolph Kattman RASMUSS/Karl Rudolf RASMUSS: German. Karl RASMUSS, a German Trade Commissioner and representative of the Nazi Party in India before the war, joined the ranks of the Abwehr in 1939. He was sent to Kabul under commercial cover in 1940 tasked with gathering intelligence on India. He was expelled from there in early 1944 and returned to Germany.

25 Ram had recently come to the attention of the British who had gleaned his pro-German activities from his former companion Harminder Singh Sodi.

26 In September 1942, the Germans installed a relay station between Kabul and Berlin to improve communications.

27 HW 41/149 (D. Division weekly progress reports).

28 This originally genuine division had been formed in 1941 to protect the Iraq supply routes to Russia. It was disbanded in Basra on 15 October 1944 and never reformed.

29 Incorrectly typed as 251 Indian Armoured Brigade.

30 Remained in PAIC.

31 Disbanded in October 1944 by conversion into Headquarters Northern Iraq Area.

32 1st Bn Gloucestershire Regiment was with 17th Indian Division.

33 1st Bn Devonshire Regiment was with 20th Indian Division.

34 2nd Bn Welch Regiment was with 19th Indian Division.

Chapter 17

1 CAB 154/99 Fleming final report.

2 Director of Intelligence SEAC.

3 No. DMI/2862/GSI(d) dated 19/1/43.

4 Lieutenant Colonel Niranjan Singh Gill.

5 This was incorrect. Gill was incarcerated by the Japanese until the end of the war and then charged with desertion by the British.

6 LCS (45) I/C/42.

7 Political warfare i.e. propaganda.

8 On 9 March 1945, 346 US B-29s dropped 2,000 tons of incendiary bombs on Tokyo over the course of forty-eight hours. Almost sixteen square miles in and around the Japanese capital were incinerated, and between 80,000 and 130,000 Japanese civilians were killed. During May 1945, XXI Bomber Command destroyed ninety-four square miles of buildings, which was equivalent to one-seventh of Japan's total urban area.

9 LCS (44) I/C/42.

10 O'Connor had been the LO of LCS in Washington since August 1943.

11 Captain Harry Thurber, one of two Naval Representatives on Joint Security Control.

Chapter 18

1 Brigadier O.C. Wingate, DSO, 'Intruder Mission', War, No.48, 10 July 1943.

2 Letters RPF to CJ 31 January 1943 and 10 February 1943 (Fleming family archives).

3 Shelford Bidwell, *The Chindit War* (London: Hodder & Stoughton, 1979), 168.

4 Letter RPF to CJ 19 December 1943 (Fleming family archives).

5 Hart-Davis, *Peter Fleming*, 290.

6 MS 1391 B/35.

7 It later transpired that Burmese foresters had laid out their trees to dry in the clearing.

8 Thirty men were killed in the landing and a further twenty-eight wounded.

9 By 13 March the build-up was complete. In seven nights about 9,000 men, 1,350 animals and 250 tons of supplies and weapons had landed behind enemy lines in Burma.

10 Including Fleming, Major R.C. Pringle, the Brigade Signals Officer, Major G.V. Faulkner, IMS and Lieutenant John Leigh Mallory, RE, the son of George Mallory, the Everest mountaineer, and nephew of Air Marshall Sir Trafford Leigh Mallory, at that time the commander of the Allied Expeditionary Air Force for Operation OVERLORD.

11 Pringle report.

12 Of sixty-one gliders despatched, only thirty-four arrived. It later transpired that of the twenty-seven gliders which had not reached their destination, six landed in enemy territory, including Fleming's.

13 Faulkner was on the advance party to set up medical services.

14 *Daily Telegraph* 1993, http://www.216parasigs.org.uk/inmemorium/documents/ColinPringle.pdf.

15 With him went the diary which Fleming had carefully kept during the past few days; he gave it to Angus because he had a waterproof tobacco pouch.

16 On the strength of his report, Pringle received a Mention in despatches.

17 Letter RPF to CJ 21 March 1944 (Fleming family archives).

18 Brigadiers Calvert, Fergusson, Brodie, Gilmour and Squadron Leader Thompson.

19 Calvert, *Prisoners of Hope*, 96.

20 Ibid, 102.

21 Letter RPF to CJ 21 March 1944 (Fleming family archives).

22 Ibid.

Chapter 19

1 This version incorporates the amendments proposed respectively by the representatives of Holland, Australia, the Philippines and France at various dates since 4 June 1943 and agreed by the Commission.

2 CAB 122.

3 Jackman took over from Col. W.R.P. Ridgway who had originally looked after the Escape and Evasion brief in GSI (d). In March 1942, it was spun out into GSI (e) which included MI9 and MI19 (WO 208/3251).

4 Including in this context Australia, Holland, France and the Philippines.

5 COS 518/5 – CAB 79/31/p. 311.

6 For instance, 2,345 Allied POWs were sent to the Sandakan camp in Borneo during the period 1942–3. In early 1945, the emaciated prisoners were forced to march through the jungle to Ranau village, 250 km away. The surviving prisoners were put to work carrying 20 kg sacks of flour over hilly terrain to Paginatan, 40 km away. By the end of July 1945, all had died of starvation or sickness or been executed. Six Australian POWs managed to escape.

Chapter 20

1 ADCOS Army WO 203/3313; Wingate to ADCOS Army 14 August 1945 WO 203/3313.

2 WO 203/3313.

3 Quoted Kate Fleming in *Celia Johnson*, 150.

4 Letter RPF to CJ 31 August 1944 (Fleming family archives).

5 According to the Regimental Headquarters War Diary, Fleming 'called' (visited) on 18 June 1943 and on 2 August and 13 November 1945.

6 Captain James Grinling (born 1899) attached Burma Defence Force 21 March 1941 to 17 November 1942.

7 Later killed in action in Italy in 1943.

8 The Scots Guards.

9 The Officers Dining Club which meets once a year.

10 13 June 1943.

11 Colonel R.B. Colvin, DSO.

12 According to the battalion's War Diary of 28 May 1940 (TNA WO 167 / 806): 'Throughout the whole battle the men, though very tired and hungry, kept extremely cheerful and were greatly helped by the adjutant, Captain Fleming, who, completely unmoved by any form of fire, came riding on his motorcycle over the rubble of demolished houses looking as though he were out for a Sunday afternoon ride and distributing cigarettes or other luxuries which he had discovered.' By the end of the battle Michael Fleming had been 'mentioned in despatches' three times. The

following day, the town of Cassel was surrounded and the Ox and Bucks ordered to march to Dunkirk by a road that was believed to be clear of enemy. This proved not to be the case for by this time the Germans were everywhere. Among the seriously wounded was Michael Fleming who suffered a very severe 'gunshot' wound in his left thigh. He was among those left behind on the line of march and was taken prisoner by the Germans. Initially treated at a POW hospital at nearby Zuydcoote, he was then taken to hospital at Lille where his wounds took a turn for the worse and he died after an operation on 1 October 1940.

13   CAB 154/99 Fleming final report.

14   Mason, *A Shaft of Sunlight*, 169.

15   History of D. Division 22 January 1947.

16   CAB 154/99 Fleming final report.

17   Wingate, *Not in the Limelight*, 217.

18   Astley, *The Inner Circle*, 96.

19   Ibid, 78.

20   Hart-Davis, *Peter Fleming*, 305.

21   Peter Fleming, *News From Tartary* (London: Jonathan Cape, 1936), 591.

22   Fleming, audio recording *The Spoken Word – Travel Writers*, August 1969.

Annexes and Notes

1   When MIR was folded into SOE, in November 1940 MIR (c) became a department in the newly formed Ministry of Defence and effectively under the wing of the prime minister who was also Minister of Defence.

2   General Sir Alan Fleming Hartley GCIE, KCSI, CB, DSO, Deputy C-in-C India.

3   Lieutenant General Lewis H. Brereton, commander US 10th Air Force in India.

4   Gen. Joseph W. Stilwell, US commander China-Burma-India area.

5   Posted SACSEA 14 November 1944.

6   He does not show up on 1944/45 Indian Army Intelligence Directorate list. Holt says he came across from A Force.

7   Does not show on 1945 RAF List (India).

8   Keen collector of butterflies of the Arakan coast!

Sources and selected bibliography

The National Archives

AB 84/4/112 (Staff)
CAB 105/27 (Telegrams re operations in India)
CAB 121/105 (Norway)
CAB 121/110 (Deception organizations)
CAB 122/733 (Afghanistan)
CAB 122/1157 (Measures against Japan)
CAB 122/693 (BASSINGTON)
CAB 122/722 (Afghanistan)
CAB 154/3 (A Force)
CAB 154/36 (Channels to the Japanese from the UK and Europe)
CAB 154/40 (Chinese leakages)
CAB 154/42 (RACKET committee)
CAB 154/44 (GODSTONE)
CAB 154/99 (Strategic deception in the Far East)
CAB 301/51 (Hanbury Williams report on SOE)
CAB 66/67119 (Strategic deception)
CAB 69/8/9 (Afghanistan)
CAB 79/31/17 (Liaison with the Russians)
CAB 80/72/19 (LCS minute)
CAB 80/8/9 (Waziristan)
CAB 80/84/90 (SACSEA memos)
CAB 84/53 (Mil Coord Committee)
CAB 91/1-4 (India Committee)
CAB 96/1-5 (Far East Committee)
HS 1/212 (Various 1942–45)
HS 1/293 (GRENVILLE)
HS 1/324 (DITB)
HS 2/238 (Norway)
HS 2/241 (Norway)
HS 8/193 (Inter Services Project Board)
HS 8/214 (Section D)
HS 8/256-63 (MIR)
HW 41/149 (D. Division weekly progress reports)
HW 41/159 (Miscellaneous papers about Far East deception)
HW 412 (Signals Intelligence SE Asia)

HW 417-20 (Signals Intelligence SE Asia)
HW 428 (Signals Intelligence SE Asia)
KV 4/197 (Records of SIME)
KV 4/332 (MI5 and DIB double agents India)
WO 106/1870 (Norway)
WO 106/1880 (Norway)
WO 106/1881 (Norway)
WO 106/1891 (Norway)
WO 106/1894–95 (Norway)
WO 106/1905 (Norway)
WO 106/1911 (Norway)
WO 106/1916 (Norway)
WO 106/1938 (Norway)
WO 106/3544 (War against Japan)
WO 106/3765 (Afghanistan)
WO 172/7192-7200 (D Force)
WO 201/1372 (Persia)
WO 201/1402B (Persia German paratroops)
WO 201/2853 (Intelligence)
WO 203/20 (ALFSEA Deception plans)
WO 203/33 (ALFSEA Deception organization – correspondence and reports)
WO 203/1197 (MINERVA)
WO 203/1207/8 (MINERVA)
WO 203/1657 (DRACULA)
WO 203/167 (Tactical deception ops)
WO 203/1075 (Miscellaneous camouflage)
WO 203/1738 (D. Division reports)
WO 203/1752 (CONCLAVE)
WO 203/20 (SEAC Deception plans)
WO 203/2029 (Airborne ops)
WO 203/24 (Units and resources)
WO 203/2480 (SEAC papers)
WO 203/260 (MINERVA)
WO 203/2827 (ZIPPER)
WO 203/33 (D. Division correspondence and reports)
WO 203/3313 (Policy, minutes and reports)
WO 203/3314 (Ops and reports)
WO 203/3377 (Airborne deception)
WO 203/34 (D. Division correspondence and reports)
WO 203/3435-36 (Sonic deception equipment)
WO 203/3452 (SEAC requirements)
WO 203/476 (Deceptions measures)
WO 203/4805-6 (Kandy)
WO 203/4821 (CKS)
WO 203/4887 (Director of Intelligence SEAC)
WO 203/5657 (Force 136 papers)
WO 203/5742-3 (SEAC deception policy 42-45; DITB)
WO 203/5746 (MULLINER)
WO 203/5747 (Liaison SWPA)

WO 203/5749 (FLABBERGAST)
WO 203/5753 (SEAC secret craft)
WO 203/5754 (STULTIFY)
WO 203/5758 (FIREFLAME)
WO 203/5759 (NETTLE)
WO 203/5760 (Clandestine Operations Directive Mar–Apr 1945)
WO 203/5762-63 (SCEPTICAL)
WO 203/5769A (MIMSY)
WO 203/6387 (Planning for clandestine operations 1945)
WO 203/67 (MINERVA)
WO 204/1561 (A Force)
WO 204/1825 (A Force)
WO 204/1913 (A Force)
WO 204/1914 A and B (A Force)
WO 208/30 (Afghanistan)
WO 208/6 (Afghanistan)
WO 216/76 (Wavell on Burma)
WO 230/52B (A Force)

British Library

Indian Army Lists 1938
Army Lists 1939–1945
Oriental and India Office, London, hold Wavell's correspondence with Col. Rt. Hon. Sir Reginald Hugh Dorman-Smith, 1943–1946 (Ref: MSS Eur E 215); correspondence with Sir Hugh Dow, 1943–1947 (Ref: MSS Eur E 372); and copies of papers relating to India, 1943–1947 (Ref: MSS Eur D 977); Report of the First Chindit Expedition Longcloth Brigade (Ref: IOR/M/5/84).

Other sources

Fleming Family Archives: Letters from RPF to CJ 1939–45.
University of Reading: Peter Fleming papers MS 1391 A/1 and A/4, B/3, B/35, 45, 46 and F/4.
University of Southampton (Hartley Library): Mountbatten papers.

Books

Aldrich, Richard J. *Intelligence and the War Against Japan*. Cambridge: Cambridge University Press, 2000.
Allen, Louis. *Burma: The Longest War 1941–1945*. London: J.M. Dent and Sons, 1984.
Allen, W.E.D. *Guerrilla War in Abyssinia*. London: Penguin Books, 1943.
Anglim, Simon. *Orde Wingate and the British Army 1922–1944*. Abingdon: Routledge, 2010.

Arnold, Ralph. *A Very Quiet War*. London: Rupert Hart-Davis, 1962.

Astley, Joan Bright. *The Inner Circle: a View of War at the Top*. London: Hutchinson, 1971.

Bailey, Roderick. *Target Italy: The Secret War Against Mussolini 1940–1943*. London: Faber & Faber, 2014.

Barstow, Diana. *Swings and Roundabouts*. Private publication, 1999.

Bayly, Christopher and Tim Harper. *Forgotten Armies: Britain's Asian Empire and the War with Japan*. London: Penguin Allen Lane, 2004.

Beamish, John. *Burma Drop*. London: Elek Books, 1958.

Bendeck, Whitney T. *A Force*. Annapolis MD: Naval Institute Press, 2013.

Bidwell, Shelford. *The Chindit War*. London: Hodder & Stoughton, 1979.

Bose, Mihir. *Lost Hero*. London: Quartet Books, 1982.

Bose, Mihir. *Raj, Secrets, Revolution: A Life of Subhas Chandra Bose*. Norwich: Grice Chapman Publishing, 2004.

Brown, Anthony Cave. *Bodyguard of Lies*. New York: Harper & Row, 1975.

Callahan, Raymond. *Burma 1942-1945*. London: Davis-Poynter, 1978.

Calvert, Mike. *Chindits: Long Range Penetration*. New York: Ballantine Books, 1974.

Calvert, Mike. *Fighting Mad: One Man's Guerrilla War*. London: Jarrolds, 1964.

Calvert, Mike. *Prisoners of Hope*. London: Jonathan Cape, 1952.

Carton De Wiart, Sir Adrian. *Happy Odyssey*. London: Jonathan Cape, 1950.

Chant, Christopher. *The Encyclopedia of Code Names of World War II*. Abingdon: Routledge Revivals, 2013.

Chinnery, Philip. *Wingate's Lost Brigade*. Barnsley: Pen & Sword Books, 2010.

Clarke, Dudley. *Seven Assignments*. London: Jonathan Cape, 1948.

Connell, John. *Wavell: Supreme Commander*. London: Collins, 1969.

Cox, Howard. *The Global Cigarette: Origins and Evolution of British American Tobacco 1880–1945*. New York: Oxford University Press, 2000.

Croft, Andrew. *A Talent for Adventure*. Self Publishing Association, 1991.

Cruickshank, Charles. *Deception in World War II*. Oxford: Oxford University Press, 1979.

Cruickshank, Charles. *SOE in the Far East*. Oxford: Oxford University Press, 1983.

Ellis, John. *The World War II Databook*. London: Aurum Press, 1993.

Falls, Cyril Bentham and Archibald Frank Becke. *Official History of the War, Military Operations Egypt and Palestine*. London: His Majesty's Stationery Office, 1930.

Fleming, Kate. *Celia Johnson*. London: Weidenfeld & Nicolson, 1991.

Fleming, Peter. *A Forgotten Journey*. London: Rupert Hart-Davis, 1952.

Fleming, Peter. *A Story to Tell*. London: Jonathan Cape, 1942.

Fleming, Peter. *Brazilian Adventure*. New York: Charles Scribner's Sons, 1933.

Fleming, Peter. *Invasion 1940*. London: Rupert Hart-Davis, 1957.

Fleming, Peter. *My Aunt's Rhinoceros and Other Reflections*. London: Rupert Hart-Davis, 1956.

Fleming, Peter. *News from Tartary*. London: Jonathan Cape, 1936.

Fleming, Peter. *One's Company*. London: Jonathan Cape, 1934.

Fleming, Peter. *The Flying Visit*. New York: Charles Scribner's Sons, 1940.

Fleming, Peter. *The Sixth Column: A Singular Tale of Our Times*. London: Rupert Hart-Davis, 1951.

Fleming, Peter. *Variety*. London: Jonathan Cape, 1933.

Fleming, Peter. *With the Guards to Mexico!*. London: Rupert Hart-Davis, 1957.

Ford, Douglas. *Britain's Secret War Against Japan 1937–45*. Abingdon: Routledge, 2006.

Fort, Adrian. *Archibald Wavell: The Life and Times of an Imperial Servant*. London: Jonathan Cape, 2009.

Fuller, J.F.C. *The Second World War*. London: Eyre and Spottiswoode, 1948.

Gage, Sir Berkeley. *A Marvellous Party*. 1989 (copyright Ulick Gage 2013).

Greene, Graham. *A Sort of Life*. 1971.

Haarr, Geirr H. *The Battle for Norway April – June 1940*. Barnsley: Seaforth Publishing, 2010.

Hart-Davis, Duff. *Peter Fleming*. London: Jonathan Cape, 1974.

Holt, Thaddeus. *The Deceivers: Allied Military Deception in the Second World War*. London: Weidenfeld & Nicolson 2004.

Howard, Sir M.E. *British Intelligence in the Second World War: Volume 5, Strategic Deception*. London: HMSO, 1990.

Hughes-Wilson, Colonel John. *Military Intelligence Blunders and Cover-Ups*. London: Robinson, 2004.

Kemp, Colonel J.C. *The History of the Royal Scots Fusiliers 1919–1959*. Glasgow: Robert Maclehose & Co, 1963.

Keswick, Maggie and Clara Weatherall. *The Thistle and the Jade*. London: Frances Lincoln, 2008.

Kirby, Maj. Gen. S.W. *The War Against Japan*. London: HMSO, 1957–1969.

Knox, James. *Robert Byron: A Biography*. London: John Murray, 2003.

Latimer, Jon. *Burma: The Forgotten War*. London: John Murray, 2004.

Linderman, A.R.B. *Rediscovering Irregular Warfare: Colin Gubbins and the Origins of Britain's SOE*. Norman OK: University of Oklahoma Press, 2016.

Lindsay, Donald. *Forgotten General: A Life of Andrew Thorne*. Wilby: Michael Russell Publishing, 1987.

Lycett, Andrew. *Ian Fleming*. London: Weidenfeld and Nicolson, 1995.

Mackenzie, William. *The Secret History of SOE 1940–1945*. London: St Ermin's Press, 2000.

Mason, Philip. *A Shaft of Sunlight: Memories of a Varied Life*. London: Andre Deutsch, 1978.

Migot, Andre (translated Peter Fleming). *Caravane vers Bouddha*. London: Rupert Hart-Davis, 1956.

Morison, Samuel Eliot. *The Rising Sun in the Pacific: 1931–April 1942*. London: Oxford University Press, 1948.

Mountbatten, Admiral the Lord Louis. (ed. Phillip Ziegler). *Personal Diary 1943–1946*. London: Collins, 1988.

Nesbit, Roy Conyers. *The Battle for Burma*. Barnsley: Pen & Sword Books, 2009.

O'Brien, Terence. *The Moonlight War: The Story of Clandestine Operations in Southeast Asia, 1944–5*. London: Arrow Books, 1987.

O'Sullivan, Donal. *Dealing with the Devil*. New York: Peter Lang Publishing, 2010.

Rankin, Nicholas. *Churchill's Wizards: The British Genius for Deception 1914–1945*. London: Faber & Faber, 2008.

Reid Scott, Malise. (ed.). *Major Alexander Reid Scott MC: War Diaries June 1941– August 1942*. Private publication, 2018.

Schofield, Victoria. *Wavell: Soldier and Statesman*. London: John Murray, 2006.

Slim, FM Viscount. *Defeat into Victory*. London: Cooper Square Press, 2000.

Smith, Michael. *The Emperor's Codes: The Role of Bletchley Park in Breaking Japan's Secret Ciphers*. London: Bantam Press, 2000.

Stannard, Martin. *The Art of Travel: Essays on Travel Writing* (ed. Philip Dodd). Abingdon: Routledge, 1982.

Thompson, Robert Smith. *A Time for War*. Upper Saddle River NJ: Prentice Hall, 1991.

Thorne, Sir Peter. *Reminiscences*. Unpublished memoir.

Toohey, Brian and William Pinwill. *Oyster: The Story of the Australian Secret Intelligence Service*. Melbourne: William Heinemann, 1989.

Van der Kiste, John. *Kings of the Hellenes*. Stroud: Alan Sutton Publishing, 1994.

Wakeman, Frederic. *Spymaster: Dai Li and the Chinese Secret Service*. Berkeley CA: University of California Press, 2003.

War Office, The. *Special Weapons and Types of Warfare: Volume III Visual and Sonic Weapons*. London: The War Office, 1953.

Ward, Arthur. *Churchill's Secret Defence Army*. Barnsley: Pen & Sword Books, 2013.

Wavell, Archibald. *Allenby: A Study in Greatness Vols I and II*. London: Harrap & Co., 1941 and 1943.

Wavell, FM Viscount. *Allenby: Soldier and Statesman*. London: Harrap & Co, 1944.

Whaley, Barton. *Stratagem: Deception and Surprise in War*. Cambridge MA: Centre for International Studies, Massachusetts Institute of Technology, 1969.

Wheatley, Dennis. *Stranger Than Fiction*. London: Hutchinson, 1959.

Wheatley, Dennis. *The Deception Planners*. London: Hutchinson, 1980.

Willmott, H.P. *Empires in the Balance*. Annapolis MD: Naval Institute Press, 1982.

Willmott, H.P. *Grave of a Dozen Schemes*. Marlborough: Airlife Publishing, 1996.

Willmott, H.P. *The Barrier and the Javelin*. Annapolis MD: Naval Institute Press, 1983.

Willmott, H.P. *The War with Japan*. Lanham MD: Rowman & Littlefield, 2002.

Wilson, Frank. *Mike the Muckshufter*. London: Jonathan Cape, 1946.

Wingate, Sir Ronald. *Lord Ismay: A Biography*. London: Hutchinson, 1970.

Wingate, Sir Ronald. *Not in the Limelight*. London: Hutchinson, 1959.

Yu, Maochun. *The Dragon's War: Allied Operations and the Fate of China, 1937–1947*. Annapolis MD: Naval Institute Press, 2006.

Index